INSPIRE / PLAN / DISCOVER / EXPERIENCE

SWEDEN

DK EYEWITNESS

SWEDEN

CONTENTS

DISCOVER SWEDEN 6

EXPERIENCE STOCKHOLM 54

EXPERIENCE SWEDEN 150

NEED TO KNOW 314

Left: The striking Emporia Shopping Centre, Malmö
Previous page: Stockholm's Gamla Stan in winter
Front cover: Hut on the shoreline in Bohuslän, Götaland

DISCOVER

Stockholm, Scandinavia's biggest city

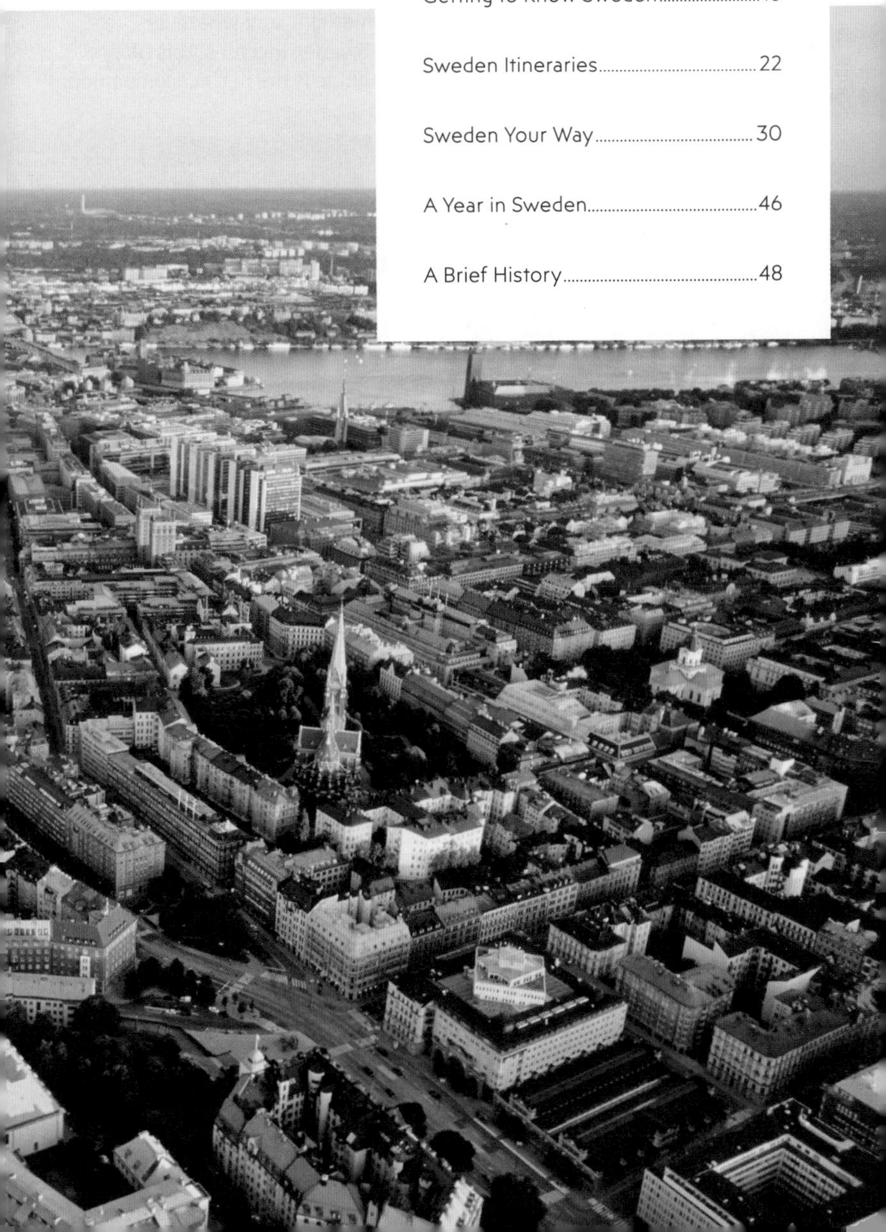

WELCOME TO
SWEDEN

Glimpsing a moose in dense woodland, eating your weight in crayfish and witnessing the spectacular Northern Lights: this is Sweden in a nutshell – inspiring, unforgettable, and as intense as any midnight sun. Whatever your dream trip to Sweden includes, this DK Eyewitness travel guide is the perfect companion.

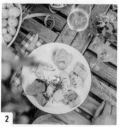

1 Horseriding on one Sweden's idyllic beaches.

2 A lunch of *smörgåsbord* with herring and potatoes.

3 The peaceful Stockholm cityscape in the morning.

4 Red huts on the edge of a lake in the High Coast.

Blessed with Viking ruins, beach-fringed islands and swoon-worthy coastal trails, Scandinavia's most populous country is far from ordinary. Culture is amped-up like nowhere else in northern Europe, and whether you're enjoying its art, theatre or music, it's easy to see why Sweden is one of the planet's happiest countries.

The best way to settle into a country as vast as Sweden is to get to grips with its great out-doors. The Allemansrätten, the right of public access to roam freely, turns even the briefest encounter with a Småland forest, a mirror-lake in Götaland or boreal plateau in subarctic Norrland into a soul-stirring micro-adventure. Flowers and berries can be collected, fishing without a license is standard and almost any land can be used for hiking, biking, canoeing and more. Here, nature is your companion.

Most journeys are bookended by stops in its two most accessible and bustling cities: Stockholm and Gothenburg. Both spectacular bases to discover rich history, here-and-now culture and new Nordic food experiences, these cities ooze culture and charm. Sing with ABBA at the chart-toppers' museum in the capital or bestride a boat prow as if a Viking voyager on a trip into the western fjords from Sweden's second city.

With so many experiences on offer, Sweden can seem overwhelming. We've broken the country down into easily navigable chapters, with detailed itineraries, expert local knowledge and colourful, comprehensive maps to help you plan the perfect visit. Whether you're staying for a weekend or longer, this DK Eyewitness guide will ensure that you see the best of the country. Enjoy the book, and enjoy Sweden.

REASONS TO LOVE
SWEDEN

With its dazzling archipelago cities, remote reindeer-inhabited landscapes, fairy tale castles and kaleidoscopic skies, there are endless reasons to love Sweden. Here, we pick some of our favourites.

1 100,000 LAKES
A haven for swimmers, kayakers and boat-trippers, the countryside is flooded with crystal-clear waters. For sheer scale and spectacle, consider lakes Vättern or Mälaren.

STOCKHOLM *2*
The capital's vast palaces, imposing cathedrals and historic Old Town are mapped in the Swedish imagination as places that define the nation and continue to inspire visitors.

3 HIKING IN THE WILDERNESS
Spectacular hikes offer unspoiled vistas in Sweden. As you glimpse a reindeer, forage for berries, or delve into a fairy tale wood, nature's welcome is your reward.

ECO-FRIENDLY LIFESTYLE *4*

With climate activist Greta Thunberg as the country's next generation pin-up, sustainability is the buzz word in Sweden. Expect carbon-free travel and tasty organic foods.

THE NORTHERN LIGHTS *5*

From October to April, nature's greatest show lights up the sky in a unforgettable rainbow of pink, red and green. Head to Kiruna *(p310)* or Abisko *(p34)* for the best spectacle.

WILD REINDEER *6*

Be it in the company of a Sami herder in the subarctic north of Lappland or encountering a bull in the Åre mountains, you'll never be alone in what feels like the world's antler capital

NOTABLE CASTLES 7

Medieval and Renaissance period pieces crown the landscape here, with fairy tale Gripsholm Castle and the grand Drottningholm Palace (p142) rivalling the natural wonders.

MIDNIGHT SUN 8

The further north you travel, the more dizzying the Swedish summer sun is. It rarely sets between mid-May and late-July above the Arctic Circle and to see it is a dazzling experience.

9 MIDSUMMER CELEBRATIONS

Ain't no party like a Swedish party in late June. As important as Christmas, the day involves a seemingly endless lunch, dancing around a pole and singing while drinking aquavit.

10 FREEDOM TO ROAM (ALLEMANSRÄTTEN)

The Swedish outdoors is an elemental experience and the country's right of public access makes it easy to explore forests, heathlands and islands on your own by bike, kayak or canoe.

VIKING HERITAGE 11

Sweden's Norse traders and raiders broke new ground in the 9th and 10th centuries and their legacy lives on at archaeological sites of burial mounds, wood huts and museums.

SMÖRGÅSBORD 12

With its belly-hugging buffet-style meals, it's impossible to eat badly in Sweden. Specialities like *kroppkakor* (potato dumplings) will excite your tastebuds.

EXPLORE
SWEDEN

This guide divides Sweden into ten colour-coded sightseeing areas, as shown on this map. Find out more about each area on the following pages.

Molde

NORWAY

Bergen

Stavanger

Kristiansand

Esbjerg

EUROPE

Norwegian
Sea

ICELAND

FINLAND

NORWAY   RUSSIA

Atlantic   SWEDEN   ESTONIA
Ocean   LATVIA

North   LITHUANIA
Sea   DENMARK

IRELAND   BELARUS

UK   NETH.   POLAND

BELGIUM GERMANY   UKRAINE

         CZECH   SLOVAKIA
         REP.   MOLDOVA

FRANCE   AUSTRIA HUNGARY
        SWITZ.   ROMANIA

                         SERBIA
                ITALY   BOSNIA-   BULGARIA
                        HERZ.

SPAIN   GREECE

GETTING TO KNOW
SWEDEN

Traditionally divided into Norrland, Svealand and Götaland, northern Europe's largest country is nestled within a beautiful and unspoiled ancient landscape. Each region is packed with its own history, cuisine and culture, brimming with natural highs, shimmering lakes and quaint villages.

STOCKHOLM

PAGE 54

A ramshackle collection of beautiful islands and beach-fringed atolls, Stockholm is a world apart from other European capitals. The historic Old Town, Gamla Stan, with its royal palace and compact squares of tightly packed New Nordic restaurants, is the main lure, while the neighbouring islands are home to an eclectic mix of sights. Stockholm is also dense with museums covering every conceivable subject: head to Djurgården for the Vasa maritime museum and the ABBA Museum, or visit Skansen for the world's oldest open-air museum.

Best for
New Nordic cuisine, artistic metro stations, museums and music

Home to
The Royal Palace (Kungliga Slottet), Stadshuset, National-museum, Drottningholm

Experience
A ferry journey to Djurgården

EASTERN SVEALAND

The waterways of Lake Mälaren and the vast archipelago extending to the Baltic both divide and unite the provinces of Uppland, Södermanland and Västmanland. An area of verdant islands and glittering bays, splendid castles and little wooden towns, and a cultural heritage that predates the Vikings, this lesser-known region is the heartland of Sweden. It's here that you'll have only-in-Sweden experiences, whether feasting on a *smörgåsbord* of seafood, enjoying the natural beauty on a bike ride or touring the castles of Lake Mälaren and the time-capsule buildings of historic Uppsala.

Best for
Ancient history and cultural heritage

Home to
Uppsala, the Stockholm Archipelago

Experience
Canoeing to an uninhabited island overrun with pine forest

EASTERN GÖTALAND

Made up of Östergötland, Småland and Öland, this region promises quintessential Sweden, with candy-red farmsteads, summer houses, Red Riding Hood forests and mirror-like lakes. Cruise the mesmerising Göta Canal, tour Växjö's kingdom of glassworks and crystal, or delve into the troll-filled woodlands of Jönköping made famous by Swedish illustrator John Bauer. In a seriously strong field of contenders, there's also Öland, an island full of time-stopped fishing villages, white beaches and lighthouses.

Best for
Glass making, cruising canals and royal history

Home to
Göta Canal

Experience
Cycling through the island of Öland

$\rightarrow$

PAGE 192

GOTLAND

For a blast of Swedish seaside fun, it's impossible to beat this Baltic-set retreat, knwon as the "Pearl of the Baltic". Sweden's largest island, Gotland is a holiday escape for mainlanders with its beach huts, isolated coves and gorgeous long sandy beaches. Hiking, cycling and boat cruising are practically human rights here, while the UNESCO-worthy capital Visby is steeped in storied medieval ruins and vaulted streets. The drama continues on the sandy beaches of Gotska Sandön and at Hoburgsgubben, the Old Man of Hoburg sea stack.

Best for
Nature, ancient history, cultural heritage, beaches and golfing

Home to
Visby

Experience
Exploring the impressive stalactites and stalagmites at Lummelunda Cave

PAGE 206

SOUTHERN GÖTALAND

Anchored by Sweden's third city, Malmö, this castle-dotted southernmost province is synonymous with maritime and Viking history. Castles and medieval sites abound, and the UNESCO World Heritage Site of Karlskrona is renowned for its naval port. For all its history, this region is also abundant with modern-day micro-adventures in its gentle, undulating hills and forests. Over in Skåne, rolling farmland reveals one of Europe's richest larders full of artisan producers and markets.

Best for
Food, biking, castles and a warmer climate

Home to
Malmö, Karlskrona

Experience
Kayaking the canals of Malmö

PAGE 226

GOTHENBURG

A maritime gateway since the Viking era, Sweden's second city is now awash with contemporary museums, buzzing entertainment venues and hipster boutiques. The coast still breathes plenty of life into the city and is responsible for a thriving crustacean industry and heavy dose of quayside culture: Barken Viking is one of the world's few preserved four-masted barques. Beyond the bustling city, flotillas cruise the Göta Älv river and surrounding fjords, before turning into the moshing North Sea.

Best for
Seafood, craft beer, fishing and maritime history

Home to
Haga Nygata

Experience
An immersive archipelago tour on a day-long boat cruise

$\rightarrow$

WESTERN GÖTALAND

PAGE 242

Sweden might be renowned for creating next year's trends, but this southwestern region has one foot firmly planted in the past. The area is smothered with prehistoric remains, including UNESCO listed Tanum, where Bronze Age people carved rock pictures. Sweden's largest lake, Vänern, and the cove-nibbled stretch of the Kattegat coast remain uncannily traditional and steadfast, too: here, where primary colour-painted wooden houses dot islands, there's a sense that summer never ends.

Best for
Lakes, fishing, beaches and prehistoric remains

Home to
Gunnebo Slott

Experience
Visiting the Bronze Age rock carvings in Tanum

WESTERN SVEALAND

PAGE 266

Fertile agricultural land spreads out around the major lakes and along the river valleys here, giving way to a predominantly forested landscape. As a result, strutting elk, bears and wolves populate this western region, but if you don't manage a wildlife safari there's still plenty to revel in. Boating and canoeing on the Fryken Lakes and fishing on the Klaralven river are regional pasttimes, but the real draw is the Vasaloppet race – when 10,000 skiers swoosh from Salen to Mora.

Best for
Red-painted wooden houses, traditional Sweden and unrivalled nature.

Home to
Örebro

Experience
Eating, drinking and maypole dancing during Midsummer celebrations

SOUTHERN NORRLAND

Brace yourself: this region rewards the intrepid. The snow-capped mountains of Härjedalen march towards Norway, presenting myriad opportunities for wild camping and mountaineering, while Åre is arguably Scandinavia's coolest adventure capital for back-country pursuits – in winter, it's renowned for skiing and telemarking. In stark contrast, the High Coast, which hugs the Baltic Sea north of Härnösand to Örnsköldsvik, has spectacular islands for summer adventures.

Best for
Unique flora and fauna, skiing and mountaineering

Home to
The High Coast, The Härjedalen Mountains

Experience
Enjoying traditional folk music and dance at a Sami village

NORTHERN NORRLAND

Stretching from the populated Baltic coast through wild forests and marshes to the open expanses of the mountains, Northern Norrland is a vast, almost untouched region. Days in Europe's most sparsely populated region are filled with meeting Sami reindeer herders or backpacking parts of the long distance hiking trail, the Kungsleden, while nights range from midnight suns to the kaleidoscopes skies of the *aurora borealis*. This is Sweden at its most visceral, yet authentic.

Best for
The Northern Lights, dramatic scenery, vast untouched landscapes and national parks

Home to
The Kungsleden Trail

Experience
Embracing the Arctic with a night at the famous ICEHOTEL

←

1 Hot-air balloons drifting over the Stockholm skyline.

2 Gathering for brunch at Michelin-starred Oaxen Krog.

3 Boxes of vintage vinyl in a SoFo record shop.

4 Demonstrating traditional glassblowing at Skansen.

Sweden's diverse regions are bursting with historic towns, dynamic cities, breathtaking natural scenery and myriad activities. These itineraries will help you make the most of your visit to this beautiful country.

2 DAYS
in Stockholm

Day 1

Morning Slap-bang in the middle of the Swedish capital, Gamla Stan is perfect for a morning stroll. The city was founded here in 1252, but the tall spires, mustard-yellow buildings and cobbled lanes are more recent. Wander past souvenir shops to Caffellini *(p75)* for barista-brewed *kaffee* – it's one of the few local haunts in this touristy part of town. Peek inside the Storkyrkan *(p70)*, the city's cathedral, then bone up on world-changing discoveries at the Nobel Prize Museum *(www.nobelprize museum.se)* nearby.

Afternoon When hunger strikes, follow your nose through Södermalm to Café String *(www.cafestring.com)*, for epic sandwiches and spicy chai lattes served in huge mugs. Fancy the vintage chair you're sitting in? Everything at this off-beat spot can be bought to take home. Later, window shop in the warren of streets of hipster-home SoFo *(p132)* and catch a glimpse of the latest Scandi fashion trends.

Evening Indulge at Urban Deli *(www. urbandeli.org)* – the vegan burgers and råbiff Koreansk (Korean-style beef) are a must. Duck into retro Bar Central *(p133)*, for a glass of wine, before a cosy night at Hotel Rival *(p77)*, an Art Deco marvel.

Day 2

Morning Wake early to breakfast on *kanelbulle* (a twisty cinnamon bun) and strong coffee at Johan & Nyström *(p133)* then ferry from Gamla Stan to leafy Djurgården, a short jaunt east, drinking in beautiful views along the way. Dance past the ABBA Museum *(p123)* on your way to the Vasamuseet *(p120)*. The marvellous maritime museum has well-curated hour-long tours to take in the highlights in a hurry, including its famous remarkably well-preserved 17th-century warship.

Afternoon Delve deeper into Djurgården to *fika (p30)* with Swedish families at farm-to-fork champions Rosenthals Trädgård *(www.rosendalstradgard.se)*. Sample the soup made using produce from the kitchen garden. Later, loaf about Skansen *(p125)*, a sprawling open-air museum. It goes all in for seasonal festivities such as Christmas and Midsummer.

Evening Revel in a uniquely Nordic dinner at two Michelin-starred Oaxen Krog *(p137)*, housed in a former boat shed by the waterfront overlooking bobbing boats. Belly full, cross back to Gamla Stan for a curative nightcap at Pharmarium *(www.pharmarium.se)*, set on the site of the city's first apothecary.

←

☐ Café-lined cobbled streets.

☐ Bright lights and bustling crowds at Liseberg theme park.

☐ A tempting sugary delight for a traditional Swedish *fika*.

☐ A hockey player lining up the puck to shoot.

2 DAYS
in Gothenburg

Day 1

Morning Ease yourself into the day with brunch at Egg and Milk (www.eggandmilk. com), a slick, American-style diner. Fuelled by waffles and maple-smoked bacon, whizz around nearby Slottsskogen (p238), Gothenburg's biggest park, on a scooter hired here and pop into the museum at the top of the hill to say "hej" to the world's only stuffed blue whale.

Afternoon Ride the tram along leafy Linnégatan and jump off at Haga. Duck into Caféva (5 Haga Nygata) to tuck into hearty soup and sourdough rolls. From here, it's a short stroll to some of Gothenburg's best shopping streets.

Evening Make a beeline for Le Pub to rub shoulders with locals over a classic Swedish "afterwork" (expect beer, snacks and lively chatter). Then wend round the corner to Andra Långgatan and take your pick of the superb restaurants for dinner. Later, kick it up a notch at legendary local music venue Pustervik. Monday nights are all about beer and ping-pong. Return to Belle Époque Pigalle (www.hotelpigalle.se) for a luxurious night's sleep.

Day 2

Morning Start your day strolling through the glasshouses and exotic plants of Trädgårdsföreningen (p233). Tucked away among pretty rose bushes is Rosenkaféet, a popular *fika* spot with plenty of outdoor seating. It's a short walk from here to Kungsportsavenyn, Gothenburg's main thoroughfare – browse the high-end boutiques or get lost among the galleries at Göteborgs Konstmuseet (p236).

Afternoon Whisk up 23 floors in the ear-popping lift to Heaven 23 (www.heaven23. se), at the top of Gothia Towers hotel. The "King Size" open sandwich served here – complete with a mountain of west coast prawns – is every bit as good as the panoramic views. If you can stomach it, the white-knuckle thrill rides at the cutesy Liseberg theme park (p234) are just across the street.

Evening If there's a game on, snap up tickets to cheer on local hockey heroes Frölunda tear up the ice at Scandinavium. Then dive into tree-lined Södra Vägen for Dinner 22 (www.dinner22.se) and feast on modern plates of reindeer and lingonberry.

7 DAYS
on the West Coast

Day 1

Get a taste for small-town life in medieval Halmstad *(p262)*, whose impressive Danish castle was built in the early 17th century. Explore its cobbled streets on foot, then strike out for Halmstad's beaches – whatever the weather. Moody winter seascapes transform into a swimmer's paradise come. Up the coast, take a dip in the open-air bathhouse in Varberg *(p263)*, then soak up the laid-back vibe with dinner and drinks at John's Place *(www.johnsplace.nu)*. Fall asleep at Gottskär Hotell *(www.gottskar hotell.com)*, on the way to Gothenburg, to the sound of waves lapping the shore.

Day 2

Arrive early at Gunnebo Slott. This huge wooden mansion, just 9 km (5 miles) outside Gothenburg, feels a world away. Tour the splendid grounds and grand rooms, *fika* in the café, then head to Gothenburg in time for lunch at Feskekörka *(p235)*, aka the Fish Church. Sample *stekt sill på knäckebröd* (fried herring on crispbread) and Västerbottenost cheese, local favourites. The nearby Stadmuseum reveals how the city's history has been shaped by the sea. Later check out Välkommen Åter *(p231)*

and snap up vintage finds. As evening descends, relax with a drink and plates of just-landed *havskräftor och räkor* (langoustines and shrimp) at Sjöbaren *(www. sjobaren.se)*, Haga's best fish restaurant.

Day 3

Grab a hearty breakfast at Kafé Marmelad *(Mariagatan 17)* in Majorna, an old working-class neighbourhood now bursting with cool bars and cafés. From here the city's edgiest exhibitions beckon at boiler-house-turned-gallery Röda Sten *(www.rodasten. com)*, just a swift tram ride away. Follow the river back to the centre to pick up provisions and the keys to a rental car. It's less than an hour to Marstrand *(p253)*, crowned by a magnificent castle. Arrive in time for dinner and a cold west-coast lager at one of the harbourfront restaurants, and watch the boats come and go as you eat.

Day 4

Breakfast on a classic *smörgås* (open-faced sandwich) – topped with sliced eggs and caviar-from-a-tube (a Swedish rite of passage). The drive up to Tjörn *(p252)* reveals one stunning view after another. At Pilane

1 Sunlight rippling across a balmy Halmstad beach.

2 The venerable Feskekörka.

3 Still waters and sunny skies at Smögen's quay.

4 Sunset over Kosteröarna.

5 Winding Dalsland canal.

Gravfält, a massive Iron Age burial site, wander the standing stones, then picnic overlooking the ancient landscape. Make time to overnight at Salt & Sill (www.salto sill.se), a floating hotel with rooms on pontoons that jut out into the mirror-smooth sea. The sauna and a glass of aquavit are all you need to relax completely.

Day 5

Start the day zipping through tiny fishing villages along Orust's (p253) west coast, to Lysekil (p250). Enjoy a hefty fika at fuss-free Café Kungsgatan (Kungsgatan 32) before joining an oyster tour with Orust Shellfish (www.orust shellfish.se). Try your hand at shucking palm-sized oysters and slurp them down on the shore. On to colourful Smögen (p250), a magnet for partying Swedes and Norwegians during the summer. Wind up the day with the freshest fish at Skärets Krog (p255), followed by great cocktails in the piano bar.

Day 6

Seal spotting and blissful wild swims make the remote Weather Islands a marvellous detour. For everyone else, the northbound road leads to Strömstad (p247) and the ferry to the Kosteröarna (p248). Upon landing, turn your steps to Kosters Trädgårdar (www.kosterstradgardar. se), an organic garden restaurant and farm shop, for a cornucopia of fresh bread, tasty soup and cinnamon buns. Later, join Skärgårdsidyllen Kayak & Outdoors (www. skargardsidyllen.se) and see how much wildlife you can spot around Kosterhavet Nationalpark, during a guided kayak trip. Enjoy supper at Rökeri i Strömstad (www. rokerietistromstad.se) back in Strömstad.

Day 7

Start the day with a self-guided stroll through Strömstad's sculpture walk, then re-join your car for the cross-country drive to Läckö Slott (p254), one of Sweden's most beautiful castles. The long ride rewards with classic Swedish scenery – all big skies, rich forests and deep lakes – plus glimpses of the snaking Dalsland Canal (p265). Drift through the castle's richly decorated rooms and out into the grounds. Come evening, indulge in a low-mileage feast at ultra-modern Hvita Hjorten (p255). End the day before a blazing log fire in one of the eco-chic rooms, gazing across at the castle.

7 DAYS

in Southern Sweden

Day 1

Start in buzzy Malmö *(p210)* with coffee at Noir Kaffekultur *(Engelbrektsgatan 6)*, a real local hangout. Then swing into nearby Moderna Museet *(p210)*. Emerge, mind fizzing with the city's hottest artists, to grab a wrap at Falafel Baghdad *(p212)* – a kingpin in Malmö's rise to becoming Sweden's falafel capital. Spend the afternoon at Malmöhus *(p211)* discovering the city's history. At dinner, feast on nose-to-tail dishes at Bastard *(www.bastardrestaurant.se)* served by tattooed staff. The canals lead north to Ohboy *(www.ohboy.se)* and a blissful sleep.

Day 2

Borrow one of the hotel's push bikes and follow easy paths to quiet Riberborg beach, camera ready. Views of the Öresund Bridge *(p213)* and Turning Torso *(p211)* are picture perfect. Nearby Ribersborgs Kallbadhus *(www.ribersborgskallbadhus.se)* is *the* place for icy swims and wood-fired saunas. From here, zip over to Saltimporten Canteen *(www.saltimporten.com)*, whose flavour-packed lunches cannot be missed. Cycle back into the centre, to catch up with the cool crowd at Belle *(belle-epoque.se)* over dinner and cocktails.

Day 3

Breakfast on a bowl of muesli and *filmjölk* (pouring yogurt), before travelling west to Lund *(p218)*, one of Sweden's oldest and best-looking cities. From the 900-year-old cathedral, home to jaw-dropping vaulted ceilings, wander to Skissernas Museum *(p219)*, home to a collection of quirky modern art. Make time for a sourdough sandwich at Broder Jakobs Stenugnsbageri *(Klostergatan 9)*, then explore the sprawling botanical gardens. As evening sets in, converted stable house Ateljé Råbygård *(www.ateljerabygard.se)*, on Lund's outskirts, is an arty refuge.

Day 4

Choose *makrill fillet* (tomatoey mackerel) on a slice of rye for breakfast – a tasty Swedish classic and great fuel for a day of exploring Skåne. Pack a picnic lunch before driving to Björnstorp, where peculiar trolley-cycles take you over old railway sleepers, past lush countryside and shaded woodland, to pretty Veberöd and back. On the road again, head towards Ystad *(p221)*, pausing for a punt on the lake at Svaneholm Slott, a 16th-century fortress with original murder holes. Fans

1 Malmö's gorgous city hall.

2 The long, wooden pier to Ribersborgs Kallbadhus.

3 Lund University building.

4 Pretty flower-filled Ystad, home to TV's *Wallander*.

5 The standing stones of ancient Ales Stenar.

of *Wallander* will recognize Ystad's winding medieval streets and the call of the night-watchman at Santka Mariekyra. Book a tour with Cineteket (*www.ystad.se/ysvc*) to check out all the show's haunts. Beyond the half-timbered buildings of the city centre, indulge in a five-course Swedish treat at Villa Strandvägen (*www.villa strandvagen.se*). After dinner, a sumptuous night's sleep awaits.

Day 5

Make an early start for megalithic Ales Stenar (*p221*), with a quick detour to Olof Viktors farm shop (*www.olofviktors.se*) and find out why it was named Sweden's best *fika* in 2018. Carry on to the mysterious ship-shaped monument, known as Skåne's Stone Henge – a tour is essential. At the bottom of the hill, venture into Kåseberga Fisk (*www.kaseberga-fisk.se*) for *varmrökta laxfilé* (hot smoked salmon) – the house specialty – and a cold local beer. Further east, snow-white dunes announce your arrival at Sandhammaren, one of Sweden's most beautiful beaches. Enjoy an arctic swim, then head up the coast to Jord & Bord (*www.jordbord.se*) for innovative garden-fresh fare (reservations required).

Day 6

Fuel up on a *smörgås* of *skinka* (ham) and Hushållsost cheese. Dive back in time at Glimmingehus (*p224*), a well-preserved medieval manor. Tour secret passages looking for one of the chateau's eleven ghosts, try your hand at medieval DIY and wander the peaceful herb garden. Lunch in the castle's café, then carry on to the Nordic Sea Winery (*www.nordicsea winery.se*), just outside Simrishamn (*p224*), for an afternoon of tastings and vineyard tours. Come evening, revel in the warm hospitality of Karnelund (*www.karnelund.se*), a laid-back minimalist restaurant-with-rooms.

Day 7

Spend the morning on a farmshop tour – smoked herring at Sjöfolket (*www.sjofolket. se*), cherry chutney at Orelund (*www. orelund.se*), creamy truckles of goat's milk cheese at Vilhelmsdal (*www.vilhelmsdal.se*) – Skåne's countryside provides an abundant larder. Stocked up on goodies, zip past the tiny villages and rust-red farmsteads of the interior back to Malmö. Park up at the Spoonery (*www.spoonery.se*), in time to lunch on moose hot pot and jackfruit chilli, before setting off on your next adventure.

Smörgåsbord

No trip to Sweden is complete without tucking into an authentic *smörgåsbord* – a full-scale, buffet-style meal consisting of hot and cold *hors d'oeuvres*. Make like the Swedes and wash yours down with a shot of *akvavit* to start, lashings of beer throughout, and a coffee to savour with dessert. During the Christmas season, many Stockholm restaurants serve a special *smörgåsbord*, known as a *julbord*, which could include everything from meatballs and sausages to smoked salmon.

→

An appetizing *smörgåsbord* feast featuring cold meats and potatoes

SWEDEN FOR
FOODIES

Sweden's humble gastronomic reputation belies a powerhouse of subtle innovation. Thanks to New Nordic cuisine and an ever-inventive approach to fine dining, it's now a top foodie destination. Expect to find epicurean adventures in the most unexpected places.

From Foraging to Fine Dining

Leave the gleaming bistros that pair wine with attentive service in the cities to join Swedish foodies in the fields and forest. Through Edible County *(www.visitsweden. com/ediblecountry)*, you can join local guides on a foraging safari to source your supper. Hand the bounty over to one of four Michelin-starred chefs and enjoy the feast gathered round a picnic table. This is DIY dining at its best, where food is cooked over smoky wood fires.

←

Checking for quality while foraging mushrooms in the Swedish countryside

EAT

Bastard
Expect nose-to-tail dining, plus foraged forest flavours.

 D7 Mäster Johansgatan 11, Malmö bastardrestaurant.se

Ⓚ Ⓚ Ⓚ

Sjöbaren
Feast on just-landed fish dishes, served in cosy, cobbled Haga.

C5 Haga Nygata 25, Gothenburg Sjobaren.se

Ⓚ Ⓚ Ⓚ

A hearty dish made using wood-fired ingredients served up at Ekstedt ↑

VEGGIE MAGIC

Swedish food has a meaty reputation, but innovative plant-based dishes are becoming increasingly popular here. Most restaurants in the north will have a couple of vegetarian dishes on their menus, but southern Sweden is where it's at for more diverse options. Hermans *(p137)* is a powerhouse on the Stockholm veggie scene, and falafel wraps are cheap and tasty in Malmö *(p212)*.

Michelin-star chef Niklaus Ekstedt crafting a dish ↑

New Nordic Cuisine

The New Nordic focus on locally sourced ingredients and a feeling of homeliness has transformed the culinary landscape. At Stockholm's Ekstedt *(www.ekstedt.nu)*, traditional cooking methods are paired with sustainably sourced produce to create birch-fired meats and wild salads of the chef's childhood. Agrikultur *(www.agrikultur.se)* goes one step further, with menus that follow the whims of the chef, creating a cosy atmosphere, as if visiting with friends.

Vikings Days

Little Vikings will get a kick out of the hands-on exhibits at Stockholm's Historiska Museet *(p116)*. This fantastic museum runs Meet the Vikings days during the summer, when kids can make bread, play Viking games and practice archery in the historic courtyard. Outside the capital, check out Birka Viking Village *(p164)*, once an important trading post. Explore replica houses and stop for a Viking-style lunch of cereals, roots and berries (there's pancakes with jam for the fussy little Vikings).

←

A longboat moored among long reeds at the splendid Birka Viking Village

SWEDEN FOR
FAMILIES

It should come as no surprise: the birthplace of Pippi Longstocking and the three-point seatbelt is very good at looking after families. Wherever you go in Sweden, you'll find that families with *barnfamiljer* (young kids) are given the red-carpet treatment.

Outdoor Adventures

Sweden bursts with family-friendly ways to get into the great outdoors. Wild camp in Tivedens National Park *(p256)*, canoe Vaxsjön lake and splash in Fårö's *(p200)* sandy shallows. Young birders will be all aflutter at birder paradise Hornborgasjön near Hjo's *(p258)*, and sea monster-spotting at Östersund *(p298)* can keep little naturalists occupied for hours.

←
Birdwatchers scanning the nesting sites around lake Hornborgasjön

←
White-knuckle thrills on a stomach-dropping ride at popular Liseberg

Fantasitc Theme Parks

Let the little ones loose at fun-filled Astrid Lindgrens Värld *(p184)*. Explore pint-sized Noisy Village, follow Don't Touch the Ground Trail and venture into Pippi Longstocking's very own VillaKulla Cottage. Enthralling scenes from the books are played out on the stage by actors - and sometimes the audience too. Travelling with older children? Give them a white-knuckle time at Liseberg *(p234)*, slap-bang in the middle of Gothenburg. It's the biggest theme park in Scandinavia, with a bone-jangling wooden coaster and games aplenty.

←
Bright lights and Christmas festivities at Liseberg, Gothenburg

TOP 5 MONEY-SAVING IDEAS

Free Travel
Take advantage of free public transport for under-7s in Stockholm, Gothenburg and Malmö.

Cheap Eats
Prices are often lower at lunchtime. For the best deal, order the *dagens rätt* (daily special).

Get a City Pass
In Sweden's biggest cities, buy a City Pass for reduced admission to top attractions.

Go Camping
Wild camping is free across the country, just be sure to follow basic safety precautions.

Stay at Hostels
Built for families, these cheap digs might be in a converted plane or boat.

Pristine Beaches

Cool, clean swimming spots abound, even in the cities, but Sweden's best are found in its remote corners. Dig your feet in the Caribbean-like sand at Stenshuvud Nationalpark, outside Kivik *(p224)*. Find an unexpected treat to the north at Piteå *(p309)*, the Nordic Riviera, where a golden arc of sand basks in endless daylight during June and July.

←

White sands and turquoise waters at Stenshuvud Nationalpark, near Kivik

SWEDEN FOR
INCREDIBLE LANDSCAPES

Sweden's dramatic geography is home to some of Europe's last truly wild spaces. Flanked by the sea on one side and hinterland on the other, the country's spectacular scenery stretches from icy mountains to unblemished sandy beaches. Be sure to make the most of Sweden's inspiring landscapes.

Did You Know?

The Kungsleden hiking trail in northern Sweden stretches for an incredible 440 km (275 miles).

Islands Getaways

Sweet tranquillity awaits at Kosterhavet National Park, in Southern Götaland, where smooth granite islands rise from the sea like whales coming up for air. Snorkel over the cold-water corals, then dine on fresh oysters and local lobster. On Gotland, enjoy a classic Swedish holiday, diving into Lummelundagrottan's (p202) caves, then into the sea at Gotska Sandön (p204), or explore medieval Visby (p196).

→

Idyllic coastal path on Gotland; Cyclists (inset) exploring the town of Visby

Wild Protected Spaces

Find smultronställe – that special place that gives you happiness – at one of Sweden's abundant national parks and nature reserves. Follow the Kungsleden Trail (p304) into Sarek National Park in the remote northwest, to find inner peace amid herds of wild reindeer, endless glacier-cut valleys and snow-splattered mountains. To the south, rugged Tivedens National Park (p256) is peppered with huge Iron Age boulders and laced with gorgeous hiking trails. Pitch a tent at Kärringaudden or Mellannäsudden, in the park, and awake to birdsong.

←

Milky lakes and snaking rivulets through the Rapa Valley in Sarek National Park

▷ Brown Bears

Unless you're very lucky - or unlucky, as the case may be - you won't encounter a wild bear by accident. Maximize your chances of a sighting with Wild Sweden *(www.wildsweden.com)*, wildlife-spotting experts. Hole up in a cosy forest hide-out during summer - complete with fresh coffee, binoculars and long-lens cameras - and play the waiting game.

◁ Birds

Half a billion migratory birds pass through southern Sweden every autumn. Head to twitcher haven Falsterbo Fågelstation *(www. falsterbofagelstation.se)*, right under their flight path - expect to spot starlings and sparrowhawks.

SWEDEN FOR
WILDLIFE ENCOUNTERS

With vast wilderness areas covering much of the country, Sweden is rich with chance wildlife encounters. An array of big mammals can all be spotted here - with a bit of effort, while birders are in for a treat.

▷ Wolves

Vilified for centuries and still hunted in parts of Sweden, today wolves are few and far between. Pitch a camp with Wild Sweden *(www.wild sweden.com)* on a guided overnight tour in August or September, for the chance to hear their howl. Campfire dinner included.

▽ Reindeer

Drive far enough to the north to encounter wild reindeer – the herds bring traffic to a halt when on the move. Take part in year-round reindeer games with Nutti Sámi Siida *(www.nutti.se)* in Swedish Lappland. Watch tiny calves take their first steps during spring then return in winter for a snowy sleigh ride with the adults.

◁ Lynx

Most active around dawn and dusk, the sleek, light-brown lynx are almost impossible to spot in the wild. The lynx is likely to climb the nearest tree if you disturb it while hiking, so looking up as you stroll through the woods is a good start. Your best chance is at Nordens Ark *(www.nordensark.se)*, a vast conservation park in Västra Götaland.

Did You Know?

An adult elk can grow to around 230 cm (7.5 ft) in height.

▷ Elk

Known by Swedes as the king of the forest (and by North Americans as the moose) *Alces alces* is a true giant. But these are typically shy beasts, and they tend to avoid human encounters. To get up close to these elusive creatures, plan a trip to Värmland Moose Park *(www.moose-world.com)* to learn about their habits and even feed bulls by hand.

The Northern Lights

Capturing the *aurora borealis* in Sweden is a test for any photographer – not least because of the cold. Good equipment helps, especially a tripod and manual exposure, but the location is important too. Try the Sky Station *(p310)* in arctic Lappland, from late September to mid-April, when the night sky is at its darkest. The park falls within in the so-called rain shadow of the Noulja mountains which ups your chances of clear skies.

$\rightarrow$

Winter camping under the Northern Lights in Kungsleden, Lappland

SWEDEN FOR
PHOTOGRAPHERS

Whether you're window shopping, island-hopping or gazing up at the Northern Lights, Sweden is sure to have you reaching for your camera. Here we reveal what's at the top of our shot list.

Capture the Coast

Wild and windswept for much of the year, the coast around Skaftö *(p251)* bursts into life in the spring. Time your shoot for the late evening on a warm day, when the skies glow red and pink. For an eerie, edge-of-the-world mood, the contorted sea stacks of Fårö *(p200)* lend themselves to dramatic shots in winter.

$\rightarrow$

Warm pink light bathing a rust-red cottage on the edge of the Bohuslan Coast near Skaftö

LINA JONN: IN FOCUS

Farmer's daughter and documentary photographer Lina Jonn opened her own studio in 1891. In vogue with trends of the late 19th century, Lina found her niche in portraiture, creating visiting cards and family albums, but continued to document rural life as it unfolded around her. Today, her images of washing shoes and King Oscar II form an unflinching portrait of Sweden as it once was.

→ Striking art in the *tunnelbana*, by Hallek and Pallarp

Stockholm

The capital's spectacular panoramas and moody weather are an invitation to keep on snapping. Gamla Stan *(p66)* is the place to start, all colourful wonky houses and winding cobbled lanes. Climb Monteliusvägen *(p133)* to snap Riddarholmskyrkan *(p74)* at its best. For an edgier vibe, jump aboard the subway – Stockholm's *tunnelbana* reveals the beating heart of the city.

↑ Glowing Gamla Stan reflected in mirror-still waters

Take to the Trails

Find yourself on the well-trod and barely-there hiking trails that snake across the country. Traipse through Skuleskogens Nationalpark *(p288)* along trails through ancient forest that break into epic clifftop views of the coast. All around Sälen *(p281)*, take your pick of 200 km (124 miles) of well-marked trails criss-crossing, ranging from family-friendly stretches to tricky mountainous treks. Further north, linger on the Kungsleden Trail *(p304)*, with wild camping or cosy, back-to-basics cabins.

$\rightarrow$

Hiking high above the cloud line in Jämtland, Southern Norrland

SWEDEN FOR
OUTDOOR ADVENTURES

The vast Swedish countryside allows for some serious outdoor fun. Gear up to enjoy thrills and spills all year long. From multi-day hikes and wild camping to skiing under the midnight sun, there's something everyone.

Cast the Net

With more than 100,000 lakes, there are fishing holes aplenty. Dive into the Jämtland mountains with Nordic Footprints *(www.nordicfootprints.se)* and try your hand at wilderness fishing. Can't get out of Stockholm? Catch & Relax *(www.catch relax.se)* have all the best fishing spots in the Stockholm Archipelago *(p158)*. Check out Svenska Fiskeregler for permit information *(www. svenskafiskeregler.se)*.

$\leftarrow$

Waiting for the big one to bite in the mirror-still waters near Norway

TOP 5 OUTDOOR EXPERIENCES

Hike Kungsleden
Trek over 440 km
(275 miles) of trails.

Ski Riksgränsen
Ski under the midnight
sun at Midsummer.

Camp Wild
Sweden's "right to roam"
lets you camp anywhere.

Fish for Food
Catch a feast aroud the
coast, lakes and streams.

Sail in Archipelagos
Hoist sails, then dive in.

Wet and Wild

In springtime the snows disappear, sending gushing meltwater through Sweden's rivers. Chase big water on the white-water Kukkola rapids near Tornedalen (p310), on the Finnish border. As summer nears, seek out wild swimming spots all around the idyllic Koster Islands (p248) and rent canoes and kayaks to drift over the still, warm waters of Lake Vättern (p258).

Kayaking towards the
glowing embers of the
sun, near Smögen ↑

SPORTLOV

Every February, skis are waxed ready for the week-long winter holiday known as *sportlov*, or sport break. It began in 1940 as an effort to save fuel by keeping children out of school for a week. By the 1950s, the government had adopted the vacation to slow the spread of winter viruses. Today it is an institution dedicated to being active, and an excuse to hit the slopes.

Zipping over perfect ↑
powder with unending
Jämtland views

Seize the Snow and Ice

Embrace the long dark winter by getting out into it. Ice skate in Kungsträdgården (p86), under the lights of Stockholm. Grab your skis in Storlien (p299) and pick between great slopes and trails near the Norwegian border. Want more? Go extreme in Skellefteå (p308), home of winter swimming, then climb frozen waterfalls with ISM (www.alpin-ism.com), under the Northern Lights.

Respect for the Environment

Fuelled by smart policymaking as well as a culture of getting out into nature, Sweden takes environmental protection seriously. Small changes make a big difference. Pitch in by cycling – using cycle-sharing scheme City Bike *(www.bike share map.com)* – and recycling whenever possible. As the Swedes have proven, it just takes one person to start a global movement.

←

Getting around Stockholm by bike, using a city-wide cycle-sharing scheme

SWEDEN FOR
THE SWEDISH LIFESTYLE

From perfecting the work-life balance to reconnecting with nature, the modern Swedish lifestyle holds a special appeal to outsiders. Here are some of the key ingredients to look out for.

Classic Scandinavian Design

Snygg (good-looking) simplicity is central to the Swedish cultural aesthetic. Functional, elegant furnishings can be found in the most unexpected places. Stop for *fika* at Café String *(www.cafestring.com)* or Café Asti *(p231)* and leave with vintage finds to take home.

NOT TOO LITTLE, NOT TOO MUCH

Loosely translated, the word *lagom* means "just the right amount". Is two cars really essential, if you already have one? Is a bigger pay cheque worth it when life is already *lagom*? Rather than compromise, Swedes know it's all about striking the perfect balance.

↑ Going for long hikes
(inset) and getting out in
the great outdoors

Love of the Outdoors

Many Swedes counter the gloom of the gruelling winter with fresh air and lots of exercise. *Friluftsliv* (literally, outdoor life) is a Swedish sensibility covering anything and everything outdoorsy. Make like a Swede by taking a trip to the Fryken Lakes *(p273)*, having a run through the Tessinparken *(p127)*, or going for a long hike on the Kungsleden Trail *(p204)*. Your mind and body will thank you.

Shall We Fika?

The Swedish concept of *fika* doesn't translate easily, but it's a fundamental part of life across Sweden. The word refers both to the activity of taking a break and the hot drink and cinnamon bun enjoyed during it. The best way to get into the *fika* state of mind is to pause, reflect and connect with others at a café or bakery. Give your *fika* a little luxury and tuck into a princess cake at Brogyllen *(p232)* in Gothenburg, or sip a coffee while you read at Stockholm's Johan & Nyström *(p133)*.

↑ Lots of light, clean lines
and pops of colour,
typifying Scandi design

→

Taking a reading break
with a cup of coffee

Traditional Cottages

What could be more Swedish than a little red summer house with white trim? Known as Falu red, the copper-rich paint that gives it its colour also protects the wooden façade from the elements. Used only for part of the year, they once lacked any amenities – all part of the getting-back-to-basics appeal. Today when you go Swedish for a summer though AirBnb.com, these cute cottages come with Scandi design, lashings of hot water and even Wi-Fi.

←

Traditional timber-build, red-painted cottages in the Swedish countryside

SWEDEN FOR
ARCHITECTURE

Modern Swedish architecture is all about creating functional spaces that take inspiration from the natural world. But the country is also peppered with traditional cottages, grand castles, and whimsical palaces, plus some very unusual hotels. Here are some of the highlights.

Modern Engineering

Head to southern Malmö to snap stunning shots of the Turning Torso (p211), a jaw-droppingly innovative residential building, flanked by the vast 8-km- (5-mile-) long Öresund Bridge (p213). Alternatively, marvel at the Kuggen in Gothenburg. Using terracotta panels and light-optimizing window bays, it astounds from all angles.

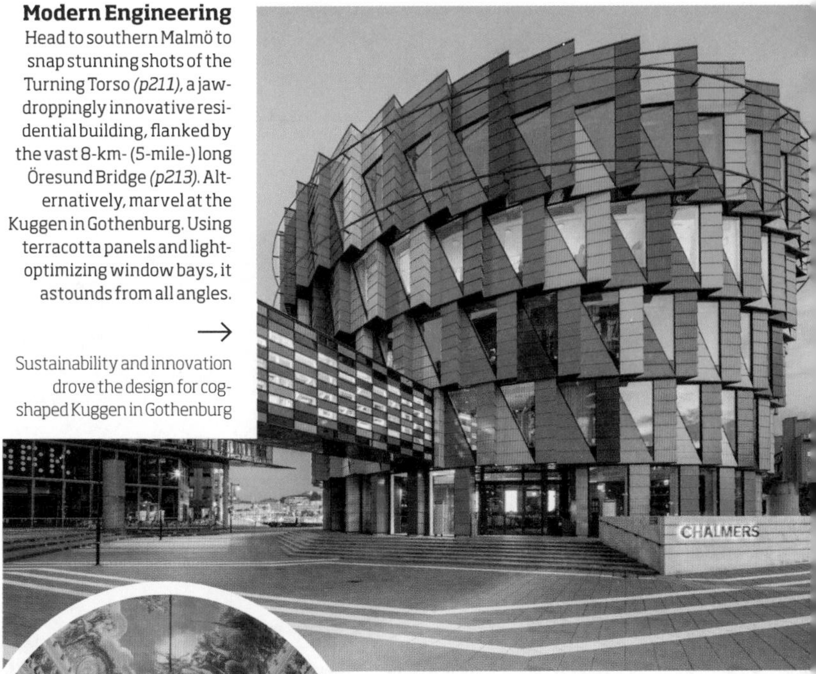

→

Sustainability and innovation drove the design for cog-shaped Kuggen in Gothenburg

←

The opulently decorated chambers of Drottningholm

Royal Abodes

Sweden's magnificent castles, peppered across the landscape, are often overlooked yet provide great days out. A driving tour (p172) around Lake Mälaren takes you past the king among Swedish palaces, UNESCO World Heritage Site Drottningholm, inspired by Versailles. Stroll through the Baroque garden, then take a guided tour of the royal family's grand private residence. Their official residence, Kungliga Slottet (p66), seems austere by comparison. Elsewhere, handsome Malmöhus Slott (p211), with its Tower-of-London-like past, and Örebro Slott (p270), sitting on a river island, are not to be missed.

←

Splendid 18th-century Drottningholm Palace aglow as the sun sets

STAY

Treehotel
Spend a night high up in the canopy in an eco-friendly bird's nest or UFO. Marvellous eco-credentials

🅰B2 🏠Edeforsvägen 2A, Harads 🅦 tree hotel.se

🄺🄺🄺

Utter Inn
Sleep with the fishes in submarine rooms under Lake Mälaren. Inflatable canoes to take you back to land included.

🅰E4 🏠Lake Mälaren, Västerås 🅦 visit vasteras.se/aktor/ hotell-utter-inn

🄺🄺🄺

A YEAR IN
SWEDEN

JANUARY

My Dog *(early Jan)*. Europe's largest dog competition; events are held over four days in Gothenburg.

△ **Kiruna Snow Festival** *(last week in Jan)*. Winter is celebrated with reindeer racing, figure skating and more at this renowned festival.

FEBRUARY

△ **Jokkmokk Winter Market** *(first weekend in Feb)*. Colourful festival with street markets, reindeer sledding and races.

Spring Salon *(Feb–Mar)*. This major art exhibition showcases work by well-known artists and new talent at Liljevalchs in Stockholm.

MAY

△ **May Day** *(1 May)*. This traditional workers' day is marked with processions and celebrations countrywide.

Elite Race *(last weekend in May)*. The world's best horses race in this traditional and prestigious international trotting competition held over two days at Solvalla.

JUNE

Stockholm Marathon *(early Jun)*. One of the world's ten biggest marathons with up to 21,500 runners.

Archipelago Boat Day *(mid-Jun)*. Steamboats assemble at Strömkajen for a round trip to Vaxholm.

△ **Midsummer Eve** *(penultimate Fri in Jun)*. A major Swedish festival celebrated by dancing around a flower-bedecked maypole.

SEPTEMBER

△ **Kivik Apple Market** *(end of Sep)*. Apples are the focus of this two-day festival in Skåne. Giant art installations created with tons of apples are a particular highlight.

Harvest Festival *(end Sep-early Oct)*. Sweden's biggest harvest festival takes place over four days in Öland, with around 900 events and local food, concerts and exhibitions.

OCTOBER

Lidingöloppet *(first weekend of Oct)*. The world's largest cross-country race, with tens of thousands of competitors.

Affordable Art Fair, Stockholm *(mid-Oct)*. A fresh collection of contemporary artworks from hundreds of established artists and rising stars.

△ **Stockholm Jazz Festival** *(mid-Oct)*. One of the city's biggest events in over 60 venues.

MARCH

△ **Vasaloppet Ski Race** *(early Mar)*. World-famous long-distance ski race.

Stockholm International Boat Show *(early Mar)*. Spring's major boat exhibition at Stockholm International Fairs in Älvsjö.

Åselenappet *(end of Mar)*. Ice-fishing competition, which is the high point of the winter market in Åsele, Lappland.

APRIL

△ **Start of Salmon Fishing Season, Mörrumsån** *(1 Apr)*. Sweden's main salmon river attracts masses of fishermen looking to catch salmon and sea trout.

Konstrundan *(Easter)*. Hundreds of artists in Skåne open their studios and workshops to visitors.

Walpurgis Night *(30 Apr)*. Around the country, bonfires and celebratory singing welcome in the new season.

JULY

△ **Stockholm Pride** *(end of Jul/early Aug)*. The Pride Parade, with over 60,000 participants, is the highlight of the week-long festival.

Skule Song Festival *(first weekend in Jul)*. One of Sweden's largest singing festivals, held at the foot of the Skule mountain on the High Coast.

Stånga Games *(mid-Jul)*. Gotland's yearly "Olympic" games are held for five days.

AUGUST

△ **Malmö Festival** *(mid-Aug)*. This eight-day street fair takes place at several venues throughout the city, with free concerts and international artists.

Gotland Medieval Week *(early Aug)*. Visby turns into a 14th-century Hanseatic city with tournaments, plays and music, plus medieval costumes.

Way out West *(mid-Aug)*. Held in Gothenburg, the west coast's biggest music festival draws famous musicians from around the world.

NOVEMBER

Gustav Adolf Day *(6 Nov)*. Gothenburg celebrates the royal founder of the city on the anniversary of his death.

△ **Stockholm Food & Wine** *(early Nov)*. The largest public fair for food and drink in the Nordic region.

St Martin's Day *(10-11 Nov)*. Parties honour St Martin of Tours and Martin Luther.

DECEMBER

△ **Christmas Markets** *(from early Dec)*. Open-air markets appear across the country. Those at Skansen and Stortorget in Stockholm are particularly atmospheric.

Lucia Celebrations *(13 Dec)*. An annual candlelit procession surrounding Lucia, a mythical figure and the bearer of light. Traditional songs fill the day and fireworks fill the evening in the country.

A BRIEF
HISTORY

Sweden has a history like no other. Bold Vikings travelled far, trading with foreign powers. Conquest catapulted Sweden into a continental superpower. Ravaged by famine, Sweden remained neutral during the World Wars; today its humanitarian efforts make it a beacon of hope for the modern age.

Prehistoric Origins

Sweden's earliest signs of human life were in the province of Skåne, left by the Hamburg culture who travelled across the Danish-Swedish land bridge to hunt reindeer. Members of the Bromme culture were the first to permanently settle here and hunt large game. Rock carvings from the Stone Age depict hunting, while those from the Bronze Age illustrate the development of agriculture. Contact with the Roman Empire improved the quality of iron tools and weapons, advancing manufacturing and agricultural techniques. Population growth and then overcrowding forced the Swedes to expand eastwards.

① Map showing Scandinavia, dated 1730.

② Vitlycke, one of the largest Bronze Age rock carvings in Scandinavia.

③ A Viking runestone photographed in winter.

④ Medieval paintings adorn the interior of a Swedish Church.

Timeline of events

c 15,500-13,100 BC

Hamburg culture hunts in Skåne for the spring and summer months.

c 12,000 BC

Bromme culture permanently settles in Skåne, near the city of Malmö.

500 BC

Iron Age: Swedes start creating stone circles and erect ship monuments.

98 AD

Tacitus, Roman historian, writes the first account of the Swedes.

Vikings Expand Eastwards

Swedes took part in some raids in the west normally associated with the Vikings, but their activity was mainly in the east. In search of silver and furs, they secured trade routes to the Eastern Roman Empire, attacking towns along the routes to ensure the safety of their merchants. Some served as mercenaries to foreign leaders, such as the Varangians, the Byzantine Emperor's bodyguards. The wealthy memorialized their service in rune-stones. Others made settlements in Russia such as Novgorod. Finns called the Swedes Rus, which is the origin of Russia's name.

Christianity and the Unification of Sweden

Within Sweden, there were two main tribes: the Swedes and the Götar. The Swedes occupied the east around Stockholm, while the Götar lived in the west around lakes Vättern and Vänern. They were united under Sweden's first Christian king, Olaf Skötkonung, thus gaining recognition from the international community. Conversion occurred over generations, and artwork shows a mixture of Christian and Viking influences. By the late 12th century, the Kingdom of Sweden was firmly established.

STONE CIRCLES

The Vikings created stone circle graves in the early and middle Iron Age, from about 500 BC to 600 AD. These were made with an odd number of stones, which represented the chairs for the judges. The odd number ensured that any deadlocks in judge-ments were avoided. The stones were often very large and there would usually be at least nine.

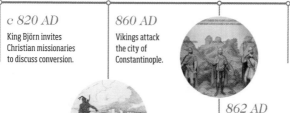

c 820 AD
King Björn invites Christian missionaries to discuss conversion.

860 AD
Vikings attack the city of Constantinople.

862 AD
Rurik, a Varangian, establishes the Rurik dynasty in Novgorod.

995 AD
Olaf Skötkonung becomes Sweden's first Christian King.

The Black Death

The Black Death first entered Scandinavia through Bergen, Norway, when labourers pulled a drifting vessel into the harbour. Its crew had perished, and within months, thousands of citizens in Bergen died. Victims suffered from dizziness, headaches, boils, and black spots on the skin. During the mid-14th century, the plague reached the Swedish province of Halland, where it continued its journey eastwards, killing one-third of the Swedish population, including King Magnus IV.

Reformation

The Papacy had immense power over Swedish monarchs. They appointed high-ranking clergymen and controlled convents and monasteries, which acted as schools and hospitals. The Swedes launched crusades against the heretical Finns and the Orthodox Christians of Novgorod with the support of the Papacy. King Gustav Vasa converted to Protestantism to centralize power around the monarchy. He confiscated church property, forcing churches to either close or convert, and had the Bible translated into Swedish from the Lutheran German version.

↑ Display at Medeltidsmuseet, Stockholm, depicting a victim of the plague

Timeline of events

1349
The Black Death reaches Sweden, killing one third of the population.

1536
Sweden adopts Protestantism with the spread of the Reformation.

1628
Vasa ship sinks on its maiden voyage.

1632
Gustavus II Adolphus is killed at the battle of Lützen.

1654
Queen Kristina, daughter of Gustavus II Adolphus, abdicates to convert to Catholicism.

Rise and Decline of the Swedish Empire

The Thirty Years' War (1618–48) was a conflict between Catholics and Protestants. King Gustavus II Adolphus and his unstoppable army entered the war on the side of the Protestants. The Swedes smashed their way into Germany, marking the height of power for the Swedish Empire. But decades of warfare and an outbreak of plague eventually weakened the empire. King Charles XII lost the battle of Poltava against Peter the Great of Russia, and sought asylum in the Ottoman Empire. In his absence, Sweden's enemies freely picked territories from the kingdom.

Emigration to the United States

In the 19th century, many Swedes left home in search of a better life. European Revolutions raised the political awareness of the poor, and they wanted freedom from oppressive monarchs. Some emigrated to escape the Lutheran Church, but most left due to desperate living conditions. Consecutive crop failures caused famine among the poor, killing thousands, and leaving many more destitute, unable to pay inflated prices for food. About 1.3 million Swedes emigrated to the US around this time.

1 Gustav Vasa addressing troops, 1836. ↑

2 Portrait of King Gustavus II Adolphus (1594-1632).

3 Poster advertising passage from Gothenburg to Chicago.

Did You Know?

For more than a century (1611-1721) Sweden was the dominant power in northern Europe.

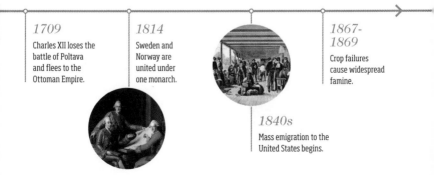

1709
Charles XII loses the battle of Poltava and flees to the Ottoman Empire.

1814
Sweden and Norway are united under one monarch.

1867-1869
Crop failures cause widespread famine.

1840s
Mass emigration to the United States begins.

Industrialization

The abolition of restrictive guild laws opened new job opportunities for men and women with manufacturers, while mechanized agriculture freed up labourers to seek employment elsewhere – many flocked to the city to work in factories. Swedish exports of natural resources such as iron, copper, and timber and manufactured goods strengthened the economy, and the government invested in modern infrastructure. By the 20th century, Stockholm had been thoroughly modernized, benefiting from water mains and sewage.

World War I and Social Reforms

Sweden remained strictly neutral and refused to negotiate trade agreements with the warring countries. Without the trade deals, the British enforced its blockade against Swedish supply vessels, causing inflated food prices and food shortages. Swedes rioted, demanding food for their families. These riots turned into peaceful protests for improved living conditions, women's suffrage, and an eight-hour workday. Women won the right to vote after the war and exercised it in the 1921 election.

1 Men at work in a huge factory in Sweden.

2 A Swedish soldier in World War II.

3 Wind turbines generating sustainable electricity, Gothenburg.

Did You Know?

The Swedish Succession Act was altered in 1980 to allow for female succession.

Timeline of events

1846-1864
Guild Laws are abolished, making craft professions available to the majority.

1901
First Nobel Prize is awarded.

1917
Hunger riots; Swedes demand an end to the food shortages.

1919
Women are granted the right to vote.

1945
Swedish Red Cross rescues concentration camp victims in Germany.

3

World War II and Humanitarian Efforts

Sweden again was neutral, but the government learned from past mistakes and negotiated trade deals. Its economy and infrastructure remained intact, allowing resources to be directed towards humanitarian efforts. Swedes got supplies over the border to help the invaded Norwegians. Countries occupied by the Nazis sent their most vulnerable to Sweden for safety. Missions were conducted to Germany to rescue concentration camp victims. After the war, the Swedish Red Cross provided medical care to civilians and soldiers in the conflicts in Vietnam and Korea.

Modern Sweden

Today, Sweden's economy remains strong from its exports of vehicles, pharmaceuticals, and natural resources, but also from its innovations. Start-ups such as Skype and Bluetooth are integrated into daily life, and companies must follow strict environmental standards, promoting sustainability. In 2018, Sweden presented its plan to the United Nations to achieve a low-carbon economy with clean energy and water.

ALFRED NOBEL

Alfred Nobel, a Swedish engineer, created dynamite for mining, inadvertently contributing to the development of weapons. Nobel was shattered that his reputation was associated with war, so upon his death he donated his fortune to establish the Nobel Peace Prize, with the hope of encouraging humanity to create a better world.

1986
Murder of Prime Minister Olof Palme sends shockwaves through Sweden.

1995
Sweden joins the European Union.

2003
Swedes votes "No" in a referendum to join the Euro.

2018
Sweden presents its climate plan to the United Nations.

EXPERIENCE STOCKHOLM

Södermalm's picturesque waterfront

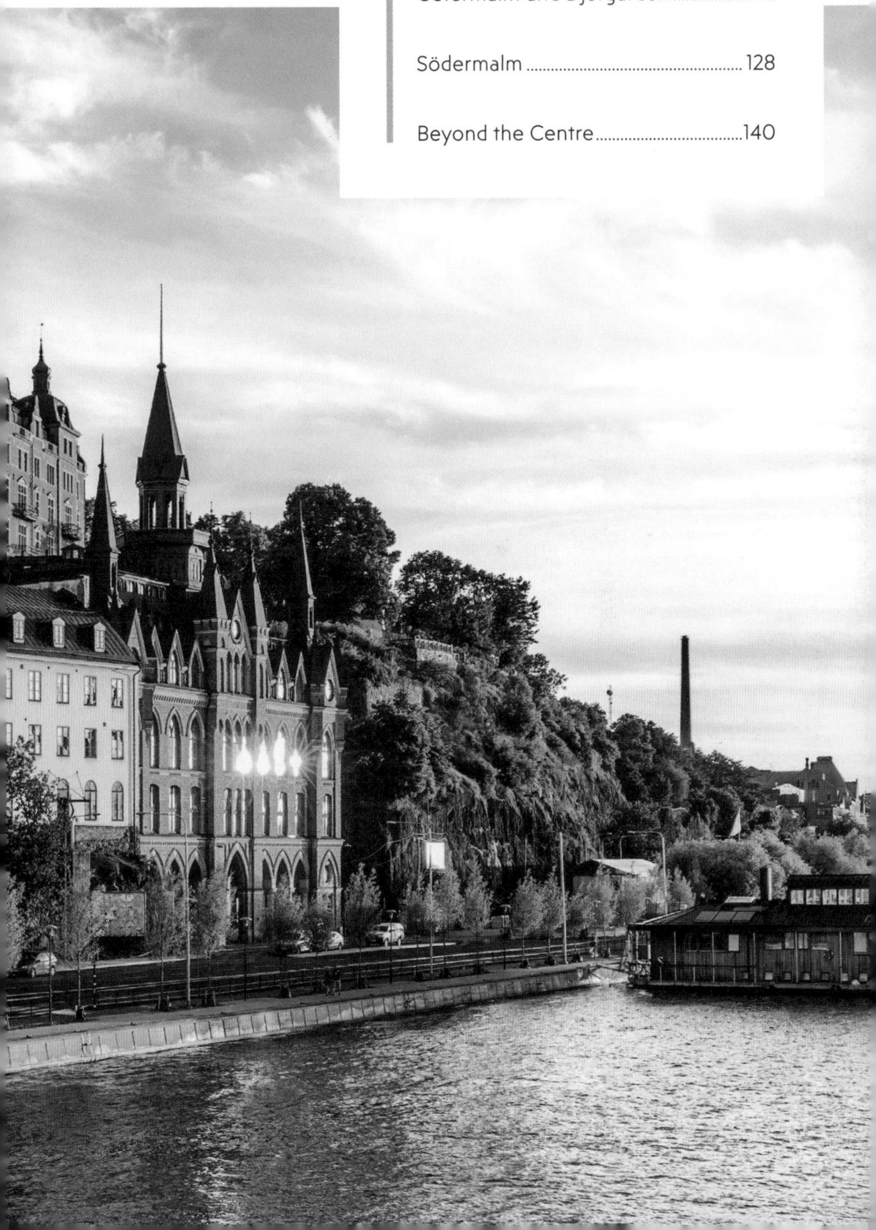

EXPLORE
STOCKHOLM

This guide divides Stockholm into five sightseeing areas, as shown on the map below, and an area beyond the centre. Find out more about each area on the following pages.

BIRKASTAN

Stadsbiblioteket

Observatorie-
lunden

Vasa-
parken

CITY
p80

Humle-
gården

Karla-
pian

Engelbrekts-
plan

NORRMALM

Östermalms-
torg

Historiska
museet

Norra
Bantorget

Konserthuset

Hötorget

Armémuseum

Kronobergs-
parken

Sergels-
torg

Norrmalms-
torg

ÖSTERMALM

Klara Kyrka

KUNGSHOLMEN

Kungliga
Operan

Blasie-
holmen

**BLAISIEHOLMEN
AND SKEPPSHOLMEN**
p98

Stadshuset

Kungliga
Slottet

Moderna
museet

Skeppsholmen

Västerbron

Riddarholmen

Riddarfjärden

GAMLA STAN
p62

Kastellholmen

Långholmen

Saltsjön

Skinnarviks-
parken

Slussen

Stadsmuseet

Mosebacke-
torg

Fotografiska

SÖDERMALM
p128

Katarina
Kyrka

SOFO

Tantolunden

Medborgar-
platsen

Nytorget

Vitabergs-
parken

SÖDERMALM

LILJEHOLMEN

Eriksdals-
lunden

ÅRSTA

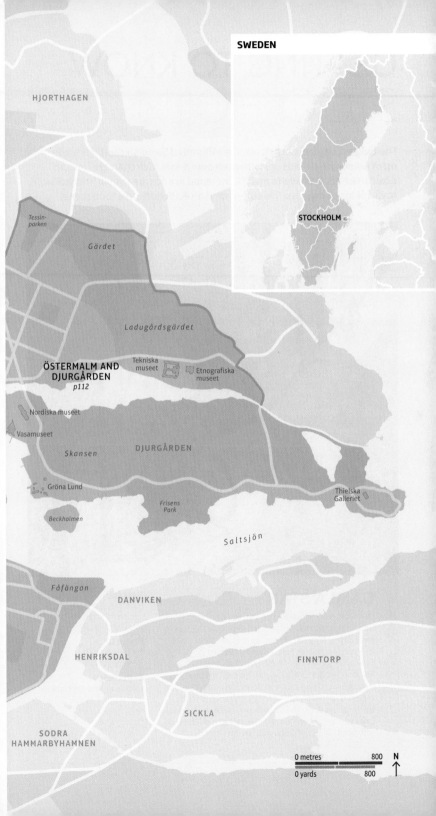

SWEDEN

STOCKHOLM

HJORTHAGEN

Tessin-
parken

Gärdet

Ladugårdsgärdet

ÖSTERMALM AND
DJURGÅRDEN
p112

Tekniska
museet

Etnografiska
museet

Nordiska museet

Vasamuseet

Skansen

DJURGÅRDEN

Gröna Lund

Frisens
Park

Thielska
Galleriet

Beckholmen

Saltsjön

Fåfängan

DANVIKEN

HENRIKSDAL

FINNTORP

SICKLA

SODRA
HAMMARBYHAMNEN

| 0 metres | | 800 |
| 0 yards | | 800 |

N
↑

GETTING TO KNOW
STOCKHOLM

The biggest city in Scandinavia, the influential Swedish capital is made up of numerous islands, all with their own distinctive character and an eco-conscious attitude to match. Crammed in each area you'll find storied royal history, edgy creative culture and an eclectic Nordic food scene.

GAMLA STAN

PAGE 62

The nucleus of old Stockholm, this historic island of Gothic steeples, royal palaces and grandiose treasury, has a strong fairy-tale like feel to it, especially at night. The stately buildings here, including the vast Royal Palace, are some of the finest examples of Roman Baroque architecture in the city, but even the pastel-coloured façades of souvenir stores and antiques shops will excite architecture and design enthusiasts. In the narrow alleys you'll find tucked-away coffee shops and cafés where *fika* (a coffee and cake break) is celebrated with Semla buns and lashings of cream.

Best for
History, regal drama, atmospheric cafés, the changing of the guard

Home to
The Royal Palace (Kungliga Slottet)

Experience
Fika *in a medieval cellar café*

PAGE 80

CITY

Stockholm's downtown core is a sprawling green oasis, interlaced with parks, leafy squares and embankments populated by fishermen reeling in the day's dinner. For lovers of art and culture, this area satisfies every desire, offering a lavish opera house, dance museum, culture house and concert hall where the Nobel Prize ceremony takes place annually. As the evening approaches, settle down with a cocktail at one of the many rooftop bars in the district to put the bustling and cool neighbourhood into perspective.

Best for
Culture, shopping and rooftop views

Home to
Stadshuset

Experience
Bagging prime tickets before glamming-up for a night at the Kungliga Operan

PAGE 98

BLASIEHOLMEN AND SKEPPSHOLMEN

This is Stockholm at its most luxurious and elegant. Swanky palaces, hotels, state residences and a castle sit alongside banks, antiques stores, art galleries and auction houses in this area. Upping the opulence of this district are its major museums and cultural institutions. Teater Galeasen is the avant-garde hub for new Scandi drama, Moderna museet is the country's leader in contemporary art, and the Nationalmuseum is home to more than half a million artifacts.

Best for
Art and antiques, naval history and museums

Home to
Moderna museet, Nationalmuseum

Experience
A boat trip from the quayside for a full-day archipelago tour

→

PAGE 112

ÖSTERMALM AND DJURGÅRDEN

These two areas forge a link between the city's perfectly preserved past and ecologically aware future. In Östermalm, the highlights are the Historiska museet (Swedish History Museum) and the lavish 19th-century mansions on Strandvagen. Djurgården, by contrast, presents a fitting tribute to all things Swedish along Saltsjön bay. Here, you can celebrate ABBA, read up on Pippi Longstocking, spot elk or board a 17th-century warship.

Best for
Diverse museums and wildlife

Home to
*Historiska museet,
Nordiska museet, Vasamuseet*

Experience
*Singing along to ABBA's hits with Agnetha,
Frida and the boys at their interactive museum*

PAGE 128

SÖDERMALM

This is where you'll be rewarded with the best views over the city. Södermalm's calling card is Fjällgatan and as "Stockholm's balcony" it presents a pixel-perfect, head-on shot of Gamla Stan and its outlying islands. But don't let the surrounding wooden houses fool you – there's a defiant indie spirit here, too, and Södermalm is as trendy as the city gets. Expect cool cafés and off-brand fashion stores, plus one-offs like an outdoor boule bar and Fotografiska, a pioneering centre for photography.

Best for
Panoramas, photography and hipster culture

Home to
Fjällgatan, Stockholms Stadsmuseum

Experience
*Relaxing on a beach in Tantolunden Park
on a midsummer's day*

BEYOND THE CENTRE

It's easy to venture beyond Stockholm, with plenty of impressive attractions warranting day trips. On an embankment 10km (6 miles) west of the city, Drottningholm offers a serene alternative to the buzz of the city centre. The private residence of the royal family, it's complemented by a theatre, park and Chinese Pavilion. Head east, on the other hand, and the wider Stockholm archipelago begins to appear. At this point, in between the bigger islands of Värmdö, Ingarö and Ljusterö and views of copper-red houses, you may feel tempted to stay an extra couple of days.

Best for
Summer houses, sailboat trips and royal gardens

Home to
Drottningholm

Experience
An overnight stay in a wooden cottage in the Stockholm archipelago

GAMLA STAN

Relics of Stockholm's early history as a town in the 13th century can still be found on Stadsholmen, the largest island in Gamla Stan (Old Town). The island is an area of huge historical heritage, with the many sights just a few metres apart.

The Royal Palace is the symbol of Sweden's era as a great power in the 17th and early 18th centuries, and its magnificent state rooms, apartments and artifacts are well matched to the Roman Baroque-style exterior. The historic buildings standing majestically around Slottsbacken underline Stockholm's role as a capital city.

Bridges lead to Riddarholmen, with its 17th-century palaces and royal crypt, and to Helgeandsholmen for the newer splendours of the Riksdagshuset (Parliament building).

GAMLA STAN

Must See

❶ The Royal Palace
(Kungliga Slottet)

Experience More

❷ Tessinska Palatset
❸ Bondeska Palatset
❹ Storkyrkan
❺ Stenbockska Palatset
❻ Tyska Kyrkan
❼ Stortorget
❽ Judiska museet
❾ Västerlånggatan
❿ Riddarholmskyrkan
⓫ Wrangelska Palatset
⓬ Medeltidsmuseet
⓭ Postmuseum
⓮ Evert Taubes Terrass
⓯ Riddarhuset
⓰ Riksdagshuset

Eat

① Café Järntorget
② Chokladkoppen
③ Caffellini Espresso Bar

Stay

④ Sven Vintappare
⑤ Scandic Gamla Stan
⑥ First Hotel Reisen

CITY

VATTUGATAN

HERKULESGATAN

RÖDBODGATAN

JAKOBSGATAN

FREDSGATAN

TEGELBACKEN

Vasabron

CENTRALBRON

Strömsborg

RIDDAR-HUSKAJEN

Riddarhuset ⓯

Stenbockska
Palatset ❺

Evert Taubes ⓮
Terrass

BIRGER
JARLS
TORG

⓫
Wrangelska
Palatset

❿
Riddarholms-
kyrkan

Riddarholmen

Riddarfjärden

SÖDER MÄLARSTRAND

Mariaberget

TIMMERMANSGATAN

BASTUGATAN

BLECKTORNSGRÄND

BELLMANSGATAN

GAMLA
STAN

BRÄNNKYRKAGATAN

HORNSGATAN

D

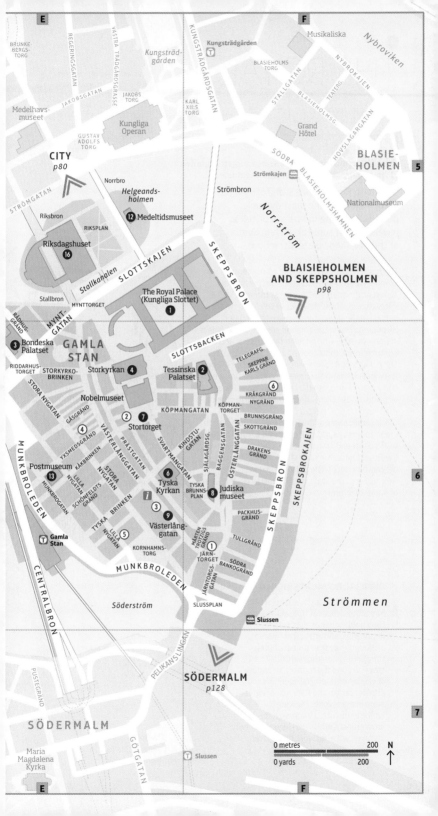

❶ ⊘ 🖾 🖰

THE ROYAL PALACE
KUNGLIGA SLOTTET

📍 E5 **Ⓐ Gamla Stan** **Ⓣ Gamla Stan, Kungsträdgården**
🕐 Times vary, check website **🌐 kungahuset.se**

The lavish Royal Palace is one of Europe's largest and most dynamic palaces. Stunning rooms and priceless jewels are just some of the highlights at the city's showpiece attraction.

The Royal Palace was originally a 13th-century Tre Kronor (Three Crowns) fortress, but evolved in the 17th century when the Vasa kings turned it into a Renaissance palace. However, in 1697, this palace burned to the ground. In its place the architect Nicodemus Tessin the Younger created a new palace in Baroque style with an Italianate exterior and a French interior, toned down to suit Swedish tastes. The palace's 608 rooms were decorated by Europe's foremost artists and craftsmen. Adolf Fredrik was the first king to move into the palace, in 1754. Though it remains the Swedish monarchy's official residence, the king no longer resides here.

The public areas of the Royal Palace are home to grand rooms of sumptuous furnishings and priceless works of art and craftsmanship. The Hall of State and the Royal Chapel are both characterized by their magnificent decor. The palace also houses the Treasury with the State regalia; Gustav III's Museum of Antiquities; and the Livrustkammaren.

OFFICIAL ROYAL RESIDENCE

King Carl XVI Gustaf and Queen Silvia have their offices at the palace, where they hold audiences with visiting dignitaries, and official ceremonies, although they spend most of their time at Drottningholm (p142). They travel around the country attending special events, official openings and anniversaries, and they make regular state visits abroad. The King is well known for his interest in the environment while the Queen is heavily involved with her work for children.

Tessin was especially proud of the two staircases, made from Swedish marble and porphyry. On the western staircase stands a bust of the gifted architect.

Stockholm's most popular tourist event is the daily changing of the guard at midday in the Outer Courtyard.

Entrance to the Royal Apartments

The Guest Apartments

The opulent Hall of State has an atmosphere of ceremonial splendour and houses the Queen Kristina's silver throne, the palace's most famous treasure.

Entrance to Treasury and Royal Chapel

The delightful Royal Chapel has a rich interior decorated by many different artists. The pulpit is the work of J P Bouchardon.

The impressive palace, home to many grand rooms ↑

The Bernadotte Apartments *(inset)* inside the vast Royal Palace

Sergel's bust of Gustav III (1779) stands in the room where the king died after being shot at the Opera.

Karl XI's Gallery is one of the most magnificent rooms in the palace and is used for banquets.

The Bernadotte Apartments are situated on the floor below Karl XI's Gallery.

Tre Kronor Museum entrance from Lejonbacken.

Carl Hårleman played a key role in the design of the palace, and his bust adorns this niche.

Gustav III's Museum of Antiquities houses statues brought home by Gustav III from his journey to Rome.

Logården is the terrace between the palace's east wings.

Livrustkammaren

APARTMENTS

The State Apartments

The Royal Family has lived at Drottningholm Palace (p142) since 1982, but official functions still take place in the State Apartments, including banquets hosted by the king during visits by foreign heads of state. The annual festivities in December to honour Nobel laureates are also held here.

The dinners are served in Karl XI's Gallery, the finest example of Swedish late Baroque. Each window is matched with a niche on the inner wall where some of the palace's priceless works of arts and crafts are exhibited. Most remarkable is the salt cellar made from ivory and gilded silver designed by the Flemish painter Rubens (1577–1640). Gustav III's State Bedchamber, where the king

died after being shot at the Opera House in 1792, is the height of Gustavian elegance. The lintels on the doors to the Don Quixote Room, named after the theme of its tapestries, are treasured pieces.

The Guest Apartments

An imposing part of the palace, these apartments are where visiting heads of state stay. The impressive rooms include the Meleager Salon, where official gifts and decorations are exchanged, the Inner Salon, whose decor was inspired by the excavations in Pompeii, and the Margareta Room, named after the king's grandmother, which displays some pictures painted by her.

The apartments contain remarkable works of craftsmanship by 18th-century masters such as Georg Haupt and Jean-Baptiste Masreliez.

> ### Did You Know?
>
> Karl XI's Gallery was modelled on the Hall of Mirrors at Versailles.

The Bernadotte Apartments

This magnificent suite has earned its name from the gallery displaying portraits of the Bernadotte dynasty. The apartments have some notable ceiling paintings and mid-18th-century chandeliers, and are used for many a ceremonial occasion. The elegant Pillar Hall is the venue for investitures, and the East Octagonal Cabinet with probably the palace's best Rococo decor, is where the king receives foreign ambassadors. Along with the western cabinet, its interior has remained just as it was planned by Carl Hårleman more than 250 years ago.

Oscar II's very masculine Writing Room, dating from the 1870s, also looks much as it did in his day. However, the palace was kept up to date with the latest technical advances: electricity was installed in 1883, and the telephone only one year later.

ROYAL GRANDEUR

The Hall of State

Rococo and Classicism were brought together in perfect harmony by the architects Nicodemus Tessin the Younger and Carl Hårleman when they designed the two-storey Hall of State.

←

Lavish gold decor, large chandeliers and ceiling frescoes in Karl XI's Gallery

The Hall provides a worthy framework for Queen Kristina's silver throne, a gift for the coronation in 1650 and one of the most valuable treasures in the palace. The canopy was added 100 years later for the coronation of King Adolf Fredrik. The throne is flanked by sculptures of Karl XIV Johan and Gustav II Adolf, while those on the cornice symbolize Peace, Strength, Religion and Justice.

Today it is used for official occasions and is also a venue for summer concerts.

The Royal Chapel

A lot of effort went into the interior decoration of the Royal Chapel. The work was carried out largely by Carl Hårleman under Tessin's supervision and, as with the Hall of State, the co-operation between the two produced a magnificent result, enhanced by the contributions of several foreign artists.

A number of remarkable artifacts have been added over the centuries. The most recent was a group of six 17th-century-style bronze crowns, as well as two crystal crowns, given by the Court to King Carl XVI Gustaf and Queen Silvia to mark their marriage in 1976.

The Treasury

At the bottom of 56 well-worn steps, below the Hall of State on the south side of the palace, is the entrance to the Treasury (Skattkammaren) where the state regalia, the most potent symbols of the monarchy, are kept. Occasionally, for an important event, King Erik XIV's crown, sceptre, orb and the keys of the kingdom are taken out of their showcase and placed beside the uncrowned King Carl XVI Gustaf. The silver baptismal font, which took the French silversmith Jean François Cousinet 11 years to make, is more than 200 years old and is still used for royal baptisms. Hanging in the Treasury is the

The exterior of the Tre Kronor Museum, built around fortress remains ↑

only undamaged tapestry dating from the 1560s, salvaged from the 1697 fire.

MUSEUMS

Gustav III's Museum of Antiquities

Opened in 1794 in memory of the king, the Museum of Antiquities initially housed more than 200 exhibits, mainly acquired during Gustav's Italian journey in 1783–4 and then supplemented with more purchases at a later date.

The most prized exhibits are in the main gallery, the best known being the sculpture of Endymion, the eternally sleeping young shepherd and lover of the Moon Goddess Selene. The 18th-century sculptor Johan Tobias Sergel is represented by *The Priestess*, ranked as the collection's second most important piece.

Tre Kronor Museum

A fascinating attraction at the Royal Palace is the Tre Kronor (Three Crowns) Museum, which is housed in the oldest parts of the ruined Tre Kronor fortress, preserved under the north side of the palace. About half of a 12th-century defensive wall and brick vaults from the 16th and 17th centuries provide a dramatic setting for the museum which illustrates the palace's history over almost 1,000 years.

Two models of the fortress show changes made during the second half of the 17th century and how it looked by the time of the fire. Among items rescued from the ashes are a *snaps* (shot) glass, amber pots and bowls made from mountain crystal.

Livrustkammaren

Founded in 1628, the Royal Armoury is Sweden's oldest museum. Housed in the cellar vaults of the Royal Palace, it is full of objets d'art and everyday items used by the Royal Family over the past five centuries. The museum also houses a a variety of royal items that illustrate events in Swedish history. Coronation ceremonies are illustrated by costumes such as those worn by King Gustav III and Queen Sofia Magdalena in 1766.

> **Founded in 1628, the Royal Armoury is Sweden's oldest museum. Housed in the cellar vaults of the Royal Palace, it is full of objets d'art and everyday items.**

EXPERIENCE MORE

②

Tessinska Palatset

📍 F6 🏛 Slottsbacken 4 🚇 Gamla Stan 🔒 To the public

The Tessin Palace on Slottsbacken is considered to be the most beautiful private residence in Sweden. It is the best-preserved palace from Sweden's era as a great power in the 17th century and was designed by and for Tessin the Younger (1654–1728), the nation's most renowned architect.

Completed in 1697, the building is located on a narrow site, which widens out towards a courtyard with a delightful Baroque garden. The relatively discreet façade with its beautiful porch was inspired by the exterior design of Roman palaces. The decor and garden were influenced by Tessin's time in Paris and Versailles.

Tessin, who became a count and state councillor, spent large sums on the building's ornamentation. Sculptures and paintings were provided by the same French masters whose work had graced the Royal Palace. Later, however, his son, Carl Gustaf, had to sell the palace for financial reasons.

The building was acquired by the City of Stockholm as a residence for its governor in

1773. In 1968 it became the residence of the governor of the County of Stockholm.

③

Bondeska Palatset

📍 E6 🏛 Riddarhustorget 8 🚇 Gamla Stan 🔒 To the public

The seat of the Supreme Court since 1949, the Bonde Palace was created in 1662–73 in the style of a French town house. The year previously, the State Treasurer Gustav Bonde had bought the site opposite Riddarhuset to build a palace with the idea of renting out most of it. Since then the Bonde Palace has had several owners and in 1730 the building became the property of the city and served as the City Hall until 1915. After that, there was little interest taken in the palace until planned renovation was begun in the late 1940s. It had even been suggested that the building should be demolished, but public opinion ensured that it remained intact. Though you cannot see inside the palace, the exterior alone is well worth a visit.

④

Storkyrkan

📍 E6 🚇 Trångsund 1 🚇 Gamla Stan ⏰ 9am–4pm daily (extended hours in summer) 🌐 storkyrkan.nu

Stockholm's 700-year-old cathedral is of great national religious importance. It was from here that the Swedish reformer Olaus Petri (1493–1552) spread his Lutheran message around the kingdom.

Originally, a small village church was built on this site

in the 13th century, probably by the city's founder, Birger Jarl. It was replaced in 1306 by a much bigger basilica, St Nicholas, which was altered over the centuries.

The Gothic character of the interior, acquired in the 15th century, was revealed in 1908 when, during restoration work, plaster was removed from the pillars, exposing the characteristic red tiling. The late Baroque period provided the so-called "royal chairs" and the pulpit, while the façade

> **🔍 HIDDEN GEM**
> ### Finska Kyrkan
>
> A two-minute walk east of Storkyrkan, Slotts-backen's oldest building (Slottsbacken 2B-C) dates from the 1640s. Originally a royal ball-games court, it has served as the religious centre for the Finnish community since 1725.

was adapted to bring it into keeping with the rest of the area around the Royal Palace. The 66-m- (216-ft-) high tower, added in 1743, has four bells, the largest of which weighs about 6 tonnes.

The cathedral houses some priceless art, including *St George and the Dragon*, regarded as one of the finest late Gothic works of art in Northern Europe. The sculpture, situated to the left of the altar, was carved from oak and moose horn by Lübeck sculptor Bernt Notke, and commemorates Sten Sture the Elder's victory over the Danes in 1471.

The 3.7-m- (12-ft-) high bronze candelabra before the altar has adorned the

cathedral for some 600 years. One of the cathedral's most prized treasures is the silver altar, which was a gift from the diplomat Johan Adler Salvius in the 1650s.

The pews nearest to the chancel, the "royal chairs", were designed by Nicodemus Tessin the Younger in 1684 to be used by royalty on special occasions. In 1705, the pulpit was installed above the grave of Olaus Petri.

On 20 April 1535, a light phenomenon was observed over Stockholm – six rings with sparkling solar halos. *The Parhelion Painting*, recalling the event, hangs in Storkyrkan and is thought to be the oldest portrayal of the capital. It shows the modest skyline dominated by the cathedral.

In 2010, the cathedral underwent a large-scale renovation ahead of the wedding of Crown Princess Victoria.

↓ Storkyrkan's interesting façade in Italian Baroque style, and the silver altar *(inset)*

5

Stenbockska Palatset

E6 **Birger Jarls Torg 4** **Gamla Stan** **To the public**

Both externally and internally the Stenbock Palace is the best-preserved building on Riddarholmen. It was built in the 1640s by the State Councillor Fredrik Stenbock and his wife, and the family's coat of arms can be seen above the porch.

6

Tyska Kyrkan

📍 E6 🚪 Svartmangatan 16
🚇 Gamla Stan ⏰ May-Aug:
10:30am-4:30pm daily;
Sep-Apr: 11am-3pm Wed,
Fri & Sat, 12:30-4pm Sun
🚫 During services
🌐 svenskakyrkan.se

The German Church is an impressive reminder of the almost total influence that Germany had over Stockholm during the 18th century. The Hanseatic League trading organization was in control of the Baltic and its ports, which explains why the basic layout of Gamla Stan resembled that of Lübeck.

The church's congregation, which today has some 2,000 members, was founded in 1571. The present twin-aisle church was built in 1638–42, as an extension of a smaller church that the parish had used since 1576. In German late Renaissance and Baroque style, the interior has a royal gallery, added in 1672 for German members of the royal household. The pulpit (1660) in ebony and alabaster is unique in Sweden and the altar, from the 1640s, is covered with paintings surrounded by sculptures of the apostles and evangelists.

The sculptures on the south porch by Jobst Hennen date from 1643 and show Jesus, Moses and three figures portraying Faith, Hope and Love.

---

7 🍴 ☕

Stortorget

📍 E6 🚇 Gamla Stan

It was not until 1778, when the Stock Exchange (Börsen) was completed, that Stortorget, ("the big square") in the heart of the old town, acquired a more uniform appearance. Its northern side had previously been taken up by several buildings that served as a town hall. Since the early Middle Ages the square had been a natural meeting point with a well and marketplace, lined with stalls on market days.

A pillory belonging to the jail, which was once on nearby Kåkbrinken, used to stand on the square. It is now in the town hall on Kungsholmen.

The medieval layout is clear on Stortorget's west side, where the red Schantzska Huset (No 20) and the narrow Seyfridtska Huset were built around 1650. The Schantzska Huset remains unchanged and has a lovely limestone porch adorned with figures of recumbent Roman warriors. The artist Johan Wendelstam was

> HIDDEN GEM
> ## 🔍 Mårten Trotzigs Gränd
>
> Climbing up the 36 steps of the city's narrowest street, a few minutes' walk southeast of Stortorget, gives a good view of the old town and how tightly the houses are packed together.

→ The 17th-century Tyska Kyrkan and the royal gallery (inset)

responsible for most of the notable porches in the old town. The 17th-century gable on Grilska Huset (No 3) is also worth a closer study. Today there are cafés and restaurants in some of the vaulted cellars.

The decision to construct the Stock Exchange was taken in 1667, but the many wars delayed it by 100 years. The architect was the young and talented Erik Palmstedt (1741–1803), who also created the decorative cover for the old well. Trading on the floor of the Stock Exchange ceased in 1990. In 2001, the **Nobelmuseet** was opened here to mark the centenary of the Prize (p91). The exhibition explores the work and ideas of more than 700 creative minds by means of short films and original artifacts. On the upper floor, the Swedish Academy holds its ceremonial gatherings, a tradition maintained since Gustav III gave his inauguration speech here in 1786.

Nobelmuseet

Jun-Aug: 10am-8pm daily; Sep-May: 11am-5pm Tue-Sun (to 8pm Tue)
w nobelmuseum.se

FREE WALKING TOURS

Stockholm is perfect for exploring on foot, and free walking tours begin in Gamla Stan. Check out: Free Walking Tour Stockholm (www. stockholmfreetour. com); Free Tour Stockholm (freetourstockholm.com); Rainbow Tours (www.freetour. com/stockholm/ stockholm-landmarks-free-tour-old-town). It is best to book ahead. Although the tours are free, a tip is expected. If the supernatural is your thing, there is also a ghost walk tour in Gamla Stan (www.stockholm-ghostwalk.com).

Judiska museet

F6 Själagårdsgatan 19
Gamla Stan 11am-5pm daily (to 8pm Thu & 4pm Fri)
w judiska-museet.se

In 1774 Aaron Isaac became the first Jewish immigrant to settle in Stockholm and practise his religion. Today, half of Sweden's Jewish population of around 18,000 live in the Stockholm area. The Jewish Museum depicts the history of the Swedish Jews from Isaac's time to the present. It focuses on Judaism as a religion, its integration into Swedish society, and the Holocaust. A comprehensive collection of pictures and other items provide an insight into Jewish life in Sweden with its traditions and customs. The beautiful *Torah* (the five books of Moses), the bridal canopy, and the collection of eight-stemmed *hanukiah* (candlesticks) are just some of the treasured spiritual artifacts.

Västerlånggatan

E6 Gamla Stan

Once a main road outside the city proper, built along parts of the original town wall, Västerlånggatan now runs through the heart of the old town, and is usually thronging with people – tourists and locals – shopping or strolling. Starting at Mynttorget in the north, by the Chancery Office (Kanslihuset) and Lejonbacken, the lively and atmospheric street finishes at Järntorget in the south, where the export of iron was once controlled. On Järntorget is Bancohuset, which was the headquarters of the State Bank from 1680 to 1906.

The building at No 7 has been used by the Swedish Parliament since the mid-1990s. Its late 19th-century façade has a distinctive southern European influence. No 27 was built by and for Erik Palmstedt, who also designed the Stock Exchange and the well at Stortorget. No 29 is a venerable building, dating from the early 15th century, and its original pointed Gothic arches were revealed during restoration in the 1940s.

No 33 is an example of how new materials and techniques in the late 19th century made it possible to fit large shop windows into old houses. The cast-iron columns that can be seen in other places also date from this period. No. 68, Von der Lindeska Huset, has a majestic 17th-century façade and a lovely porch with sculptures.

↑ Västerlånggatan, Gamla Stan's most popular shopping street

↑ Riddarholmskyrkan's vaulted ceiling and its iconic tower *(inset)*

10 ♦ Ⓜ

Riddarholmskyrkan

📍E6 🏠Birger Jarls Torg
📞08-402 61 00 🚇Gamla
Stan 🕐Mid-May-Sep:
10am-5pm daily; Oct-Nov:
10am-4pm Sat & Sun

This church on the island of Riddarholmen is best known as a place for royal burials. Its interior is full of ornate sarcophagi and worn gravestones, and by the altar are the tombs of the medieval kings Karl Knutsson and Magnus Ladulås.

Built on the site of the late 13th-century Greyfriars abbey, founded by Magnus Ladulås, the majestic brick church has been gradually enlarged over the centuries. After a serious fire in 1835, it acquired its present lattice-work cast-iron tower.

Inside, burial vaults, dating back to the 17th century, surround the church. The coffins rest on a lower level with space for a memorial above. The most recent was built in 1858–60 for the Bernadotte dynasty.

The vaults contain the remains of all the Swedish sovereigns from Gustav II

Adolf in the 17th century to the present day with two exceptions: Queen Kristina, who was buried at St Peter's in Rome in 1689, and Gustav VI Adolf, who was interred at Haga in 1973. The most magnificent sarcophagus is that of the 19th-century king, Karl XIV Johan, which was towed here by sledge from his porphyry workshops in northern Sweden. Particularly moving are the graves of royal children, including the many small tin coffins that surround the last resting place of Gustav II Adolf and his queen, Maria Eleonora.

11

Wrangelska Palatset

📍E6 🏠Birger Jarls
Torg 16 🚇Gamla Stan
🚫To the public

Only two parts of Gustav Vasa's fortifications from 1530 remain – Birger Jarls

Tower and the southernmost tower of what became the iconic Wrangel Palace. Built as a residence for the nobleman Lars Sparre in 1652–70, it was remodelled a few decades later by the Swedish statesman Carl Gustaf Wrangel. A field marshal in the Thirty Years War, Wrangel chose Nicodemus Tessin the Elder as his architect. The result was Stockholm's largest privately owned palace, and one of the most visited.

In 1697 the Royal Family moved into the Wrangel Palace after the Tre Kronor fortress *(p66)* was ravaged by fire. It became known as the King's House, and it was here in the same year that the 15-year-old Karl XII took the oath of office after the death of his father. Gustav III was born here in 1746 and in 1792 his assassin was incarcerated in the dungeons. The Svea Court of Appeal (Svea Hovrätt) now uses this building.

12 🚇 🏛

Medeltidsmuseet

📍 E5 🏛 Strömparterren 3, Norrbro 🚇 Kungsträdgården 🕐 Noon-5pm Tue-Sun (to 8pm Wed) 🌐 medeltidsmuseet. stockholm.se

This fascinating museum of medieval Stockholm is built around some of the capital's archaeological remains, mainly parts of the city wall that date from the 1530s. They were discovered in 1978–80. Completely underground, the dimly lit, atmospheric museum includes finds that evoke Stockholm's early history. Among them is the 22-m- (72-ft-) long Riddarholm ship, dating from the 1520s, which was discovered off Riddarholmen in 1930.

The museum provides a good picture of Stockholm's early days. From the entrance, a 350-year-old tunnel leads into a reconstructed medieval world. There is a pillory in the square and gallows with the tools of the executioner's trade. The city has been recreated with a church, harbour and a square. You can also see a 55-m- (180-ft-) long section of the original city wall, complete with a skeleton that had been concealed there.

---

13 🚇 🍴 🖥 🏛

Postmuseum

📍 E6 🏛 Lilla Nygatan 6 🚇 Gamla Stan 🕐 11am-4pm Tue-Sun (Sep-Apr: to 7pm Wed) 🌐 postmuseum.se

An attraction in itself, the Postmuseum building takes up a whole area bought by the Swedish Post Office in 1720. About 100 years later the majestic-looking post office was built, incorporating parts of the 17th-century buildings. Stockholm's only post office until 1869, it was turned into a museum in 1906, and continues to attract many visitors today.

Letters have been sent in Sweden, in an organized way, since 1636, and the museum's permanent exhibits include a portrayal of early "peasant postmen" fighting the Åland Sea in their boat *Simpan*. Also on display is the first post bus, which ran in northern Sweden in the early 1920s, and a stage-coach used in eastern Sweden.

The collection includes Sweden's first stamp-printing press and no fewer than four million stamps, among which are the first Swedish stamps, produced in 1855. Also on show here is an example of the "Penny Black", the world's first stamp dating from 1840, and the world's first colonial stamps, issued by Mauritius in 1847.

There is a philatelic library holding 51,000 volumes and stamp collections, as well as computers and multimedia equipment for research. A special creative workshop for children, The Little Post Office (closed for restoration), is in the basement. Here kids can make a postcard, sort and deliver post and load the postal van.

Kids enjoying the exhibits at the
↓ Postmuseum

→

The Parliament building, with striking views over the water

14

Evert Taubes Terrass

🗺 D6 🚇 Norra Riddarholmshamnen 🚇 Gamla Stan

A statue of Evert Taube, Sweden's much-loved singer and ballad writer, stands on the terrace below Wrangelska Palatset looking out over the waters of Riddarfjärden. In an ideal position, given the poet's close links to the sea, the bronze sculpture was created by the Swedish sculptor and artist Willy Gordon in 1990. It's also a lovely spot to relax in and watch the city go by.

←

The Swedish musician, Evert Taube (1890–1976)

Close by stands Christer Berg's granite *Solbåten* (Sun Boat), an elegant sculpture in granite unveiled in 1966. Inspired by the shape of a shell, from some angles it also resembles a sail.

15

Riddarhuset

🗺 E6 🚇 Riddarhustorget 10 🚇 Gamla Stan ⏰ 11am–noon Mon–Fri (mid-Jun–Aug: 10am–1pm) 🚫 Public hols 🌐 riddarhuset.se

Often regarded as one of Stockholm's most beautiful buildings, Riddarhuset (House of Nobility) stands on Riddarhustorget, which until the mid-19th century was Stockholm's city centre.

Built in 1641–7 on the initiative of the state chancellor, Riddarhuset provided the knights with a base for meetings and events. The building is a supreme

example of Dutch Baroque design by the renowned architects Simon and Jean de la Vallée, Heinrich Wilhelm and Justus Vingboons.

Inscribed over the entrance on the northern façade is the knights' motto *Arte et Marte* (Art and War) with Minerva, Goddess of Art and Science, and Mars, God of War, flanking either side.

The sculptures on the vaulted roof symbolize the knightly virtues. On the south side is *Nobilitas* (Nobility) holding a small Minerva and spear. She is flanked by *Studium* (Diligence) and *Valor* (Bravery). Facing the north is the male equivalent, *Honor*, flanked by *Prudentia* (Prudence) and *Fortitudo* (Strength).

The interior of Riddarhuset is equally magnificent. The lower hall is dominated by an impressive double staircase that leads up to the Knights' Room. This has a masterly painted ceiling by the renowned Swedish artist David Klöcker Ehrenstrahl (1628–98) and Riddarhuset's foremost treasure, a sculpted ebony chair, from 1623. The walls are covered with coats of arms.

Riksdagshuset

🅚 E5 🏠 Riksgatan 1,
Helgeandsholmen
🚇 Kungsträdgården 🕐 For
tours & meetings in the
Chamber: check website for
details 🌐 riksdagen.se

The Parliament House building (Riksdagshuset) and Bank
of Sweden (Riksbank), located
on Helgeandsholmen were
inaugurated in 1905 and 1906
respectively. Since 1983, when
Parliament returned here
after 12 years at Sergels Torg,
the two buildings have been
combined. They were restored
and a modern extension built
to house a new, single debating
chamber. Riksdagshuset's
chamber is truly Nordic in its
decoration, with benches of
Swedish birch and wall
panelling in Finnish birch. A
large tapestry, *Memory of a
Landscape* (1983), by Elisabeth
Hasselberg-Olsson, covers

54 sq m (581 sq ft) of wall and
took 3,500 hours to make.
Parliamentary debates can
be watched from the public
gallery, which holds up to 500
spectators, and there are
guided tours of the building.

The original two-chamber
Parliament is used for meetings of the majority party.
The former First Chamber
has three paintings by Otte
Sköld (1894–1958); the other
chamber contains works by
Axel Törneman and Georg
Pauli, who realized Törneman's
sketches after his death.
Between the chambers is a
45-m- (148-ft-) long hall with
an elegant display of coats
of arms, paintings and
chandeliers. The Finance
Committee meets in the oak-
panelled library surrounded
by old prints and *Jugendstil*
(Art Nouveau-style) lamps.

Facing the old entrance at
Norrbro, the magnificent stairwell still retains its features
from 1905. Other impressive

> **Riksdagshuset's chamber is truly
> Nordic in its decoration, with benches
> of Swedish birch and wall panelling
> in Finnish birch.**

survivors from these opulent
days include eight columns, a
floor, steps and balusters in
various marbles. The present
entrance was the Bank of
Sweden's main hall until 1976.
It has fine columns, too, made
from polished granite, and
some outstanding paintings
from the Parliamentary collection of some 3,000 works.

A SHORT WALK
SLOTTSBACKEN

Distance 1 km (0.5 miles) **Nearest metro**
Kungsträdgården **Time** 15 minutes

Slottsbacken is much more than just a steep hill
linking Skeppsbron and the highest part of Gamla
Stan (Old Town). The area provides the background
for the daily changing-of-the-guard and is also the
route for visiting heads of state and foreign ambassadors when they have an audience with the king
at Kungliga Slottet (the Royal Palace). Louis Jean
Desprez's striking Obelisk stands next to palace's
southern facade. Added to the site in 1799, the spire
represents the state's ambition to make Stockholm
a leading European city in architectural terms.

The Obelisk, by Louis Jean
Desprez, was erected in 1799
to thank the citizens for
supporting Gustav III's
Russian war in 1788–90.

Outer Courtyard

Named after the Swedish
statesman, **Axel Oxenstiernas**
Palats *(1653) is an unusual*
example in Stockholm of the style
known as Roman Mannerism.

Storkyrkan *(p70), an impressive*
cathedral with a late Gothic
interior, it is full of treasures
from many different eras.

The Olaus Petri statue *stands in*
front of a tablet telling the
cathedral's history since 1264.

Stock Exchange

TRÅNGSUND

STORTORGET

Stortorget *(p72) is the heart of the "city*
between the bridges", with a well dating
from 1778. The square was the scene of
the Stockholm Bloodbath in 1520.

←
The old square of Stortoget lined
with colourful buildings illuminated
in the amber street light

The southern façade of the the **Royal Palace** (p67) has a triumphal central arch with four niches for statues, created by French artists in the 18th century.

START

Sweden's oldest museum, **Livrustkammaren** (p67), displays royal weaponry, clothing and carriages from over five centuries.

Locator Map
For more detail see p64

Gustav III's statue was sculpted by J T Sergel in 1799 in memory of the "gallant king" who was murdered in 1792.

Built by Nicodemus Tessin the Younger, architect of the Royal Palace, in 1694–7, **Tessinska Palatset** (p70) has been the residence of the Governor of Stockholm County since 1968

In a 16th-century setting, **Kungliga Myntkabinettet** (the Royal Coin Cabinet) has the world's largest stamped coin, dating from 1644.

SKEPPSBRON

SLOTTSBACKEN

ÖSTERLÅNGGATAN

FINISH

KÖPMANGATAN

Köpmantorget has a statue of St George Slaying the Dragon (1912).

Finska Kyrkan, Slottsbacken's oldest building, dates from the 1640s. Originally a royal ball-games court for the palace, since 1725 it has been the religious centre for the Finnish community.

0 metres 100
0 yards 100
N ↑

↑ A guard standing duty in the cobbled courtyard of Livrustkammaren

CITY

Considered the central part of town and known as City, this area was where, in the mid-18th century, the first stone-built houses and palaces outside Gamla Stan started to appear for the burghers and nobility. After World War II, the run-down buildings around Hötorget were demolished to form what is now Sergels Torg; many homes were replaced by modern high-rise office blocks.

In the 21st century, though, the area has livened up and become the true heart and commercial centre of Stockholm. A hub for public transport and banking, City is the place for the best department stores and shopping malls, exclusive boutiques and nightspots. The unique landscape surrounding Stockholm permeates even City, offering sudden unexpected glimpses of water complete with bustling boat life and a string of anglers along the embankments.

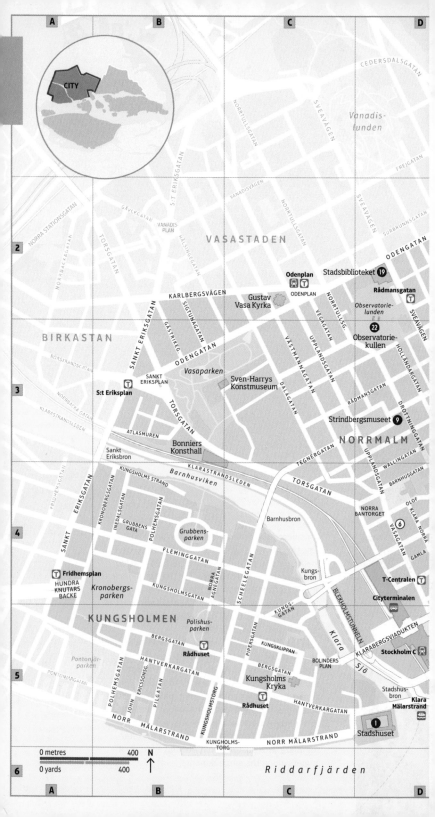

CITY

Must See
1. Stadshuset

Experience More
2. Nordiska Kompaniet (NK)
3. Kungsträdgården
4. Jacobs Kyrka
5. Kungliga Operan
6. Dansmuseet
7. Arvfurstens Palats
8. Klara Kyrka
9. Strindbergsmuseet
10. Medelhavsmuseet
11. Adolf Fredriks Kyrka
12. Kulturhuset and Stadsteatern
13. Konserthuset
14. Kungliga Biblioteket
15. Scenkonstmuseet
16. Hovstallet
17. Armémuseum
18. Humlegården
19. Stadsbiblioteket
20. Kungliga Dramatiska Teatern
21. Hallwylska museet
22. Observatoriekullen

Eat
1. Frantzén
2. Östermalmshallen
3. Eskstedt
4. StikkiNikki

Drink
5. Brasseriet
6. Duvel Café
7. Kung Carls Bakficka

❶ ⬦ Ⓜ ⓨ ⬚

STADSHUSET

📍 D5 🏛 Hantverkargatan 1 🚇 Ⓣ Rådhuset ⏰ For guided tours. Tower: daily 🚫 Some hols and for special events 🌐 stockholm.se/stadshuset

Undeniably Sweden's biggest architectural project of the 20th century, the City Hall was completed in 1923 and has become a symbol of Stockholm. Climb to the top of the 106-m- (348-ft-) tall tower for superb views over the city from the terrace.

Designed by Ragnar Östberg (1866–1945), the leading architect of the Swedish National Romantic style, the Stadshuset displays influences of both the Nordic Gothic and Northern Italian schools. Several leading Swedish artists also contributed to the rich interior design. Though the building can be viewed by guided tour only, you can stroll at leisure through the courtyard and well-manicured gardens, as well as climb the tower. The famous cellar restaurant, Stadshuskällaren (stadshuskallaren sthlm.se), offers a wide range of classic Swedish dishes.

> **Did You Know?**
>
> Some of the annual Nobel Prize festivities held in December take place in the Blue Hall.

↑ The imposing red-brick City Hall dominating Riddarfjärden bay

The Byzantine-inspired wall mosaics by Swedish artist Einar Forseth (1892–1988) in the Golden Hall are made up of 18.6 million pieces of glass and gold.

The Blue Hall is a banqueting room constructed from handmade bricks. The name derives from the initial plan to paint the bricks blue, but the architect changed his mind.

📷 PICTURE PERFECT
Capture the City Hall

Take the best photos of Stadshuset at night from across the water by walking eastwards to the path on the central railway bridge, Centralbron.

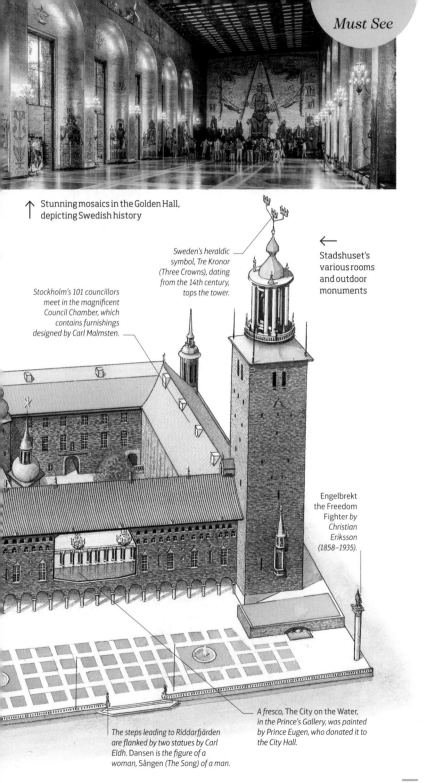

↑ Stunning mosaics in the Golden Hall, depicting Swedish history

Sweden's heraldic symbol, Tre Kronor (Three Crowns), dating from the 14th century, tops the tower.

← Stadshuset's various rooms and outdoor monuments

Stockholm's 101 councillors meet in the magnificent Council Chamber, which contains furnishings designed by Carl Malmsten.

Engelbrekt the Freedom Fighter by Christian Eriksson (1858–1935).

A fresco, The City on the Water, in the Prince's Gallery, was painted by Prince Eugen, who donated it to the City Hall.

The steps leading to Riddarfjärden are flanked by two statues by Carl Eldh. Dansen is the figure of a woman, Sången (The Song) of a man.

EXPERIENCE MORE

② 🍴 🍽 🛍
Nordiska Kompaniet (NK)

📍E4 🚇Hamngatan 18-20
🚇T-Centralen 🕐10am-8pm
Mon-Fri, 10am-6pm Sat,
11am-5pm Sun 🌐nk.se

The vast granite palace on Hamngatan houses the department store Nordiska Kompaniet (NK). Opened in 1915, NK was – and still is – aimed at an exclusive clientele. It made its name as a showcase for Swedish arts and crafts, writing design history when the textiles department, Textilkammaren, opened in 1937. The manager was the textile artist Astrid Sampe, who commissioned leading artists and designers to supply work. Olle Baertling, Arne Jacobsen, Alvar Aalto and Viola Gråsten all contributed patterns. Sampe also introduced new fabric-printing techniques.

Today at NK you can find almost everything from perfume, clothing and sporting equipment to glass, silver and porcelain, but above all, the store is, as its founder Josef Sachs described it, a commercial and cultural theatre.

③
Kungsträdgården

📍E5 🚇Kungsträdgården

The "King's Garden" is a popular meeting place for Stockholmers, and there is something for everyone going on all year round. This open urban space is bordered by tree-lined promenades, with a modern fountain in the middle. At the Strömgatan end there is a square named after Karl XII with J P Molin's statue of the warrior king, unveiled in 1868, at its centre. In Kungsträdgården itself there is a statue of Karl XIII (1809–18) by Erik Göthe. During the summer, the park is the venue for food festivals, concerts, dancing and street theatre, while in winter the skating rink attracts children and grown-ups alike. Also to be seen is Molin's fountain, made from gypsum in 1866 and cast in bronze.

It is the city's oldest park, starting as the royal kitchen garden in the 15th century. During Erik XIV's reign in the 16th century, it was transformed into a formal Renaissance garden. Queen Kristina built a stone summer

The late Renaissance-style Kungliga Operan; performance (inset) ↑

house here in the 17th century, which stands at Västra Träd-gårdsgatan 2, by the cobble-stoned Lantmäteribacken.

---

④ 🎨
Jacobs Kyrka

📍E5 🚇Jakobs Torg 5
📞08-723 30 00
🚇Kungsträdgården
🕐11am-5pm Mon-Wed
& Sat-Sun, 11am-6pm
Thu & Fri

In medieval times there was a small chapel where Kungsträdgården now lies. Dedicated to St Jacob, the patron saint of wayfarers, the chapel and another modest-sized church were pulled down by King Gustav Vasa in the 16th century. His son, Johan III, wanted to provide two new churches in Norra Malmen, as the area was then called, and work to build the churches of St Jacob and St Klara (p88) started in 1580. St Jacob's was consecrated first, in 1643. It has been restored several times since then, in some cases rather clumsily. However, several valuable items have been preserved, including

An amazing display of ↑
cherry blossom in
Kungsträdgården

porches by the stonemasons Henrik Blom and Hans Hebel. The organ's façade was created by the architect Carl Hårleman and the large painting on the west wall of the southern nave is by Fredrik Westin, Sweden's most distinguished historical painter of the early 19th century.

Kungliga Operan

◉ E5 ⌂ Gustav Adolfs Torg 2 Ⓣ Kungsträdgården ◷ Box Office: 3pm-6pm Mon-Fri, noon-3pm Sat 🆆 operan.se

Opera has been staged in Sweden since 18 January 1773, when a performance took place at Bollhuset on Slottsbacken (p78). Kungliga Operan (the Royal Opera House) on Gustav Adolfs Torg was inaugurated on 30 September 1782, but by the late 19th century it had become a fire hazard. The architect Axel Anderberg was commissioned to design a new opera house, which was given to the State in 1898 by a consortium founded by the financier K A Wallenberg.

The colouring of the building in late Renaissance style is in keeping with the Royal Palace and Parliament building, and some details of the architecture are common to all three. The beautiful staircase with ceiling paintings by Axel Jungstedt was inspired by the Paris Opera. The same artist's portrait of Oscar II hangs in the 28-m- (92-ft-) long golden foyer, where Carl Larsson was responsible for the decorative paintings. The wings at either side of the stage have been retained, as has the width of the proscenium arch. Also saved was J T Sergel's group of angels above the stage. An angel in Vicke Andrén's ceiling painting holds a sketch of the Opera House.

Dansmuseet

◉ E5 ⌂ Drottninggatan 17 Ⓣ Kungsträdgården ◷ 11am-5pm Tue-Fri, noon-4pm Sat & Sun 🆆 dansmuseet.se

In the heart of Stockholm, the Dance Museum is housed in a former bank building on Drottninggatan. The museum was originally established in Paris in 1953 by the Swedish aristocrat Rolf de Maré (1888–1964). He was a noted art collector and the founder of the renowned avant-garde company Les Ballets Suédois. The collection features all aspects of dance – beautiful costumes and masks, scenery sketches, art and posters, books and documents – and includes an archive on popular dance. Apart from the exhibition hall, there is a data bank – the Rolf de Maré Study Centre – which contains video/DVD facilities, a library and archives. The museum shop stocks Sweden's largest collection of dance DVDs.

EAT

Frantzén
Reserve a spot at Sweden's very own Michelin three-star restaurant. Chef Björn Frantzén's menu blends the Nordic kitchen with a Japanese touch.

◉ D4 ⌂ Klara Norra Kyrkogata 26 ◷ Sun-Tue & mid-Jun-mid-Jul 🆆 restaurantfrantzen. com

Ⓚ Ⓚ Ⓚ

→ Overlooking the water, Arvfurstens Palats, now the Swedish Foreign Office

DRINK

Brasseriet
Fresh juices and home-made syrups are used in the delectable cocktails.

⦿E5 ⌂Strömgatan 14 🕒Sun 🌐brasseriet.se

Duvel Café
A wide selection of experimental cocktails, such as a Willy Wonka Fashioned.

⦿D4 ⌂Vasagatan 50 🕒Sun 🌐duvelcafe.com

Kung Carls Bakficka
Cocktails from past and present, all made with fresh ingredients and the best spirits.

⦿E4 ⌂Norrlandsgatan 28 🌐kungcarls bakficka.se

❼
Arvfurstens Palats

⦿E5 ⌂Gustav Adolfs Torg 1 🚇Kungsträdgården 🚫To the public

Opposite the Royal Opera House, on the other side of Gustav Adolfs Torg, stands Arvfurstens Palats (Prince's Palace), built for Gustav III's sister Sofia Albertina and completed in 1794. She commissioned the architect Erik Palmstedt to carry out the work. He was a pupil of Carl Fredrik Adelcrantz, designer of the original opera house.

The palace and its decor are shining examples of the Gustavian style, thanks to the contributions of artists and craftsmen such as Louis Masreliez and Georg Haupt and their pupils Gustaf Adolf Ditzinger, J T Sergel and Gottlieb Iwersson. In 1906 the building was taken over by the Swedish Foreign Office.

Nearby stands the elegant Sagerska Palatset, built in 1894 in French Renaissance style. Since 1996, following renovation to make it fit for purpose, the palace has been used by the prime minister as an official residence.

❽ 🖼
Klara Kyrka

⦿D4 ⌂Klarabergsgatan 37 🚇T-Centralen 🕒8am-5pm Mon-Fri, 11am-3pm & 5-7:30pm Sat, 10am-5pm Sun 🌐clarakyrka.se

The convent of St Klara stood on the site of the present church and cemetery until 1527, when it was pulled down on the orders of King Gustav Vasa. Later, his son Johan III commissioned a new church, which was completed in 1590.

The church was ravaged by fire in 1751. Its reconstruction was planned by two of the period's most outstanding architects, Carl Hårleman and Carl Fredrik Adelcrantz. The pulpit was made in 1753 to

> **Gods and people from ancient cultures around the Mediterranean rub shoulders in Medelhavsmuseet (the Museum of Mediterranean and Near East Antiquities).**

Hårleman's design, and J T Sergel created the angelic figures in the northern gallery. A pair of identical angels adorn the chancel, based on the gypsum originals.

In the 1880s, the 116-m (380-ft) tower was added. The 20th-century church artist, Olle Hjortzberg, created the paintings in the vault in 1904.

Music recitals are held on Saturday evenings in the church, but if you're only visiting in the week, stop by at lunchtime to hear beautiful hymns and classical music.

Strindbergsmuseet

📍D3 🚪Drottninggatan 85
🚇Rådmansgatan ⏰10am–4pm Tue–Sun (Sep–Jun: from noon) 🚫6 & 21–23 Jun
🌐strindbergsmuseet.se

The world-famous dramatist August Strindberg (1849–1912) lived at 24 different addresses in Stockholm over the years.

He moved to the last of these in 1908, and gave it the name Blå Tornet (the Blue Tower). By then he had gained international recognition.

The apartment, now housing Strindbergsmuseet, was newly built with central heating, toilet and lift, but lacked a kitchen. Instead he relied on Falkner's Pension, in the same building, for food and other services. On his last few birthdays the great man would stand on his balcony and watch his admirers stage a torchlight procession in his honour.

Opened in 1973, the museum displays the author's home with his bedroom and dining room and his study as it was on his death, as well as 3,000 books, photographic archives, press cuttings and posters. Inside the adjoining premises is a permanent exhibition that portrays Strindberg as author, theatrical director, artist and photographer. A number of fascinating temporary exhibitions and other activities are often held here throughout the year.

🔟 ⓧ 🖥 🏛

Medelhavsmuseet

📍E5 🚪Fredsgatan 2
🚇Kungsträdgården
⏰11am–8pm Tue–Fri, 11am–5pm Sat & Sun
🌐medelhavsmuseet.se

Gods and people from ancient cultures around the Mediterranean rub shoulders in Medelhavsmuseet (the Museum of Mediterranean and Near East Antiquities). Its many treasures include a large group of terracotta figures discovered by archaeologists on Cyprus in the 1930s. There is an extensive display covering ancient Egypt, where you can go on a journey through 7,000 years of Egyptian history, and meet the people who lived alongside the Nile. On display are bronze weapons, tools and burial chambers where mummies can be investigated in closer detail using the lastest interactive technology.

Models made of unusual materials, such as cork, show how houses were once constructed, and the museum also has a fascinating gold room with objects from the Near East, Cyprus, Greece and Rome. Greek and Islamic culture and Roman and Etruscan art are all represented, and complemented by temporary exhibitions.

Medelhavsmuseet is housed in a former bank, which was originally built in the 17th century for Field Marshall Gustav Horn, a decorated general in the Thirty Years War. The Neo-Classical interior has a beautiful stairwell, dating from 1905, and the peristyles and colonnade around the upper part of the hall are worth a visit in themselves.

↑ An exhibition room inside the Neo-Classical interior of Medelhavsmuseet

⑪ Ⓜ ▣ 🏛

Adolf Fredriks Kyrka

📍D3 🏠Holländargatan 16
📞08-20 70 76 🚇Hötorget
🕐1–6pm Mon, 10am–4pm
Tue–Wed & Fri–Sun,
10:30am–4pm Thu

King Adolf Fredrik laid the foundation stone of this church in 1768 on the site of an earlier chapel dedicated to St Olof. Designed by the Swedish architect Carl Fredrik Adelcrantz, in Neo-Classical style with traces of Rococo, the church was built in the shape of a Greek cross and has a central dome.

The interior has undergone a number of changes, but both the altar and pulpit have remained intact. The famous sculptor Johan Tobias Sergel created the altarpiece, which is considered his most important work, and also the memorial dedicated to the French philosopher Descartes, who died in Stockholm in 1650. The paintings in the dome were added in 1899–1900 by Julius Kronberg. More recent acquisitions include altar silverware by Sigurd Persson.

The cemetery is the final resting place of many renowned figures, including the assassinated prime minister Olof Palme (1927–86), as well as the politician Hjalmar Branting, a key figure of the Social Democratic movement. J T Sergel is also buried here.

💬 INSIDER TIP
Summer in the Parks

During the summer, Kulturhuset and Stadsteatern host Parkteatern *(www. kulturhusetstadsteatern.se/parkteatern)*, free musical events as well as theatre and dance performances in the city's parks.

⑫ ⊘ 🍴 ▣ 🏛

Kulturhuset and Stadsteatern

📍E4 🏠Sergels Torg 3
🚇T-Centralen 🕐11am–7pm Mon–Sun (to 5pm Sat & Sun) 🌐kulturhusetstad steatern.se

The distinctive glass façade of Kulturhuset (Cultural Centre), at the heart of Stockholm's cultural life, fronts the south side of Sergels Torg. The winning entry in a Nordic architectural competition, Kulturhuset has become a symbol of Swedish Modernism. Typical of its era, the centre was designed by Peter Celsing and opened its doors in 1974.

Refurbished to meet the needs of the new millennium, the complex contains several galleries that mount regularly changing exhibitions. In the auditorium, a varied schedule of music, dance, drama and lectures is presented.

In the Children's Room, youngsters can read books, draw pictures, listen to stories

↑ Kulturhuset, blending well into its setting on Sergels Torg

or watch films. "Lava" focuses on youth culture nationwide. There is a library for fans of strip cartoons, and reading rooms providing computers, newspapers and magazines.

Among the shops here is Designtorget, selling items of contemporary Swedish design. The centre also has a variety of cafés and eateries, including the top-floor Café Panorama that offers fantastic city views and Nooshi, which specializes in authentic cuisine from China, Japan and Thailand.

Kulturhuset is also home to Stadsteatern (City Theatre), whose main auditorium opened in 1990. This part of the building was formerly occupied by Parliament while its chamber on Helgeands-holmen was being rebuilt. The theatre was designed by architects Lars Fahlsten and Per Ahrbom and contains six stages of varying size and style.

13 Ⓜ ⊡ 🛍

Konserthuset

📍E4 🏠Hötorget 8
🚇Hötorget 🎫Ticket Office:
11am-6pm Mon-Sat (to 3pm
Sat) and an hour before a
concert 🌐konserthuset.se

A Nordic version of a Greek
temple, Konserthuset (the
Concert Hall) is a masterpiece
of the architect Ivar Tengbom
(1878–1968) and is an outstanding example of the Neo-
Classical style of the 1920s.
Tengbom's tradition has been
carried on by his son Anders
(1911–2009), who was in
charge of its renovation in
1970–71, and his grandson
Svante (b 1942), who had a
similar task in 1993–5.

Constructed in 1923–6, the
main auditorium has undergone major reconstruction
and modernization to over-
come acoustic problems. It is
now the city's principal venue
for music performances in
winter. Its interior is very
simple, in contrast to the
Grünewald Hall, by the artist

Isaac Grünewald (1889–1946),
which is in the more lavish
style of an Italian Renaissance
palace. The four marble statues
that stand in the main foyer
are by Carl Milles, also the
creator of the *Orpheus*
sculpture group outside.
Simon Gate and Edward Hald
also contributed to the decor.

Konserthuset has been the
home of the internationally
acclaimed Swedish Royal
Philharmonic Orchestra since
it first opened. The orchestra
gives some 70 concerts every
year, and international star
soloists perform here regularly.
It is also the venue for the
Nobel Prize presentations.

THE NOBEL PRIZES

Alfred Nobel (1833–96) was an
outstanding chemist and inventor.
He left his fortune to endow
the prestigious Nobel Prizes -
consisting of a monetary
award and a medal - which
have been presented
every December since
1901. The ceremony takes
place in Konserthuset, where
prizes are awarded for physics,
chemistry, physiology or
medicine, and literature. Since
1969 the Bank of Sweden has
given a prize for economic sciences
in Nobel's memory. In 1901 each
prize was worth 150,000 Kr; in
2012 the figure was 8 million Kr.

ALFRED NOBEL

14

Kungliga Biblioteket

📍F3 🏠Humlegårdsgaten 26 🚇Östermalmstorg ⏰9am-6pm Mon-Thu, 9am-5pm Fri, 11am-3pm Sat (except Jul) 🌐kb.se

This is Sweden's national library and an autonomous government department in its own right. Ever since 1661, when there were only nine printing presses in Sweden, copies of every piece of printed matter have had to be lodged with Kungliga Biblioteket (Royal Library). Since 1993 this requirement has also applied to electronic documents. As there are now some 3,000 printers and publishers in Sweden,

the volume of material is expanding rapidly. The stock of books is increasing at the rate of 35,000 volumes a year. The Department of Audiovisual Material (previously the Swedish National Archive of Recorded Sound and Moving Images) is also here.

The imposing original building, dating from 1865–78, had to be expanded in the 1920s, and again in the 1990s. The major extension provided an auditorium and, most importantly, two underground book storage areas covering 18,000 sq m (193,750 sq ft).

The library is in a beautiful setting in Humlegården, created by Gustav II Adolf in 1619 to grow hops for the royal household. Ever since the 18th century, the park has been a favourite recreation area for Stockholmers.

15

Scenkonstmuseet

📍F4 🏠Sibyllegatan 2 🚇Östermalmstorg, Kungsträdgården ⏰11am-5pm Tue-Sun 🌐scenkonstmuseet.se

In 2017, following an extensive renovation project, Stockholm's Museum of Music reopened as Scenkonstmuseet – the national performing arts museum. Housed in a 300-year-old building that was once a royal bakery, the museum's collection across three floors celebrates music and performing arts, in all art forms. Exhibits include musical instruments, set design models, puppets and costumes, with some pieces dating back to the 16th century.

The museum places emphasis on interactive exhibits to engage visitors and inspire the next generation of performers. The museum also has its own concert venue where visitors are encouraged to participate.

Kungliga Biblioteket, set in a park created by Gustav II Adolf ↓ *(inset)*

Hovstallet

🅕F4 ⏣Väpnargatan 1 Ⓣ Östermalmstorg ⒼFor guided tours, check website; courtyard and café: Jul & Aug ⓦkungahuset.se

Formerly on Helgeandsholmen, the Hovstallet (Royal Stables) moved here in 1893, when the new Parliament building was being constructed. The Royal Stables looks after transport for the Royal Family and royal household. It maintains about 40 carriages, a dozen cars, carriage horses, and a few horses used for riding.

Did You Know?

The first royal car was an 1899 Daimler, with a 5-horsepower engine and room for four people.

There are many treasures among the carriages, such as the glass-panelled State Coach known as a "Berliner". It was built in Sweden at the Adolf Freyschuss carriage works and made its debut at Oscar II's silver jubilee in 1897. It is still used today on ceremonial occasions.

Incoming ambassadors travel to the Royal Palace for their formal audience with the monarch in Karl XV's coupé. Open horse-drawn carriages from the mid-19th century are normally used for royal processions.

Armémuseum

🅕F4 ⏣Riddargatan 13 Ⓣ Östermalmstorg Ⓞ10am–5pm daily ⓦarmemuseum.se

The old armoury on the grand Artillerigården has been the home of the Armémuseum (Royal Army Museum) since 1879. During the 1990s, the 250-year-old building and its displays underwent extensive renovation to create one of the capital's best-planned and most interesting museums.

The fascinating exhibits are arranged over three floors, presenting the collection of some 80,000 items in an exciting and comprehensive way. Dramatic life-size settings have been made to portray Sweden's history of war and defence, showing not only what took place in battle and the living conditions of the soldiers involved but how the lives of the women and children at home were affected by the events. Diaries, intelligence manuals, rifles, flags, banners and even cutlery add a strong note of reality.

Processions of royal visits in the city start from the Armémuseum, and during the summer, guardsmen march from here to the Royal Palace at 11:45am every day during the changing of the guard ceremony.

INGMAR BERGMAN

The playwright and producer Ingmar Bergman was born at Östermalm in 1918. His long series of masterly films have made him world famous, but he started his career in the theatre. From 1963 to 1966 he was Director of Kungliga Dramatiska Teatern. His breakthrough as a film producer came with *Smiles of the Summer Night* (1955), and *The Seventh Seal* (1957) was a cinematic milestone. *Fanny and Alexander* (1982) was his last major film, after which he wrote screen plays and published his autobiography, *Magic Lantern*. Ingmar Bergman died in 2007.

18
Humlegården

🅟 F3 🏠 Karlavägen 32
🚇 Karlaplan ⏱ 24 hrs
🌐 stockholm.se

Just a stone's throw away from Stureplan square, the broad, oak tree-lined paths and lawns of Humlegården, or "Hop Garden", are a welcome retreat from the busy city centre. This former royal garden has been a public park since 1869, featuring a large play area and, in the summer, popular outdoor clubs and bars. A statue of Swedish naturalist Carl von Linné looks out over the middle of the park. The beautiful park is also home to the National Library of Sweden.

19
Stadsbiblioteket

🅟 D2 🏠 Sveavägen 73
🚇 Odenplan, Rådmansgatan
🕐 10am–5pm Mon–Fri,
noon–4pm Sat
🌐 biblioteket.stockholm.se

Gunnar Asplund's masterpiece, the Stadsbiblioteket (City Library), is one of the capital's most architecturally important buildings. Asplund, the champion of the Functionalist style prevalent in the 1930s, designed a public library dominated by Classical ideals. It was opened in 1928.

Internally, the furnishings were designed by Asplund himself. The work of Swedish artists is well represented: in the entrance hall are Ivar Johnsson's stucco reliefs with themes from Homer's *Iliad* and the sparkling mural in the children's section, *John Blund*, is by Nils Dardel. Hilding Linnquist was responsible for the huge tapestry, and for four mural paintings using ancient fresco techniques.

The library lends more than a million books every year and also organizes author sessions.

---

20 🍽 🍴
Kungliga Dramatiska Teatern

🅟 F4 🏠 Nybroplan
🚇 Östermalmstorg
🎟 Ticket Office: noon–7pm Tue–Sat, noon–4pm Sun
🌐 dramaten.se

When plans were drawn up in the early 20th century to build the present Kungliga Dramatiska Teatern (Royal

---

┃ **GUNNAR ASPLUND**

Gunnar Asplund (1885-1940) was a dominant figure among Swedish and internationally renowned architects in the 1930s. His first major commission was the chapel at the Skogskyrkogården Cemetery, designed in National Romantic style. His last work was Heliga Korsets Kapell, the cemetery's crematorium (1935–40). Regarded as a masterpiece in the Functionalist style, it has earned a place on the UNESCO World Heritage list.

↑ Inside the City Library, and the Neo-Classical façade *(inset)*

Dramatic Theatre), the State refused to give financial aid, so it was funded by lotteries instead. The results exceeded all expectations, giving the architect Fredrik Lilljekvist generous resources.

The lavish theatre, known as Dramaten, took six years to build and opened in 1908. The Jugendstil façade, inspired by Viennese architecture, is in costly white marble. Swedish sculptors Christian Ericsson created the powerful relief frieze, Carl Milles the centre section and John Börjesson the statues *Poetry* and *Drama*.

The ceiling in the foyer is by Carl Larsson, while the upper lobby's back wall was painted by Oscar Björk, and the auditorium's ceiling and stage lintel by Julius Kronberg. The central painting in the marble foyer is by Gustav Cederström.

When Gustav III founded the Royal Dramatic Theatre in 1788, it performed in a building on Slottsbacken.

The colour scheme there – blue, white and gold – was chosen for the venue it is housed in today, but was changed to "theatre red" in the 1930s. The original colours were reinstated in 1988.

---

21 🏛 🏛

Hallwylska museet

📍F4 🏠Hamngatan 4 🚇Östermalmstorg 🕐Jul-Aug: 10am-7pm Tue-Sun; Sep-Jun: noon-4pm Tue-Fri (to 7pm Wed), 11am-5pm Sat & Sun 🔒Some public hols 🌐hallwylska museet.se

The impressive façade of Hamngatan 4 is nothing in comparison with what is concealed behind the heavy gates. The Hallwyl Palace was built from 1892 to 1897 as a residence for the wealthy Count and Countess Walther and Wilhelmina von Hallwyl. When the Countess died in 1930, the State was left a fantastic gift: an unbelievably ornate palace whose chatelaine had amassed a priceless collection of *objets d'art*. Eight years later the doors opened on a new museum with 67,000 catalogued items.

The architect Isak Gustav Clason (1856–1930) had no worries about cost and nor did the artistic adviser Julius Kronberg. Every detail had to be perfect. An example is the billiards room which has gilt-leather wallpaper with billiard balls sculpted into the marble fireplace.

The paintings in the gallery, mostly 16th- and 17th-century Flemish, were bought over a period of only two years.

22

Observatoriekullen

📍D3 🏠Drottninggatan 120 🚇Odenplan

Several institutions connected with science and education

can be found on and around the Observatoriekullen (Observatory Hill). The oldest is the former observatory designed by Carl Hårleman and opened from 1753 to 1931, when astronomical research was moved to Saltsjöbaden in the Stockholm archipelago. The grove that surrounds the old observatory began to take shape in the 18th century. It is now an idyllic enclosed area, first opened to the public in the 20th century.

On top of the hill is Sigrid Fridman's statue *The Centaur*.

A park stretches down to Sveavägen, where a pond is fed by a hillside stream. At the southern entrance of the park is Nils Möllerberg's sculpture *Youth*.

A SHORT WALK
AROUND KUNGSTRÄDGÅRDEN

Distance 1.5 km (1 mile) **Nearest metro** Kungsträdgården
Time 20 minutes

With a history going back to the 15th century, the King's Garden (Kungsträdgården) has long been the city's most popular meeting place and recreational centre. Both visitors and Stockholmers gather here for summer concerts and festivals, or just to enjoy a stroll under the lime trees. Around the park is a wealth of shops, including the upmarket department store Nordiska Kompaniet, boutiques, churches, museums and restaurants. A short walk takes you to Gustav Adolfs Torg, flanked by the Royal Opera House and other stately buildings, including the Swedish Foreign Office.

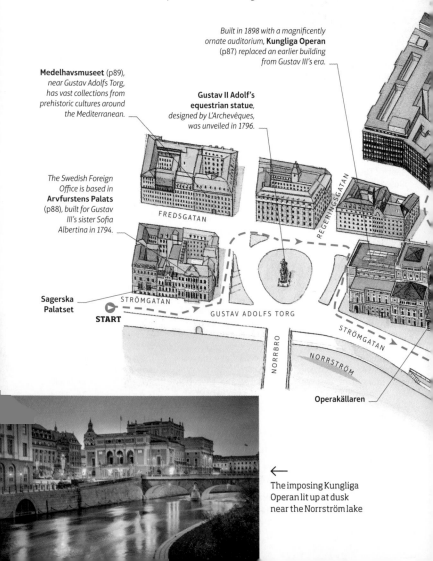

Built in 1898 with a magnificently ornate auditorium, **Kungliga Operan** *(p87) replaced an earlier building from Gustav III's era.*

Medelhavsmuseet *(p89), near Gustav Adolfs Torg, has vast collections from prehistoric cultures around the Mediterranean.*

Gustav II Adolf's equestrian statue, *designed by L'Archevêques, was unveiled in 1796.*

The Swedish Foreign Office is based in **Arvfurstens Palats** *(p88), built for Gustav III's sister Sofia Albertina in 1794.*

FREDSGATAN

REGERINGSGATAN

Sagerska Palatset

STRÖMGATAN

START

GUSTAV ADOLFS TORG

STRÖMGATAN

NORRBRO

NORRSTRÖM

Operakällaren

← The imposing Kungliga Operan lit up at dusk near the Norrström lake

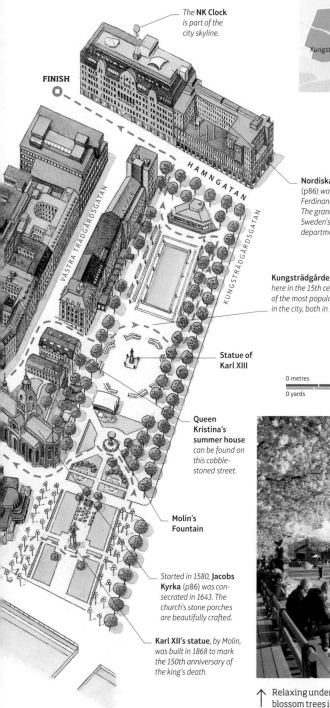

The **NK Clock** is part of the city skyline.

FINISH

Locator Map
For more detail see p82

H A M N G A T A N

VÄSTRA TRÄDGÅRDSGATAN

KUNGSTRÄDGÅRDSGATAN

Nordiska Kompaniet (NK) (p86) *was designed by Ferdinand Boberg in 1915. The granite palace houses Sweden's most exclusive department store.*

Kungsträdgården (p86) *was sited here in the 15th century. Today it is one of the most popular recreation centres in the city, both in summer and winter.*

Statue of Karl XIII

Queen Kristina's summer house *can be found on this cobble-stoned street.*

Molin's Fountain

Started in 1580, **Jacobs Kyrka** (p86) *was consecrated in 1643. The church's stone porches are beautifully crafted.*

Karl XII's statue, *by Molin, was built in 1868 to mark the 150th anniversary of the king's death.*

↑ Relaxing under a row of blossom trees in leafy Kungsträdgården

BLASIEHOLMEN AND SKEPPSHOLMEN

Opposite the Royal Palace on the eastern side of the Norrström channel lies Blasieholmen, a natural springboard to the islands of Skeppsholmen and Kastellholmen. Several elegant palaces were built at Blasieholmen during Sweden's era as a great power in the 17th and early 18th centuries, but the area's present appearance was acquired in the period between the mid-19th century, when buildings such as Nationalmuseum were erected, and just before World War I. In the early 1900s, stately residences such as Bååtska Palatset became overshadowed by smart hotels, opulent bank buildings and entertainment venues.

Skeppsholmen is reached by a wrought-iron bridge with old wooden boats moored next to it. In the middle of the 17th century the island became the base for the Swedish navy and many of its old buildings were designed as barracks and stores. Today they house some of the city's major museums and cultural institutions.

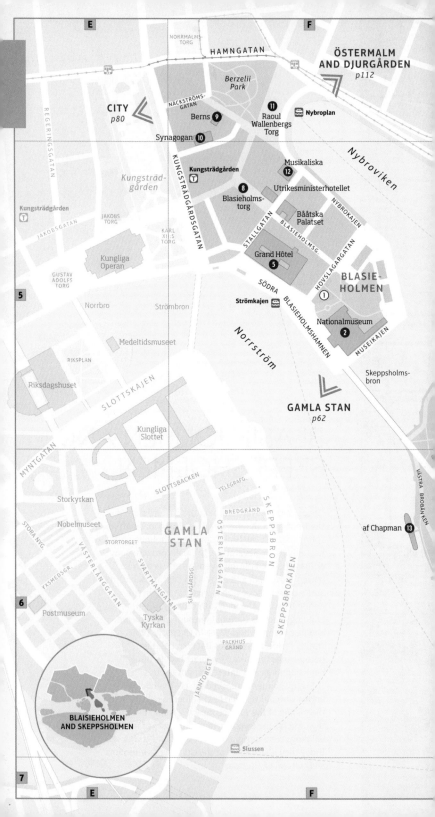

ÖSTERMALM
AND DJURGÅRDEN
p112

NORRMALMS-
TORG

HAMNGATAN

*Berzelii
Park*

CITY
p80

NÄCKSTRÖMS-
GATAN

Berns **9**

Raoul **11**
Wallenbergs
Torg

Nybroplan

Synagogan **10**

Nybroviken

Kungsträdgården Ⓣ

Musikaliska **12**

KUNGSTRÄDGÅRDSGATAN

REGERINGSGATAN

*Kungsträd-
gården*

Blasieholms- **8**
torg

Utrikesministerhotellet

Båätska
Palatset

NYBROKAJEN

Kungsträdgården
Ⓣ

JAKOBS
TORG

JAKOBSGATAN

KARL
XII:S
TORG

STALLGATAN

BLASIEHOLMSG.

Grand Hôtel
5

BLASIE-
HOLMEN **1**

HOVSLAGARGATAN

Kungliga
Operan

GUSTAV
ADOLFS
TORG

5

Norrbro   Strömbron

Strömkajen 🚢

SÖDRA
BLASIEHOLMSHAMNEN

Nationalmuseum
2

MUSEIKAJEN

Medeltidsmuseet

Norrström

Skeppsholms-
bron

RIKSPLAN

SLOTTSKAJEN

Riksdagshuset

GAMLA STAN
p62

MYNTGATAN

Kungliga
Slottet

SLOTTSBACKEN

TELEGRAFG.

VÄSTRA
BROBÄNKEN

Storkyrkan

BREDGRÄND

SKEPPSBRON

af Chapman **13**

STORA NYG.

Nobelmuseet

**GAMLA
STAN**

ÖSTERLÅNGGATAN

VÄSTERLÅNGGATAN

STORTORGET

SJÄLAGÅRDSG.

6

YXSMEDSGR.

Postmuseet

SVARTMANGATAN

Tyska
Kyrkan

SKEPPSBROKAJEN

PACKHUS
GRÄND

JÄRNTORGET

**BLAISIEHOLMEN
AND SKEPPSHOLMEN**

Slussen 🚢

7

E   F

BLASIEHOLMEN AND SKEPPSHOLMEN

Must Sees
❶ Moderna museet
❷ Nationalmuseum

Experience More
❸ Östasiatiska museet
❹ Arkitektur och designcentrum
❺ Grand Hôtel
❻ Kastellholmen
❼ Bergrummet
❽ Blasieholmstorg
❾ Berns
❿ Synagogan
⓫ Raoul Wallenbergs Torg
⓬ Musikaliska
⓭ af Chapman

Stay
① Lydmar Hotel
② Hotel Skeppsholmen

RIDDARGATAN
SKEPPARGATAN
GREVGATAN
STURMANSGATAN
STRANDVÄGEN

Ladugårdslandsviken

Fotografins Hus

❸ Östasiatiska museet

TYGHUSPLAN

SLUPSKJULSPLAN

Spritmuseum

❼ Bergrummet

SVENSKSUNDSVÄGEN

❶ Moderna museet

EXERCISPLAN

❹ Arkitektur och designcentrum

SKEPPSHOLMEN

Svenskundsparken

Skeppsholmen

LÅNGA RADEN

②

GRÖNA GÅNGEN

AMIRALSVÄGEN

Allmänna gränd

6

SÖDRA BROBÄNKEN

Kastellholmsbron

KASTELLHOLMSKAJEN

Kastellholmen

❻

KASTELLBACKEN

ÖRLOGSVÄGEN

Kastellet

Kastellparken

0 metres 200
0 yards 200

N ↑

7

① 〈🛴〉〈🚫〉〈🍴〉〈🖥〉〈🛍〉

MODERNA MUSEET

📍G5 🚇Exercisplan 🚆Kungsträdgården ⛴Djurgårdsfärja 🕐10am-6pm Tue-Sun (to 8pm Tue & Fri) 🌐modernamuseet.se

The Museum of Modern Art is an airy, contemporary building, designed by the Catalan architect Rafael Moneo in 1998. The museum has a top-class collection of international and Swedish modern art, as well as photography and film, from 1900 to the present day.

Built partly underground, the complex has around 140,000 artworks displayed on various levels. The photographic library is the most comprehensive collection of its type in northern Europe and there is also a collection of video art and art documentaries. A wide choice of books on art, photography, film and architecture can be found in the bookshop, and the restaurant has attractive views over the water. The large room on the entrance level is used for temporary exhibitions. Three rooms on the same level have an alternating selection of collections from the eras 1900–45, 1946–70 and 1971 to the present day. The middle level has an auditorium, cinema and study gallery. Another entrance is at the lower level.

RAFAEL MONEO

Rafael Moneo (b 1937) is one of the world's leading contemporary architects. As a young architect, he took part in the project to build the Sydney Opera House. His flair for adapting building design to sensitive surroundings was recognized in 1998 when his was chosen out of 211 entries as the winner of the competition to design the new Moderna museet.

→ The *Narcissus Garden* by the Japanese artist Yayoi Kusama, which grabs much attention

1 The permanent exhibition of works by Niki de Saint-Phalle is a highlight.

2 The museum's logo is made up of a distinctive signature that resembles graffiti, which appears on its long façade.

3 Minimalist galleries provide the perfect setting in which to display the museum's contemporary art.

Did You Know?

The collection comprises over 140,000 works in various media; only a fraction can be displayed.

2 🖌️ 🖥️ 🏛️

NATIONALMUSEUM

📍F5 🏛️ Södra Blasieholmshamnen 2 🚇 Kungsträdgården 🕐 11am–5pm Tue–Sun (to 9pm Thu) 🌐 nationalmuseum.se

The Nationalmuseum is a landmark standing on the southern side of Blasieholmen. The location by the Strömmen channel inspired the 19th-century German architect August Stüler to design a handsome building in the Venetian and Florentine Renaissance styles.

Completed in 1866, the museum houses Sweden's largest art collection, with some 16,000 classic paintings and sculptures. Drawings and graphics from the 15th century up to the early 20th century bring the total to 500,000. Set in one of the world's oldest museums, the collection includes works by great masters, such as Rembrandt, Renoir, Goya, Rubens, Degas and Gauguin and those by Swedish masters Anders Zorn and Carl Larsson. Other exhibits include a 500-year-old tapestry and examples of work by master furniture-makers, such as Georg Haupt. Space is also devoted to the development of modern Swedish handicrafts and design.

After five years of renovation, the museum reopened in 2018. The renovations cost 1.2 billion kronor and it was the first time that the museum had undergone total renovations since it first opened. Exhibition spaces have been transformed and a sculpture courtyard, restaurant and creative workshops are new additions. The restaurant not only offers culinary experiences but art and design, and has been thoughtfully curated and designed by a team of over 30 designers.

GALLERY GUIDE

The collection is set out chronologically and follows a timeline. Arts, crafts and design sit side by side, providing a greater perspective on the eras. Each era has a main hall, where the features of the art and the relevant cultural and social influences are presented. The adjacent rooms provide space for delving deeper into the issues that relate to the time period.

① The upper staircase is adorned with monumental murals and art work.

② Though now housed in the Nationalmuseum, Rembrandt's *The Conspiracy of the Batavians under Claudius Civilis* (1661–2) was intended for Amsterdam.

③ The Nationalmuseum building, designed in Venetian and Renaissance styles, is pleasingly sited overlooking the water.

Must See

Visitors studying a life-size sculpture in one of the museum's galleries

105

EXPERIENCE MORE

3

Östasiatiska museet

G5 🚏 **Tyghusplan**
🚇 **Kungsträdgården**
⛴ **Djurgårdsfärja** 🕙 **11am-5pm Tue-Sun (to 8pm Tue)**
🌐 **ostasiatiskamuseet.se**

Devoted to archaeology and art from China, Japan, Korea and India, Östasiatiska museet can claim one of the world's foremost collections of Chinese art outside Asia.

On a visit to the Yellow River valley in China in the early 1920s, the Swedish geologist Johan Gunnar Andersson discovered hitherto unknown dwellings and graves containing objects dating from the New Stone Age.

He was allowed to take a selection of items back to Sweden, and these formed the basis for the museum, founded in 1926. A key figure in its development was the then Crown Prince, later to become King Gustav VI Adolf, who was both interested in and knowledgeable about archaeology. Later, he bequeathed to the museum his own large collection of ancient Chinese arts and crafts. The museum has been located on Skeppsholmen since 1963, when it was moved into a restored house that had been built in 1699–1700 as a depot for Karl XII's bodyguard.

←
A Chinese artifact on display at Östasiatiska museet

THE SKEPPSHOLMEN CANNONS

A salute battery of four 57-mm rapid-fire cannons is sited on Skeppsholmen and is still in use. Salutes are fired to mark national and royal special occasions at noon on weekdays and 1pm at weekends: 28 January - the King's name day; 30 April - the King's birthday; 6 June - Sweden's National Day; 14 July - Crown Princess Victoria's birthday; 8 August - the Queen's name day; 23 December - the Queen's birthday.

4

Arkitektur och designcentrum

G6 🚏 **Exercisplan 4**
🚇 **Kungsträdgården**
⛴ **Djurgårdsfärja** 🕙 **10am-6pm Tue-Sun (to 8pm Tue & Fri)** 🌐 **arkdes.se**

The Swedish Architecture and Design Centre shares an entrance hall and restaurant with Moderna museet. It has also reclaimed its earlier Neo-Classical home, a one-time naval drill hall.

In the permanent exhibition, more than 100 architectural models guide visitors through the history of Swedish building. They include the oldest and simplest of wooden houses to the highly sophisticated construction techniques and innovative styles of the present day.

It is fascinating to move from an almost 2,000-year-old longhouse to a modern super-market, interspersed with examples of architecture in Gothenburg from the 17th century to the 1930s. Models

---

The exclusive five-star Grand Hôtel on Blasieholmen ↑

of historic architectural works worldwide, from 2000 BC up to the present day, are also on show.

The museum offers an ambitious programme – albeit only in Swedish – alongside the permanent and temporary exhibitions, including lectures, study days, city walks, guided tours, school visits and family events on Sunday afternoons, which involve model-building.

5

Grand Hôtel

F5 🚏 **Södra Blasieholmshamnen 8**
🚇 **Kungsträdgården**
🌐 **grandhotel.se**

Oscar II's head chef, Régis Cadier, founded the Grand Hôtel, one of Stockholm's leading five-star hotels, in 1874. Since 1901, the hotel has accommodated the Nobel Prize winners each year.

Delicious traditional Swedish delicacies are served in an abundant smörgåsbord in the elegant Veranda. The hotel also has a Michelin-starred restaurant and the Cadier Bar, which is named after its founder.

The Grand Hotel is praised for its 24 good banqueting and conference suites, the best known of which is the lofty Vinterträdgården (Winter Garden), which can accommodate up to 800 people. The impressive Spegelsalen (Hall of Mirrors) is a copy of the hall at Versailles and was where the Nobel Prize banquet was held until 1929, when it became too big and was moved to Stadshuset (City Hall, p84).

6

Kastellholmen

📍G6 🚇Kungsträdgården
⛴Djurgårdsfärja

Right in the middle of Stockholm, Kastellholmen is a typical archipelago island with granite rocks and steep cliffs. From Skeppsholmen, this peaceful spot is reached by crossing a bridge built in 1880. Every morning since 1640 a sailor has hoisted the three-tailed Swedish war flag at the medieval-style castle, which was built in 1846-8. Whenever a visiting naval vessel arrives, the battery's four cannons fire

a welcoming salute from the castle terrace.

The charming brick pavilion by the bridge was built in 1882 for the Royal Skating Club, which once used the water between the two islands when it froze.

7 ⊘ ▢ ▢

Bergrummet

📍F6 🚇Svensksundsvägen
5 🚇Kungsträdgården
🕙10am-5pm daily
🌐bergrummet.com

Located in the underground tunnels of Skeppsholmen, the Tidö collection of toys and comics is the largest in Northern Europe, housing more than 40,000 items. Highlights of the collection include original Marvel Comics illustrations, 15th-century dolls and model cars. The museum also puts on temporary exhibitions throughout the year.

You can also pick up toys and treasures such as games, books and comic books in the well-stocked shop, while the café is a lovely spot to relax in while the kids explore the museum.

↑ Elegant dining room inside the Grand Hôtel

STAY

Lydmar Hotel
A refined hotel offering understated luxury and cutting-edge designs.

📍F5 🚇Södra
Blasieholmshamnen 2
🌐lydmad.com

Ⓚ Ⓚ Ⓚ

Hotel Skeppsholmen
This hotel combines the atmosphere of a 17th-century building with modern design.

📍G6 🚇Gröna gången 1
🌐hotelskepps
holmen.se

Ⓚ Ⓚ Ⓚ

8

Blasieholmstorg

F5 **Kungsträdgården**

Two of the city's oldest palaces are located on Blasieholmstorg, which is flanked by two bronze horses. The palace at No 8 was built in the mid-17th century by Field Marshal Gustaf Horn. It was rebuilt 100 years later and acquired the character of an 18th-century French palace.

Foreign ambassadors and ministers lodged here when they visited the capital, hence it became known as the Ministers' Palace. Later it became a base for overseas administration and soon earned its present name of Utrikesministerhotellet (Foreign Ministry Hotel). Parts of the building are used as offices by the Musical Academy and the Swedish Institute.

Bååtska Palatset stands nearby at No 6. Its exterior dates from 1669 and was designed by Tessin the Elder. In 1876–7 it was partly rebuilt by F W Scholander for the Freemasons, who still have their lodge here.

After dark, colourful lights enhance Berns entertainment venue ↓

Another interesting complex of buildings can be found on the square at No 10. The façade which faces on to Nybrokajen, along the water's edge, is an attractive example of the Neo-Renaissance style of the 1870s and 1880s.

9

Berns

F4 **Näckströmsgatan 8**
08-566 322 00
Kungsträdgården, Östermalmstorg

This has been one of the city's most legendary restaurant and entertainment venues since 1863. The building's halls, with their stately galleries, magnificent crystal chandeliers and elegant mirrors, were restored to their original splendour by the British designer and restaurateur Terence Conran to mark the new millennium.

Berns is one of Stockholm's biggest restaurants, with seating capacity for 400 diners. The gallery level, with its beautifully decorated dining rooms, was made famous by August Strindberg's novel *The Red Room* (1879). In addition to its

> **Two of the city's oldest palaces are located on Blasieholmstorg, which is flanked by two bronze horses.**

various restaurants, there are a number of bars, plus a rooftop terrace (open in summer), making this a great place for a night out, with live music, international DJs and fantastic cocktails on offer. The building also has a luxury hotel.

10

Synagogan

F4 **Wahrendoffsgatan 3B** **08-587 858 24**
Kungsträdgården

It took most of the 1860s to build the Conservative Jewish community's synagogue on land reclaimed from the sea. When it was inaugurated in 1870, the building was standing on 1,300 piles that had been driven down to a depth of 15 m (50 ft). It is built in what the architect, F W Scholander, called "ancient Eastern style". The synagogue can be visited on guided tours during the summer. Alongside is the congregation's assembly room and library. Outside is a monument erected in 1998 in memory of 8,000 victims of the Holocaust whose relations had been rescued and taken to Sweden during World War II.

There is also an interesting Orthodox synagogue in Södermalm. Its entrance is just around the corner from Ragvaldsgatan 14C.

⓫ Raoul Wallenbergs Torg

☑ F4 ⓣ Östermalmstorg ⛟ 7

This square is dedicated to Raoul Wallenberg (1912–unknown), who during World War II worked as a diplomat at the Swedish Embassy in Budapest. By using Swedish "protective passports" and safe houses throughout the city he helped a large

number of Hungarian Jews to escape deportation to the Nazi concentration camps.

In 1945, when Budapest was liberated, Wallenberg was imprisoned by the Soviet Union and according to Russian sources he died in Moscow's Lubianka prison in 1947. His fate has never been satisfactorily explained despite strenuous efforts by the Swedes to seek the truth.

The small square adjoins Berzelii Park and Nybroplan and faces the Nybrokajen waterfront, and great efforts have been made to ensure that the square continues to remain a worthy memorial to Wallenberg.

⓬ Musikaliska

☑ F5 ⓝ Nybrokajen 11 ⓣ Kungsträdgården, Östermalmstorg ⛴ Djurgårdsfärja ◑ For concerts, check website for details ⓦ musikaliska.com

Constructed in the 1870s, this building facing the waters of Nybroviken once housed the Musical Academy. Its concert hall, which opened in 1878,

⚠ GREAT VIEW
Bridge over to Skeppsholmen

Take a stroll across the wrought-iron bridge to Skeppsholmen and pause by the golden crown at the middle of the bridge. From here there is a stunning view of the Royal Palace across the water.

was the first in the country, and was used to present the inaugural Nobel Prize in 1901. Designed in Neo-Renaissance style complete with cast-iron pillars, the hall has a royal box and galleries, and can seat up to 600 people. Musikaliska is a popular venue for choral and chamber concerts, jazz and folk music.

⓭ af Chapman

☑ F6 ⓝ Västra Brobänken ⓒ 08-463 22 66 ⓣ Kungsträdgården ⛴ Djurgårdsfärja

The sailing ship *af Chapman* may have been converted into a youth hostel – one of the most attractive and unusual in Stockholm – but visitors staying in more conventional accommodation in the city can nonetheless admire the iconic boat from a café nearby.

The three-masted ship was built in 1888 at the English port of Whitehaven and used as a freight vessel. She made voyages between Europe, Australia and the west coast of North America. In 1915, she came to Sweden and saw service as a sail training ship until 1934. The City of Stockholm bought the vessel after World War II and she has been berthed here since 1949. She is named after Fredrik Henrik af Chapman, a master shipbuilder who was born in Gothenburg in 1721.

A SHORT WALK
SKEPPSHOLMEN

Distance 1 km (0.5 miles) **Nearest ferry terminal** Skeppsholmen **Time** 15 minutes

Skeppsholmen has long since lost its importance as a naval base and has been transformed into a centre for culture. Many of the naval buildings have been restored and traditional wooden boats are moored here, but pride of place now goes to the Moderna museet. The island is ideal for a full-day visit, with its location between the waters of Strömmen and Nybroviken acting as a breathing space in the centre of Stockholm. The attractive buildings, the English-style park and the view towards Skeppsbron and Strandvägen also make Skeppsholmen a pleasant place for those who would just prefer to have a quiet stroll.

The **Östasiatiska museet** (p106) *has a fine collection of arts and crafts from China, Japan, Korea and India.*

▶ **START**

The **Skeppsholmsbron** *bridge*

Skeppsholmen Church *(1824–42) is well-preserved in the Empire style.*

Salute battery

Admiralty House

Built in 1888, **af Chapman** *(p109), the full-rigged former freighter and school ship, has served as a popular youth hostel since 1949.*

SVENSKSUNDVÄGEN

VÄSTRA BROBANKEN

Youth Hostel

Swedish Society of Crafts & Design

The first part of **Kungliga Konsthögskolan** *(the Royal College of Fine Arts) was completed in the 1770s, but its present appearance dates to the mid-1990s.*

Paradise *(1963), a sculpture group by Jean Tinguely and Niki de Saint Phalle, stands outside Moderna museet.*

↑ The elegant af Chapman ship moored next to a pleasant promenade in autumn

Teater Galeasen *is Stockholm's avant-garde theatre for new Swedish and international drama.*

This loading crane was built in 1751 and is the oldest of its type in Sweden.

The festival area on the quayside is the venue for the International Jazz & Blues Festival, which takes place for a week in July each year.

Designed by Rafael Moneo, **Moderna museet** *(p102) was opened in 1998 when Stockholm was Cultural Capital of Europe.*

Arkitektur och designcentrum
(p106) highlights thousands of years of building, with a collection of models showing masterpieces worldwide.

Monument commemorating the battle at Svensksund in 1790

Locator Map
For more detail see p100

BLASIEHOLMEN AND
SKEPPSHOLMEN

Skeppsholmen

0 metres   100
0 yards   100

N

ÖSTRA BROBANKEN

SVENSKSUNDSV

AMIRALSVÄGEN

LÅNGA RADEN

SÖDRA BROBANKEN

FINISH

Hotel Skeppsholmen *is part of a complex of buildings dating back to around 1700. Today it serves as a hotel and restaurant.*

Did You Know?

Hotel Skeppsholmen originally accommodated King Karl XII's bodyguard.

ÖSTERMALM AND DJURGÅRDEN

During the 15th century, Östermalm was known as Ladugårdslandet, or "The Barn Land", when the monarchy used the area as a royal farm. With the rise of the Swedish Empire, its open fields were used for military training, until the mid-1800s, when the district underwent extensive redevelopment to become a residential area for the wealthy. In 1885, officials adopted Östermalm as the new name. Today, visitors stroll along Strandvägen to admire the historic buildings and indulge in the lovely restaurants and exclusive shopping.

South of Östermalm lies Djurgården, an island owned by the monarchy since medieval times. In 1897, Stockholm hosted the World's Fair on the island, where officials built numerous structures and museums for the event. Most of the buildings for the exposition were torn down, but some were converted to tourist attractions such as Skansen and the Nordic Museum. There are now strict laws in place to protect the island's cultural and natural heritage.

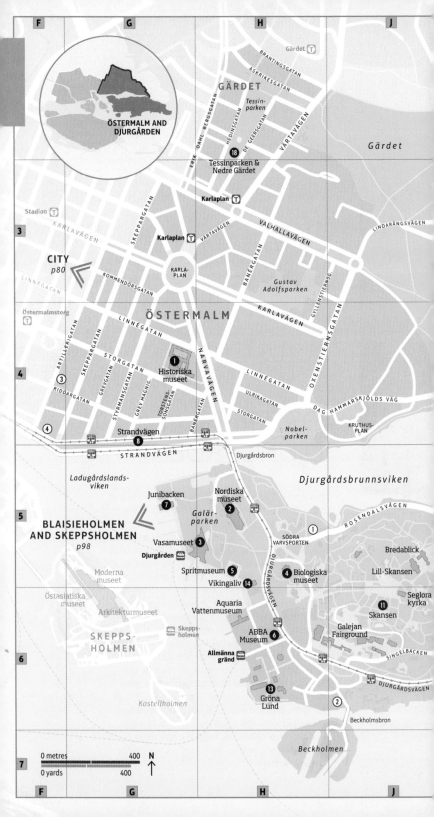

ÖSTERMALM AND DJURGÅRDEN

Must Sees
1 Historiska museet
2 Nordiska museet
3 Vasamuseet

Experience More
4 Biologiska museet
5 Spritmuseum
6 ABBA Museum
7 Junibacken
8 Strandvägen
9 Waldemarsudde
10 Thielska Galleriet
11 Skansen
12 Etnografiska museet
13 Gröna Lund
14 Vikingaliv
15 Tekniska museet
16 Sjöhistoriska museet
17 Kaknästornet
18 Tessinparken & Nedre Gärdet

Eat
1 Villa Godthem
2 Oaxen Krog
3 Gastrologik

Stay
4 Hotel Diplomat

Exhibits displayed in a
modern, open space
inside Historiska museet ↑

① 🖉 🚫 🖥 🏛

HISTORISKA MUSEET

📍G4 🏛 Narvavägen 13-17 🚇 Karlaplan 🕐 Sep-May: 11am-5pm Tue-Sun (to 8pm Wed); Jun & Aug: 10am-6pm daily 🌐 historiska.se

Designed by Bengt Romare and Georg Sherman, the Swedish History Museum has a wealth of material behind its richly detailed bronze gateways. Without doubt its most significant highlight is the spectacular Gold Room.

Opened in 1943, the museum originally made its name with its prominent collection from the Viking era, as well as its outstanding treasures from the early Middle Ages.

The Gold Room

Since the early 1990s the museum's many priceless gold artifacts have been on show in Guldrummet, an underground vault built in two circular sections with 250 tons of reinforced concrete to ensure security. The inner part houses the main collection, with 50 kg (110 lb) of gold treasures and 250 kg (550 lb) of silver from the Bronze Age to the Middle Ages. The Gold Collars were found between 1827 and 1864; the

three-ringed collar in a stone quarry in eastern Sweden; and the seven-ringed hanging on a spike in a barn. The Elisabeth Reliquary was originally a drinking goblet mounted with gold and precious stones in the 11th century. In about 1230 a silver cover was added to enclose the skull of St Elisabeth. Sweden seized it in 1631, as a trophy in the Thirty Years' War.

> **The Elisabeth Reliquary was originally a drinking goblet mounted with gold and precious stones in the 11th century.**

Kungliga Myntkabinettet

Located in the same building, the Royal Coin Cabinet *(www.myntkabinettet.se)* is a fabulous museum holding a priceless collection of currency and highlighting the history of money from the 10th century to the present day – from the little cowrie shell via the drachmaw and denarius to the current cash card. The museum also gives an insight into the art of medal design over the past 600 years and shows both traditional portrait medals and modern examples such as those that have been awarded to Nobel laureates.

The Elisabeth Reliquary ↑
drinking goblet

←

Door to the museum, decorated by Bror Marklund (1907-77)

2 🚲 🎨 🍴 🖥 📷 🛍

NORDISKA MUSEET

📍H5 🏠Djurgårdsvägen 6-16 🚌7 ⛴Djurgårdsfärja 🕐10am-5pm daily (to 8pm Wed; Jun & Aug: 9am-6pm) 🎫Some public hols 🌐nordiskamuseet.se

A monument to Swedish cultural history, Nordiska museet portrays everyday life in Sweden from the 1520s to the present day. It has more than 1.5 million exhibits, with everything from clothing and jewellery to furniture and children's toys, as well as replicas of period homes.

In 1872, Artur Hazelius (1833–1901), the founder of Skansen (p125), began collecting objects that would remind future generations of the old Nordic farming culture. The present museum, resembling an extravagant Renaissance castle, was designed by Isak Gustav Clason and opened in 1907.

Displayed are re-created period homes and furnishings, including parts of a drawing room from the 1880s and a Swedish interior from the 1950s. There is also a bedchamber where the lord of the manor at Ulvsunda would accommodate prominent guests at the end of the 17th century. The museum owns the largest single collection of August Strindberg's paintings in the world – sixteen of these are exhibited. The Sámi are Europe's northernmost indigenous people and an exhibition here examines their traditional way of life and influences on Swedish culture.

→ Visitors admiring a photography exhibition

↑ The huge main hall, a fitting entrance to the museum

GALLERY GUIDE

The museum is set up over four floors. From the entrance, stairs lead up to the temporary exhibitions in the main hall on the second level. As visitors enter this huge hall they are greeted by a monumental statue of King Gustav Vasa, made in painted and gilded oak by Carl Milles in 1924. The third floor houses the Strindberg collection, doll's houses, table settings, traditions and the fashion and textile galleries. On the fourth floor are sections dealing with folk art, interiors, Swedish homes, small objects and a section covering the Sami people and culture.

Did You Know?

Nordiska is one of the first museums to work on preserving collections for generations to come.

↑ Nordiska museet, set in an imposing Renaissance-style building

3 ⚐ 🏛 🍴 ☕ 🖥 🛍

VASAMUSEET

⚐ H5 🏠 Galärvarvsvägen 14 🚌 7 ⛴ Djurgårdsfärja ⏰ 10am–5pm daily (to 8pm Wed; Jun–Aug: 8:30am–6pm) 🌐 vasamuseet.se

The Vasa Museum is the most visited museum in Scandinavia and tells the story of the 17th-century warship *Vasa* and her recovery. A number of models and reconstructions bring it to life, and getting up close to the vessel is a unique experience.

After a maiden voyage of just 1,300 m (1,422 yd) in calm weather, the warship *Vasa* capsized and sank in Stockholm's harbour on 10 August 1628. About 30 people went down with what was supposed to be the pride of the navy, only 100 m (109 yd) off the southern tip of Djurgården. It was discovered that the *Vasa* had a fatal flaw – she was top heavy, with insufficient ballast. Almost all the guns were salvaged from the vessel in the 17th century but it was not until 1956 that a private researcher's persistent search led to the rediscovery of the *Vasa*. In 1961 her remarkably intact hull was raised after 333 years under water, followed by a 17-year conservation programme. This popular museum opened in 1990, less than a nautical mile from the scene of the disaster. The ship is now preserved under controlled conditions to prevent decay.

↑ The *Vasa* in dry dock after being salvaged between 1956 and 1961

The carefully restored ship, revealing skilled carving along the prow ↑

Key features of Vasa

THE SALVAGE OPERATION

The marine archaeologist Anders Franzén had been looking for the *Vasa* for many years. On 25 August 1956 his patience was rewarded when he brought up a piece of blackened oak on his plumb line. From the autumn of 1957, it took divers two years to clear space beneath the hull for the lifting cables. The first lift, using six cables, was a success, after which the ship was raised in 16 stages into shallow water. Plugs were inserted into holes left by rusted iron bolts, then the final lift began and in 1961 the *Vasa* was towed into dry dock.

Bronze Cannon

More than 50 of the *Vasa's* 64 original cannons were salvaged in the 17th century, using a diving bell for the recovery operation. Three of the largest bronze cannons are on display in the museum.

Sculpture

▶ More than 200 carved ornaments and 500 sculpted figures decorate the *Vasa*. Particularly noteworthy is the gun-port lion.

Gun Deck

Although visitors cannot board the ship, there is a full-size replica of a part of the upper gun deck, which gives a good idea of what conditions on board were like and the powerful artillery it was armed with.

Gun Ports

The *Vasa* carried more heavy cannons on its two gun-decks than earlier ships of the same size. This contributed to its capsizing.

Stern

◀ Many of the ship's 500 sculptures were centred on the stern, a symbol of Sweden's might. The *Vasa's* stern was badly damaged, but has been painstakingly restored to reveal the ship's magnificent ornamentation.

Upper Deck

Skilled carpenters restored the destroyed upper deck in the 1990s. While new parts were needed, original timber has been used as much as possible.

Lion Figurehead

▶ King Gustav II Adolf, who commissioned the *Vasa*, was known as the Lion of the North, so a springing lion was the obvious choice for the figurehead. It is 4 m (13 ft) long and weighs 450 kg (990 lb).

← Biologiska museest's wooden façade, inspired by Nordic medieval design

natural surroundings. Within a few months of opening in 1893, Kolthoff had delivered 2,000 stuffed animals, as well as birds' nests, young and eggs, to the museum.

4

Biologiska museet

📍 H5 🏠 Hazeliusporten 2
🚋 7 🔒 For restoration
🌐 skansen.se

The National Romantic artistic influences of the late 19th century inspired the architect Agi Lindegren when he designed the Museum of Biology in the 1890s.

Behind the museum was zoologist and conservationist Gustaf Kolthoff (1845–1913). In 1892, he persuaded the industrialist C F Liljevalch to develop and maintain a biological museum to include all the Scandinavian mammals and birds as stuffed specimens in

5

Spritmuseum

📍 H5 🏠 Djurgårdsvägen 38
🚇 Karlaplan 🚋 7
⛴ Djurgårdsfärja 🕐 10am–5pm Mon–Wed, 10am–7pm Thu–Sat, noon–5pm Sun
🌐 spritmuseum.se

The Spritmuseum (Spirits Museum) is in Stockholm's two

remaining 18th-century naval buildings on the island of Djurgården. Exhibits explore Swedish people's relationship with alcohol. Visitors follow a through-the-year itinerary, discovering the pleasure that can be derived from sipping a chilled beer on a park bench on a summer's evening, as well as the warming effects of a glass of red wine during the winter months. The visit also illustrates the processes linked to alcohol production, attitudes towards drinking and the art of the Swedish drinking song.

The museum hosts temporary exhibitions, too. Past successes include the Absolut Art Collection (images used in Absolut Vodka's advertising campaigns). Such artworks were commissioned from the likes of Andy Warhol, Ralph Steadman and Pierre et Gilles.

6 ABBA Museum

📍 H6 🏠 Djurgårdsvägen 68 🚌 7 ⛴ Djurgårdsfärja 🕐 Times vary, check website 🌐 abbathemuseum.com

This museum is dedicated to ABBA, Sweden's best-known and loved pop band, which enjoyed enormous success all over the world in the 1970s.

The interactive experiences here include the chance to sit at a piano that is connected to Benny Andersson's own piano in his music studio; when the composer tinkles the ivories, the museum piano also starts playing. Other fun experiences include auditioning to be ABBA's fifth member at a replica of the band's Polar Studio and recording a video.

Did You Know?

Sweden is one of the world's most successful exporters of popular music.

← Café at the ABBA Museum, ideal for a pitstop after exploring the memorabilia

ASTRID LINDGREN

Born on 14 November 1907 in Vimmerby in southern Sweden, Astrid Lindgren wrote around 100 children's books, and is one of the world's most-read children's authors. Publishers turned down her first book about Pippi Longstocking, but she went on to win a children's book competition in 1945, and her headstrong character Pippi soon won the hearts of children. Astrid continued writing until the age of 85.

7 Junibacken

📍 G5 🏠 Galärvarvsvägen 8 🚌 7 ⛴ Djurgårdsfärja 🕐 10am–5pm daily (summer: to 6pm) 🌐 junibacken.se

At this tribute to the much-loved author, Astrid Lindgren, a mini-train takes you from a mock-up of the station at Vimmerby to meet some of her characters, finishing with a visit to Pippi's home in Villekulla Cottage. Creations of other Swedish children's authors also make an appearance.

8 Strandvägen

📍 G4 🚇 Östermalmstorg, Karlaplan 🚌 7

The palatial houses along this quayside boulevard were built in the early 20th century by Stockholm's ten richest citizens. This was a muddy, hilly stretch prior to the 1897 Stockholm Exhibition, when a campaign began to create a grand avenue with no equal in Europe. Lined with lime trees, Strandvägen became the elegant boulevard envisaged and is a pleasant place for a stroll, to admire the façades and watch the boats.

EAT

Villa Godthem

This place is known for its signature "Plank Steak".

📍H5 🏠Rosendalsvägen 9 🌐villagodthem.se

ⓀⓀⓀ

Oaxen Krog

Here, creative dishes are made using ethically produced ingredients.

📍J6 🏠Beckholmsvägen 26 🕐Sun & Mon 🌐oaxen.com

ⓀⓀⓀ

Gastrologik

This restaurant has an inventive tasting menu using seasonal produce.

📍F4 🏠Artillerigatan 14 🕐Sun & Mon 🌐gastrologik.se

ⓀⓀⓀ

Traditional windmill in the grounds at Prince Eugen's Waldemarsudde ↓

⑨ 🖉Ⓜ🍴🖵🛍
Waldemarsudde

📍K7 🏠Prins Eugens Väg 6 🕐11am–5pm Tue–Sun (to 8pm Thu) 🌐waldemarsudde.se

One of Sweden's most visited art galleries, Prince Eugen's Waldemarsudde passed into State ownership after his death in 1947. The prince was trained as a military officer, but then became one of the leading landscape painters of his generation. Among his paintings hanging in his former palace are three of his most prized: *Spring* (1891), *The Old Castle* (1893) and *The Cloud* (1896).

Together with works by his contemporaries, the gallery holds an impressive collection of early 20th-century Swedish art and works by younger artists, including Isaac Grünewald and Leander Engström. Sculptors of the same era are represented, particularly Per Hasselberg, whose works are in the gallery and park.

Prince Eugen and his architect, Ferdinand Boberg, drew up the sketches for the palace, completed in 1905. The same architect later designed the gallery, which now includes parts of the collection of some 2,000 works, as well as the Prince's paintings.

Waldemarsudde's guest apartments remain largely unchanged, and the two upper floors with the Prince's studio at the top are used for temporary exhibitions. The buildings are surrounded by beautiful gardens, which feature a windmill that dates back to the 18th century.

---

⑩ 🖉Ⓜ🖵
Thielska Galleriet

📍M6 🏠Sjötullsbacken 8 🕐Noon–5pm Tue–Sun (to 8pm Thu) 🌐thielska-galleriet.se

When the apartments of the banker Ernest Thiel (1860–1947) on Strandvägen started to overflow with his comprehensive collection of Nordic art from the late 19th and early 20th centuries, he commissioned a villa on Djurgården. However, during World War I Thiel lost most of his fortune. His collection was bought by the

State, which opened Thielska Galleriet in his villa in 1926.

There are paintings by all the major Swedish artists who formed an artists' colony at Grèz-sur-Loing, south of Paris, including Carl Larsson and August Strindberg. The gallery also shows works by Eugène Jansson, Anders Zorn and Prince Eugen. Thiel also acquired pieces by foreign artists, not least his good friend Edvard Munch.

11

Skansen

J6 **Djurgårdsslätten 49–51** **Djurgårdsfärja** **Times vary, check website** **24 & 25 Dec** **skansen.se**

The world's first open-air museum, Skansen was established in 1891 to show an increasingly industrialized society how people once lived. It has around 150 houses and farm buildings from all over Sweden. Skansen also plays an important role in nurturing the country's folklore and traditions. Sweden's National Day, Midsummer, Walpurgis Night, Christmas and New Year's Eve celebrations take place here.

In the Town Quarter, complete with 19th-century wooden town houses, glass-blowers, bookbinders and other craftspeople demonstrate their skills. The 300-year-old Älvros farmhouse, from the Härjedalen region, represents rural life with an intriguing collection of everyday tools. At the other end of the scale,

> **INSIDER TIP**
> **Picnic in the Park**
>
> Take a stroll through Rosendals Trädgården, 1.2 km (0.7 miles) east of Skansen. In the spring you can have a picnic under the blossoming apple trees.

Skogaholm Manor, a Carolean manor from 1680, shows how the wealthy lived.

You can see Nordic animals such as wolves in the zoo, and snakes in the aquarium.

12

Etnografiska museet

L4 **Djurgårds-brunnsvägen 34** **11am–5pm Tue–Sun (to 8pm Wed)** **etnografiska.se**

The National Museum of Ethnography is a showcase for the collections brought home to Sweden by enterprising travellers and scientists from the 18th century to the present day. Another aspect is to reflect the multicultural influences on Sweden brought about by immigration into the country during the late 20th century.

The explorer Sven Hedin (1865–1952), the last Swede to be ennobled (in 1902), contributed many exhibits to the museum including Buddha figures, Chinese costumes and Mongolian temple tents. Another section of interest shows masks and totem poles from western Canada.

A Japanese tea house was opened in 1990, which is a work of art in itself. You can take part in traditional tea ceremonies during the summer.

The museum runs an educational programme with lectures, courses and workshops. It also displays themed temporary exhibits.

↑ Gröna Lund funfair seen across the water from Kastellholmen

---

13

Gröna Lund

H6 **Lilla Allmänna Gränd 9** **Djurgårdsfärja** **Late Apr–mid-Sep: Times vary, check website** **gronalund.com**

A tavern called Gröna Lund (Green Grove) existed on this site in the 18th century, and it was one of the haunts of the renowned troubadour Carl Michael Bellman.

Jakob Schultheis used the tavern's name for the modest-sized funfair that he opened here in 1883, with a two-level horse-drawn roundabout as the main attraction. Today Gröna Lund is Sweden's oldest amusement park.

The 130-day season, starting around the end of April, is short but hectic. Gröna Lund draws up to 18,000 visitors a day to its attractions, which include a thrilling roller-coaster and haunted house. Popular ride "Insane" is a vertical roller-coaster that can reach speeds of 60 km/h (47 mph), and it is considered to be one of the highest and longest of its kind in the world.

The park also has several good restaurants and cafés, two stages, a cabaret restaurant, a theatre and beautiful gardens.

⑭ 🛹 🏄 🍴 🛍
Vikingaliv

📍H5 📫Djurgårdsvägen 48
🕐Daily 🌐vikingaliv.se

At Stockholm's excellent Viking Museum you can learn about how Vikings lived, what they ate and what made them infamous seafarers. Feel the weight of a Viking sword and helmet, find out about their conquests around the world, the toils of their everyday life and separate fact from fiction in this interactive exhibition.

The captivating adventure ride "Ragnfrid's Saga" takes you on a journey through Viking age Europe, where you will follow Harald and his crew on a dramatic quest for silver.

The museum's fantastic restaurant, Glöd, has one of Stockholm's best locations with a view over the water in the Wasa marina.

⑮ 🛹 🏄 🍴 🖥 🛍
Tekniska museet

📍K4 📫Museivägen 7
🕐10am–5pm daily (to 8pm Wed) 🚫1 Jan, Midsummer, 24, 25 & 31 Dec 🌐tekniska museet.se

A wealth of fantastic exhibits connected with Sweden's technical and industrial history can be explored at the Museum of Science and Technology. It also houses the Teknorama science centre, with hands-on experiments designed for children.

The machinery hall features the country's oldest preserved

steam engine. Built in 1832, it was used in a coal mine in southern Sweden. The classic Model T Ford and early Swedish cars from Volvo, Scania and Saab are also on display. Swinging from above is Sweden's first commercial aircraft (1924). The museum also has sections on electric power, computing, technology in the home, and the Swedish forestry, mining, iron and steel industries.

⑯ 🏄 🖥 🛍
Sjöhistoriska museet

📍K4 📫Djurgårdsbrunns vägen 24 🕐10am–5pm Tue–Sun 🌐sjohistoriska.se

The National Maritime Museum focuses on shipping, shipbuilding and naval defence. It is housed in an attractive building, designed by the architect Ragnar Östberg in 1938, beside the calm waters of Djurgårdsbrunnsviken.

There are some 100,000 exhibits, including more than 1,500 model ships. The oldest

← Visitors hands-on *(inset)* at Tekniska museet's innovative exhibits

Swedish model is a reproduction of the "Cathedral ship" from the early 1600s. The model collection comprises every conceivable type of ship from small coasters to oil tankers, coal vessels, dinghies, full-riggers and submarines. A series of models on a scale of 1:200 shows the development of ships in Scandinavia since the Iron Age.

Life-size settings provide a good idea of life on board the various ships. Among them are the exquisite original cabin and elegant stern from the royal schooner *Amphion*. Designed by the leading shipbuilder F H af Chapman and built at the Djurgården shipyard, *Amphion* was Gustav III's flagship in the 1788–90 war with Russia.

The museum has some notable examples of ship decoration from the late 17th century. They include part of the national coat of arms recovered by divers in the 1920s from the stern of the *Riksäpplet*, which sank at Dalarö in 1676. A large relief portrayal of Karl XI on horseback from the stern of *Carolus XI* – an 82-cannon ship launched from the shipyard in 1678 – is also on show. It is thought that the relief was removed years later when the ship was renamed *Sverige*. There are many fine figureheads in the collection, including one depicting Amphion, the son of Zeus, playing his lyre, which adorned the schooner of the same name.

The museum often hosts temporary exhibitions that focus on themes such as piracy, shipping and treasure recovered from shipwrecks.

Linked to the museum is the Swedish Marine Archaeology Archive, containing an extensive collection of maritime documents and photographs.

↑ The 34-storey Kaknästornet TV tower looming over the city

⑰ Kaknästornet

◉ L4 ⌂ Ladugårdsgärdet
◷ To the public

Anchored by 72 steel poles, driven 8 m (26 ft) into the rock, the iconic 34-storey Kaknästornet soars to a height of 155 m (508 ft) above the city. Though no longer open to the public, the tower, designed by the renowned Swedish architects Bengt Lindroos and Hans Borgström, is worth a visit. Opened in 1967, it was erected as a centre for the country's television and radio broadcasting and also contains technical equipment to conduct conferences by satellite between European cities. Five dishes to the left of the tower – the largest of which has a diameter of 13 m (43 ft) – relay signals to and from satellites. The main hall containing the transmitters and receivers has been blasted out of the rock below the dishes.

⑱ Tessinparken & Nedre Gärdet

◉ H3 Ⓣ Karlaplan, Gärdet

Opened in 1931, Tessinparken runs from north to south and is attractively designed with lawns, play areas, paths and ponds. The adjoining houses, built between 1932 and 1937, have their own gardens and blend in such a way that they give the impression of being part of the park itself.

The earliest houses, nearest to Valhallavägen, still show signs of 1920s Classicism, although Gärdet's real hallmark is Functionalism. The lower white houses along Askrikegatan, marking the northern boundary of the park, are Functionalist in style and noticeably different from other buildings in Gärdet.

A statue of a woman with a suitcase, *Housewife's Holiday*, stands in the part of Tessin Park adjoining Valhallavägen. It was made by Olof Thorwald Ohlsson in the 1970s. At the other end of the park is a colourful concrete statue, *The Egg*, by Egon Möller-Nielsen.

> The Sjöhistoriska museet often hosts temporary exhibitions focusing on themes such as piracy, shipping and treasure recovered from shipwrecks.

SÖDERMALM

Stockholm extended its borders in the 14th century to include the large island of Södermalm, often shorted to Söder (South), to accommodate the increasing population. Most of the island was used for grazing, until the mid-1700s, when wooden housing for both working-class and wealthy families was built. In 1759, a baking accident started the Great Stockholm Fire, destroying 300 houses in Södermalm. Afterwards, officials placed heavy restrictions on wooden buildings, preferring stone and brick. This mixture of wooden and stone buildings survives today.

By the 1800s, industrialization transformed the island into a working-class residential area, but it had become rundown. Despite its impoverished state, Södermalm attracted creative minds, which enticed investors to revitalize the area. Old industrial buildings were turned into places of creativity such as the Fotografiska museum. Södermalm's renaissance invited bohemian and hipster subcultures to flourish, generating trendy shops and hangouts, while other artistic minds found inspiration from the beautiful surroundings, particularly at Fjällgatan.

SÖDERMALM

Experience
1 Västerbron
2 SoFo
3 Långholmen
4 Monteliusvägen
5 Medborgarplatsen
6 Stadsmuseet
7 Mariatorget
8 Fotografiska
9 Katarinahissen
10 Mosebacke
11 Katarina Kyrka
12 Fåfängan
13 Vita Bergen
14 Tantolunden

Eat
1 Meatballs for the People
2 Hermans
3 Deli di Luca
4 King Scoopa
5 Restaurant Pelikan

Drink
6 Kvarnen
7 Johan & Nyström
8 Erik's Gondolen
9 Snotty Sounds

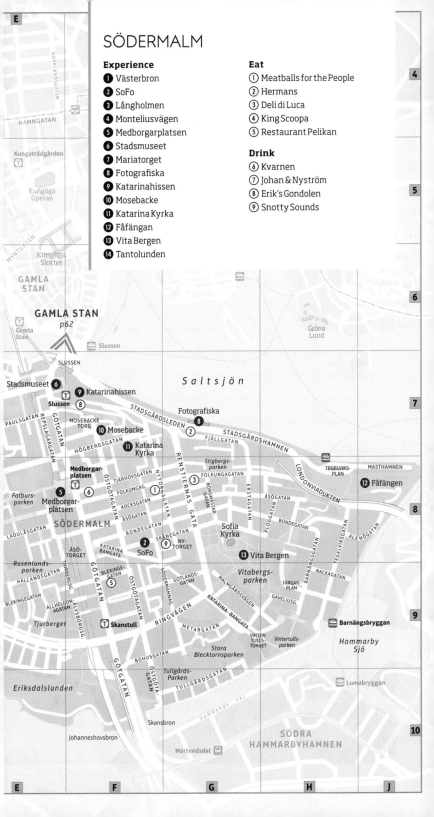

EXPERIENCE

❶

Västerbron

📍 A6

As Stockholm expanded and car use increased in the 1920s, it became necessary to build an additional bridge between the northern and southern shores of Lake Mälaren. Västerbron bridge was completed in 1935, and was broadened 20 years later. The bridge is built in two spans of 168 m (551 ft) and 204 m (669 ft).

The attractive design blends well with the landscape. There are footpaths and cycle lanes on each side and a walk to the centre offers a stunning view of central Stockholm.

Lovers attach padlocks on the railings at the apex of the bridge, symbolizing the hope that their relationship will last forever. Despite the romantic intention, though, it is feared that this tradition will eventually damage the bridge.

❷ 🍴 🛍️

SoFo

📍 F8 🌐 sofostockholm.se

The name SoFo is short for "South of Folkungagatan", a nod to the Soho districts of London and New York. The quarter is densely packed with quirky and interesting shops specializing in everything from clothing and design to jewellery, vintage, homeware, music and much more. Skånegatan, one of the city's hippest streets with designer shops and alternative bars, is the focal point of SoFo.

Families fill the area around Nytorget square during the day, and it is only a short stroll to Vitabergsparken, which stages free open-air music and dance events during the summer. The area is lively at night, even on weekdays, due to a thriving restaurant and bar scene. It's worth visiting on the last Thursday of every month for SoFo Night, when many retailers are open late and often offer special deals.

❸ 🍴 🖥️

Långholmen

📍 A6 🚇 Hornstull, then 10-minute walk

Below the majestic Västerbron bridge is the island of Långholmen, which is linked to Södermalm by two bridges. Långholmen is best known for the various prisons that have stood here since 1724. During the 20th century it was the site of the largest prison in Sweden, which closed in 1975.

The island has now become a popular recreational area. The prison buildings have been demolished, but the former royal jail, dating from 1835, remains. The one-time cells now form both a hotel and a prison museum. There is also a youth hostel and restaurant, as well as a museum to the poet C M Bellman with a café in the gardens, which run down towards Riddarfjärden. Långholmen's park has an

> Constructed in 1998 on a precipice, Monteliusvägen has charming old houses on one side and wonderful views on the other, as well as benches and picnic tables.

open-air theatre, and offers excellent swimming from the beaches and the rocks.

Monteliusvägen

◉D7 🚇Mariatorget

This 500-m- (1,640-ft-) long walking path, adjacent to popular Ivar Los Park, offers magnificent views of Lake Mälaren, Stadshuset, Gamla Stan and Riddarholmen.

Constructed in 1998 on a precipice, Monteliusvägen has charming old houses on one side and wonderful views on the other, as well as benches and picnic tables. The path has areas of clay planks that can be slippery in winter. On Blecktornsgränd, towards the eastern end of the walk, there are several cafés.

Medborgarplatsen

◉E8 🚇Medborgarplatsen

Södermalm's natural centre, Medborgarplatsen, or "Citizen Square", lives up to its name with a host of activities in and around it. In summer it comes alive with outdoor bars and restaurants; in winter there is an ice-skating rink. It is also a gathering place for protests and the starting point for the May Day Parade (p46).

The square was formerly called Södra Bantorge but was renamed Medborgarplatsen in 1939, on completion of Medborgarhuset. This building was designed in Functionalist and Neo-Classical styles, and contains an auditorium, gym, swimming pool and library.

In 1984 the Göta Ark offices were added on the northwest side. Alongside the stairway to Södra Station is the Södertorn apartment block designed by the Danish architect Henning Larssen. At the entrance is *Nana's Fountain* by Niki de Saint-Phalle, who also created a large sculpture group at the Moderna museet (p102).

The western corner of the square features a fine 17th-century gateway. Closer to Götgatan is Gustaf Nordahl's *The Source of Life* (1983), while Stefan Thorén's sculpture *Dawn* is a dominant feature on the square outside. On the west side is Söderhallarna, a popular shopping centre.

DRINK

Kvarnen
Old-fashioned Swedish beer hall that becomes a popular bar-nightclub on weekends.

◉F8 🏠Tjärhovsgatan 4
📞08-643 03 80

Johan & Nyström
The concept store of these specialist coffee roasters.

◉E7 🏠Swedenborgs-gatan 7 📞08-530 22 440

Erik's Gondolen
The views of the city's skyline are outstanding. Good cocktails, too.

◉F7 🏠Stadsgården 6
🌐eriks.se/gondolen

Snotty Sounds
Great selection of ales and local craft beers, and alternative live music.

◉G8 🏠Skånegatan 9
📞08-644 39 10

←

Hanging out at a hip café in trendy SoFo, an area known for its creative shops

Stadsmuseet

E7 **Ryssgården**
Slussen **Noon-6pm
Tue-Fri, 10am-4pm Sat-
Sun** **stadsmuseet.
stockholm.se**

Hemmed in between the
traffic roundabouts of Slussen
and the steep hill up to Mosebacke Torg is Stockholm's
Stadsmuseet (City Museum).
It is housed in a late 17th-
century building originally
designed by Tessin the Elder
as Södra Stadshuset (Southern City Hall). After a fire, it
was completed by Tessin the
Younger in 1685. It has been
used for various purposes
over the centuries, including
law courts and dungeons,
city-hall cellars, theatres and
churches, until it became the
city museum in the 1930s.

The museum documents
the fascinating history of
Stockholm. The city's main
stages of development are
described in a slideshow and
a series of four permanent
exhibitions. The first starts
with the Stockholm Bloodbath
of 1520 *(p73)* and continues
through the 17th century.
The eventful 18th century is
illustrated with exhibits that
include the Lohe Treasure –
20 kg (44 lb) of silver that was
discovered in Gamla Stan in
1937. The other sections depict

industrialization in the 19th
century and the tremendous
growth in the 20th century
with the emergence of a new
city centre and new suburbs.

Mariatorget

D/E7 **Mariatorget**

A pretty, quiet square with a
gently splashing fountain,
Mariatorget is a popular
meeting place year round and
attracts plenty of sunbathers
in summer. It is the perfect
spot to rest your tired feet.
Mariatorget and the streets
around it, St Paulsgatan,
Krumarkargatan and
Swedenborgsgatan, are
popular with locals for
shopping and dining.

INSIDER TIP
Literary Tours

Södermalm became
famous with the
popularity of Stieg
Larsson's Millennium
trilogy - particulary
after *The Girl With the
Dragon Tattoo* film
series. You can take in
the key locations used
in the books with the
superb "millennium
walks" hosted by the
Stadsmuseet.

Fotografiska

G7 **Stadsgårdshamnen
22** **9am-11pm daily
(to 1am Thu-Sat)**
fotografiska.com

Fotografiska is one of the
world's largest meeting places
for contemporary photo-
graphy. Focusing on the work
of well-known Swedish and
international photographers,
as well as new talents. The
gallery presents four unique
large exhibitions and around
20 smaller ones annually;
there are no permanent
exhibitions so there is always
something new to see. The
museum aims to engage and
inspire dialogue on photography via its exhibitions,
seminars, and courses.

The galleries are housed
in an industrial Art Nouveau-
style building on Stockholm's
waterfront, which was built in
1906 and was designed by
famous Swedish architect
Ferdinand Boberg. The
brick façade of the former

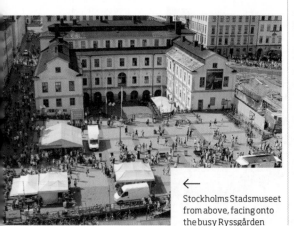

← Stockholms Stadsmuseet
from above, facing onto
the busy Ryssgården

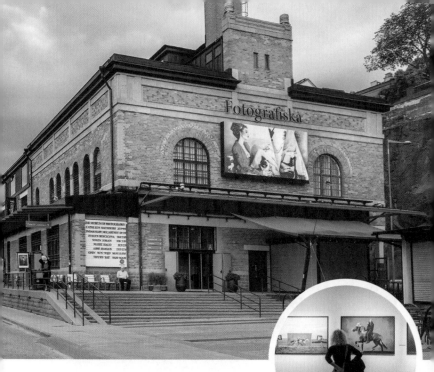

↑ A temporary exhibition *(inset)* in Fotografiska

customs building is intact but the interiors have been totally renovated. There is also a photo gallery and a well-stocked shop on site. Concerts are sometimes held here too.

In the top floor café, you will find one of Stockholm's very best viewing points. The award-winning restaurant is run by well-known chef Paul Svensson. The concept focuses on green seasonal dishes, and Svensson even collaborated with Nya Carnegiebryggeriet to brew an organic Belgian blonde beer, Echo, which is sold in the restaurant.

9 🍽
Katarinahissen

📍F7 🏠Stadsgården 🚇Slussen 🔓To the public

Katarinahissen is the oldest of Stockholm's "high-rise" attractions. The 38-m- (125-ft-) high lift was opened to the public in March 1883 and is still a prominent silhouette on the

Söder skyline. The first Swedish neon sign was erected here in 1909 – a legendary advertisement for Stomatol toothpaste. In the 1930s, the sign was moved to a nearby rooftop. The original lift was driven by steam, but it switched to electricity in 1915 and was replaced by a new lift in the 1930s.

Although the original lift stopped operating in 2010, there is another, albeit less iconic, lift inside the building, which transports diners up to a gourmet restaurant, Gondolen, which is located high above the city's port. The sweeping views over the city from here are spectacular,

and it's worth reserving a table just before the sunset.

🔟 🍴
Mosebacke

📍F7 🚇Slussen

The district of Mosebacke has become a popular cultural centre thanks to Södra Teatern, which hosts music and theatrical events, and its bar. In milder weather, Södra Bar is crowded every evening. Mosebacke Torg, the square, is more peaceful – an oasis with a summer café selling cinnamon buns.

> **The district of Mosebacke has become a popular cultural centre thanks to Södra Teatern, which hosts music and theatrical events, and its bar.**

Katarina Kyrka

🅰F7 🏠Högbergsgatan 13A
🚇Slussen,
Medborgarplatsen
🕐11am-5pm Mon-Sat,
8:30am-5pm Sun
🌐svenskakyrkan.se

The buildings surrounding the hilltop on Katarinaberget date partly from the 18th century, although there have been churches on the site since the late 1300s. The most impressive of all the buildings is Katarina Kyrka, designed by one of the era's greatest architects, Jean de la Vallée (1620–96). King Karl X Gustav was also deeply involved in the project, and specified that the church should have a central nave with the altar and pulpit positioned right in the middle. Construction began in 1656 and the church was finally completed in 1695. In 1723 it was badly damaged by fire, along with large parts of the surrounding area, but it

was restored over the next couple of decades. The architect Göran Josua Adelcranz designed a larger, octagonal tower.

Major restoration was carried out in the 20th century, and a new copper roof was added in 1988. Then two years later, on the night of 16 May 1990, there was another fire and the interior and virtually all its fittings were destroyed. Only the outer walls survived.

The architectural practice of Ove Hidemark was commissioned to design a new church which, as far as possible, was to be a faithful reconstruction of the original.

In order to carry out such a detailed reconstruction, the architects resorted to the use of 17th-century building techniques. Experts and craftsmen skilfully joined heavy timbering on to the central dome in the traditional way, and the church's central arch was rebuilt with bricks specially made in the 17th-century style.

↑ Katarina Kyrka, beautifully restored after a devastating fire in 1990

In 1995, Katarina Kyrka was reconsecrated and, in the eyes of many people, looked more beautiful than ever. The altar was sited exactly where it was originally planned.

The reconstruction cost 270 million kronor, of which 145 million kronor was covered by insurance. The remainder of the funds was raised through public donations.

Fåfängan

🅰J8 🏠Södermalm

Fåfängan, at Södermalm's most easterly point, provides a grandstand view of the boats using Stockholm's harbour.

The hill and its park were given the name Fåfängan in the 1770s. The wholesale merchant Fredrik Lundin

Stockholmers and visitors alike meet for swimming and picnics in the large Tantolunden park by the waters of Årstaviken bay in summer.

owned the area at that time, and he built a pavilion, which still stands on the hilltop in a garden filled with flowerbeds. The word "Fåfängan" ("Vanity") originally denoted an area of land that was not worth using. But in Stockholm it has a special meaning: "The pavilion on the hilltop with a marvellous view." It is a delightful place for a coffee break while exploring Söder.

13

Vita Bergen

📍 G8 🏠 Södermalm

Famous today for its popular open-air theatre performances, this park is also an opportunity to see houses originally built for workers at Söder's harbours and factories. They were simple homes, often with a small garden and surrounded by a fence. In 1736 the building of new wooden houses was forbidden because of the fire risk, but slum districts, as this was then, were exempted.

Around 1900, when Sofia Kyrka was built, the area was turned into a leafy hillside park with allotment-garden cottages to the east. The park has a bronze statue, *Elsa Borg*, by Astri Bergman Taube (1972), wife of the great troubadour Evert Taube *(p76)*.

---

14 🖼️

Tantolunden

📍 C8 🚇 Zinkensdamm

Stockholmers and visitors alike meet for swimming and picnics in the large Tantolunden park by the waters of Årstaviken bay in summer and for sledding in winter. There is a fantastic playground, a beach volleyball court and golf, plus excellent cafés. The park is often used as a festival area, most notably for the annual Stockholm Pride festival *(p47)*. Move away from the crowds and wander up the hill to see more than 100 allotment gardens and cottages.

Taking in the view of Årstaviken from Tantolunden ↑

EAT

Meatballs for the People

The classic Swedish dish is done 14 different ways at this trendy spot.

📍 F8 🏠 Nytorgsgatan 30 🌐 meatball.se

Ⓚ Ⓚ Ⓚ

Hermans

With an all-you-can-eat vegetarian buffet, this place offers great variety.

📍 G7 🏠 Fjällgatan 23B 🌐 hermans.se

Ⓚ Ⓚ Ⓚ

Deli di Luca

A taste of Italy with a Nordic twist. Sit in for meals or buy to take away for picnics.

📍 G8 🏠 Folkungagatan 110 🌐 delidiluca.se

Ⓚ Ⓚ Ⓚ

King Scoopa

Treat yourself to their ice cream burger – a donut filled with a scoop of ice cream, cookies and sauce.

📍 B8 🏠 Hornsgatan 156 🚫 Mon 🌐 kingscoopa.com

Ⓚ Ⓚ Ⓚ

Restaurant Pelikan

A traditional Swedish beer hall serving all the usual Swedish favourites, from herring platter to fish stew. Pelikan has one of the best selections of Swedish beer in the city.

📍 F9 🏠 Blekingegatan 40 🌐 pelikan.se

Ⓚ Ⓚ Ⓚ

A SHORT WALK
FJÄLLGATAN

Distance 1 km (0.5 miles) **Nearest metro**
Medborgarplatsen **Time** 15 minutes

Per Anders Fogelström (1917–98), probably Söder's best-known author, wrote: "Fjällgatan must be the city's most beautiful street. It's an old-fashioned narrow street which runs along the hilltop with well-maintained cobblestones…and with street lights jutting out from the houses. Then the street opens up and gives a fantastic view of the city and the water…" This historic area offers an experience of the authentic Söder, with its calm and creative atmosphere.

Did You Know?

Locals call Fjällgatan 'Stockholm's balcony' due to its panoramic view of the city.

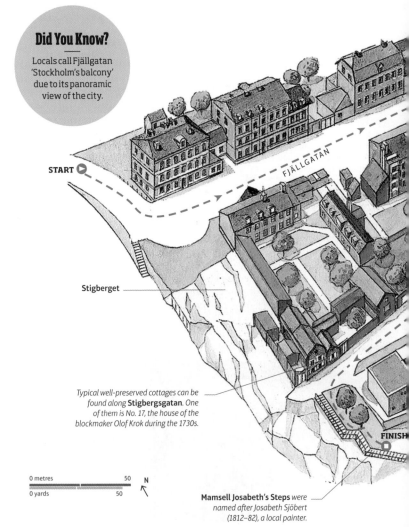

START

FJÄLLGATAN

Stigberget

*Typical well-preserved cottages can be found along **Stigbergsgatan**. One of them is No. 17, the house of the blockmaker Olof Krok during the 1730s.*

FINISH

0 metres   50
0 yards   50

N

Mamsell Josabeth's Steps were named after Josabeth Sjöbert (1812–82), a local painter.

↑ Gazing at the city from the famous waterfront viewpoint in Söder

Locator Map
For more detail see p130

Historic café

Viewpoint with magnificent vista across the city.

This alley of steps was once known as Mikaelsgränd after a 17th-century executioner. Later it was named **Sista Styverns Trappor** *after the inn on the harbour.*

Most of the houses were built along **Fjällgatan** *after a devastating fire in 1723. No. 34 is said to be the area's oldest.*

STIGBERGSGATAN

Norwegian Church

↑ Picturesque old cottages in Söder cloaked in a golden blanket of leaves

BEYOND THE CENTRE

Must See

① Drottningholm

Experience More

② Naturhistoriska Riksmuseet
③ Hagaparken
④ Ulriksdal
⑤ Millesgården
⑥ Stadion
⑦ Skogskyrkogården
⑧ Bellevueparken
⑨ Karlbergs Slott
⑩ Ericsson Globe

Just beyond central Stockholm are many opportunities to appreciate the landscape's natural beauty and cultural heritage. Around 8 km (5 miles) northeast of Stockholm lies Millesgården, the former home of the famous sculptor Carl Milles and his artist wife, Olga Milles. Their home was transformed into a museum that exhibits an extensive collection of antiques and sculptures. Milles's sculptures can be found in the inner city such as the Orpheus Fountain and Gustav Vasa statue in the Nordic Museum. The outskirts of Stockholm also include a handful of well-preserved castles such as the Karlberg and Drottningholm Palace. Both palaces were built in the 1600s, with Karlberg acting as a military institution. Drottningholm was listed as a UNESCO World Heritage Site in 1991.

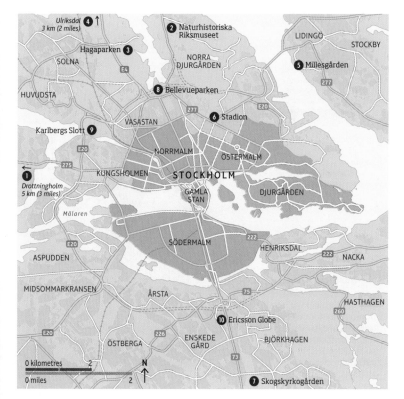

DROTTNINGHOLM

⌂ 10 km (6 miles) W of Stockholm ⓣ Brommaplan, then bus 301 or 302
🚌 Late Mar-Oct ⊙ Times vary, check website 📅 14-30 Dec 🌐 royalcourt.se

A UNESCO World Heritage Site since 1991, the unique Baroque and Rococo environment of Drottningholm – its palace, theatre, park and Chinese Pavilion – have been perfectly preserved. Parts of the palace have been the home to the Royal Family since 1982.

This royal palace emerged in its present form towards the end of the 17th century, and was one of the most lavish buildings of its era. Contemporary Italian and French architecture inspired the renowned Swedish architect Tessin the Elder (1615–81) in his design, which was also intended to glorify royal power. The project was completed by Tessin the Younger, while architects such as Carl Hårleman and Jean Eric Rehn finished the interiors.

The palace of Drottningholm is complemented by the Court Theatre (Slottsteatern), the world's oldest theatre still in active use, and the elegant Chinese Pavilion (Kina Slott), which has one of the finest European Rococo interiors with chinoiserie. The complex is situated on the shores of Lake Mälaren, surrounded by Baroque and Rococo gardens, and lush English-style parkland. In the summer you can enjoy performances of opera and ballet in the beautiful theatre.

Standing in the Queen's Salon is a writing table by Swedish cabinet maker Georg Haupt. This masterpiece was commissioned by King Adolf Fredrik as a gift to Queen Lovisa Ulrika.

The bronze statue of Hercules (1680s) by the Dutch Renaissance sculptor Adrian de Vries adorns the parterre in the palace's Baroque Gardens.

The Upper South Bodyguard Room, an ante-room to the State Room, was decorated with stucco works by artists Giovanni and Carlo Carove.

> 💬 INSIDER TIP
> **Boat Tour**
>
> A historic ship takes you on a beautiful journey from central Stockholm, across Lake Mälaren, to the elegant Drottningholm Palace. To find out more, visit www.stromma.com.

The lavish façade of Drottningholm and one of its art-filled salons *(inset)* ↑

Queen Lovisa Ulrika's commissioned Jean Eric Rehn (1717–93) to decorate this splendid library, which illustrates her influence on art and science in Sweden in the 18th century.

Morning receptions ("levées") were held in Queen Hedvig Eleonora's State Bedroom.

← Drottningholm's impressive palace and its apartments

Did You Know?

When translated, the name Drottningholm means "Queens islet".

EXPLORING DROTTNINGHOLM

The Palace Apartments

The first thing that meets the eye on entering the apartments is a Baroque corridor with a view that frames part of the gardens in all their splendour. The central part of the palace is dominated by the grand staircase, with ceiling paintings by David Klöcker Ehrenstrahl. Marble statues of the nine muses and their protector, Apollo, are placed at the corners of the balustrades.

There are many beautiful salons to explore. The Green Salon, which marks the beginning of the main ceremonial suite, is reached from the lower vestibule via the Lower Northern Body-guard Room. Queen Hedvig Eleonora (1636–1715) held audiences in the Ehrenstrahl Salon, named after the artist whose paintings dominate the walls. Hedvig Eleonora's Meissen porcelain can be seen in the Blue Cabinet; the Library has her collection of more than 2,000 books.

The Chinese Salon was King Adolf Fredrik's private bed-room. It is above the Queen's State Bedroom and a hidden staircase links the two floors.

After the General's Room, Karl XI's Gallery, and the Golden Salon, comes the Queen's Salon. The portraits in this salon are of European queens. This floor finishes with the Upper South Bodyguard Room, an ante-room to the State Room and lavishly decorated by the Carove stucco artists.

←

Tessin the Elder's grand marble staircase dominates the central part of the palace

functionality: the pilasters, for example, are made from gypsum and the supports from papier mâché. The scenery, with its wooden hand-driven machinery, is still in working order. In the 1920s, the machinery ropes were replaced, electric lighting was installed, and the original wings were refurbished.

Every summer there are about 30 performances, mainly opera and ballet from the 18th century. The theatre is open daily, and there are also guided tours.

The Palace Park

The palace's three gardens are each of a completely different character but still combine to provide a unified whole. The symmetrical formal garden started to take shape in 1640, and was designed to stimulate the senses with sights, sounds and smells.

The avenues of chestnut trees were laid out when the Chinese Pavilion was completed, along with the Rococo-inspired garden area – a cross between the formal main garden and the freer composition of the English park. The English park has natural paths and a stream with small islands, as well as trees and bushes at "natural" irregular intervals. Gustav III added four statues that he had bought during his travels in Italy. The first 300 of a total of 846 lime trees were planted in the avenues flanking the Baroque garden as early as 1684.

The Chinese Pavilion

On her 33rd birthday in 1753, Queen Lovisa Ulrika was given a Chinese pavilion by her husband. It had been manufactured in Stockholm, shipped to Drottningholm and assembled near the palace. When it had to be taken down after ten years because rot had set in, it was replaced by the present Chinese Pavilion (Kina Slott), which is still one of the major attractions here.

The Chinese Pavilion is a mixture of what was considered 250 years ago to be typical Chinese style along with artifacts from China and Japan. Four smaller pavilions belong to the building. In the northeastern pavilion the king had his lathe and a

carpenter's bench. Next to this is the Confidencen pavilion, where meals were taken if he wished to be left undisturbed. The adjoining Turkish-style "watch tent" was built as a barracks for Gustav III's dragoons. It now houses a museum about the estate.

The Court Theatre

The designer of the Chinese Pavilion, Swedish architect Carl Fredrik Adelcrantz, was also responsible for the Court Theatre (Slottsteatern), which dates from 1766. Commissioned by Queen Lovisa Ulrika, this simple wooden building is now the world's oldest theatre still preserved in its original condition. The interior and fittings are masterpieces of simple

> **The palace's three gardens are each of a completely different character but still combine to provide a unified whole.**

EXPERIENCE MORE

2

Naturhistoriska Riksmuseet

📍 Frescativägen 40
🚇 Universitetet 🕐 10am–6pm Tue–Sun 🌐 nrm.se

Completed in 1916, the vast Naturhistoriska Riksmuseet (Swedish Royal Museum of Natural History) was founded in 1739 by Carl von Linné as part of Vetenskapsakademien (the Academy of Science). It is one of the ten largest museums of its kind in the world, and over the centuries, the number of exhibits has risen to 17 million.

During the 1990s the museum was modernized, and there are both permanent and temporary exhibitions on a wide range of themes from dinosaurs and sea creatures to the human body. The popular Cosmonova is both a planetarium and an IMAX cinema. Erected in 1930, the Vega Monument marks the 50th anniversary of explorer Adolf

---

THE ROYAL NATIONAL CITY PARK (EKOPARKEN)

Ekoparken – the world's first National City Park – was established by the Swedish Parliament in 1995. It has enabled the capital to safeguard the ecology of its "green lung", a 27-sq-km- (10.5-sq-mile-) area for recreation. The park threads through Stockholm's central districts, including Skeppsholmen and Djurgården, and continues northwest to Hagaparken, Brunnsviken and Ulriksdal. It also encompasses the islands of Fjäderholmarna.

↑ Picknicking on the lawns in front of the Echo Temple in Hagaparken

Erik Nordenskiöld's return from the first voyage through the Northeast Passage.

3

Hagaparken

📍 4 km (2.5 miles) N of city centre, along E4
🌐 visithaga.se

King Gustav Vasa decided to create a royal park in the popular Haga area in the mid-18th century, and his vision was realized by the architect of the moment, Fredrik Magnus Piper. The result was an English-style park with unusual buildings, including the Chinese Pagoda and the Roman battle tent, Koppartälten, part of which holds the **Haga Parkmuseum**. Today, the park is part of Ekoparken.

Gustav III's Pavilion, a Gustavian masterpiece designed by Olof Tempelman, with an interior by Louis Masreliez, is the park's greatest architectural attraction, while **Fjärilshuset Haga Ocean** has colourful butterflies and birds flying freely around a tropical greenhouse, plus a shark tank.

Haga Parkmuseum
📞 08-402 60 00
🕐 Mid-May–Sep: 11am–5pm daily; Oct–mid-May: 10am–3pm Fri–Sun

Gustav III's Pavilion
⊗ 📞 08-402 61 30 🕐 For tours; mid-Jun–mid-Aug: noon–4pm daily

Fjärilshuset Haga Ocean
⊗ 📞 08-730 39 81
🕐 10am–4pm Mon–Fri, 10am–5pm Sat & Sun
🚫 Midsummer Eve

4

Ulriksdal

📍 7 km (4 miles) N of Stockholm 🕐 Palace: Jun–Aug: noon–3pm Sat & Sun; Orangery: Jun–Aug: noon–4pm Tue–Sun 🌐 rappne.se

Situated on a headland in the bay of Edsviken, this palace and its attractive buildings and leafy surroundings are well worth a detour north of Hagaparken. At the entrance to the grounds is one of Stockholm's best restaurants, Ulriksdals Vardshus.

The original palace was built in the 1640s and designed by Hans Jakob Kristler in German/Dutch Renaissance style. The owner, Marshal of the Realm Jakob de la Gardie, named the palace Jakobsdal. It was bought in 1669 by the Dowager Queen Hedvig Eleonora. Fifteen years later, she donated the palace to her grandson Ulrik as a christening gift, and it was renamed

> **Situated on a headland in the bay of Edsviken, Ulriksdal's attractive buildings and leafy surroundings are well worth a detour.**

Ulriksdal. Around this time the architect Tessin the Elder suggested some rebuilding work, but only a few of his proposals saw the light of day. The palace acquired its beautiful Baroque exterior in the 18th century.

After being a popular place for festivities in the time of Gustav III (1746–92), it began to lose its glamour. Interest was revived under Karl XV (1826–72), and furnishings and handicrafts many hundreds of years old are held in his rooms.

The park was laid out in the mid-17th century, and has 300-year-old lime trees, as well as one of Europe's most northerly beechwoods. Carl Milles' two sculptures of wild boars stand by the pool in front of the palace. A stream is crossed by a footbridge, which is supported by Per Lundgren's *Moors Dragging the Nets*.

More art can be seen in the Orangery, designed by Tessin the Elder in the 1660s for Queen Hedvig Eleonora. It now houses a sculpture museum. The palace chapel, a popular place for weddings, was designed by F W Scholander and built in 1865 in Dutch Neo-Renaissance style. The riding school, built in 1671, was converted into a theatre by Carl Hårleman and C F Adelcrantz in the 1750s, and performances are still staged here in summer.

---

⑤

Millesgården

🏛 Herserudsvägen 32, Lidingö 🚇 Ropsten 🕐 May–Sep: 10am–5pm daily; Oct–Apr: 11am–5pm Tue–Sun 🌐 millesgarden.se

In 1906 Carl Milles (1875–1955), one of the 20th century's greatest Swedish sculptors and the best known internationally, purchased land on the island of Lidingö on which he built a house, completed in 1908. He lived here with his wife for many years and in 1936 they donated the property to the people of Sweden.

The Millesgården complex extends over a series of terraces filled with sculptures and includes Milles' studios with originals and replicas of his work. There is a superb garden – a work of art in itself – and a fine view over the water.

⑥

Stadion

📍 Lidingövägen 1–3 📞 07-392 190 07 🚇 Stadion 🕐 7am–9:30pm Mon–Fri, 8am–6pm Sat, 8am–9:30pm Sun

A new main arena was built for the 1912 Olympic Games in Stockholm, the towers of which have become a familiar landmark on the capital's skyline. The architect of Stadion, Torben Grut (1871–1945), followed the National Romantic influences of the day and the complex is richly decorated. The clock tower has two figures by Carl Fagerberg: Ask and Embla, the counterparts of Adam and Eve in Nordic mythology. There are also busts of Victor Balck, the man behind the 1912 Olympics, and P H Ling, the father of Swedish gymnastics.

Four notable sculptures were added in the 1930s. The painter and gymnast Bruno Liljefors created *Play* at the main entrance, Carl Eldh made *The Runners*, and Carl Fagerberg provided *Relay Runners* and *The Shot-Putter*.

Stadion is an important venue for athletics events and an international athletics gala is staged every summer. In 1990 it hosted the World Equestrian Championships.

Cycling past Ulriksdal Palace and its well-maintained gardens
↓

Skogskyrkogården

📍 6 km (3.5 miles) S of Stockholm 🚇 Skogskyrkogården ⏰ For tours; Jun–Sep: 10:30am Sun 🌐 skogskyrkogarden.se

Nature and architecture have combined to give the Skogskyrkogården Cemetery a place on the UNESCO World Heritage list. The cemetery is the creation of architects Gunnar Asplund (p94) and Sigurd Lewerentz, winners of a design competition for the site in 1915. It is set amid

GRETA GARBO

The legendary Greta Garbo, one of the 20th century's outstanding film stars, was born in 1905 in Södermalm. At the age of 17 she joined the theatre academy of Dramaten and made her film debut in Peter the Tramp. Her breakthrough came in 1924 in Mauritz Stiller's film The Atonement of Gösta Berling. The following year she moved to Hollywood. Garbo appeared in 24 films, including Anna Karenina (1935) and Camille (1936). She never married and lived a solitary life until her death in 1990. Her ashes were interred at the Skogskyrkogården Cemetery in 1999.

pinewoods which provide a framework for the various chapels and crematorium, all of which are examples of Sweden's National Romantic and Functionalist styles.

Asplund's first work, Skogskapellet (Woodland Chapel), featuring a steep shingled roof, was opened at the same time as the cemetery in 1920, and was decorated by Carl Milles (p147). His last masterpiece, Skogskrematoriet (Woodland Crematorium), was completed in 1940, along with its three chapels, representing Faith, Hope and the Holy Cross.

Skogskyrkogården is the final resting place of many notable figures, including the film star Greta Garbo.

Bellevueparken

📍 South of Brunnsviken Lake, Ekoparken

This park is part of Ekoparken (p146), Stockholm's Royal National City Park. Built by architect Fredrik Magnus Piper, Bellevue offers winding paths, groves, tree-lined avenues and open green areas. It is

> Nature and architecture have combined to give the Skogskyrkogården Cemetery a place on the UNESCO World Heritage list.

also home to 200-year-old lime trees and rare medicinal plants. The name (French for "beautiful view") came from Baron Carl Sparre, who purchased a villa on Bellevue Hill in 1782, which is now used as a conference centre.

On Bellevue Hill is the Lögbodavägen viewpoint, which looks out over the Brunnsviken inlet and is close to the monument The Young Strindberg in the Archipelago by Carl Eldh (1873–1954). This sculptor's studio, in an unusual wooden building dating from 1919, is now preserved as the Carl Eldhs Ateljémuseum and is located nearby. Eldh was one of Sweden's most prolific sculptors. The plaster casts of his sculptures are on show in his studio and include the Branting Monument at Norra Bantorget and The Runners at Stadion (p147).

Carl Eldhs Ateljémuseum

🏠 Lögbodavägen 10 📞 08-
6126560 🕐 May & Sep:
noon–4pm Thu–Sun; Jun–
Aug: noon–4pm Tue–Sun;
Apr & Oct: noon–4pm Sun

---

⑨
Karlbergs Slott

🏠 Karlsbergs Slottsväg
📞 08-746 10 00 🚇 St
Eriksplan 🚪 To the public

Admiral Karl Karlsson
Gyllenhielm started to build
Karlbergs Slott in the 1630s,
during the Thirty Years War.
From 1670 the palace was
extended and rebuilt. When
Karlberg became royal property in 1688, it was one of
Sweden's most majestic
palaces. It was where the
"hero King" Karl XII (1682–
1718) grew up, and it was here
that he lay in state after his
death at the Battle of
Fredrikshald. In 1792 the
architect C C Gjörwell converted the property into the
Royal War Academy, which
later became the Karlberg
Military School, and since
1999 it has been the
site for a military
academy.

Though closed to the public,
the interior decorations
include Carl Carove's magnificent stucco-work in the grand
hall. The palace church has
been renovated several times,
but the 17th-century lanterns
are original.

---

⑩
Ericsson Globe

🏠 3 km (2 miles) S of
Stockholm 🚇 Globen
🕐 During events; gondola
ride by appt 🌐 stockholm
live.com

In 1989 Stockholm acquired a
new symbol in the shape of the
indoor arena Ericsson Globe,
which has a circumference of
690 m (2,260 ft) and a height of
85 m (279 ft). The arena offers
a wide programme of events,
from international sports to
performances by musicians
from all over the world.

The spectacular Skyview
ride enables you to travel up
the outside wall of the arena
in glass gondolas.

EAT

Landet
This trendy place is a
restaurant, bar, club
and live music venue
in one. Landet's is
popular with Stockholm
foodies. Try the
exquisite veal entrecôte
or the steak tartare.

🏠 LM Ericsson's vag 27,
Midsommarkransen
📅 Sat am & Sun
🌐 landet.nu

Sjöpaviljongen
Set in lovely waterside
surroundings,
Sjöpaviljongen serves
seasonal Swedish
cuisine. It has a terrace
to eat on in summer.

🏠 Tranebergs strand 4,
Bromma
🌐 sjopaviljongen.se

The illuminated Ericsson
Globe, dominating the
city skyline ↓

EXPERIENCE
SWEDEN

Hiking the Kungsleden Trail, Lappland

EASTERN SVEALAND

This area was the cradle of ancient Svea, as can be seen in the rock carvings, burial mounds and standing stones in the shapes of ships that dot the landscape. It was from the town of Birka on Lake Mälaren and from Roslagen in Uppland that the Vikings headed east on plundering raids and trading missions around Europe and beyond. The centre of the ancient pagan Æsir cult in Uppsala held out against Christianity until the 12th century. Many beautiful, small medieval churches, richly decorated with paintings depicting biblical scenes, testify to the fact that Christianity finally dominated, however. Uppsala itself became a cathedral city and the seat of the archbishop in 1273.

The many castles and fortresses that guard the waterways are an eye-catching sight. Several of these date back to the Middle Ages, but the most important, such as Skokloster, are the result of the great wealth that flooded into the country after Sweden's victories in the various European wars of the 17th century. Shipping brought further prosperity to the region, with centres such as Arboga lying on the iron route between Bergslagen, Stockholm and the Uppland harbours. There are well-preserved ironworks in all three provinces, including Engelsbergs Bruk, a UNESCO World Heritage Site.

An extensive archipelago stretches between the coasts of Uppland and Södermanland, and Lake Mälaren itself is so full of islands that the archipelago appears to continue inland uninterrupted.

EASTERN SVEALAND

Must Sees
1. Uppsala
2. Stockholm Archipelago

Experience More
3. Österbybruk
4. Grisslehamn
5. Öregrund and Östhammer
6. Forsmarks Bruk
7. Norrtälje
8. Sigtuna
9. Skokloster
10. Enköping
11. Birka
12. Södertälje
13. Trosa
14. Ytterjärna
15. Flen
16. Nyköping
17. Strängnäs
18. Mariefred
19. Eskilstuna
20. Julita Gård
21. Västerås
22. Arboga
23. Köping
24. Sala
25. Fagersta
26. Kopparberg
27. Grythyttan
28. Nora

↑ The twin spires of Domkyrkan, the seat of the Archbishop of Uppsala

①

UPPSALA

🅰F4 ⚑Uppsala ✈25 km (16 miles) S of city centre 🚇
🚌Kungsgatan ℹStationsgatan 20A; destinationuppsala.se

This seat of learning on the idyllic Fyrisån river long remained a small town, despite housing Scandinavia's first university in 1477 and hosting parliaments and coronations. It wasn't until industrialization and the expansion in education that Uppsala became Sweden's fourth largest city. The Gothic cathedral, castle, historic university, botanical gardens and ancient Gamla (Old) Uppsala make this one of Sweden's foremost sights.

①

Domkyrkan

🏠Domkyrkoplan 2 📞018-430 36 30 🕐8am-6pm daily

The first sight on approaching Uppsala is the 119 m (390 ft) high twin spires of the largest cathedral in the Nordic region. Many monarchs have been crowned here and kings Gustav Vasa and Johan III, as well as botanist Carl von Linné, are buried here. The chapel contains the remains of St Erik, patron saint of Stockholm, in a golden shrine.

The cathedral treasury, Skattkammaren, has a superb collection of textiles and silver.

②

Gustavianum

🏠Akademigatan 3
🕐Times vary, check website
🔒Public hols
🌐gustavianum.uu.se

Named after King Gustav II Adolf, this is the oldest preserved building of Uppsala University. The Gustavianum mounts exhibitions connected with the work of the university since its foundation. One of the gems on show is the Augsburg Art Cabinet from the early 17th century. Various archaeological collections from Egypt and the classical world are also on display.

③

Universitetshuset

🏠Biskopsgatan 3 📞018-471 17 66 🕐Mon-Fri and for events

The university's imposing main building was constructed in 1887 in Neo-Renaissance style. It contains an attractive auditorium.

④

Carolina Rediviva

🏠Dag Hammarskjölds Väg 1 📞018-471 39 00
🕐17 Jun-30 Aug: 9am-noon Mon-Fri 🔒Public hols

In 1841, the university library moved into this building, which houses 5 million printed books and 4 km (2 miles) of shelving holding handwritten manuscripts. Rarities include

Did You Know?

Since the 1970s, every night at 10pm students in Uppsala's Flogsta neighbourhood let out a collective scream.

the Silver Bible from the 6th century and Olaus Magnus's Carta Marina (1539).

---

⑤ Ⓜ 🍴 🖵 🏛

Uppsala Slott

🏠 Slottsbacken
⏰ Art Museum: 11:30am–4pm Tue–Sun (to 8pm Thu)
🌐 uppsalakonstmuseum.se

Standing on a glacial ridge, this Vasa castle competes with the cathedral for domination of the city. Built as a fortress in 1549, it was added to several times, but never finished. A city fire in 1702 destroyed much of the castle. It now houses Uppsala's art museum, the governor's residence and the House of Peace, a museum exploring world conflicts and Sweden's history of neutrality.

---

⑥ Ⓜ 🖵 🏛

Botaniska Trädgården

🏠 Villavägen 8 ⏰ Daily
🚫 Public hols 🌐 botan.uu.se

The botanical gardens hold more than 130,000 plants, many exotic, in a beautiful setting that includes several greenhouses. The first garden was established on the banks of the Fyrisån river in 1655. In 1741, Carl von Linné took it over and made it one of the leading gardens of its time.

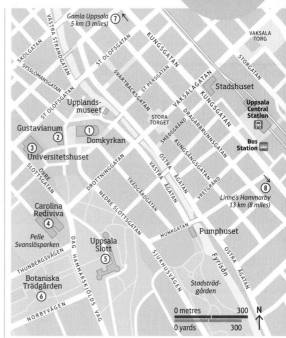

⑦ 🚶 Ⓜ 🖵 🏛

Gamla Uppsala

🏠 Route 290 or E4, 5 km (3 miles) N of city centre
☎ 018-239 301 ⏰ Jan–Mar, Oct–Dec: noon–4pm Mon, Wed, Sat & Sun; Apr–Sep: 10am–4pm daily (Jun & Aug: to 5pm) 🚫 1 Jan, Mid-summer's Eve, 24, 25, 31 Dec

Gamla Uppsala is like a time capsule, with royal burial

mounds rising up from the plain as they have done for 1,500 years. This was a centre for worshipping the Norse gods long into the 11th century, with a temple which was clad entirely in gold. In the early 12th century, the heathen temple gave way to a Christian church, then a cathedral. You can learn more in the museum. Nearby is also Disagården, an open-air museum about the lives of 19th-century farmers.

---

⑧ 🚶 Ⓜ 🖵

Linné's Hammarby

🏠 13 km (8 miles) SE of Uppsala ⏰ May–Aug: 11am–5pm Tue–Sun; Sep: 11am–5pm Fri–Sun
🚫 Whitsun, Midsummer Eve 🌐 hammarby.uu.se

The Hammarby farm estate was Linné's rural retreat and where he grew plants that could not survive in the botanical gardens. It is now owned by the state and run by the university.

CARL VON LINNÉ

"God created, Linné organized," goes the saying about the Swedish king of plants. It is thanks to Linné's ground-breaking *Systema Naturae*, first published in 1735, that the world has the familiar system of binomial nomenclature, giving all plants and animals two Latin names. In 1741, Linné became professor of medicine at Uppsala and his spirit has suffused the city ever since. At his country house in Hammarby, Linné tutored students. He would often greet them dressed in his nightshirt, for the morning's nature walk. According to Linné "nature does not wait for powder and wigs".

② STOCKHOLM ARCHIPELAGO

🅰F4 🚌SL traffic information in Eng, 08-600 10 00 🚤Strömma Kanalbolaget, 08-587 140 00; Vaxholmsbolaget, 08-679 58 30 🌐stockholmarchipelago.se

Extending 80 km (50 miles) east from the waters of Stockholm to the open sea, the archipelago comprises tens of thousands of islands of all shapes and sizes, some inhabited, others not. The majority of them, with their traditional wooden houses and cosy hotels, can be reached by an extensive network of scheduled ferries from Stockholm, Vaxholm, Stavsnäs and Dalarö.

① Fjäderholmarna

🅰6 km (4 miles) E of Stockholm 🚤May–Sep from Nybrokajen and Slussen

With the inclusion of the Fjäderholmarna islands in the Royal National City Park, the city's "green lung" has acquired a small part of Stockholm's archipelago.

The main island, Stora Fjäderholmen, has an attractive harbour, restaurants, an art gallery, and museums devoted to boating and angling, as well as the Baltic Sea Museum, home to virtually every type of aquatic creature from Stockholm to Landsort. Local handicrafts include metalwork, weaving, wood-carving and glassmaking. The other three islands have rich birdlife.

② Vaxholm

🅰25 km (16 miles) NE of Stockholm 🚌670 🚤From Strömkajen and Nybrokajen

The archipelago's main community, Vaxholm, is easily reached by boat from Stockholm on a delightful one-hour journey. **Vaxholm Fortress**, on the nearby island of Vaxholmen, guards this busy port. First fortified in 1548 by Gustav Vasa, the more recent 19th-century citadel houses a military museum.

The wooden buildings and shops around the square and along Hamngatan provide a pleasant stroll.

Vaxholm Fortress

🅰Vaxholmen 📞08-541 718 90 🕐Mid-Jun–Sep: 11:30am–5:30pm daily

EXCURSIONS BY STEAMBOAT

Traditional steamboats are a familiar feature on the waters around Stockholm. Both in the archipelago and on Lake Mälaren visitors can still enjoy the tranquil atmosphere of a steamboat voyage. One of the veterans, SS *Blidösund*, built in 1911, serves mostly the northern archipelago. Some routes, for instance Stockholm-Mariefred, are operated partly or completely by steamers. Most of the other passenger boats from the early 20th century have instead been fitted with oil-fired engines, but still provide a nostalgic journey back in time.

↑ Colourful houses lining Vaxholm's harbour in the archipelago

a pub with guest rooms. There are chalets to rent, a camp site and a youth hostel.

---

④
Finnhamn

🏠 40 km (25 miles) NE of Stockholm 🚢 From Strömkajen and Nybrokajen

These islands lie two and a half hours by boat from the city. The main island has a wooden villa designed by Ernst Stenhammar (1912). Today it is the largest youth hostel in the archipelago. There is a restaurant, chalets, and a camp site. Smaller islands nearby are accessible by rowing boat.

---

⑤
Möja

🏠 50 km (31 miles) E of Stockholm 🚌 670 to Vaxholm, then boat 🚢 From Strömkajen and Nybrokajen

Fishing and strawberry-growing were the mainstays of this idyllic corner of the

archipelago. Now there are few strawberry growers and only one fisherman living here. Instead, picturesque harbours attract the sailing fraternity. Nature reserves around Möja shelter rich wildlife. Services are good in the summer, with boats and cottages for hire.

---

⑥
Sandhamn

🏠 50 km (31 miles) E of Stockholm 🚌 433, 434 to Stavsnäs, then boat 🚢 From Nybrokajen 🌐 destinationsandhamn.se

Sandhamn is home to The Royal Swedish Yacht Club, and every summer the world's yachting elite flock here.

A pretty village with narrow alleys and decorated houses, Sandhamn has shops, crafts centres and a swimming pool.

Camping is not permitted, but there are plenty of hotels, B&Bs and chalets. There are also great sandy beaches.

---

③
Grinda

🏠 30 km (19 miles) E of Stockholm 🚌 670 to Vaxholm, then boat 🚢 From Strömkajen and Nybrokajen

Grinda is a leafy island, typical of the inner archipelago. It has excellent beaches for swimming, and good fishing. Architect Ernst Stenhammar built a villa here, which is now

⑦
Utö

🏠 50 km (31 miles) SE of Stockholm 🚢 From Strömkajen 🌐 utoturistbyra.se

Utö, one of the area's best seaside resorts, was inhabited before the Viking era and has a rich history. The Mining Museum and the view from the windmill are of note.

> 💬 INSIDER TIP
> **Closest islands**
>
> If you're a bit short on time but want to explore the archipelago, you can visit the closest spots - Fjäderholmarna and Vaxholm - which are less than an hour from Stockholm.

EXPERIENCE MORE

Österbybruk

F3 **Uppland**
Ånghammaren;
www.roslagen.se

Iron played a key role in the region and nowhere is this more apparent than at Österbybruk. It is the area's oldest ironworks, dating back to the 15th century, but things only really took off when Dutchman Louis de Geer bought the foundry in 1643. With the help of migrant Walloon blacksmiths, he developed the iron industry so crucial to Sweden's position as a great power.

As the world's only fully preserved Walloon forge, the 15th-century **Vallonsmedjan** uses puppets, sound and light to recreate life in the hammer mills. Surrounding it are 18th- and 19th-century streets.

The 18th-century manor house was home to wildlife painter Bruno Liljefors in the early 20th century. In summer, his popular animal paintings are exhibited in **Liljeforsateljén** in the gardens.

Just 3 km (2 miles) from Österbybruk, **Dannemora Gruva** was the mine on which local ironworking was built. Gaping opencast pits (closed to the public) are relics of an industry that has gone on here since the Middle Ages. Above the mine is the building in which Sweden's first steam engine was built in 1726.

Vallonsmedjan
Österbybruk **Jun-Aug: daily by appt only**

Liljeforsateljén
Österbybruk **May-Sep: noon-4pm Sat & Sun (mid-Jun-mid-Aug: to 5pm dail)y**

Dannemora Gruva
2 km (1 mile) W of Österbybruk **0295-214 92** **Jun-Sep: daily**

4
Grisslehamn

F3 **Uppland**

The choppy Åland Sea constantly batters the red granite cliffs of northern Väddö at Grisslehamn. This is the closest point in Sweden to Finland and the reason for the town's existence. Today's ferry crossing to Eckerö takes only two hours, but things were much tougher in the 17th and 18th centuries when this was the main link with the eastern outposts of the Swedish empire. Until 1876, the post was rowed across the water by local fishermen in open boats. To commemorate the "post rowers", a race is held across the Åland Sea every year in similar boats.

Today, apart from those making the ferry crossing, the sleepy fishing port of Grisslehamn attracts Väddö's many holidaymakers. You can stroll along the waterfront

Lighthouse across
from Grisslehamn,
where sailors *(inset)*
prepare to race

→
Typical wooden buildings lining the waterfront in Öregrund

enjoying the sea views, and pause to purchase delicious fresh fish from the red sheds on the harbourside.

In 1902, the renowned Swedish painter and writer Albert Engström (1869–1940) moved to Grisslehamn. He became much loved for his priceless characters such as the tramp, Kolingen, and the Roslagen figure, Österman. The **Albert Engströmsmuseet**, a fine reconstruction of Engström's home containing his art and memorabilia, was moved to Augustberg in 2006. There are also temporary exhibitions on display here. The cartoonist's interesting cliffside studio was painted white on the side facing the sea to serve as a marker for seafarers.

Albert Engströmsmuseet
🎨🎭💻 🏠 Augustberg ⏰ Late Jun-Aug: 11am-5pm daily; Sep-Jun: by appt only 🌐 albert engstrom.se

5
Öregrund and Östhammer

🗺 F3 🏠 Uppland 🛈 Harbour Square, Öregrund; Rådhusgatan 6, Östhammar; www. roslagen.se

The twin towns of Öregrund and Östhammar are closely linked geographically and historically. At the end of the 15th century, the citizens of Östhammar founded Öregrund in order to create a better harbour. Seafaring and iron-exporting became vital to the town.

In 1719, Öregrund was burned by the Russians, but the wooden buildings were rebuilt according to a town plan from 1744. The fine town hall dates from 1829. At the end of the 19th century, the sleepy area became a seaside resort and continues to attract visitors to this day.

The lovely Öregrund and Östhammar region is home to many well-preserved old ironworking communities, including Harg and Gimo. Built in 1763–70, Gimo Manor was the first in Sweden to be designed in Gustavian style by the Swedish architect Jean Eric Rehn.

On the outskirts of Gimo lies **Skäfthammars Kyrka**, a medieval church particularly renowned for its lectern, which was built for the Gimo smiths.

Skäfthammars Kyrka
🏠 Gimo, 16 km (10 miles) SE of Östhammar 📞 0173-40077 ⏰ Times vary, call ahead

---

6 🍽🍴🏪🛍
Forsmarks Bruk

🗺 F3 🏠 Uppland 🛈 Next to Brukscaféet; www.visitforsmark.se

The historic ironworks of Forsmarks Bruk retains its well-preserved streets with their beautiful, whitewashed rows of houses and a manor house built in 1767–74.

The nuclear power station of **Forsmarks Kärnkraftverk** lies on the coast, 3 km (2 miles) north from the ironworks. It provides one seventh of Sweden's electricity. Guided tours include such features as the vast biotest lake where the environmental impact of the cooling water is studied.

Louis de Geer's Walloon ironworks empire also included the impressively preserved **Lövstabruk**, an 18th-century manor set amid leafy grounds.

Forsmarks Kärnkraftverk
🚫 🏠 3 km (2 miles) N of Forsmark 📞 0173-81000 ⏰ Mid-Jun-mid-Aug: Mon-Fri; other times by appt

Lövstabruk
🚫🍴💻 🏠 16 km (10 miles) N of Forsmark ⏰ Summer: daily 🌐 lovstabruk.com

> An idyllic town, built of wood, Norrtälje is the natural hub of Roslagen, the area which covers large swathes of the Uppland coast.

⑦ Norrtälje

🅰F4 **🅾Uppland**
ℹ Lilla Brogatan 3;
www.norrtalje.se

An idyllic town, built of wood, Norrtälje is the natural hub of Roslagen, the area that covers large swathes of the Uppland coast. Norrtälje received its town charter from Gustav II Adolf in 1622, when an important armaments factory was established here. In the second half of the 19th century, the town became a seaside resort, not least due to the health-giving properties of the mud found in Norrtälje Bay.

Thousands of summer residents from Stockholm still head for Norrtälje. The charming town centre and the buildings along the Norrtäljeån river retain their 18th-century features. The church was built in 1726 and the town hall dates from 1792. Along with a good selection of shops, cafés and pubs, the brilliant range of attractions here include the interesting **Roslagsmuseet** in the old armaments factory, focusing on seafaring and coastal life. **Pythagoras** is an unusual museum in a former diesel engine factory and one of Sweden's best preserved industrial relics.

Roslagsmuseet
🅰Faktorigatan
📞0705-566 555

Pythagoras
♿⊗⊘ **🅰Verkstadsgatan 6**
🕐Mid-Jan–mid-Dec: noon–4pm Tue-Sun **🌐pythagoras-museum.se**

⑧ Sigtuna

🅰F4 **🅾Uppland** **⊗**
🚉To Märsta C, then bus
ℹ Stora Gatan 33; www.destinationsigtuna.se

Sweden's second oldest town, after Birka, was founded in 980 and soon became a centre of Christianity. Ruins of three of the original seven churches in medieval Sigtuna, St Per, St Lars and St Olof, still remain. The attractive main street, Stora Gatan, is lined with colourful wooden buildings and follows the original route. Still in use today is the 13th-century church of St Maria, with its medieval paintings. It is the oldest brick-built church in Mälardalen.

Sigtuna has Sweden's smallest town hall, built in 1744, and Lundströmska Gården, an early 20th-century home furnished in the style of the period. There are around 150 11th-century rune stones in the surrounding region.

The area is well endowed with stately homes. These include Skokloster and the lavish royal palace of **Rosersberg**, with some of Europe's best-kept interiors from the period 1795–1825.

East of Sigtuna is **Steninge Slott**, the renowned Swedish architect Tessin the Younger's Italianate Baroque master-piece built in the 1690s. The attractive house and gardens were a popular tourist spot, but the site is now being transformed into a residential area with more than 600 homes.

Rosersbergs Slott
♿⊗⊙⊘ **🅰15 km (9 miles) SE of Sigtuna** **🕐For guided tours only; May-Sep: 11am–3pm (Jun-Aug: to 4pm)** **🌐rosersbergsslott.se**

Steninge Slott
♿⊗⊙⊘ **🅰7 km (4 miles) E of Sigtuna** **🕐Palace: Jun-Aug daily** **🌐steningeslottsby.se**

⑨ ⊘Ⓜ▣🛍
Skokloster

🅰F4 **🅾Uppland** **🚆SL train from Stockholm to Bålsta, then bus 311** **🚌From Uppsala** **🕐May & Sep: 11am-4pm Sat & Sun; Jun-Aug: 11am-5pm daily** **🌐skoklostersslott.se**

One of the best-preserved Baroque castles in Europe, Skokloster, on Lake Mälaren, contains a unique collection of furniture, art, weapons, textiles and books.

Construction was started in 1654 for army commander Carl Gustav Wrangel, who accumulated incredible treasures during the Thirty Years' War (1618–48). This magnificent building was a way for Wrangel to show off his success, but he only ever lived here for a few weeks. Time seems to have stood still at the castle: the Banquet Hall, for example, remains incomplete, with all the tools lying where the craftsmen left them. The most sumptuous

Sigtuna's main street, Stora Gatan, lined with wooden buildings ↑

←

Baroque Skokloster Castle, beautifully situated on Lake Mälaren

rooms, however, are the armoury, with a collection of some 2,000 items, and the library. There is also a lathe workshop that features an unique collection of Dutch woodworking tools.

Standing next to the castle is Sweden's second oldest brick church. Built in the 13th century for nuns of the Cistercian order, it still contains a triumphal cross from this era. In the 1600s, it became the Wrangel family church. The churchyard contains several runestones, some of which are signed by the Viking rune-master, Fot, who was active in the mid-11th century.

10

Enköping

F4 Uppland
Rådhusgatan 3; www.enkoping.se

This centrally located town on Lake Mälaren calls itself Sweden's "nearest town". Another name is "Horseradish Town", which originates from the vegetable production that made the town famous in the 19th century. And Enköping still remains a city of greenery with its host of beautiful parks and gardens.

Enköping was granted a town charter in 1300. It was a spiritual centre with three churches and a monastery. Of these, only the remodelled Vårfrukyrkan remains.

A short drive northeast of Enköping, the medieval church of **Härkeberga** is a real gem. At the end of the 15th century, its star chamber was decorated by the Swedish master painter Albertus Pictor. The walls and ceilings are covered with colourful frescoes of biblical stories, every-day life and fantasy creatures.

Härkeberga Kyrka
10 km (6 miles) NE of Enköping Mar-Oct: daily

995

The year that Sweden's first coin was minted in Sigtuna, for Olof the "Tax King".

⓫ 🚲 Ⓜ 🍴 🖥 🛍

Birka

🅰F4 🚇Uppland 🚢From Stockholm during summer only ⏰Times vary; check website 🌐birkaviking gastaden.se

The trading post of Birka on the island of Björkö in Lake Mälaren was established in the 8th century. Thought to be the oldest town in Scandinavia, the town's founder was the Svea king, whose royal residence was on nearby Adelsö.

About 100 years later, Birka is described by a writer as having "many rich merchants and an abundance of all types of goods and a great deal of money and valuables". It was thought to have had 1,000 inhabitants, including crafts-men of every kind, whose products attracted merchants from distant countries.

The town was planned on uncomplicated lines. People lived in modest houses, which stood in rows overlooking the long jetties. At these lay the ships that took the Vikings out on trading missions and war expeditions. In 830 the arrival of a monk named Ansgar marked the start of Sweden's conversion to Christianity. But Birka's moment of greatness soon passed. In the 10th cen-tury, the town was abandoned in favour of Sigtuna, on the nearby mainland.

Today, Björkö is a green island with meadows and juniper-covered slopes. It has

a fascinating museum and ongoing archaeological digs. The museum shows how Birka would have looked in its hey-day, along with some of the finds. In summer, services are held in the Ansgar Chapel.

Did You Know?

Ancient Birka's trade links reached as far as the Byzantine Empire.

There is a harbour, restaurant, and good places to swim.

⓬

Södertälje

🅰F4 🚇Stockholms län 🚉🚌 ℹSaltsjögatan 1; www.destination sodertalje.se

Good communications are the key to the economic success of Södertälje, one of Sweden's oldest cities. In the 9th cen-tury, a fall in sea levels made the sound between the Baltic Sea and Lake Mälaren unnavi-gable, and so Tälje became a reloading point. The town flourished in the Middle Ages but fires, war and plague almost eradicated it in the 17th and 18th centuries. Fortunes improved with the construc-tion of the canal in 1819, and with the arrival of the railway

←

Boats moored at a hidden jetty among the reeds at Birka

↑ Neat wooden houses lining the Trosa's harbour canal

in 1860, industrialization took off. Today, major companies such as vehicle-maker Scania form the basis of a booming commercial life.

Södertälje's history is the focus of **Torekällbergets museet**, an open-air museum with animals, historic buildings and a craft quarter. **Marcus Wallenberg-hallen** holds a large collection of veteran vehicles from Scania's 100-year production history.

Tom Tits Experiment is a science centre with many fun activities, both indoors and outdoors, for kids of all ages.

Torekällbergets museet
ⓣ🅰 🅰Källgatan 🄲08-523 014 22 🄾May-Aug: 10am-4pm daily

Marcus Wallenberg-hallen
🅰Scania Vagnmakarvägen 2 🄲08-553 825 00 🄾Jul-mid-Dec: 8am-4:30pm Mon-Fri

Tom Tits Experiment
🄰ⓣ🅰🅰 🅰Storgatan 33 🄾10am-6pm Mon-Sun 🅀1 Jan, 23-26 & 31 Dec 🆆tomtit.se

13
Trosa

🅰F4 🅰Södermanland 🅰To Vagnhärad or Södertälje, then bus ℹ️Västra Langgatan 4; www.trosa.com

Known as the end of the world, idyllic Trosa is something of a geographical dead end if you are not venturing into the Trosa archipelago beyond. It was burned to the ground by the Russians in 1719, although its church, dating from 1711, was spared. Groups of red wooden buildings can be found mainly in Kåkstan, where Garvaregården is an arts and crafts museum.

Nearby, **Tullgarns Slott** was the favourite summer residence of Gustav V (1858–1950). The beautiful 18th-century palace has magnificent interiors and gardens.

Tullgarns Slott
🄰🄰 🅰On E4, 10 km (6 miles) N of Trosa 🄲08-551 720 11 🄾May-Sep: 11am-5pm Tue-Sun

14
Ytterjärna

🅰F4 🅰Stockholms län 🅰To Järna, then bus 🆆ytterjarna.se

Since the 1960s, Ytterjärna has become the centre for Swedish anthroposophists, followers of the teachings of Austrian philosopher Rudolf Steiner (1861–1925).

Anthroposophists focus on the development of the whole human being, particularly in the fields of art, music, farming and medicine. There are a number of Steiner organizations here, including schools, the Vidarkliniken hospital, biodynamic farms and market gardens.

Kulturhuset is renowned as a centre for art, music and theatre, and for the building's audacious design by architect Erik Asmussen, with its intertwined colour and shape.

Kulturhuset
🄰ⓣ🅰 🅰Pl 1800 🄾10am-5pm daily 🅀Public hols 🆆kulturhuset.nu

⑮
Flen

🅐E4 🅐Södermanland 🅐
ℹ Södra Järnvägsgatan 2;
Malmköping (summer);
www.visitflen.se

One of the youngest towns in Sweden, Flen only gained its royal charter in 1949. Although the town centre has little to offer, it makes a good base from which to explore attractions in the area.

On Lake Valdemaren, 10 km (6 miles) east of the town, lies Stenhammar's beautiful castle, renowned as the residence of Prince Vilhelm in the early 1900s. The castle is now used by Carl XVI Gustav, however, and is not open to the public.

Northwest of Flen is the prime minister's summer residence, Harpsund, where the gardens are open to visitors. The old regimental town of Malmköping, 14 km (9 miles) northwest of Flen, is home to Malmahed, a former military site that is now a museum and nature centre. There are several military museums, as well as **Museispårvägen**, displaying veteran trams and other public transport vehicles. Visitors can also enjoy a short tram ride through the countryside.

Museispårvägen

⊛ 🅐Malmköping,
17 km (11 miles) N of Flen,
Road 55 🅐Late May-end
Jun: 11am-5pm Sat & Sun;
end Jun-Aug: 11am-5pm
daily 🅦muma.se

💬 **INSIDER TIP**
Gone Fishing

To try your hand at fishing, contact Fishing in the Middle of Sweden. They will connect you with quality fishing destinations, guides, and accommodation in central Sweden *(www.fishinginthe middleofsweden.com)*.

Riding horses around ↑
the grounds by Lake
Valdemaren in Flen

⑯
Nyköping

🅐F4 🅐Södermanland 🅔🅐
ℹ Rådhuset, Stora Torget;
www.visit
nykoping.se

Södermanland's county town is best known for the notorious Nyköping Banquet in 1317. King Birger invited the Dukes Erik and Valdemar to a banquet at which the disputes between the brothers were to be resolved. Instead, Birger had the dukes thrown into Nyköpinghus's dungeon, and left to die. The story is retold in summer in a pageant at the castle. A fire in 1665 destroyed the original castle and only the tower remains. In the adjoining county governor's residence, the **Sörmlands Museum** contains a lively mix of historical exhibitions.

A pleasant way to see the sights in the summer is to take the Tuffis tourist train, which departs from Stora Torget. On the coast north of the town, Nynäs Slott nature reserve is also worth a visit.

Sörmlands Museum

⊛⊕ 🅐Nyköpingshus
🅐10am-5pm daily (to 8pm
Wed) 🅐Sep-May: Mon
🅦sormlandsmuseum.se

---

⑰
Strängnäs

🅐E4 🅐Södermanland 🅐
ℹ Nygatan 10 (Jun-Aug);
www.strangnas.se

As keeper of the keys of the Kingdom, Strängnäs was an important centre in the Middle Ages. It was mentioned as an episcopal see as early as 1120 and is dominated by the imposing tower of its Gothic cathedral, **Domkyrkan**, completed in 1280. It was here that Gustav Vasa was chosen as king on 6 June 1523, the date which was to become Sweden's National Day. Quaint wooden buildings surround the cathedral. To its east is Roggeborgen, the bishop's palace from the 1480s.

Gyllenjelmsgatan, the street that runs from the city centre to the mighty gates of the cathedral, was described by the poet Bo Setterlind as the most beautiful in Sweden.

Strängnäs Municipality includes the largest island in Lake Mälaren, Selaön. There are more rune stones here than in any other part of Södermanland, indicating that this was a major cultural centre in ancient times.

→

Gripsholms Slott in
Mariefred, site of the
National Portrait Gallery

One of the best ways to visit Mariefred is by the boat that crosses Lake Mälaren. The 1903 steamer S/S _Mariefred_ plies the three-and-a-half-hour voyage from Stockholm.

Nowadays the island has no connections to the mainland.

The renovated Mälsåkers Palace, which dates from the 17th century, is another of Selaön's attractions.

Domkyrkan

⊗ 🏠 Biskopsgränd 2
📞 0152-245 00 🕐 Daily by appt or for services on Wed & Sun

Mariefred

🅰 F4 🏠 Södermanland 🚉🚌
ℹ Rådhuset; www. imariefred.nu

This town should ideally be approached from the water to get the best view of the splendid **Gripsholms Slott**. The first fortress on this site was built in the 1380s by the Lord High Chancellor, Bo Jonsson Grip, who gave the castle its name. Work on the present building, initiated by Gustav Vasa, started in 1537, but extensive alterations were made by Gustav III in the late 18th century. It was during this period that the National Portrait Gallery was set up. It now contains 4,000 portraits, representing the celebrities of the past 500 years.

Gripsholms Slott has a number of well-preserved interiors from various periods, with highlights including Gustav III's theatre and the White Salon. The town of Mariefred, which grew up in the shadow of the castle, derives its name from a medieval Carthusian monastery. An inn has stood on the site of the monastery since the early 17th century.

The peaceful old streets of Mariefred with their delightful wooden buildings are a pleasure to stroll around. Art enthusiasts should head for Grafikens Hus on a hill leading up to the former royal farm, where stables and haylofts have been converted into attractive galleries.

One of the best ways to visit Mariefred is by the boat that crosses Lake Malären. The 1903 steamer S/S _Mariefred_ plies the three-and-a-half-hour voyage from Stockholm.

There is a Railway Museum in the town and **ÖSLJ** (Östra Södermanlands Järnväg museum society) operates authentic narrow-gauge steam trains that depart from the harbour on a 20-minute historical trip to Läggesta and, on certain days, on to Taxinge. There is a pleasant café and shop located at the station.

Gripsholms Slott

⊗⊗⊕ 🏠 500 m (546 yd) SW of the centre 🕐 Early May–Sep: 10am–4pm daily; Apr, Oct & Nov: noon–3pm (check website for days)
🆆 gripsholmsslott.se

ÖSLJ

⊗⊕ 🏠 Storgatan 21, 500 m (546 yd) W of the centre
🕐 Check website for departure times 🆆 oslj.nu

Did You Know?

The cover photo for ABBA's album _Waterloo_ was taken at Gripsholms Slott.

Pretty houses
in Eskilstuna along
the riverbank →

⑲
Eskilstuna

🅰E4 🏛Södermanland
🚌 ℹFristadstorget 1;
www.eskilstuna.se

The town is named after
St Eskil, the Englishman
who became Svealand's first
Christian bishop and built his
church on the riverbank along
Eskilstunaån at the end of the
10th century. During Sweden's
Age of Greatness in the 17th
century, Eskilstuna flourished
after Karl X Gustav gave master
smith Reinhold Rademacher
a 20-year monopoly on the
manufacture of items such as
cannons, knives and scissors.
Rademachergatan still has a
few forges kept as they were
in the 1650s, where visitors
can play at being a blacksmith.

Today's modern industrial
town and centre of learning
features over 200 items of
public art, including Carl Milles'
Hand of God in Stadsparken.

Parken Zoo is one of the
country's leading zoos, home

to animals from all around the
world, including some endangered species. There is also a
heated outdoor pool and an
amusement park, which is
popular with young children.

North of Eskilstuna is
Torshälla, a small town of
cobbled streets, well-kept
wooden houses and a superb
12th-century church.

Parken Zoo

🦊🐒🐒😀😀 🚶1 km (half
a mile) W of centre ⏰Times
vary, check website
🖥parkenzoo.se

---

⑳
Julita Gård

🅰E4 🏛Södermanland
📞08-519 547 30 🚌To
Katrineholm, then bus 405
📅May & Sep: 11am–4pm
Sun & Sun; Jun–Aug: 10am–
5pm daily

This extensive Södermanland
estate on Lake Öljaren is said
to be the world's largest

open-air museum. It was
created in the first half of the
20th century by the romantic
Lieutenant Arthur Bäckström
and in 1941 was donated to
Stockholm's Nordiska museet.
Julita is a working estate farm
with parks and gardens, and
an 18th-century manor house
built on the site of a medieval
Cistercian monastery.

The estate has a collection
of buildings reflecting rural life
in Södermanland. Threatened
national species are cared for
at the Swedish agricultural
museum. There is also a dairy
museum. Children can pop into
the house of the much-loved
children's literary character,
Pettson, and his cat Findus.

㉑
Västerås

🅰E4 🏛Västmanland 🚌🚆
ℹKopporbergvägen 10,
021-390 100

Strategically situated at
the point where the Svartån
river meets Lake Mälaren, the
county town of Västerås has
been an important trading
centre since Viking times.
Construction of the castle and
cathedral began in the 13th
century, and in 1527

> Strategically situated at the point where
> the Svartån river runs into Lake Mälaren,
> the county town of Västerås has been an
> important trading centre since Viking times.

Parliament was convened here. The cathedral, **Domkyrkan**, contains the sarcophagus of Erik XIV (r. 1561–69), the king who was allegedly poisoned by his brother Johan III, by pea soup laced with arsenic.

Around the cathedral lies the town's old centre of learning, where Johannes Rudbeckius opened Sweden's first upper secondary school in 1623. In the 17th and 18th centuries

↑ Cycling alongside colourful buildings in the town of Arboga

Västerås became a major port for the Bergslagen region. Today it is an industrial centre and headquarters of the engineering giant Asea-Brown-Boveri (ABB).

To the east of the town lies the 7th-century Anundshögen mound where Bröt-Anund, the king who settled Bergslagen, is said to be buried. Standing stones in the shapes of ships 50 m (164 ft) long can be seen around the mound.

Northwest of the town is **Skultuna Messingsbruk**, Europe's oldest active brass-works, founded in 1607 and renowned for its cannons and stylish candlesticks.

Domkyrkan

⊛ ⌂ Västra Kyrkogatan 6 ☎ 021-81 46 00 ⌚ aily

Skultuna Messingsbruk

⊛ ⊜ 🖰 ⌂ 16 km (10 miles) NW of Västerås ⌚ Daily
🅆 skultuna.com

㉒
Arboga

🅰 E4 🄐 Västmanland ▸▪
🅆 arboga.se

Red-painted iron warehouses, Ladbron quay and the railway line recall Arboga's great age as the chief shipping port for iron from Bergslagen. Fahlströmska Gården is a 16th-century warehouse with a huge loft.

Arboga was the site of Sweden's first parliament in 1435. Churches from the period include the hospital chapel on Stortorget. The 14th-century Heliga Trefaldighets Kyrka on Järntorget has a splendid Baroque pulpit.

㉓
Köping

🅰 E4 🄐 Västmanland
🄑 🄸 Barnhemsgatan 2; www.koping.se

The port of Köping on Lake Mälaren has been a vital link

EAT

Hambergs Fisk
Upscale bistro and fish market with a good selection of dessert cheeses. Try the seafood platter.

🅰 F4 🄐 Fyristorg 8, Uppsala ⌚ Sun
🅆 hambergs.se

⊛⊛⊛

Villa Anna
Intimate restaurant serving Swedish cuisine with exciting flavour combinations.

🅰 F4 🄐 Odinslund 3, Uppsala ⌚ Sun & Mon
🅆 villaanna.se

⊛⊛⊛

Båthuset Krog & Bar
The menu at this floating restaurant is dominated by seafood and traditional Swedish dishes.

🅰 F4 🄐 Hamngatan 2, Sigtuna ⌚ Mon
🅆 bathuset.com

⊛⊛⊛

for transporting products to and from the mines and forests of Bergslagen since medieval times. The city burned down in 1889, but buildings to the west of the river were saved, including the 17th-century Nyströmska Gården, a joiner's yard where visitors can see how the town's special tilt-top table was made. Other attractions include the motor museum, **Bil och Teknikhistoriska Samlingarna**.

Bil och Teknikhistoriska Samlingarna

⊛ ⊜ 🖰 ⌂ Glasgatan 19 ⌚ May-Oct: 11am-4pm Tue-Sat (Jun-Aug: also Sun)
🅆 biloteknik.se

24
Sala

**▲E4 ❖Västmanland ▣
🛈 Stora Torget ; www.
destinationsala.se**

During the 16th century, the
silver mine in Sala was one
of the richest in the world;
200 tonnes were mined here
up to 1570, providing valuable
funds for the state coffers.
The former **Silvergruva** mine
is open to the public for
guided tours down to levels
of 60 m (200 ft) and 155 m
(508 ft). There is a "mine suite"
at the lower level, where you
can spend the night below
ground. Above ground, there
are beautiful walks around
the old pits and canals, and
treasure hunts are organized
for children.

Aguélimuseet showcases
the work of Sala's own artist,
Orientalist Ivan Aguéli (1869–
1917), and other Modernists.

Silvergruva
🟡🟡🟡🟡🟡 ❖Drottning
Christinas Väg ⏰Times
vary, check website ◫salas
silvergruva.se

Aguélimuseet
🟡🟡🟡 ❖Vasagatan 17
⏰11am–4pm Wed–Sat
◫aguelimuseet.se

25
Fagersta

**▲E4 ❖Västmanland
▣ 🛈Vastmannavagen 12;
0223-131 00**

Iron-working has shaped
Fagersta for centuries. In
Dunshammar, just south
of the town, Iron Age blast
furnaces show how iron used
to be extracted from bog ore.
Today Fagersta is home to
metal-manufacturing and
stainless-steel industries.

At the privately owned
UNESCO World Heritage Site
of **Engelsbergs Bruk**, the
blast furnace and ironworks
have been preserved in full
working order and give a
remarkable impression of
how the site operated
between the 17th and 19th
centuries. Oljeön, the world's

oldest preserved oil refinery
(1875–1902), is 1.5 km (1 mile)
from the ironworks.

Flowing through Fagersta is
the 200-year-old Strömsholm
canal from Lake Mälaren to
Smedjebacken in Dalarna.
Completed in 1795, it was
once a vital transport link for
the Bergslagen foundries.
Twenty-six locks, six of them
in Fagersta, raise boats a total
of 100 m (330 ft). Passenger
ferries operate on the canal.

Engelsbergs Bruk
🟡🟡🟡🟡 ❖15 km (10 miles)
E of Fagersta 📞070-211 76
60 ⏰For tours only; call
ahead to book

26
Kopparberg

**▲E4 ❖Västmanland
🛈Gruvstugutorget 3;
www.bergslagen.se**

The discovery of copper in the
early 17th century attracted
miners from Falun, who called
the place Nya Kopparberget
(New Copper Hill). Today, the
town shares its name with the
famous brand of pear cider,
which is produced locally. The
2.5-km (1.5-miles) Kopparstigen

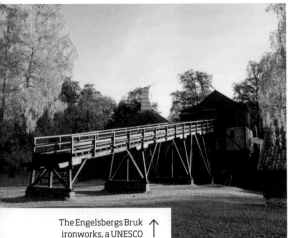

The Engelsbergs Bruk
ironworks, a UNESCO
World Heritage Site ↑

(Copper Trail) takes in 28 places of interest. Along the way is **Kopparbergs muséer**, a complex including an 1880s photography studio, gold-smiths' museum and postal museum. Also notable are the 17th-century courthouse and a wooden church from 1635.

Kopparbergs muséer
⊜ 🅰Gruvstugutorget
📞0580-715 19 🕒Jun-Aug: daily

Grythyttan
🅰D4 🅰Västmanland
🚉To Örebro, then bus

A local vein of silver brought prosperity and town status to Grythyttan in 1649, but when the silver ran out 33 years later, the town charter was withdrawn. Today, Grythyttan has awakened from its long slumber and is now a gastronomic centre.

It all started when the inn, built in 1640, was given a new lease of life in the 1970s, thanks to inspired innkeeper Carl Jan Granqvist. Now, in addition to Grythyttan's wooden houses and red-painted church, there

↑ Industrial building at Silvergruva open-air museum, and exploring the mine *(inset)*

is a catering college centred on **Måltidens Hus i Norden**. It occupies Sweden's spectacular pavilion built for EXPO 1992 in Seville. Various activities offer focus on food and cooking, alongside exhibitions and a cookery book museum.

South of Grythyttan lies **Loka Brunn**, a classic Swedish spa founded in the 1720s. The site has modern facilities, but the old spa, with its gardens and spring, has been preserved in the Swedish spa museum. You can sample the spring water and view the restored bathhouse, pharmacy, clinic and royal kitchen built in 1761.

Måltidens Hus i Norden
🕒🍴😊🏛 🅰Sörälgsvägen 4
🕒End of Jun-mid-Aug: daily; other times: Mon-Fri
🌐maltidenshus.com

Loka Brunn
😊😊🍴😊🏛 🅰15 km (9 miles) S of Grythyttan 🕒Pool: daily; museum: summer only
🌐lokabrunn.se

Nora
🅰E4 🅰Västmanland
🚉To Örebro, then bus
ℹJarnvagsgatan 1;
www.nora.se

This idyllic wooden town is an ideal place to stroll around, with its cobbled streets and charming shops, many in 18th-century buildings. Göthlinska Gården (1793) is an interesting museum furnished in the style of a middle-class family home from around 1900.

The highlight of the Nora mining area's monuments is Pershyttan, 3 km (2 miles) west of the centre, where the charcoal blast furnace dates from 1856. In summer, a steam train runs from Nora on the Nora Bergslags Veteranjärnväg, Sweden's first normal-gauge railway. Nora's train sheds house historic steam trains, diesel engines and carriages.

A DRIVING TOUR
MÄLARDALEN'S CASTLES

Length 500 km (300 miles) **Recommended route**
This tour lasts three days, despite the generally good roads. An option is to select a group of palaces close to each other. For more information, see www.malarslott.nu

There are more than 100 sturdy castles, opulent palaces and ravishing country houses around Lake Mälaren, of which this driving tour takes in 10 of the best. Often strategically located near Iron Age and Viking settlements, they highlight the significance of this extensive waterway. Wik's 15th-century castle and the Vasa kings' solid, 16th-century fortress of Gripsholm show how long the need for defences lasted. From the mid-17th century, the grand palaces of Sweden's Age of Greatness, such as Skokloster, predominated, as manifestations of their owners' wealth.

EASTERN SVEALAND

Mälardalen's Castles

Locator Map
For more detail see p154

The medieval castle of **Engsö** *was reworked in French Rococo style in the 1740s. It has many beautiful interiors.*

Heby

Svartån

Surahammar

Tillberga

Västerås

Stockholm Västerås Airport

Hallstahammar

Kolbäck

Strömsholm

Tidö

Engsö

With its beautiful pastureland and bridle paths, **Strömsholm** *has been known for equestrianism since the 16th century. The palace was built in the 1670s in Baroque style.*

Köping

Kungsör

Arboga

Mälaren

Sundbyholm

Torshälla

Söderfjärden

Eskilstuna

Tidö, *Lord Chancellor Axel Oxenstierna's country house, built in 1642, is a fine example of a Baroque manor. A museum displays 30,000 antique toys.*

Hjälmaren

Hälleforsnäs

Malmköping

0 kilometres   15
0 miles   15

N
↑

← Exploring the Renaissance Gripsholm Castle

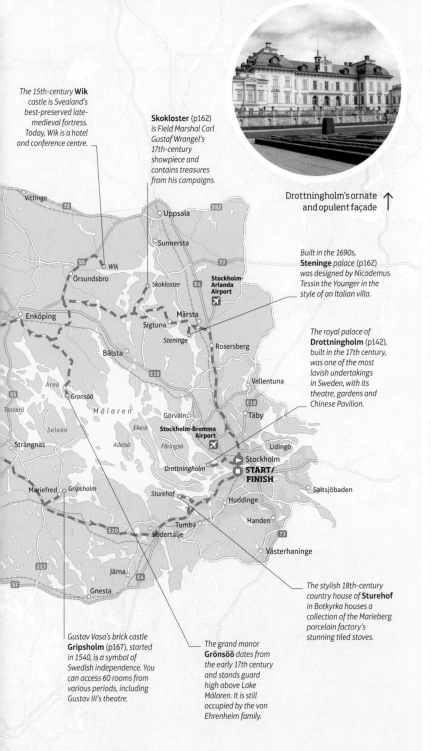

The 15th-century **Wik** castle is Svealand's best-preserved late-medieval fortress. Today, Wik is a hotel and conference centre.

Skokloster (p162) is Field Marshal Carl Gustaf Wrangel's 17th-century showpiece and contains treasures from his campaigns.

Drottningholm's ornate and opulent façade ↑

Built in the 1690s, **Steninge** palace (p162) was designed by Nicodemus Tessin the Younger in the style of an Italian villa.

The royal palace of **Drottningholm** (p142), built in the 17th century, was one of the most lavish undertakings in Sweden, with its theatre, gardens and Chinese Pavilion.

The stylish 18th-century country house of **Sturehof** in Botkyrka houses a collection of the Marieberg porcelain factory's stunning tiled stoves.

Gustav Vasa's brick castle **Gripsholm** (p167), started in 1540, is a symbol of Swedish independence. You can access 60 rooms from various periods, including Gustav III's theatre.

The grand manor **Grönsöö** dates from the early 17th century and stands guard high above Lake Mälaren. It is still occupied by the von Ehrenheim family.

Vittinge
72
Uppsala
282
Sunnersta
77
55
Wik
Örsundsbro
Enköping
Skokloster
E4
Stockholm-Arlanda Airport ✈
Sigtuna
Märsta
Steninge
Bålsta
Rosersberg
E18
Arnö
55
Gronsöö
Tosterö
Mälaren
Selaön
Vallentuna
Görväln
E18
Täby
Ekerö
Stockholm-Bromma Airport ✈
Adelsö
Färingsö
Lidingö
Strängnäs
Drottningholm
Stockholm
START/ FINISH
Saltsjöbaden
Mariefred
Gripsholm
Sturehof
Huddinge
Handen
Tumba
Södertälje
E20
Västerhaninge
73
223
Järna
E4
57
Gnesta

EASTERN GÖTALAND

The provinces of Östergötland, Småland and Öland together make up Eastern Götaland. In north Östergötland lie the major towns of Norrköping and Linköping. But once you travel south from the steep hills of Kolmården, which form the northern border of the state, flat agricultural land extends as far as the eye can see. Besides being the granary of Sweden, this is historical soil – it was here that the royal Folkung dynasty had its roots and where Birgitta Gudmarsson (St Bridget) advised the political and religious leaders of the 14th century.

The hills north of Gränna and the ruins of Brahehus castle mark the beginning of Småland. For a long time Småland formed the border with Denmark and it was from this region that Nils Dacke led a peasants' revolt in the 16th century. The land is poorer and stonier than Östergötland, supporting crofters and their small farms. Mass emigration drained the area of thousands of people during the famine of the 19th century. However, Småland has had its success stories: it is the ideal location for one of its major industries, glassworking, which relies on timber and water.

The region's archipelago stretches south from the Sankta Annas islands in Östergötland through the Kalmarsund between Småland and Öland. Thanks to Ölandsbron bridge, the long, narrow island of Öland is easily accessible. Holiday makers are drawn to its sandy beaches, while botanists head for the Alvar plain and ornithologists for Ottenby bird station.

EASTERN GÖTALAND

Must See

❶ Göta Canal

Experience More

❷ Kolmårdens Djurpark
❸ Norrköping
❹ Linköping
❺ Medevi Brunn
❻ Vadstena
❼ Gränna
❽ Omberg
❾ Jönköping
❿ Oskarshamn
⓫ Vimmerby
⓬ Eksjö
⓭ Växjö
⓮ Västervik
⓯ Färjestaden
⓰ Kalmar
⓱ Blå Jungfrun
⓲ Borgholm
⓳ Öland's Southern Cape
⓴ Byxelkrok
㉑ Ölands Museum
㉒ Eketorps Borg
㉓ Stora Alvaret

WESTERN
GÖTALAND
p242

EASTERN
GÖTALAND

Ett vackert naturområde speglas i vattnet vid en kanal.

Ett vackert naturområde speglas i vattnet vid en kanal.

1

GÖTA CANAL

◳ Östergötland and Västergötland 🚌🚆 ℹ AB Göta Kanalbolag in Motala; www.gotakanal.se

Opened in 1832, the Göta Canal provided a vital link for transporting timber and iron between Stockholm and Gothenburg. But it was another 100 years before leisure traffic took off on the waterway.

In summer, from May to August, the canal bustles with small craft and passenger boats and it is possible to cruise the entire length on the classic white boats such as *M/S Diana* (1931), *Wilhelm Tham* (1912) and *Juno* (1874). Built in 1874, Juno is one of the oldest boats afloat with sleeping accommodation still in use. Other boats take passengers along shorter stretches and there are special packages available, such as combining cycling holidays with canal trips. Guest marinas offer services along the canal. Motala is regarded as the "capital" of the canal, and the man behind its construction, Baltzar von Platen (1766–1829), is buried here. At Borensberg, the Göta Hotell is an idyllic summer spot beside the water, which offers food and accommodation to passers-by.

FROM THE BALTIC TO LAKE VÄNERN

"The Blue Band of Sweden" as the Göta Canal is known, is the high point of Swedish engineering history. It took 58,000 men and 22 years to build a waterway across Sweden from the Baltic Sea to the already completed Trollhättan Canal (p254), and provide a route to the Kattegatt. The problem was coping with a difference in height of around 92 m (301 ft), and the mammoth project took advantage of the latest technological innovations. The canal has 58 locks between Mem on the Baltic and Sjötorp on Lake Vänern.

Did You Know?

A staircase of seven locks at Berg raises boats to an impressive total of 18 m (59 ft).

① Roads cross under the canal, an odd sight when a boat passes overhead.

② From May to August traditional white boats, such as *M/S Diana,* take passengers cruising on the Gota Canal.

③ The spectacular opening of the flight of locks named Berg Slussar attracts a large audience.

↑ Trees on the river bank mirrored in the still waters of the Göta Canal

EXPERIENCE MORE

② ✦🎿🍴☕🛍
Kolmårdens Djurpark

🅰E5 🏛Östergötland
Junction from E4, 12 km
(7 miles) N of Norrköping
🚆 🕐Mid-May-Aug: 10am-
6pm (to 8pm Midsummer)
🌐kolmarden.com

Kolmårdens Djurpark is no
ordinary animal park – the
enclosures are large and attractively landscaped. Creatures
of the savannah live here
alongside Nordic species such
as brown bears and wolves.

Snakes and crocodiles live
in the outdoor Tropicarium,
while the Aparium is designed
so that the apes can be
viewed indoors and out. Tiger
World, offers a unique walk-
through experience close to
the big cats. A cable-car ride
provides a bird's-eye view of
the grounds.

Sitting alongside are thrill
rides and shows. There are a
variety of accommodation
options available for visitors,
including African tents on the
savannah and a youth hostel
with a mixture of shared
dorms with nice views. There's
also a great themed spa to
enjoy on-site.

③
Norrköping

🅰E5 🏛Östergötland E4 🚆
🛈Drottninggatan 7-9;
www.upplev.norrkoping.se

In the 17th century the skills
of entrepreneur Louis de
Geer, combined with water
power from the Motala Ström
river system, transformed
Norrköping into Sweden's first
industrial town. Norrköping
and neighbouring Linköping
make up Sweden's fourth
largest urban region.

Although Norrköping is an
industrial town, the mix of old
and new buildings, parks and
trams make it an attractive
place to visit. On a small island
in Motala Ström sits **Arbetets
museet** (Museum of Labour),
in an old spinning mill known
as Strykjärnet (the Iron).

The area around Norrköping
has a long history of habitation;
around 1,650 carvings can be
seen at Himmelstalund on
the edge of town.

Arbetets museet
🎿🍴☕🛍 🏛Laxholmen
🕐Times vary, check website
🚫Public hols 🌐arbetets
museum.se

④
Linköping

🅰E5 🏛Östergötland E4
🚆🚍 🛈Storgatan 15; www.
visitlinkoping.se

The county capital and
cathedral city of Linköping lies
in the middle of the Östgöta
plain. First populated 3,000
years ago, Linköping is now
Sweden's fifth largest city, and
is known for its university and
high-tech industry.

Construction of the
Domkyrkan (Cathedral) started in the mid-13th century.
The interior contains superb
medieval stone carvings and
a Renaissance altarpiece is
by the Dutch painter M J Van
Heemskerck (1498–1574).
The old town open-air
museum, **Gamla Linköping**,
is a collection of 80 buildings

> **First populated
> 3,000 years ago,
> Linköping is now
> Sweden's fifth
> largest city, and
> is known for its
> university.**

← Norrköping after dark with the lights of Strykjärnet reflected in the water

(6 miles) southeast of the centre, lies the castle of Sturefors, which is renowned for its 18th-century interiors and beautiful grounds. The castle is a private residence, but parts of the grounds are open to the public.

Domkyrkan

🕭 🏠 St Persgatan 📞 013-
🕒 Daily; call for times

Gamla Linköping

🕭🕭🕭 🏠 2 km (3 miles)
W of Linköping 📞 013-12 11
10 🕒 Daily 🌐 gamla
linkoping.info

Flygvapenmuseum

🕭🕭🕭🕭 🏠 4 km (3 miles)
W of Linköping 🕒 Jun-Aug:
11am-7pm daily (to 8pm
Thu); Sep-May: 11am-5pm
Tue-Sun (to 8pm Thu) 🌐 fly
gvapenmuseum.se

5
Medevi Brunn

🅰 E5 🏠 Östergötland Road
50 🅿 ℹ 0141-911 00;
www.medevibrunn.se

In the 17th-century the scientist and doctor Urban

Hjärne analyzed water from the Medevi spring and declared it to be "superior to other medication". Thus began the transformation of Medevi Brunn into a health spa. Today, the season at Medevi starts at Midsummer and lasts for seven weeks. Throughout this time the traditional brass sextet Brunnsorkester performs daily concerts, and there are various activities going on that you can take part in.

South of Medevi, on the edge of Lake Vättern, lies **Övralid**, the former home of poet and Nobel laureate Verner von Heidenstam (1859–1940). Designed by Heidenstam himself, the house has stunning views across the lake.

Övralid

🕭🕭🕭 🏠 10 km (6 miles)
N of Motala, Road 50 🕒 15
May-31 Aug: daily; tours
10am-5pm on the hour
🌐 ovralid.se

from the city and surrounding

area. This charming setting, complete with picturesque wooden buildings, cobbled streets and gardens, is a window on a past way of life.

Malmen, site of Sweden's first military flying school (1911), is now home to the **Flygvapenmuseum** (Swedish Air Force Museum). Exhibits include examples of Swedish military aircraft.

Kaga Kyrka, one of the region's best-preserved medieval churches, is located on the Svartån river south of Linköping. Dating from the 12th century, its walls are decorated with frescoes. On Erlången lake, 10 km

← The attractive health spa of Medevi Brunn powdered with snow

6

Vadstena

E5 Östergötland Road 50 upplevvadstena.se

Situated on Lake Vättern, Vadstena is dominated by St Birgitta's abbey, which dates back to the 14th century, and the mid-16th-century castle of the Vasa kings. Cobbled streets, wooden buildings and glorious gardens add to the town's character.

The moated **Vadstena Slott** was built in 1545 as a fortress against the Danes. As well as being a museum, the castle also hosts opera, theatre performances and concerts.

The abbey complex includes the original abbey, Vadstena Kloster, established in 1384 and dissolved after the Reformation in 1595, and **Vadstena Klosterkyrka** (1430). This abbey church houses the relics of St Bridget. It is also the site of the Pax Mariae convent, founded in the 1980s, which is home to around ten nuns.

Vadstena Slott

Hamngatan 4
Apr–Oct: noon–4pm daily
Apr–mid-May & Sep–Oct: Sat & Sun vadstena slott.com

Vadstena Klosterkyrka

Lasarettsgatan 5
Daily 0143-29850

7

Gränna

D5 Småland E4
Södra Strandgatan 13B; www.jkpg.com

Gränna was at its height in the 17th century in the days of Count Per Brahe, who founded the town and whose plan is still evident today. On the square in the centre of Gränna, **Grenna Museum** has tales to tell of the tragic expedition to the North Pole headed by the town's famous son Salomon August Andrée in the hot-air balloon *Örnen*. Inspired by Andrée, Gränna has become a centre for balloon flights. The town is also known for its *polkagris* (peppermint rock). The red and white sweet originated in 1859 when widow Amalia Eriksson started a bakery here.

Along the beautiful stretch of the E4 beside Lake Vättern, just north of Gränna, lies the ruined Brahehus castle, built for Count Per Brahe in the 1640s. On a clear day Brahehus offers magnificent views over Vättern towards Västergötland

↑ An aerial view of the Alvastra Kloster ruins, southeast Omberg

on the other side of the lake and Visingsö. This flat island can be reached by boat from Gränna. Here you can visit the ruined castle of Visingsborg and explore old oak forests.

Grenna Museum

Brahegatan 38-40 10am–4pm daily (Sep–Apr: Tue–Sat) 1 Jan, 24, 25 & 31 Dec grennamuseum.se

---

8

Omberg

E5 Östergötland 20 km (12 miles) S of Vadstena upplevvadstena.se

Rising mountain-like from the wide Östgöta plains is Omberg. Its highest point is 175 m (574 ft) above Lake Vättern. It is the legendary home of Queen

←

The interior of Vadstena Kloster, part of the stately castle complex at Vadstena

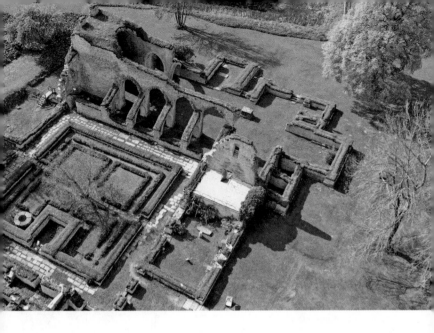

Omma, whose name means "steam", and indeed the fog that often surrounds the hill gives it a mythical quality. Orchid marshes, beech woodlands and ancient forest flourish on the limestone-rich rock. Walking trails cross the area. To the south lies author Ellen Key's home, **Strand**, and the nature reserves of Bokskogen and Stora Lund. On the plains southeast of Omberg is the ruin of Alvastra Kloster, where St Bridget once stayed.

Strand
🏛 🅰4.5 km (2.7 miles) SW of Omberg 🕐 Early May & Sep: Sat & Sun; mid-May–Aug: 11am–noon, 2–3pm Tue–Sun; 🌐 ellenkey.se

---

9
Jönköping
🅰D5 🅰Småland E4 🚍🚄
🅸 Södra Strandgatan 13; www.jkpg.com

King Magnus Ladulås granted Jönköping its charter in 1284, by which time the town was already an important trading centre. For years Småland formed Sweden's southern border with Denmark, but when the Danes invaded in 1612 the people set fire to Jönköping and fled to Visingsö.

In the 19th century the town became known for matchstick production; the first factory was opened here in the 1840s. **Tändsticksmuseet** (the Match Museum) is set in a former match factory (1848). Local history comes under the spotlight at **Jönköpings Läns Museum**, which houses works by the local artist John Bauer.

Tändsticksmuseet
🏛🏛🏛 🅰Tändsticksgränd 27 🕐Jun–Aug: 10am–5pm daily (to 3pm Sat & Sun); Sep–May: 11am–3pm Tue–Sat 🚫Public hols 🌐match museum.jonkoping.se

Jönköpings Läns Museum
🏛🏛🏛🏛 🅰Dag Hammarskjölds Plats 2 🕐10am–5pm Mon–Fri, 11am–3pm Sat & Sun 🌐jonkopingslans museum.se

---

ST BRIDGET

At the age of only 13, Bridget (c 1303–73) was married to a local dignitary and became lady of the manor of Ulvåsa. Even as a child, she had religious visions and as an adult made pilgrimages to Spain, Rome and Jerusalem. In 1370 she gained the Pope's consent to found a monastic order, the Brigittine Order. Canonized in 1391, Bridget is the patron saint of Sweden, and in 1999 became one of the patron saints of Europe.

Did You Know?

King Oskar I gave his name to Oskarshamn, which gained its charter in 1856.

⑩

Oskarshamn

Ⓐ E6 **Ⓐ** Småland E22 **Ⓐ**
ℹ Biogränd 7; www.
oskarshamn.com

Previously known as Döderhultsvik, Oskarshamn grew up around the harbour and today is still an important place with a lively seafaring industry. The old areas of Besväret and Fnyket have wooden 19th- century houses and are ideal for a leisurely exploration on foot. There are great views over the water and the island Blå Jungfrun (p187) from Långa Soffan, an extraordinarily long 72-m- (79-yd-) bench built close to the harbour in 1867.

Oskarshamn has several museums. On display at **Döderhultarmuseet** are the original wooden figures by sculptor Axel Petersson, also known as "Döderhultarn", together with a description of his life in late-19th-century Småland. **Oskarshamns Sjöfartsmuseum** (Maritime Museum) displays a superb collection of local maritime history.
Biologiska museet has a botanical collection that focuses mainly on Swedish plants.

→

Sculpture by Axel Petersson, Döderhultar-museet

→

Kids exploring (inset) at Vimmerby's Astrid Lindgrens Värld

Döderhultarmuseet
🅰🅰🅰🅰
Ⓐ Hantverksgatan 18
📞 0491-880 40 **Ⓓ** Daily

Oskarshamns Sjöfartsmuseum
🅰🅰🅰🅰
Ⓐ Hantverksgatan 18
📞 0491-880 40 **Ⓓ** Mon-Sat (Jun-Aug: daily)

Biologiska museet
Ⓐ Gyllings väg 9 **Ⓓ** Tue-Fri
Ⓦ bimon.se

⑪

Vimmerby

Ⓐ E5 **Ⓐ** Småland Road 33/34 **Ⓐ** **ℹ** Rådhuset 1; 0492-310 10

The small town of Vimmerby began as a marketplace on the "King's Road" between Stockholm and Kalmar. It was strategically important and constantly fought over by the Danes, who burned it to the ground on many occasions. Few old buildings remain, but on Storgatan there is the austere Neo-Classical-style Rådhuset (town hall) from the 1820s. Like the houses of Tenngjutargården and Grankvistgården, it is a historical monument.

Vimmerby is associated with Astrid Lindgren (p123), who was born in Näs and set many of her popular children's books in this area. All her beloved characters can be encoun-tered in **Astrid Lindgrens Värld** (Astrid Lindgren's World). The park here also includes the Astrid Lindgren Centre with an exhibition on the author's life and work.

Norra Kvill National Park, 20 km (12 miles) northwest of Vimmerby, is an area of virgin forest with pine trees over 350 years old. The park slopes down to a small lake.

Astrid Lindgrens Värld
🅰🅰🅰🅰🅰 **Ⓐ** Fabriksgatan
Ⓓ Mid-May-end of Aug: daily
Ⓦ astridlindgrensvarld.se

← Miniature houses at Astrid Lindgrens Värld, in the town of Vimmerby

made in 2002 by the glass artist Bertil Vallien. **Smålands Museum**, with Sveriges Glasmuseum (Glass Museum), tells the story of the glassworks. Next to it is **Utvandrarnas Hus**, which focuses on the mass emigration in the 19th century.

Smålands Museum

⊛⊛⊜⊜ ◻Södra Järnvägsgatan 2 ◻10am–5pm Tue–Fri, 11am–4pm Sat & Sun (Jun–Aug: also Mon) ◻Public hols ◼kultur parkensmaland.se

Utvandrarnas Hus

⊛⊛⊜⊜ ◻Vilhelm Mobergs Gata 4 ◻10am–5pm Tue–Fri, 11am–4pm Sat & Sun (Jun–Aug: also Mon) ◼kultur parkensmaland.se

---

⑫
Eksjö

◮E5 ◻Småland Road 32/40 ◻ ◻Österlånggatan 31; www.visiteksjo.se

The small town of Eksjö, in the highlands of southern Sweden, is the country's most genuine wooden town. This was border country until the 17th century and Eksjö was burned down by its own people in conjunction with a Danish retreat. In the 1560s Erik XIV drew up a new town plan for Eksjö, which largely remains today. Gamla Stan (the old town) escaped the fire and its buildings remain intact and have been sympathetically renovated.

About 13 km (8 miles) east of Eksjö, the Skurugata nature reserve has an impressive canyon in porphyritic rock, 800 m (2,625 ft) long and 35 m (115 ft) deep. From Eksjö to the neighbouring town of Nässjö is just over 20 km (12 miles). Nässjö owes its existence to the coming of the railway in the 1860s. Today the railway companies Statens Järnvägar and Banverket are still the main employers.

---

⑬
Växjö

◮E6 ◻Småland Road 23/25/27/30 ◻◻ ◻Residenset, Stortorget; www.vaxjo.se

A bishopric as early as the 12th century, Växjö was granted its town charter by King Magnus Erikson in 1342. For some time the town lay on the border with Denmark and it was from here that Nils Dacke led his peasant revolt against the king of Sweden in the 16th century. Devastating fires, the most recent in 1843, destroyed the town, which has since been rebuilt. The cathedral dates from the late 12th century, but has been remodelled over the centuries. It contains an altarpiece in glass and wood

---

⑭
Västervik

◮E5 ◻Småland E22 ◻◻ ◻Rådhuset, Stora Torget 4; www.vastervik.com

Frequent Danish attacks eventually destroyed Västervik in 1677. Rebuilt, it became a major seafaring centre. The area known as Gamla Norr contains the oldest preserved houses in Västervik, including Aspagården and the former poor-house, Cederflychtska Huset. **Västerviks Museum** outlines the history of the town. Part of the museum is in the open air with traditional buildings. The railway line was closed in 1984, but train enthusiasts have reopened the part from Västervik to Hultfred, to preserve it as part of Sweden's industrial heritage.

Västerviks Museum

⊛⊛⊜ ◻Kulbacken ◻Jun–Aug: 11am–4pm daily; Sep–May: 10am–4pm Mon–Fri & Sun ◼vasterviksmuseum.se

---

About 13 km (8 miles) east of Eksjö, the Skurugata nature reserve has an impressive canyon in porphyritic rock, 800 m (2,625 ft) long and 35 m (115 ft) deep.

⓯
Färjestaden

🅰E6 **🚗 Öland Road 136**

The Ölandsbron Bridge connects Färjestaden on Öland with the mainland. The first turning to the north in Färjestaden leads to **Ölands Djurpark**, a popular place for families. The zoo has 200 species of animals, a water world and amusement park, circus and theatre productions.

Beijershamn, south of Färjestaden, is an interesting reed-covered birdwatching area with wetland and archipelago species. Not far

---

INSIDER TIP
Viktoria Dagen

The annual Victoria Day celebrations take place on 14 July in Öland, where the Swedish Royal Family spend their summer holiday. Expect crowds singing "Happy Birthday" and a fantastic concert.

---

from here is Karlevistenen, a remarkable 11th-century runestone dedicated to a hero named Sibbe the Wise.

Vickleby village street, on road 136 to the south, is the epitome of idyllic Öland. Next to the church is Capellagården School of Craft and Design, founded by furniture designer Carl Malmsten in the 1950s and currently a centre for various design-related courses.

Ölands Djurpark

🐾🎡🎪🎭🐘 🚗3 km (2 miles) N of Färjestaden 📅Easter-Sep: 10am–6pm daily 🌐olandsdjurpark.com

---

⓰
Kalmar

🅰E6 **🚗Småland E22** **✈🚆** **ℹ️Ölandskajen 9; www. kalmar.com**

Founded in the 12th century, Kalmar's key position on Kalmarsund made it a flourishing trading post and a target for Danish attack. To prevent the latter, **Kalmar Slott** was

built in 1200 and it was here that the Kalmar Union was formed in 1397, binding the Scandinavian kingdoms for 130 years. The restored castle contains furnished apartments and exhibitions.

With its twisting streets and attractive buildings, the area around the castle, Gamla Stan (old town), is made for walking. Next to the castle is **Kalmar Konstmuseum** (Art Museum), showing Swedish art.

The Italian Baroque Domkyrkan (cathedral) on the island of Kvarnholmen dates from the second half of the 17th century and was designed by Tessin the Elder. Kvarnholmen is also home to **Kalmar Läns Museum** which displays local art.

Kalmar Slott

🐾🐘🎡🎭🍴 🚗Kungsgatan 1 📅May–Sep: daily; Oct–Apr: Sat & Sun 🌐kalmarslott.se

Kalmar Konstmuseum

🐾🐘🍴 🚗Stadsparken 📅11am–5pm Tue–Sun 🔒Some public hols 🌐kalmarkonstmuseum.se

Kalmar Läns Museum

🐾🐘🎡🍴 🚗Skeppsbrogatan 51 📞0480-451 300 📅10am–5pm daily 🔒Some public hols

> **Blå Jungfrun is mainly bare pink granite, polished smooth by ice and water, with deciduous forest in the south.**

↑ Boathouses on Öland, with Blå Jungfrun in the distance

🄱
Blå Jungfrun

🄰F6 🄰Småland 20 km (12 miles) E of Oskarshamn ⛴From Oskarshamn & Byxelkrok 🄸Oskarshamn Tourist Office; 0491-770 72

Located in the northern part of Kalmarsund, the sound separating the mainland from the island of Öland, the national park Blå Jungfrun (the Blue Maiden) encompasses an island about 800 m (875 yd) in diameter and the waters surrounding it. Blå Jungfrun's highest point is 86 m (282 ft) above sea level, making it easily visible from the mainland and from Öland.

According to legend, the island is the site of Blåkulla, where witches would gather, and is the subject of many a dark tale. Carl von Linné (p157) described it as "horrible". Others have found it romantic, including the poet Verner von Heidenstam, who was married here in 1896. Blå Jungfrun is mainly bare pink granite, polished smooth by ice and water, with deciduous forest in the south and a population of black guillemots. It is unlikely that it was inhabited, although a stone labyrinth was built here and there are caves. Boats run from Oskarshamn or Byxelkrok (p188) to Blå Jungfrun, once a day, weather permitting. The journey takes 90 minutes from Oskarshamn.

←

The magnificent Kalmar Castle at sunset; internal courtyard within the castle walls (inset)

🄱
Borgholm

🄰E6 🄰Öland Road 136

In summer Borgholm town centre bustles with shoppers and boats fill the guest harbour. Borgholm became a seaside resort at the end of the 19th century and some of the older buildings still have their ornamented wooden verandas.

Dominating the town is **Borgholms Slottsruin**, a vast ruined medieval castle with a museum inside. Guides recount the history of the ruins and offer special tours for children in summer. Also in summer, the castle stage is a popular venue for concerts.

Just south of the centre lies **Sollidens Slott**, the summer residence of the Swedish Royal Family, completed in 1906. On 14 July each year, the birthday of Crown Princess Victoria is celebrated here with various events. Exhibitions are held in the pavilion.

Borgholms Slottsruin
🄰🄰🄰🄰🄰🄰 🄰1 km (half a mile) S of Borgholm 🄾Apr-Sep: daily; Oct-Mar: by appt 🄦borgholmsslott.se

Sollidens Slott
🄰🄰🄰🄰🄰 🄰1.5 km (1 mile) S of Borgholm 🄾Mid-May-mid-Sep: daily 🄦sollidens slott.se

→

A black-tailed godwit *(inset)* and Långe Jan at Öland's southern cape

19

Öland's Southern Cape

A E7 **A** Öland **i** Ottenby Naturum; 0485-66 12 00 (Jun-Aug: daily)

In the mid-16th century the area around Öland's southern cape became a royal hunting ground, and descendants of the fallow deer introduced by Johan III in 1569 can be spotted even today. The northern boundary of his land is marked by Karl X's wall, built in the 1650s to prevent local people and their animals from entering the grounds. To the south, Sweden's oldest and tallest lighthouse, Långe Jan, stands 41.6 m (136 ft) high, and offers amazing views.

At the southernmost tip of the island is a nature reserve, Ottenby Naturum, along with **Ottenby Fågelstation** (the bird station). Ornithologists come here to study migratory birds close up and conduct research. The station has many bird-related exhibitions and offers guided tours around the nature reserve.

Ottenby Fågelstation

⊘⊘😊 **A** Öland's southern cape **O** Mar-Oct: daily; set guided bird tours mid-Mar-mid-Nov **w** ottenby.se

20

Byxelkrok

A F6 **A** Öland Road 136

Almost at the northernmost end of Öland's west coast on Kalmarsund is the popular old fishing village of Byxelkrok. Boats to Blå Jungfrun *(p187)* depart from here.

A few miles north is Neptuni Åkrar, an area of ridged stones resembling ploughed fields with ancient monuments, including the Iron Age stone ship Forgallaskeppet.

Nearby Löttorp is home to a paradise for car-mad kids – **Lådbilslandet** (Boxcar Country). Here youngsters can drive a real car, ranging from buses to trucks, around a miniature city. There is also an amusement park.

Böda, 10 km (6 miles) north of Löttorp, has wonderful sandy beaches. It is also the site of **Skäftekärr Järnåldersby**, a reconstructed Iron Age village. Complete with goods, animals, houses and costumed guides, it provides an insight into Iron Age life. The village also has an arboretum with a collection of *Thuja occidentalis* (cypress) planted in the 19th century.

Lådbilslandet

⊘⊘😊⊕ **A** 40 km (25 miles) N of Borgholm **O** Mid-Jun-mid-Aug: daily **w** ladbilslandetoland.com

Skäftekärr Järnåldersby

⊘⊘😊⊕ **A** 50 km (31 miles) N of Borgholm **C** 070-634 19 50 **O** End Jun-Aug: daily; other times: call to check

STAY

㉑

Ölands Museum

🅐E6 **🄺Öland 20 km (12 miles) NE of Färjestaden** **🕐Jun-Aug: 11am-5:30pm daily; Sep: 11am-5pm Sat & Sun** **🆆olandsmuseum.se**

Himmelsberga, in the middle of the island, is home to Ölands Museum, an open-air museum of art and cultural history. It centres on a well-preserved linear village with 18th- and 19th-century farms. The interiors of the houses show how life was once lived, and pigs, chickens and sheep are kept in the grounds. A shop sells crafts and books about Öland. Next to the museum is a gallery showing work by local artists. North of Himmelsberga, Gärdslösa Kyrka is one of the most interesting churches on Öland. It dates from the mid-13th century and has fine limestone murals, a beautiful votive

→

Gateway to the fort at Eketorps Borg, housing an informative museum

ship and a 17th-century pulpit. The fort of Ismantorps Borg in Långlöt has been dated to the 5th century. Archaeological finds show that it was probably an important marketplace and cult site. It is encircled by a wall up to 6 m (19 ft) thick and 3 m (10 ft) high with nine gates.

Öland's best preserved row of windmills can be seen in Lerkaka, just to the south of Himmelsberga. The mills are widely considered to be among the country's most beautiful; one is open to visitors.

㉒

Eketorps Borg

🅐E6 **🄺Öland** **🕐May-Aug; times vary, check website** **🆆eketorp.se**

The only one of Öland's ancient forts to have been completely excavated, Eketorps Borg was built in three stages. It originated in the 4th century to protect the population and was later converted to a fortified farming village with military functions, but was abandoned in the 7th century. It was thrust into use again at the end of the 12th century in the war between the royal houses of Erik and Sverker.

The fort has been partly reconstructed to show how people lived and worked in the Iron Age. In the museum numerous artifacts uncovered on the site are on display, including jewellery and weapons.

Around 10 km (6 miles) north of Eketorp lies Seby Gravfält with no fewer than 285 visible ancient monuments in the form of different kinds of burial sites, mainly dating from the Iron Age.

㉓

Stora Alvaret

🅐E6 **🄺Öland**

The extraordinary limestone plain of Stora Alvaret dominates southern Öland. Here, the bedrock is around 400 million years old and is covered in a thin layer of soil that was used from prehistoric times as grazing land. In the year 2000 the area was declared a UNESCO World Heritage Site.

In spring the ground is covered in pasque flowers (*Pulsatilla pratensis*). The dominant grass species include meadow oat-grass (*Helictotrichon pratense*) and sheep's fescue (*Festuca ovina*). Juniper bushes are common and lichen inches over rock.

The extreme climate has created almost desert-like conditions to which the flora and fauna have had to adapt. Mountain and Mediterranean plants grow here as well as a unique species of rock-rose (*Helianthemum oelandicum*). The island is a resting place for cranes, but conditions on the plain are so harsh that only a few birds, such as the skylark and wheatear, have adapted to the environment.

A DRIVING TOUR
KINGDOM OF CRYSTAL

Length 140 km (85 miles) **Stopping-off points** Many glassworks have a café/restaurant and some of the larger ones hold herring evenings **Route** Växjö–Nybro, Road 25

Växjö, home to the Swedish Glass Museum *(p185)*, is an ideal starting point for a driving tour of at least nine of the famous glassworks set in the beautiful countryside between Växjö and Nybro. Access to timber and water accounts for the concentration of glassworks in this area of Småland, where forest, lakes and waterways dominate the landscape. The glassworks are mostly only 20–30 km (12–20 miles) apart, and many have shops offering discounted items and displays of the designers' latest creations.

Locator Map
For more detail see p176

Bergdala's signature is blue-edged glass, but designers are pushing the boundaries when it comes to colour and shape. The temperature of the smelting oven is a constant 1,150° C (2,102° F).

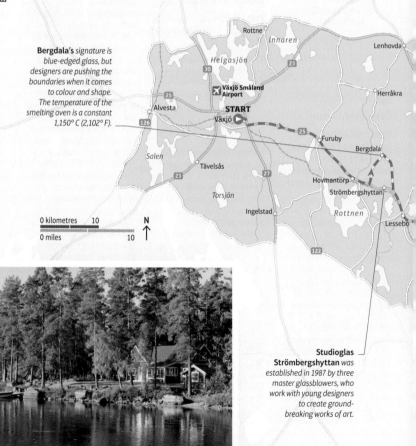

0 kilometres   10
0 miles   10

N ↑

Studioglas **Strömbergshyttan** *was established in 1987 by three master glassblowers, who work with young designers to create ground-breaking works of art.*

↑ The beautiful province of Småland is rich in lakes and forests

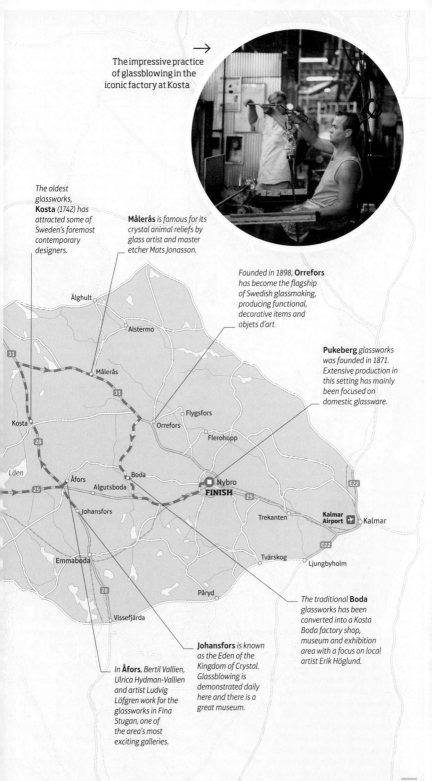

→ The impressive practice of glassblowing in the iconic factory at Kosta

The oldest glassworks, **Kosta** (1742) has attracted some of Sweden's foremost contemporary designers.

Målerås is famous for its crystal animal reliefs by glass artist and master etcher Mats Jonasson.

Founded in 1898, **Orrefors** has become the flagship of Swedish glassmaking, producing functional, decorative items and objets d'art.

Pukeberg glassworks was founded in 1871. Extensive production in this setting has mainly been focused on domestic glassware.

Älghult

Alstermo

Målerås

Flygsfors

Kosta

Orrefors

Flerohopp

Läen

Åfors

Boda

Algutsboda

□ Nybro
FINISH

Johansfors

Trekanten

Kalmar Airport ✈ ○Kalmar

Emmaboda

Tvärskog ○Ljungbyholm

Påryd

Vissefjärda

The traditional **Boda** *glassworks has been converted into a Kosta Boda factory shop, museum and exhibition area with a focus on local artist Erik Höglund.*

Johansfors is known as the Eden of the Kingdom of Crystal. Glassblowing is demonstrated daily here and there is a great museum.

In **Åfors**, Bertil Vallien, Ulrica Hydman-Vallien and artist Ludvig Löfgren work for the glassworks in Fina Stugan, one of the area's most exciting galleries.

GOTLAND

In geological terms, the island of Gotland is fairly old. It consists of layers of rocks that were deposited in a tropical sea during the Silurian period around 400 million years ago. Fossils can still be found washed up along the shore. At the northern- and southernmost tips of the island, the limestone comes to the surface and plant life is sparse. The high limestone cliffs with their large bird population are broken by sandy beaches, and standing offshore are numerous extraordinary sea stacks, known as *raukar*.

A wealth of archaeological finds have been uncovered on the island, from the ship burials of the Bronze Age to the silver treasure of the Viking period. More than 90 medieval churches dot the landscape and the museums have numerous artifacts from the Hanseatic period and the Danish King Valdemar Atterdag's capture of Visby in 1361.

In the centre of the island forest dominates. The warm autumns and mild winters allow trees such as walnut and apricot to survive in sheltered spots. No fewer than 35 different orchids can be found on the island and the flower meadows that blossom at midsummer are beautiful. The island's fauna lacks the large mammals of the mainland, but there is a herd of *russ*, Gotland's little wild ponies.

Gotlanders have their own dialect, *Gutamål*, and their own traditions. These are especially reflected in the games of the annual Gotland Olympics and in the Medieval Week in Visby.

GOTLAND

Must See

1 Visby

Experience More

2 Fårö
3 Slite
4 Bunge
5 Tingstäde
6 Lummelundagrottan
7 Bro Kyrka
8 Roma
9 Lojsta
10 Ljugarn
11 Gotska Sandön
12 Karlsöarna
13 Fröjel Kyrka
14 Petes
15 Hoburgen

Nynäshamn

Irevik

Stenkyrka

LUMMELUNDAGROTTAN 6

TINGSTÄDE 5

149   148

Visby Airport
BRO
7 KYRKA

1 VISBY

Vatlings
Gård

Hogklint

Follingbo

← Oskarshamn,
Västervik

Stenkumla

143

Dalhem

Gnisvard   140

142

8 ROMA

Mästerby

Tofta Strand

GOTLAND   143

Västergarn

Sanda   Hejde   Buttle

Klintehamn   141   Lojsta Hed

Etelhem

Lilla
Karlsö   13
FRÖJEL
KYRKA   9 LOJSTA   144

KARLSÖARNA 12

Stånga   Lau Kyrka

Stora
Karlsö

När

Hemse

PETES 14   140   142   Rone

Ronehamn

Havdhemn

Kattlunds

Baltic
Sea

Burgsvik

142   Faludden

Vändburg

HOBURGEN 15

0 kilometres   15
0 miles   15

N
↑

1

VISBY

F5 **Gotland** 🚌🚢 **Donnerska huset, Donners plats 1; www.gotland.com**

A town of roses and ruins, the walled city of Visby is a UNESCO World Heritage Site as well as a popular party town in summer. Its cobbled streets are lined with picturesque cottages, haunting medieval ruins and a multitude of cafés and bars. Away from the busy, more touristy parts of Strandgatan, Stora Torget and around the pleasure boat harbour, the evocative ambience recalls the town's medieval history.

① 🍴 🖥
Stora Torget

At the heart of Visby lies Stora Torget (Big Square) from which the roads to the town gates radiate. This is still a focal point for visitors to Visby, despite the development of a modern town centre outside Österport, and there is a lively market here in summer. Several attractive medieval houses surround the square, including the restaurants of Gutekällaren, with its characteristic stepped gable, and Munkkällaren, with its deep vaulted cellars and inner courtyard.

The ruins of the church of Sta Karin (St Catherine), dating from the 1230s, form a dramatic backdrop on the southern side of Stora Torget. In the shadow of the ruins is Rosengård, a café where generations have come to enjoy good coffee and delicious pastries.

② 🎨 🖌 🖥 🛍
Gotlands Museum

Strandgatan 14 **May-Sep: daily; Oct-Apr: Tue-Sun** **gotlandsmuseum.se**

Gotland's long history, going back to prehistoric times, has made this collection one of Sweden's richest regional museums. It is housed in a former royal distillery, built in the 1770s.

The Hall of Picture Stones contains an impressive array of carved stones from the 5th to the 11th centuries, some with runic inscriptions. Next door, the Gravkammaren (Grave Room) shows burial customs from ancient times to the Vikings. Several skeletons are on display, including the 8,000-year-old Stenkyrkamannen (Stenkyrka Man). One of the most remarkable sights is the collection of Viking silver treasure – no fewer than 700 items have been recovered from sites around the island.

Church art is also well represented. The museum holds the original, Gothic Öja Madonna (Öja church in southern Gotland has to make do with a copy). A large gallery displays medieval furniture and collections from later periods.

0 metres 300
0 yards 300
N

*Baltic
Sea*

Town Walls

Botaniska Trädgården ④

⑤ Ruins of St Nicolai

③ Ruins of Helge And

St Drotten
Gotlandssmycken St Lars
Domkyrkan Sta Maria

Almedalen

Gotlands Museum ②
① Stora Torget

i DONNERS PLATS
Kvinnfolki
Konstmuseum

Harbour

Kranku Te & Kaffe
Ruins of St Hans

Town Walls

Bus Station

↑ The pretty rose-lined lane of Fiskargränd leads up from Strandgatan

SHOP

Kranku Te & Kaffe

This charming tea shop, founded in 1977, is known for its own blends. It also sells coffee and confectionary.

🏠 St Hansplan 4
📞 0498-217 481

Kvinnfolki

This place sells crafts, furniture and jewellery.

🏠 Donners plats 4
🌐 kvinnfolki.se

Gotlandssmycken

Stunning handmade jewellery is on offer here.

🏠 Strandgatan 32
🌐 gotlandssmycken.se

③

Ruins of Helge And

🏠 Helge Ands Plan
ℹ️ Gotlands Museum, 0498-292 700.

Helgeandstiftelserna was a religious order founded in the early 13th century to take care of the poor and the sick. The ruin of Helge And (Church of the Holy Spirit) is one of Visby's most striking church ruins and dates from this period. The octagonal building has two floors. Two large staircases lead up to the first floor, which were designed in this way to allow patients from the hospital to reach the church via a passage from the upper floor. Today the ruins are used for cultural events and are open to visitors in the summer.

④

Botaniska Trädgården

🏠 Strandgatan ⏰ 24 hrs daily 🌐 visbybotan.se

Gotland's botanical garden was founded in 1856 by the Badande Wännerna (Society of the Bathing Friends), a gentlemen's club. To reach the garden, follow the promenade along the shore from the harbour and go through Kärleksporten (Gate of Love).

Inside the gate, the lush park offers a spice-scented herb garden and a pretty rose garden (at its peak Jul & Aug). There are more than 16,000 species including many plants and trees that are exotic to the Nordic countries, such as walnut, mulberry and ginkgo. In its midst stand the ivy-clad ruins of St Olof's church and there is a water-lily pond, and a small pavilion making an ideal resting place.

⑤

Ruins of St Nicolai

🏠 St Nicolaigatan 📞 0498-269 000

The ruins of St Nicolai are all that remains of a Dominican monastery founded in Visby in 1228. The Black Friars expanded it and built a Gothic cathedral that they dedicated to the patron saint of sailors and merchants, St Nicholas. When the people of Lübeck stormed Visby in 1525 much of the cathedral was destroyed.

Between 1929 and 1990 a pageant, *Petrus de Dacia*, was performed here every summer. Today, musical and theatrical events are staged in the ruins and the Gotland Chamber Music Festival is usually held here each summer.

VISBY'S TOWN WALL

The medieval inner town of Visby is shaped by its mighty town wall, almost 3.5 km (2 miles) in length. Construction of the wall began at the end of the 13th century. It was originally 5.5 m (18 ft) high and designed to protect against attack from the sea. On the inland side, the wall was surrounded by a deep moat. Within the ramparts, narrow cobbled streets are lined with tightly packed houses, wealthy merchants' homes and the ruins of historic churches. UNESCO described it as the "best fortified commercial city in northern Europe" and declared it a World Heritage Site in 1995.

A SHORT WALK
VISBY

Distance 1 km (0.5 miles) **Time** 15 minutes

Within the walls, Visby is relatively small and the sights are within easy walking distance. The main streets run north to south: Strandgatan with historic sights and nightlife spots, St Hansgatan with its churches, and Adelsgatan, the shopping street leading from Söderport (South Gate) to Stora Torget, the main square. North of here are quieter residential streets and alleyways, making for a lovely stroll. Near Norderport (North Gate) it is possible to climb up on the ramparts and admire the magnificent wall. As you wander through the warren of cobbled streets, take your time to soak up the town's medieval beauty and stop at one of the pretty cafés to enjoy a coffee and a slice of cake.

Locator Map
For more detail see p196

↑ A narrow medieval street in Visby's town centre

Visby town wall *has 19 towers and gates, including Kruttornet (Gunpowder Tower).*

Gotlands Museum *is devoted to the island's past from ancient times to modern day.*

START

PACK-HUS PLAN

Burmeisterska Huset *was built by Hans Burmeister, a wealthy merchant from Lübeck, in the 17th century. It is one of the best-preserved examples of its kind in Visby.*

RIGAGRAND

LYBSKA GR.

BIRGERS GRAND

STRANDGATAN

DUBBGR

STRANDGATAN

MELLANGATAN

DONNERS PLATS

Did You Know?

In August, Visby hosts events for Medieval Week, including jousting, concerts and fire shows.

St Drotten is the sister church to St Lars.

St Lars is also known as the church of Sta Anna after the mother of the Virgin Mary.

Kapitelhusgården, a leafy medieval courtyard, provides a lovely setting where the public can try their hand at medieval crafts. During the summer, it can become busy, especially during Medieval Week.

Domkyrkan Sta Maria, completed in 1225, was the church of the German merchants. It is the only one of Visby's 17 medieval churches which is not in ruins.

FINISH

VÄRKROGATAN

SKOLGATAN

S:T DROTTENS GATA

SKYROGATAN

MELLANGATAN

S:T HANSGATAN

STORA TORGET

Entertainment focuses on the main square, **Stora Torget**. Munkkällaren, with a terrace on the square, is one of the many restaurants and bars here.

Franciscan monks built the church and monastery of **Sta Karin** (St Catherines) in 1233. Rebuilt in the 14th century, it was destroyed in 1525 by an army from Lübeck.

0 metres		50	N ↑
0 yards		50	

On display in the **Konstmuseet** (Museum of Art) is Visby Town Wall, a painting by Hanna Pauli (1864–1940).

→ Ruins of Sta Karin Church along one side of Stora Torget, Visby's town square

EXPERIENCE MORE

2 Fårö

🅰 G5 🅰 Gotland ℹ Mar-Sep at Fårö church; Oct-Feb at Donnerska huset, Donners plats 1; www.gotland.com

A summer paradise for visitors from the mainland and further afield, Fårö appears exotic even to a Gotlander from the main island. Lying at the northern tip of Gotland, the little island of Fårö has a language and traditions all of its own. In the summer months car ferries shuttle back and forth on the 15-minute trip from Fårösund to Broa. At other times of year the service is more limited.

Sparse, low pine forest and moorland with swamp and marshland cover the island. There are sheep everywhere.

Off the northwest coast are the spectacular limestone stacks, known as *raukar*, of Langham-mars and Diger-huvud. The sand dune of Ullahau is at the island's northern end, and Sudersand's long sandy beach is popular with holiday-makers. The easternmost cape of Holmudden is topped by the 30-m (98-ft) high lighthouse, Fårö Fyr. Roughly in the centre of the island, **Fårö Kyrka** offers views over the inlet of Kyrkviken. The church contains paintings dating from 1618 and 1767, which depict seal hunters being rescued from the sea.

Fårö Kyrka

⊛ 🏠 5 km (3 miles) N of Broa 📞 0498-221 074 🕓 Jun-Aug: daily; Sep-May: Sat & Sun

3 Slite

🅰 F5 🅰 Gotland Road 147 ℹ Donnerska huset, Donners plats 1; www. slitestrandby.se

Occupying a stunning setting in a bay facing its own archipelago is the town of Slite. Slite had a long and troubled history from the Viking period onwards, and development only really took off in the late 19th century with an upturn in seafaring. Today the cement factory is a major employer.

In summer, the fine sandy beaches, harbour, tennis courts, stunning stone stacks and lime kiln attract holiday-makers. The islands offshore are perfect for short trips, including Enholmen with Karlsvärd fortress, which dates from 1853–6.

On the opposite side of the bay is Hellvi, with the old

harbour of Kyllaj. The quiet beach is in a beautiful setting overlooking weathered sea stacks.

Northwest of Slite is **Lärbro Kyrka**, a mid-13th century church with an 11th-century watch tower next to it. Buried in the churchyard are 44 former prisoners of war from the German concentration camps, who came to the hospital at Lärbro in 1945.

St Olofsholm, nearby, is dedicated to Olav the Holy, who visited Gotland in 1029 to convert the island to Christianity. In medieval times it was a place of pilgrimage. This is also the site of Ytterholmen's large group of limestone stacks and a glorious pebble beach.

Fascinating shapes *(inset)* formed by eroded stacks on Färö's coast

Lärbro Kyrka

Ⓐ Ⓑ 🏠 10 km (6 miles) N of Slite 📞 0498-222 700 🕐 Mid-May-mid-Sep: daily

---

④
Bunge

🅰F5 🏠 Gotland Road 148

The village of Bunge is known for its 14th-century church, **Bunge Kyrka**, built in Gothic style. Its tower was constructed in the 13th century to defend an earlier church – holes from pikes and arrows in the north wall bear witness to past battles.

Inside are notable limestone paintings dating from around 1400, which are thought to depict the Teutonic Knights fighting the Vitalien brothers, pirates of Mecklenburg who occupied Gotland in the 1390s. In the chancel is a poor box in limestone signed by stone-mason Lafrans Botvidarson, dating from the 13th century.

Standing next to the church is **Bungemuseet**, one of Sweden's largest rural museums. It was created in 1917 by Bunge schoolteacher Theodor Erlandsson, who wanted to demonstrate how the people of Gotland used to live. In the fields next to the school he gathered together cottages, buildings and cultural objects from different parts of Gotland covering the 17th, 18th and 19th centuries as well as four carved stones from the 8th century. The museum hosts many events in the summer, including medieval tournaments, markets and handicraft festivals. In Snäckersstugan cottage, with the date 1700 carved into the gable, visitors can enjoy a cup of coffee and attempt to make out the Gotland proverbs that are painted on the ceiling.

Just north of Bunge is the busy Fårösund, one of the larger towns in northern Gotland, with around 1,000 inhabitants. For many years

↑ Building at Bungemuseet with a thatched roof of Gotland sedge

the area was dominated by the military, and countless young men were drilled here in defence of the island.

Bunge Kyrka

🏠 60 km (37 miles) N of Visby 📞 0498-222 700 🕐 Mid-May-mid-Sep: 9am-noon Mon, Tue & Thu, 1-3pm Wed

Bungemuseet

Ⓐ Ⓑ Ⓒ Ⓓ 🏠 2 km (1 mile) E of Bunge 🕐 Mid-May-mid-Sep: 11am-4pm daily 🌐 bungemuseet.se

---

⑤
Tingstäde

🅰F5 🏠 23 km (14 miles) N of Visby 🛈 Donnerska huset, Donners plats 1; 0498-201 700

Halfway between Visby and Fårösund on Road 148 lies Tingstäde, a community best known for its sea rescue radio station and its marsh. The church here dates from the 13th and 14th centuries and has one of the highest towers on the island.

Tingstäde marsh is, in fact, a shallow lake and popular, child-friendly bathing spot. Submerged in the centre of the lake is Bulverket, a 10th- to 11th-century fortress surrounded by a palisade of 1,500 stakes.

Lummelundagrottan

⚐F5 **🚗Road 149, 13 km
(8 miles) N of Visby**
📞0498-27 30 50 **🕐May–
Sep, plus some weekends;
call ahead to book**

In 1948 two local school
boys discovered an opening
in the ground in Martebo
marsh and crawled in. They
had chanced upon the
entrance to a network of
caves and passageways, now
the major tourist attraction
of Lummelundagrottan.

Today the entrance is at
Lummelundas Bruk. Exploration of the caves continues,
but the part that is open for
viewing provides a fantastic
show of stalactites and
stalagmites, magic mirrors
of water and spine-tinglingly
tight openings. There are
various tour options, including
the Cave Adventure aided
by small boats, and an hour-
long tour for children aged
4 to 6 years.

Immediately to the south
of the caves is the lovely
Krusmyntagården, a herb
garden designed in
traditional monastic style
with wonderful views over
the sea.

Krusmyntagården

🎨🍷🛍️🍴 **🚗Road
149, 10 km (6 miles)
N of Visby**
🕐May–Sep: daily
🌐krusmynta.se

⑦ Bro Kyrka

⚐F5 **🚗Road 148, 11 km
(7 miles) NE of Visby** **📞08-
584 808 80** **🕐Mid-May–
mid-Sep: 9am–5pm daily**

Tradition has it that Bro
Kyrka is built over a votive
well, and in medieval times it
was a famous votive church,
particularly among sailors.
The building dates from the
13th and 14th centuries.
Inside the church, the prayer
chamber contains notable
5th-century picture stones.

About 1 km (half a mile)
north of Bro Kyrka, on Road
148, are two picture stones
known as "Bro Stajnkällingar".
According to legend, two
elderly women were turned
to stone for arguing on the
way to the Christmas Mass.

From Bro, a turning leads
to Fole church on Road 147,
and a short detour takes you
to **Vatlings Gård**. The estate
has Gotland's best-preserved
medieval stone house
outside Visby and is well
worth a visit. Note the
steep saddle roof and
stone staircase inside.

Vatlings Gård
🚗Road 147, 18 km
18 km (11 miles) E
of Visby 🕐Daily
📞0498-292 700

⑧ Roma

⚐F5 **🚗18 km (11 miles)
SE of Visby** **ℹ️Roma
Kungsgård; 070-543 33 34**
**🕐May–Aug: 10am–6pm
daily**

Cistercian monks from Nydala
monastery in Småland founded Roma Kloster in 1164. The
monastery was built on the
pattern of the French mother
monastery and became a
religious centre for the entire
Baltic region. The three-aisle
church in the Fontenay style
was completed in the 13th
century. The monastery was
abandoned during the
Reformation in 1530 and
ended up in the ownership of
the Danish crown as a royal
manor under Visborg Castle.

When Gotland came under
Swedish rule in 1645, the
monastery was practically in
ruins. The county governor
used materials from the site
to build his residence, Roma
Kungsgård, in 1733. Only the
church remained intact, and
that was used as a stable. In
1822, Roma Kungsgård served
as an army store.

The ruins of Roma mona-
stery bear witness to the
monks' skill in construction
techniques. The beautiful
vaulted ceilings are reminiscent of Roman aqueducts.

↓ The fine medieval
exterior of Bro Kyrka

Beautiful Gotland ponies running freely around the Lojsta Hed area ↑

In the summer, Romateatern performs Shakespearian plays on an open-air stage that is set among the ruins.

---

⑨
Lojsta

🅰F6 🏠15 km (9 miles) S of Visby 🛈 Donnerska huset, Donners plats 1; 0498-201 700

Like so many of Gotland's churches, Lojsta Kyrka dates from the mid-13th century. The choir has ornamental paintings and the figures above the triumphal arch are by the master known as "Egypticus" in the 14th century.

On Lojsta Hed, an area of forest and heath north of the church, lives a herd of semi-wild Gotland ponies (russ), the stubborn little horse native to the island. The animals are owned by local farmers and by Gotlands Läns Hushållnings-sällskap. Several annual events are organized, such as the release of the stallion in early June, and the high point of the year, the Gotland pony judging, at the end of July.

A few miles from Lojsta near Etelhem is a large building with a sedge roof, Lojstahallen. This is a superb reconstruction of a late Iron Age hall building. Next to it is a medieval fortress, Lojsta Slott.

⑩
Ljugarn

🅰F6 🏠40 km (25 miles) SW of Visby 🛈 Donnerska huset, Donners plats 1; 0498-201 700

This cheerful resort was Gotland's first and makes a good centre for touring the southeast of the island. There was a harbour here long before Russian forces raided Ljugarn on their way to laying waste to the east coast of Sweden in 1714–18. By 1900, the small community, with its long sandy beach, limestone sea stacks and guesthouse, had become a popular bathing spot.

South of Ljugarn is the 13th- to 14th-century Lau Kyrka. This large church has a triumphal crucifix from the 13th century and excellent acoustics for the concerts held there.

Northwest of Ljugarn, Torsburgen fortress was built in the 3rd or 4th century. It is protected by naturally steep slopes and a wall 7 m (23 ft) high and up to 24 m (79 ft) wide. To reach it, take the forest road from the 146 towards Östergarn, 2 km (1 mile) east of Kräklingbo church.

About 6 km (4 miles) south of Ljugarn, at Guffride, are seven Bronze Age stone-settings, in the form of ships, and are the largest on Gotland.

GAME OF VARPA

This outdoor game dates back to the Viking Age and has survived in Gotland. Its concept is similar to boules and horseshoes except it is played with a flat heavy object that is called a "varpa" instead of balls. The object of the game is to throw the varpa as close to a stick as possible. "Varpa" is an old word meaning "to throw".

Birds gathering on the rocks around Stora Karlsö's nature reserve

11

Gotska Sandön

🗺️ G5 🚩 40km (25 miles) N of Fårö 🚢 From Nynäshamn and Fårösund ℹ️ Donnerska huset, Donners plats 1; 0498-201 700; booking: 0498-240 450

The most isolated island in the Baltic, Gotska Sandön is one of Sweden's national parks and features a unique landscape of deserted, constantly changing sandy beaches and dunes, pine forests and a rich flora. There are migratory birds and unusual beetles, but only one mammal, the hare. The island became a national park in 1909.

Gotska Sandön has been inhabited since the dawn of civilization, although the population has never been large. Colonies of grey seals led seal hunters to settle on the island and the dangerous waters offshore attracted wreck plunderers. In the 17th and 18th centuries, sheep were grazed here and later crops were grown. As recently as the 1950s, a few lighthouse

keepers and their families (and one female teacher) lived here, but now the lighthouse is automated and the only permanent resident is a caretaker.

There is no harbour and boat traffic from Fårösund or Nynäshamn is infrequent and dependent on the weather conditions. It is possible to camp or stay in a shared sleeping hut or cottage, but accommodation must be booked before arrival.

12

Karlsöarna

🗺️ F6 🚩 Gotland 🚢 Stora Karlsö: from Klintehamn during summer season only; Lilla Karlsö: from Klintehamn ℹ️ Donnerska huset, Donners plats 1; 0498-201 700 or 0498-240 500

Several myths have been spun around Stora and Lilla Karlsö, the rocky islands together known as Karlsöarna that lie 6.5 km (4 miles) off the west coast of Gotland.

Stora Karlsö covers 2.5 sq km (1 sq mile) and is a nature reserve with steep cliffs, caves such as "Stora Förvar", moorland, leafy groves, and rare flowers and birds. Between the bare rocks in May and June, the orchids *Adam och Eva (Dactylorhiza sambucina)* and *Sankt Pers nycklar (Orchis mascula)* form carpets of blooms. Sea birds such as auks, gulls and eider duck can be seen. Razorbills lay their eggs among the stones on the beach, while guillemots prefer the shelves of the steep cliffs.

A guided tour lasts for a couple of hours and is included in the price of the boat crossing. There is also a museum in Norderhamn.

Did You Know?

Stora Karlsö is the world's second oldest nature reserve after Yellowstone National Park in the US.

Like Stora Karlsö, Lilla Karlsö is also a nature reserve. The island has been grazed by sheep since the Bronze Age. It is home to guillemots, razorbills and gulls, while eider duck, little terns and velvet scoters nest on the flat land. The Swedish Society for Nature Conservation organizes informative guided tours. There is a youth hostel on the island, which must be booked in advance.

---

13 🎧

Fröjel Kyrka

🅰F6 🚗40 km (25 miles) S of Visby 📞0498-240 005 🕐Daily

Set in a stunning location, high up overlooking the sea, is the saddle-roof church of Fröjel Kyrka, built in the 12th and 13th centuries. Inside is a triumphal crucifix by the craftsman who created the rood screen of Öja church. The churchyard has an ancient maze, which indicates that the site was used long before the arrival of Christianity.

North of the church lies the magnificent Gannarve Skeppssättning (Gannarve Ship Barrow), which is considered to be one of the best in Gotland. This has been dated to the late Bronze Age (1000–300 BC) and is 30 m (98 ft) long and 5 m (16 ft) wide.

14

Petes

🅰F6 🚗Gotland ℹGotlands Museum (mid-Jun–mid-Aug: 11:30am–2:30pm daily); 0498-292 700

To the southwest of Gotland, just before Hablingbo church on coastal road 140, there is a turning to the seaside community of Petes. Here, the well-preserved houses show Gotland's architecture from the 18th and 19th centuries.

For younger visitors, Barnens Petes displays classic toys such as stilts, wooden rifles, hobby horses, hoops and wooden dolls.

15

Hoburgen

🅰F6 🚗80 km (50 miles) S of Visby

Far to the south lies Hoburgen, a 35-m- (115-ft-) high steep cliff of fossil-rich limestone with seams of the local red Hoburgen marble. On the clifftop is a lighthouse that was built in 1846. From here it is 176 km (97 miles) to the northernmost lighthouse on the island of Fårö.

Below the lighthouse is one of Sweden's most famous sea stacks, Hoburgsgubben (the Old Man of Hoburg), standing guard outside the caves of Skattkammaren (the Treasure Chamber) and Sängkammaren (the Bed Chamber).

Hoburgen is a favourite spot for ornithologists, who come to study the multitude of birds that swoop over Gotland's southernmost outpost all year round. There is a restaurant nearby, which is only open in summer.

→

The prominent Hoburgen lighthouse marks the southern tip of Gotland

SOUTHERN GÖTALAND

Sweden's two southernmost provinces, Skåne and Blekinge, together form southern Götaland. Skåne has an undeserved reputation for being completely flat but, apart from the plain of Söderslätt, the countryside is surprisingly hilly with the rocky ridges of Söderåsen, Linderödsåsen and Romeleåsen. To the northwest, the area is bounded by the imposing Hallandsåsen ridge. Blekinge, criss-crossed by rivers and lakes, is known as the Garden of Sweden. It has its own island archipelago with sheltered harbours. North, towards the border with Småland, the wilder forest landscape predominates.

Throughout southern Götaland the Danish influence prior to 1645 is still evident, not least in the architecture, which differs greatly from elsewhere in Sweden. A common sight in rural Skåne is the traditional, often half-timbered farmhouse with a thatched roof, built around a cobbled courtyard. Castles and manor houses, in many cases built by the Danish nobility, are a feature of the countryside. In the coastal communities, former fishing huts are today cherished by their summer residents.

Having been sparring partners in the long-distant past, Sweden and Denmark are now linked by the Öresund Bridge from Malmö to Copenhagen. Both sides of the sound are collaborating on the development of the Swedish–Danish region, Öresund.

SOUTHERN GÖTALAND

Must Sees

① Malmö

② Karlskrona

Experience More

③ Bjärehalvön

④ Kullabygden

⑤ Helsingborg

⑥ Klippan

⑦ Bosjökloster

⑧ Frostavallen

⑨ Dalby

⑩ Lund

⑪ Landskrona

⑫ Trelleborg

⑬ Kristianstad

⑭ Skanör/Falsterbo

⑮ Ystad

⑯ Sölvesborg

⑰ Kristianopel

⑱ Karlshamn

⑲ Ronneby

Kayaking down the crystal-clear canal in the centre of Malmö ↑

❶

MALMÖ

⌖ D7 **⌂ Skåne** **✈ 30 km (19 miles) E of city centre**
🚉 Skeppsbron **🚌 Skeppsbron 10** **ℹ Carlsgatan 4A;**
www.malmotown.com

Sweden's gateway to Europe, Malmö is the country's third largest city. It was founded in the mid-13th century and was under Danish rule from 1397 to 1658. Malmö has a lively, European atmosphere and has become a centre for art and design. The old town is centred on Stortorget with its historic town hall and governor's residence.

①

Rådhuset

⌂ Stortorget
🚫 To the public

The centre of Malmö is its main square Stortorget, laid out in the 1530s. Stortorget is dominated by Rådhuset, the town hall, originally built in Renaissance Dutch style in 1546. Only the cellar remains of the medieval building, which served both as a prison and an inn. In 1860 architect Helgo Zettervall renovated the town hall, giving it a new look and making changes in the cellars (including the removal of the prisoners). The inn still stands today and is one of the most popular bars in Malmö.

②

Jörgen Kocks Hus

⌂ Stortorget
🚫 To the public

Jörgen Kocks Hus, a large six-storey building with a stepped gable roof, was constructed in 1525. Jörgen Kock was appointed mint-master for Denmark in 1518. Four years later he was elected mayor of the city, and became one of the most powerful men in Malmö. He was involved in the rebellion over the Danish succession and was captured and sentenced to death; however, he escaped and was later reinstated as mayor of Malmö in 1540.

③

Residenset

⌂ Stortorget **🚫 To the public**

In the mid-18th century two buildings, Kungshuset and Gyllenpalmska Huset, were combined to form the new governor's residence. Years later it was given a new façade by architect F W Scholander. Today, the building is home to the county governor.

④ ✍

St Petri Kyrka

⌂ Göran Olsgatan 4 **🕐 Daily**
🌐 svenskakyrkanmalmo.se

In a street behind Stortorget is Malmö's cathedral, St Petri Kyrka. Built in the 12th century, the church is modelled on St Mary's in Lübeck. The high tower, built in the late 19th century, after two older towers collapsed, is prominent in Malmö's skyline.

The cathedral has treasures from the 16th and 17th centuries when Malmö's prosperity was high. The magnificent 15-m- (49-ft-) high altar in Renaissance style is beautifully ornamented, painted and gilded. The pulpit dating from 1599 is in sandstone and black limestone. Later additions include the organ front, a masterpiece designed in 1785. The original medieval organ is one of the oldest working organs in the world and is now in Malmö Museum.

(5) (M)

Turning Torso

🏛 Lila Varvsgatan 14
🚪 To the public 🌐 skyhigh meetings.com

The Turning Torso, a futurist residential skyscraper, is the tallest building in Scandinavia. It stands in the exclusive neighbourhood of the Western Harbour and is visible for miles. Designed by architect Santiago Calatrava, the building was based on one of his earlier sculptures *The Twisting Torso*, a white marble piece resembling the shape of a twisting human being.

Completed in 2005, the skyscraper is 190 m (623 ft) tall with 54 storeys, and has a 90-degree twist throughout. Group tours to the top floors can be booked.

(6) (🎨) (M) (🖼) (🛍)

Malmö Museum

🏛 Malmöhusvägen 6
📞 040-344 400 🕐 10am–5pm daily 🚫 1 Jan, 1 May, Midsummer Eve, Midsummer, 24, 25 & 31 Dec

Originally built in 1434, the fortress of Malmöhus was largely destroyed as a result of war. It was rebuilt in 1537. Today it is the oldest preserved Renaissance castle in the Nordic region. After restoration in 1932, Malmö Museum moved into the building. Its collections cover archaeology, ethnography, the history of art and handicrafts, and zoology. The Stadsmuseet (City Museum), on the same site, illustrates the history of Malmö and surrounding Skåne with tools, weapons and domestic objects.

The Museum's aquarium is home to typical marine life from southern Sweden, as well as tropical fish including the unusual lungfish. There is also a jellyfish aquarium, terrariums with snakes and a Nocturnal Hall of bats.

Malmö's smallest museum, **Ebbas Hus**, is a tiny terraced house that has been preserved just as it was in the early 20th century.

Ebbas Hus

🏛 Snapperupsgatan 10
🕐 Wed

> Malmö Museum's aquarium is home to typical marine life from southern Sweden, as well as tropical fish including the unusual lungfish.

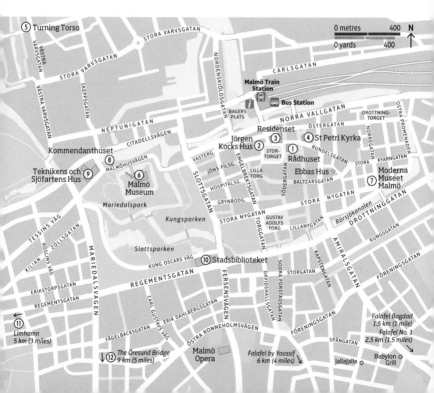

EAT

Malmö is the Swedish city of falafel. These deep-fried balls of ground chickpeas or fava beans with herbs, are a tasty snack. You'll find falafel stands all over the city, but these are some of the best.

Falafel Bagdad
🏠 Annelundsgatan 57

Ⓚ Ⓚ Ⓚ

Falafel No. 1
🏠 Västra Kattarpsvägen 41

Ⓚ Ⓚ Ⓚ

Falafel by Youssif
🏠 Stenyxegatan 24
🕒 Sat & Sun

Ⓚ Ⓚ Ⓚ

Jallajalla
🏠 Bergsgatan 16

Ⓚ Ⓚ Ⓚ

Babylon Grill
🏠 Amiralsgatan 33

Ⓚ Ⓚ Ⓚ

↑ The vibrant exterior of Moderna Museet Malmö, once a former power station

⑦ 〰 🖵

Moderna Museet Malmö

🏠 Ola Billgrens plats 2–4
🕒 11am–6pm Tue–Fri, 11am–5pm Sat & Sun 🔒 Some public hols 🌐 moderna museet.se/malmo

The Moderna Museet is one of Europe's leading museums of modern and contemporary art, and the only one north of Amsterdam with an international collection covering the entire 20th century. The gallery is housed in an old power station that was built in 1900. Architecturally striking

in its combination of past and present design styles, the Moderna Museet hosts rotating exhibitions that range from the Russian avant-garde to contemporary Swedish art.

⑧ 〰 🖵 🏛

Kommendanthuset

🏠 Malmöhusvägen
📞 040-344 400 🕒 Daily
🔒 1 Jan, 1 May, Midsummer Eve, Midsummer, 24, 25 & 31 Dec

In the latter part of the 18th century the storage buildings in the Malmöhus courtyard had fallen into disrepair and Gustav III ordered the construction of a new armoury. It was built outside the fortress in the Bastion Banér and was completed in 1794. By 1814 the fortress's military days were over and it had become a prison. Kommendanthuset (the Governor's House) became the quarters first for the prison's doctor and priest and later the prison governor.

In the 20th century the city of Malmö took over the building and restored it to its original appearance, incorporating it into Malmö Museum. It now houses Fotografins rum, an exhibition hall for photography. It also organizes a number of events and activities for children.

⑨ 〰 🖵 🏛

Teknikens och Sjöfartens Hus

🏠 Malmöhusvägen 📞 040-344 438 🕒 Daily 🔒 1 Jan, 1 May, Midsummer Eve, Midsummer, 24, 25 & 31 Dec

The Museum of Technology and Seafaring is part of Malmö Museum. Its exhibits cover virtually everything to do with technological development and seafaring, as well as the history of roadbuilding and aviation, engines – and steam engines in particular – just to name a few examples. Among the exhibits is the delta-winged fighter plane J35 Draken from the 1960s. The technically curious can experiment in the kunskapstivoli interactive test lab.

The museum also covers the industrial and seafaring history of Skåne. Here, the star exhibits include experiencing the U3 submarine and the steam launch Schebo. For those who have never been in a submarine, it is a chance not to be missed. This exhibit is very popular with children.

The shipbuilding and shipping industry and the development of the ports from the 17th century onwards are highlighted, as is ferry traffic, so vital to Skåne. There is also an interactive knowledge park, where you have the chance to do your own science experiments.

---

⑩ 🎐 🖵

Stadsbiblioteket

🏠 Kung Oscars väg 11
📞 040-660 85 00 🕐 Daily
🚫 Public hols

The City Library moved into the "castle" on Kung Oscars Väg in 1946. Danish architect Henning Larsen renovated and extended the old edifice, adding the cylindrical entrance building and the airy Calendar of Light hall.

The library offers free use of computers, Wi-Fi and a media collection. Tools for digital needs such as editing, scanning and printing are available in the Learning Centre. The library puts on various events for people of all ages and draws almost a million visitors a year.

⑪ 🖉 🖵 🏛

Limhamn

🏠 5 km (3 miles) SW of city centre

To the south of Malmö lies Limhamn, a shipping port for lime since the 16th century. Today it is home to one of Sweden's largest marinas, with views over the Öresund Bridge.

One of Limhamn's most fascinating sights is the disused limestone quarry, a huge gaping hole that is now a nature reserve. The Limhamn Museum Society runs various events during holidays.

---

⑫ 🖉 🖵 🏛

The Öresund Bridge

🏠 E20, 6 km (4 miles) SW of city centre

The idea of a bridge between Sweden and Denmark had been discussed for many years,

THE BRIDGE

This Nordic-noir crime TV series takes place in both Sweden and Denmark. When a dead body is found in the exact centre of the Öresund Bridge, the police forces of both nations have to work together to solve the crime. Fans will find many of the film locations dotted around the city, including the Västra Hamnen district.

but it was only in July 2000 that this dream was realized.

The Öresund Bridge is 8 km (5 miles) long, linking Lernacken in Sweden, south-west of Malmö, and the Danish island of Peberholm, south of Saltholm. The highest part rests on four pylons, 204 m (670 ft) tall, and the roadway is around 30 m (100 ft) wide. The E20 runs along the upper level with a railway along the lower level. The link plunges into a long tunnel leading to Copenhagen's international airport.

← Rows of bookshelves in the light and airy Stadsbiblioteket, and its striking glass etxerior (inset)

↑ Small, typical Swedish cottages lining the water's edge, Karlskrona

❷
KARLSKRONA

Ⓐ E7 **Ⓐ** Blekinge **✈** 25 km (15 miles) W of town centre **🚌** Jarnvagsstationsgatan **⛴** Verkö (Gdynia) **🛈** Stortorget 2; www.visitkarlskrona.se

The naval town of Karlskrona is built over several islands in the Blekinge archipelago. It is said to have been inspired by both Versailles and Rome, and centres around two squares, Stortorget on the island of Trossö, and Amiralitetstorget. Karlskrona has a number of outstanding sights from Sweden's Age of Greatness (1632–1718), and is a UNESCO World Heritage Site on account of its naval architecture.

① 🖼 🍴 🖥 🛍
Grevagården/ Blekinge Museum

Ⓐ Borgmästaregatan 21 **Ⓞ** Jun–Aug: daily; rest of the year: Tue–Sun **🕐** Some public hols **ⓦ** blekinge museum.se

Grevagården is the main building of Blekinge Museum. It dates from the early 18th century and was the home of Admiral-General Hans Wachtmeister – the café is set in what was once his kitchen. The museum focuses on the history of Blekinge and Karlskrona's heyday. There is a small Baroque garden.

②
Stortorget

This imposing square is said to be the largest in northern Europe. It is flanked by two impressive churches. Fredrikskyrkan is a large basilica consecrated in 1744, but characterized by the 17th-century taste for Baroque lines. Its 35 bells ring three times a day. The other church, Heliga Trefaldighetskyrkan (Holy Trinity), was completed in 1709 and is also known as the German Church after Admiral-General Hans

Wachtmeister, who inspired it and is buried in the crypt.

The town hall, completed in 1798, has been rebuilt several times. Today it is the seat of Karlskrona district court.

Vattenborgen, the water tower, was built in 1863 to supply Trossö with fresh water. It was replaced by a tower outside the town in 1939.

③ 🖼 🎭 🍴 🖥 🛍
Marinmuseum

Ⓐ Stumholmen **Ⓞ** Jan–Apr & Oct–Dec: Tue–Sun; May–Sep: daily **🕐** Some public hols **ⓦ** marinmuseum.se

The fascinating naval museum, opened in 1997, stands on the harbour on Stumholmen, an island which for almost 300 years has been part of the main base of the Swedish navy.

← Statue of Hans Wachtmeister at Alamedan, erected in 1930

Originally founded in 1752, Marinmuseum covers every imaginable aspect of maritime activity. It holds a particularly impressive collection of figureheads, weapons and uniforms. From an underwater glass corridor it is possible to see the wreck of an 18th-century ship lying on the bottom of the sea.

One of the world's smallest full-rigged ships, *Jarramas*, is moored on the quay outside the museum, along with the minesweeper *Bremön* and the torpedo boat *T38*. The Sloop and Long-Boat Shed contains an exhibition of working boats and often allows visitors to see how old boats are restored.

---

④

Gamla Örlogsvarvet

🏠 Högvakten, Amiralitetstorget 1 🕐 Jun–Aug: daily 🌐 orlogsstaden karlskrona.se

The Karlskrona shipyard, founded in 1679, became one of the country's foremost military shipyards. Fortifications were constructed to build, equip and repair warships. The only way to see this vast naval harbour and its 18th-century buildings is to take a guided tour. Among the most interesting sights in Gamla Örlogsvarvet are the 300-m- (984-ft-) long Rope Walk, where the rigging for the fleet was manufactured, the Wasa Shed and Polhem Dock on Lindholmen and Five-Finger Dock and the Old Mast Crane in the western part of the shipyard. It is the existence of these buildings, and the fact that Karlskrona is such a good example of a late 17th-century planned naval base, that earned the town its World Heritage Site status.

---

⑤

Kungsholm Fortress

Located on a tiny island in the Blekinge archipelago, this remarkable circular fortress has guarded the entrance to Karlskrona from the sea for more than 300 years. It was part of a vast complex of fortifications that included the Drottningskär citadel, towers and powder magazines. Guided tours can be booked via the tourist office.

Must See

EAT

Bourbon Burgers Cigars and Lounge
This rock lounge serves superb burgers and plays everything from The Beatles to Guns N' Roses.

🏠 Ronnebygatan 21
📞 0455-350 350
🕐 Sun & Mon

Ⓚ Ⓚ Ⓚ

Nya Skafferiet
This place is known for its lunches made with seasonal ingredients.

🏠 Rådhusgatan 9 🕐 Sun
🌐 nyaskafferiet.se

Ⓚ Ⓚ Ⓚ

Vinberga Vinkiosk
This small wine bar serves fresh and simple food and wine.

🏠 Borgmästaregatan 19
🕐 Sun-Tue 🌐 vinberga vinkiosk.com

Ⓚ Ⓚ Ⓚ

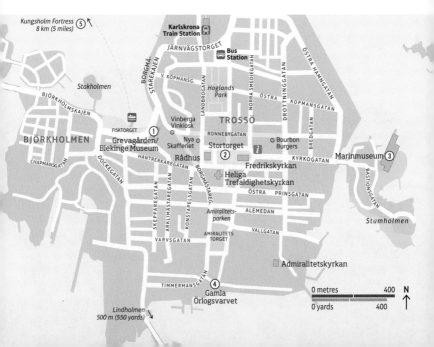

EXPERIENCE MORE

3

Bjärehalvön

🅰D6 🚉Skåne Road 105
🚫🚏 *i* Båstad Tourist
Office: Köpmansgatan 1,
www.bastad.com; Torekov
Tourist Office: Hamnplanen
2; 0431-36 31 80

There are several popular
resorts around the peninsula
of Bjärehalvön, between the
bays of Skälderviken and
Laholmsbukten. The medieval
town of Båstad is has beautiful
old houses and glorious
beaches. Just over 10 km
(6 miles) to the west is the old
fishing village of Torekov. Boat
trips run from Torekov to the
nature reserve Hallands
Väderö, a remnant of the
Hallandsåsen ridge now left
3 km (2 miles) out to sea. Of
special note is the alder marsh.

On the northern cape of the
peninsula is Hovs Hallar, a
geologically interesting area
with dramatic rocks and caves.
The area is a nature reserve
popular with birdwatchers
and walkers. Hovs Hallar is
the westernmost end of the
Hallandsåsen ridge, which
forms the border between
the Bjärehalvön peninsula
and Halland. With its lovely
meadows and varied flora,
the ridge is ideal for walking.

West of Båstad is
Norrvikens Trädgårdar, a
paradise for garden lovers
created by architect Rudolf
Abelin in the early 20th century.
There are several different
gardens, including a Baroque
and a Japanese garden.

The town of Ängelholm,
between the Bjärehalvön and
Kullahalvön peninsulas at the
end of the bay of Skälderviken,
has a sandy beach. Historically,
Ängelholm was known for its
pottery industry and today
clay cuckoos, the town's
symbol, are made here.

Norrvikens Trädgårdar

🌸🍴🏛 🚩5 km (3 miles) W of
Båstad 🕐May–Aug: daily

4

Kullabygden

🅰D7 🚉Skåne Road
111/112 🚏 *i* Centralgatan
20, Höganäs; 042-337 774

The beautiful Kullen Peninsula
has been inhabited since the
Bronze age. Today, the pretty
medieval fishing villages of
Arild, Mölle, Höganäs and Viken
have become popular seaside
resorts. Höganäs is best
known for its ceramics.

Krapperups Slott, located
just north of Höganäs, dates
from the mid-16th century;
the castle houses an art
gallery and museum.

Krapperups Slott

🌸🍴🏛 🚩7 km (4 miles) N
of Höganäs 🕐Castle: by
appt; gallery & museum:
Apr–May: Sat & Sun; Jun–
mid-Aug: daily 🌐krapper
up.se

5

Helsingborg

⚐D7 ⚐Skåne E4 🚆🚗🚌
**🛈Kungsgatan 11; www.
visithelsingborg.com**

Known as the "Pearl of the
Sound", Helsingborg is a lively
town, spectacularly located
on the shores of the Öresund
within sight of the Danish
coast. The town's strategic
position at the narrowest
point of the sound led to a
stormy history, and the 34-m
(111-ft) tower **Kärnan** is all that
remains of its 12th-century
fortress. The brick tower of the
town hall (1897) also features
on the skyline. It was designed
by architect Alfred Hellerström
and contains glass paintings
by Gustav Cederström.

Built in 1641, Jacob Hansen's
half-timbered house is the
oldest house in Helsingborg.

Did You Know?

Båstad in Bjärehalvön
is best known for hosting
the annual Swedish Open
tennis tournament.

The **Dunkers Kulturhus**, by
Danish architect Kim Utzon,
encompasses a museum, art
gallery and theatre. The open-
air **Fredriksdal Friluftsmuseum** displays historical
buildings from the region and
has a botanical garden with
the wild plants of Skåne.

Ramlösa Brunn, 5 km
(3 miles) southeast of Helsingborg, is known for its spring
water, which is on offer in
the Water Pavilion.

The castle of **Sofiero** was
bequeathed to Helsingborg
municipality by Gustav VI Adolf.
The park is famous for its Royal
Gardens with more than 300
varieties of rhododendron.

Kärnan

⊛ ⚐Slottshagen 📞042-
105 000 ⊙Daily

Dunkers Kulturhus

⊛⊛☺ ⚐Kungsgatan 11
📞042-107 400 ⊙Tue-Sun

Fredriksdals
Friluftsmuseum

⊛☺ ⚐Gisela Trapps Vag 1
📞042-104 500 ⊙Daily

Sofiero

⊛⊛☺ ⚐Sofierovägen 131,
5 km (3 miles) N of Helsingborg
📞042-10 25 00 ⊙Mid-Apr-
mid-Sep: 10am-6pm daily;
mid-Sep-mid Apr: park only

←

Rocky Hovs Hallar on
the northern cape of the
Bjärehalvön peninsula

↑ The modern Dunkers
   Kulturhus building
   in Helsingborg

6

Klippan

**⚐D6/7 ⚐Skåne Road 21
🚗 🛈Trädgårdsgatan 12;
0435-281 76**

Located on the Söderåsen
ridge, 30 km (19 miles) east of
Helsingborg, Klippan is known
for having Sweden's oldest
operating paper mill, built
in the 16th century.

Söderåsen National Park
offers leafy forests, dramatic
screes, babbling brooks and
stunning views from Koppar-
hatten and Hjortsprånget.
The Skåneleden trail runs
through the park.

The 17th-century mansion
Vrams Gunnarstorp, 10 km (6
miles) west of Klippan, is built
in Dutch Renaissance style. The
park with its noted hornbeam
avenue is open to the public.

> 🔺 GREAT VIEW
> **Kullaberg**
>
> Near the town of Molle
> on the Kullabygden
> peninsula, the Kullaberg
> Nature Reserve affords
> dramatic views of steep
> cliffs rising from the sea
> and the rocky ridges
> above. There are also
> expansive views over
> Öresund and Kattegatt.

7

Bosjökloster

🏛D7 🚗Skåne Road 23
🕐May-Sep: 8am-6pm daily;
Oct-Apr: 10am-5pm daily
🌐bosjokloster.se

On a peninsula between the lakes of Östra and Västra Ringsjön lies one of Sweden's most remarkable houses. Bosjökloster was built around 1080 as a convent and soon became one of the wealthiest in Skåne. Rich families paid a great deal to secure a place for their daughters, often donating goods and land. This all came to an end with the Danish Reformation in 1536, when its possessions were transferred into private ownership.

In 1875–79 Bosjökloster was reconstructed to a design by architect Helgo Zettervall and became the prime example of his skill for renovating manors.

In the early 20th century the property was bought by Count Philip Bonde and today it is owned by his grandson. The stately home was opened to the public in 1962. There are parks and gardens, a restaurant, café, mini-zoo, boats for hire and fishing, too. You can see a 1,000-year-old oak tree in the park, while the oldest room in the house, Stensalen, is devoted to exhibitions of arts and crafts.

8

Frostavallen

🏛D7 🚗Skåne 3 km (2 miles) N of Höör on Road 21 🚉To Höör 🛈Höör Tourist Office; www.visitmittskane.se

The beautiful countryside around Höör in central Skåne offers something for everyone, from hiking, canoeing and swimming to fishing from the shore or by boat on Vaxsjön lake. With its many restaurants, cafés, hotels and camp sites, Frostavallen is ideal for a day trip or a longer stay. There are playgrounds and leisure equipment is available for hire.

Nearby is **Skånes Djurpark**, a zoo specializing in Nordic animals. Popular with children, it has more than 1,000 wild and domesticated Nordic animals.

A different kind of experience is offered at **Höörs Stenåldersby**, where visitors can see for themselves what life was like in a Stone Age village. You can even try flint-knapping and bow-making.

Skånes Djurpark

🏛Frostavallen
🕐Daily 🌐skanesdjurpark.se

Höörs Stenåldersby

🏛Next to Skånes Djurpark
☎0413-553270 🕐Jul by appt

9

Dalby

🏛D7 🚗Skåne 🛈Lund Tourist Center, Bangatan 1; www.visitlund.se

Dalby is most best known as the home of the oldest preserved stone church in Scandinavia. The Holy Cross Church was consecrated in 1060, when Denmark was divided into nine dioceses.

←
Bosjökloster, originally a Benedictine convent, viewed through an arch

Did You Know

The dialect in the south is "skånska". Whether it is Swedish, Danish or a separate language is a puzzle.

The Söderskog National Park, situated just northwest of Dalby, is another highlight. In spring it is the perfect place to see wildflowers and hear the songbirds while exploring. There is also an old quarry east of the city, Stenbrottet, which is a popular place for swimming.

10

Lund

🏛D7 🚗Skåne E 22 ✈Sturup 🚉 🛈Bangatan 1; www.visitlund.se

Founded by King Sven Tveskägg more than 1,000 years ago, the university town of Lund was once Denmark's capital. In the Middle Ages it was a religious, political and cultural centre and site of a cathedral, **Lund Domkyrka**, which was consecrated in 1145. Over the centuries it has been rebuilt, most recently by Helgo Zettervall, 1860–80. Look out for the 14th-century astronomical clock and a sculpture in the crypt of the giant Finn supporting the cathedral's vaulting.

Lund University was established in 1666, in the grounds of the bishop's palace, Lundagård. Now the university is the second largest seat of learning in Sweden with around 47,000 students.

In the heart of the partly medieval city centre lies **Kulturen**, an open-air museum with perfectly preserved streets, cottages and town houses. The 14th-century chapel of Laurentiikapellet, in central Lund, is thought to

Visitors admiring the stunning nave inside Lund Domkyrka

have been the library of the monastery of St Laurence.

Historiska Museet, containing Domkyrkomuseet, is one of Sweden's largest museums of archaeology, and includes an exhibition about the history of the cathedral. **Lunds Konsthall**, designed by Klas Anshelm, displays contemporary art, while the **Museum of Sketches** shows the development of the creative process through original sketches and models.

Lunds Domkyrka

🕙 ⌂Kyrkogatan ☎046-71 87 00 ⏰Daily

Kulturen

🕙🕙🕙😑🖪
⌂Tegnerplatsen 6 ⏰May-Aug: daily; Sep-Apr: Tue-Sun
🔲kulturen.com

Historiska Museet

🕙🕙 ⌂Krafts Torg 1 ⏰Noon-5pm Tue-Sun (to 8pm Thu)
🔲historiskamuseet.lu.se

Lunds Konsthall

🕙😑🖪 ⌂Mårtenstorget 3
⏰Times vary, check website
🔲lundskonsthall.se

Museum of Sketches

🕙 ⌂Finngatan 2 ⏰Tue-Sun
🔲skissernasmuseum.lu.se

TYCHO BRAHE

Astronomer Tycho Brahe was born in Skåne in 1546. Inspired by an eclipse of the sun in 1560, he took up astronomy. He believed that the old methods of measurement to determine the position of the planets were not exact and designed a new system. His discoveries in astronomy paved the way for a new view of the universe. Brahe died in Prague in 1601.

---

⑪

Landskrona

🅰D7 ⌂Skåne 🚉
🛈Drottninggatan 7; 0418-47 30 00

In 1549, Danish king Christian III built the **Landskrona Slott Citadellet** (Citadel) to protect the shipbuilding town against the Swedes. This fortress surrounded by a moat dominates the town. Most sights are in the area around it, including **Landskrona Museum**, with its local history collection, and Konsthallen (Art Gallery).

In the sound between Sweden and Denmark lies the island of Ven, where Tycho Brahe set up his underground observatory, Stjärneborg, in the 1580s. The Tycho Brahe Museum features multimedia shows about the observatory.

Landskrona Slott Citadellet

🕙 ⌂Slottsgatan ⏰Courtyard and exhibition: daily
🔲citadellet.com

Landskrona Museum

⌂Slottsgatan ⏰Noon-5pm Tue-Sun (from 10pm Sat)
🔒Some public hols
🔲landskrona.se

← Colourful wooden huts on the beach, Skanö/Falsterbo; Falsterbo Lighthouse *(inset)* on the headland

⑫

Trelleborg

Ⓐ D7 **Ⓐ Skåne E22** 🚌🚆
ⓘ Kontinentgatan 2; www. visittrelleborg.se

The town of Trelleborg was at its most prosperous in the Middle Ages, when German merchants came to trade salt for herring. Some of the old Skåne houses can be seen in the quarter around Gamla Torg (Old Square) and in Klostergränden, where the ruins of a 13th-century Franciscan monastery still stand. Stadsparken, the town park, boasts a gorgeous rose garden and is worth a visit.

Trelleborgen is a reconstruction of a Viking fortress, situated exactly where a fortress thought to have been built by King Harald Blue Tooth in the 10th century, once stood. Other attractions include **Trelleborgs Museum**, focusing on local history, **Trelleborgs Sjöfartsmuseum** (Seafaring Museum) and **Axel Ebbes Konsthall** (art gallery), with its collection of sculptures by the Skåne artist Axel Ebbe.

Trelleborgen
🌀😊🕐 **Ⓐ Västra Vallgatan 6** **Ⓒ Times vary, check website** **Ⓦ trelleborg.se**

Trelleborgs Museum
🌀😊🕐 **Ⓐ Stortorget 1** **Ⓒ 0410-733 045** **Ⓒ Tue–Sun**

Trelleborgs Sjöfartsmuseum
Ⓐ Gråbrödersgatan 12 **Ⓒ Apr– Nov: Sat & Sun** **Ⓦ trelleborgs- sjofartsmuseum.se**

Axel Ebbes Konsthall
🌀🕐 **Ⓐ Hesekillegatan 1** **Ⓒ 0410-733 045** **Ⓒ Jun–Aug: Tue–Sun; Sep–May: Sat & Sun**

---

⑬

Kristianstad

Ⓐ D7 **Ⓐ Skåne E22** ✈🚆
ⓘ Västra Storgatan 12; www.kristianstad.se/ turism

The Danish King Christian IV built the town of Kristianstad in the early 17th century, and the original street layout with two gates can still be seen today. The town's main sight is Heliga Trefaldighetskyrkan (the Church of the Holy Trinity) from the same period, an excellent example of Renaissance architecture. A more recent attraction is the eco-museum **Naturum Vattenriket**, a 35-km (22-mile) stretch of wetlands on the Helgeån river. It is best seen on a guided river tour. Fishing permits can be bought.

Naturum Vattenriket
🌀🕐😊 **Ⓐ Naturumsvägen 2** **Ⓒ Daily** **Ⓒ Mon (winter) and some public hols** **Ⓦ vattenriket.kristianstad. se/naturum**

⑭

Skanör/Falsterbo

Ⓐ D7 **Ⓐ Skåne Road 100** ✈ **Sturup** **ⓘ Falsterbo Strandbad turistcenter; www.visitskane.com**

Today the twin towns at the far end of Skåne's southwestern cape are idyllic seaside resorts, but they owe their development to the lucrative herring

industry in the Middle Ages. Sights include Falsterbo Museum, with its local history collection, the ruins of the 14th-century fort of Falsterbohus, and Falsterbo Konsthall, an art gallery in the old railway station. On the headland is Falsterbo Lighthouse, which was built in 1793 and is still in working order. Skanör town hall dates from 1777 and the church is 13th century.

Bärnstensmuseet, the Amber Museum in Höllviken, near the Viking earthworks of Kämpinge Vall, is worth a visit.

Bärnstensmuseet

⊛ ⊗ ⏹ Kämpinge, 10 km (6 miles) E of Falsterbo ⏰ Times vary, check website ⓦ brost.se

---

🅕
Ystad

🅐 D7 ⏹ Skåne E65 🚃🚌
🅳 St Knuts Torg; www.visitystadosterlen.se

In Ystad the impact of Danish rule and contact with the German Hanseatic League are apparent and the medieval church and monastery communities have also left their mark on the town. Among the many old buildings is the 13th-century Sta Mariakyrkan, where every night the watchman in the tower declares that all is well by blowing his horn. In Karl XII's Hus on Stora Västergatan the warrior king is said to have spent the night in 1715 following his return from Turkey.

Ystad has several museums, but if you're pushed for time, visit **Ystads Konstmuseum** (Art Museum). A fine theatre on the harbourside offers a repertoire ranging from opera to stand-up comedy.

High above the fishing community of Kåseberga lies the largest stone ship in Sweden, **Ales Stenar**. The 67-m (220-ft) site comprises 59 stones.

East along the coast from Ystad, Sandhammaren is best known for its sandy beaches, but in the past was feared by sailors as new reefs formed around the cape. The lighthouse dates from 1862.

Marsvinsholms Slott is an estate dating back to the 14th century. The castle is not open to the public, but in summer visitors can enjoy the park within the grounds or see a play at the open-air theatre.

💬 INSIDER TIP
Indulgent Day

Treat yourself to a spa day at Saltsjöbad (www.ysb.se) or a traditional sauna and sea dip. This hotel and spa are located by the Baltic Sea in Ystad. You can book a spa morning, afternoon or for a whole day.

Ystads Konstmuseum

⊛ ⊜ ⊕ ⏹ St Knuts Torg ⏰ Tue–Sun 🚫 Public hols ⓦ konstmuseet.ystad.se

Ales Stenar

⏹ Kåseberga Road 9, 20 km (12 miles) E of Ystad 📞 0411-577 681 ⏰ Daily

Marsvinsholms Slott

⊜ ⏹ On E65, 12 km (8 miles) NW of Ystad ⏰ Park: daily in summer ⓦ marsvinsholm.se

Facing out over the sea, Ales Stenar is particularly ↓ dramatic at sunset

Typical red wooden houses in an idyllic waterside setting near Kristianopel ↑

16

Sölvesborg

🅰E7 🏠Blekinge E22 🚊
ℹRepslagaregatan 1;
www.solvesborg.se

In the Middle Ages, Sölvesborg, on the cape of Listerlandet, was an important trading centre protected by a castle. The town has a Danish feel to it and retains its medieval charm.

In a former granary and distillery, **Sölvesborgs Museum** traces the history of Lister. The town's oldest building is St Nicolai Kyrka, a church with parts dating from the 13th century.

Southeast of Sölvesborg and at the far end of the cape lies the old fishing village of Hällevik with its traditional wooden houses, harbours and smokery. It also has a great little fishing museum.

Ferries run from Nogersund to the attractive island of Hanö in Hanöbukten bay. The island served as an English naval base in the Napoleonic Wars in the early 19th century and includes a graveyard for British seamen.

Sölvesborgs Museum
🏠Skeppsbrogatan 3
📞0456-81 61 81 🕐Mid-Jun-mid-Aug: Tue-Sun; rest of the year: by appt

---

17

Kristianopel

🅰E6 🏠Blekinge E22 🚊
ℹStortorget 2, Karlskrona;
www.kristianopel.se

Enjoying a beautiful location on a peninsula in Kalmarsund, the little fortified town of Kristianopel has become a popular summer haunt with a guest harbour and tourist facilities. The town was built by the Danish King Christian IV and gained its charter in 1600. At the Peace of Roskilde in 1658 it became Swedish.

Brömsebro is 8 km (5 miles) north of Kristianopel, just inland from the coast. Here, on the border between Blekinge and Småland, is where peace with Denmark was declared in 1645, when Jämtland, Härjedalen and Gotland once more became Swedish provinces. The negotiations were held on an islet in Brömsebäcken river and a commemorative stone was raised here in 1915. At the mouth of the river are the ruins of Brömsehus, a fortress that was captured in 1436 by Swedish rebel Engelbrekt.

18

Karlshamn

🅰E7 🏠Blekinge E22
🚊🚌 ℹPirgatan 2; www.karlshamn.se

Founded in 1664, this town was planned as a naval base, and Kastellet, on the island of Frisholmen, was built to defend

> 💬 INSIDER TIP
> ### Sweden Rock Festival
>
> This hard-rock music festival (www.sweden rock.com) is held in Norje (north of Sölvesborg) early June. Artists who have performed include Black Sabbath, Iron Maiden, Aerosmith and Guns N' Roses.

that, it was the main town of Blekinge and a busy trading centre. In 1564, during the Seven Years War with the Danes, it was overrun by the army of Erik XIV and burned. About 3,000 inhabitants – the majority of the population – were slaughtered in what became known as the Ronneby Bloodbath. In the early 19th century the town gained a new lease of life thanks to the Kockums foundry and enamel works in Kallinge and the Ronneby Brunn spa.

There are a few old buildings in the Bergslagen district, and the beautiful 18th-century spa park has been restored. The park's diverse landscape offers green spaces, water features, natural forest and various themed gardens. Visitors can taste the healing waters by operating the hand pump at the old spring.

Just east of Ronneby is the 13th-century church Edestads Kyrka, which once served as a defensive fort. Lying 7 km (4 miles) east of the town is the remarkable 4-m- (13-ft-) high, 8th-century runestone, Björketorpsstenen. The text inscribed on the stone is said to be a curse.

Hjortsberga Grave Field on the Johannishus ridge contains 120 ancient burial mounds. About 12 km (7 miles) north-east of Ronneby is Johannishus Åsar, a nature reserve that is set in beautiful pasture land.

it. However, the naval port role went to Karlskrona (p214) and Karlshamn became a trading centre with a reputation for the production of *punsch*. A reconstruction of Punschfabriken, the factory that produced the alcoholic drink "Flaggpunsch", is part of **Karlshamns Museum**.

Other places of interest include Skottsbergska Gården, a merchant's house built in 1763 where both the living quarters and tobacco shop can be seen as they were in the 18th century. **Kreativum** is a science centre that will appeal to people of all ages. Asschierska Huset, on the square, was Karlshamn's first town hall. The Mörrumsån salmon fishing river runs through the municipality.

Around 15 km (9 miles) east of Karlshamn is Eriksbergs Vilt-och Naturpark, a large wildlife and nature sanctuary that is home to golden eagles, sea eagles and deer.

Karlshamns Museum

🖉 🕙 🏛 Vinkelgatan 8 🕙 Mid-Jun–mid-Aug: 1–5pm Tue–Sun; Sep–May: 1–4pm Mon–Fri 🔳 karlshamnsmuseum.se

Kreativum

🏛 Strömmavägen 28 🕙 10am–4pm Sat & Sun; daily during school holidays and by appt 🔳 kreativum.se

---

⑲

Ronneby

🅰 E7 🏛 Blekinge E22 ➕ 🏠 🛈 Västra Torggatan 1; www.ronneby.se

Founded in the 13th century, Ronneby did not become Swedish until 1658. Prior to

---

SALMON FISHING IN MÖRRUMSÅN

Every year the salmon fishing in the Mörrumsån river attracts enthusiasts from all over the world. Fishing here dates back to the 13th century when the king held all the rights. The river flows through a beautiful landscape from Lake Vrången in the north to the sea at Elleholm via the lakes of Helgasjön and Åsnen. A fishing permit is required and these cost between 300 and 1,200 Kr per day. During the 2003 season 1,160 salmon were caught here, the record catch weighing in at 18.36 kg (40.34 lbs). Laxens Hus (Salmon World) in Mörrum gathers together everything to do with fishing and mounts a variety of exhibitions on, for example, the animal life of the river, and the history of the sport.

A DRIVING TOUR
ÖSTERLEN

Length 80 km (50 miles) **Stopping-off points** Cafés and restaurants are found in most towns

The name Österlen means "the land to the east" and refers to the southeast corner of Skåne from Ravlunda south to Ystad and west to the Linderödsåsen ridge. The land is the most fertile in Sweden and across the rolling plains are many of the country's most treasured ancient monuments, grandest castles and forts and oldest churches. Along the coast, idyllic fishing villages are dotted like pearls on a string and the entire region has become a haven for painters and writers. Major roads on this route are of a good standard, but country roads can be in poorer condition.

SOUTHERN GÖTALAND

Österlen

Locator Map
For more detail see p208

Kivik *is best known for its annual market and apple orchards, but it is also a charming fishing village with half-timbered houses.*

Brösarps Backar
nature reserve is awash with rare flowers. The area has lots of excellent walking trails.

Brösarps Backar

START ⏵ Brösarp

Vitemölla

Vitaby · Kivik

Tomelilla *is an ideal starting point for a tour of Skåne's rolling countryside. The town is also famous for its art museum.*

Lövestad

Sankt Olof

Rörum

Vik

Old low-rise houses give **Simrishamn** *its character. Craftsmen lived around the square and fishermen made their home by the harbour.*

Onslunda

Baskemölla

Tomelilla

Gärsnäs · Östra Tommarp

Simrishamn

Smedstorp

Hammenhög

Sövestad

Glimmingehus

Stora Herrestad

Tosterup Castle

Skillinge

Ystad
FINISH
Nybrostrand

Glemmingebro

Löderup

Borrby

The evocative 16th-century knight's manor of **Glimmingehus** *offers exciting ghost trails and a taste of medieval cooking.*

Kåseberga

Sandhammaren

0 kilometres 10
0 miles 10

N ↑

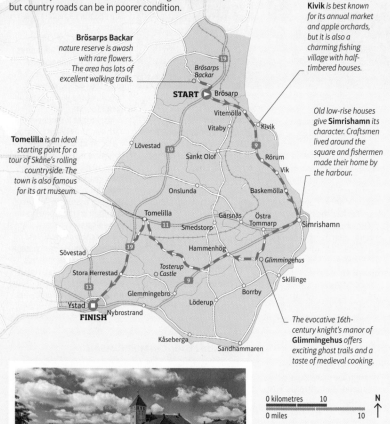

←
Tosterup Castle in its idyllic rural setting south of Tomelilla

↑ Traditional town houses lining the pretty cobbled streets in Simrishamn

GOTHENBURG

The people of Gothenburg (Göteborg in Swedish) have nicknamed their city "the face of Sweden". This maritime metropolis has for centuries been one of Sweden's gateways to the outside world. Historically, the Göta Älv river was the country's only outlet to the west, as can be seen by the remains of fortresses and earthworks that once protected it. Gothenburg is still Sweden's most important port and holds fast to its maritime past.

Today's Gothenburg was preceded by four earlier towns along the Göta Älv river. These were pawns in a period of constant conflict between Sweden and Denmark. The first town was built by Dutch settlers on the island of Hisingen in the early 17th century. It was hardly established before Gustav II Adolf decided in 1619 that it should be moved to the area where the suburbs of Vallgraven and Nordstaden now stand. Gothenburg's 17th-century incarnation was as a fortified town created by the architect and field marshal Erik Dahlbergh. The 18th century saw Gothenburg become even more cosmopolitan thanks to German, English and Scottish immigration.

With the advent of steam power, the shipping industry flourished in the mid-19th century, and the city became a prominent shipbuilding centre. The shipyards have mostly gone, but Gothenburg is still a major industrial city and home of the car manufacturer Volvo.

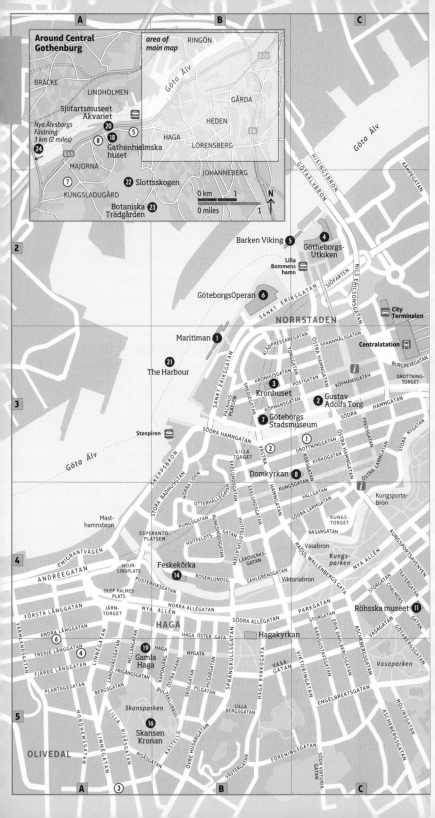

Around Central Gothenburg

BRÄCKE

LINDHOLMEN

RINGÖN

area of main map

Göta Älv

GÅRDA

HEDEN

HAGA

LORENSBERG

Sjöfartsmuseet Akvariet ⑳

Nya Älvsborgs Fästning
3 km (2 miles)

⑧ ⑱ ⑤

Gathenhielmska huset

㉔

MAJORNA

JOHANNEBERG

⑦

KUNGSLADUGÅRD

㉒ Slottsskogen

Botaniska Trädgården ㉓

0 km   1
0 miles   1

N

RINGÖN

Barken Viking ⑤

Götheborgs-Utkiken ④

Lilla Bommens hamn

GöteborgsOperan ⑥

NORRSTADEN

SANKT ERIKSGATAN

HISINGSBRON

GÖTAÄLVBRON

NILS ERICSONSGATAN

City Terminalen

Maritiman ①

The Harbour ㉑

SANKT ERIKSGATAN

PACKHUS-PLATSEN

SMEDJEGATAN

KRONHUSGATAN

Kronhuset ③

POSTGATAN

KÖPMANSGATAN

KÖPMANSGATAN

KLÄDPRESSAREGATAN

TORGGATAN

ÖSTRA HAMNGATAN

SPANNMÅLSGATAN

Gustav Adolfs Torg ②

Göteborgs Stadsmuseum ⑦

Centralstation

BURGREVEGATAN

DROTTNING-TORGET

ⓘ

Stenpiren

SÖDRA HAMNGATAN

LILLA TORGET

VÄSTRA HAMNGATAN

DROTTNINGGATAN

②

①

KUNGSGATAN

KÖPMANSGATAN

KYRKOGATAN

SÖDRA HAMNGATAN

FREDSGATAN

STORA NYGATAN

STORA BADHUSGATAN

SKEPPSBRON

Domkyrkan ⑧

NORRA LIDEN

OTTERHÄLLEGATAN

EKELUNDSGATAN

EKELUNDSGATAN

HAMNGATAN

KUNGSGATAN

SÖDRA LARMGATAN

VALLGATAN

KUNGS-TORGET

Kungsports-bron

ⓘ

Göta Älv

Mast-hamnsbron

EMIGRANTVÄGEN

ANDRÉEGATAN

KUNGSGATAN

ESPERANTO-PLATSEN

HEUR-LINSPLATS

HVITFELDTS-PLATSEN

HVITFELTSGATAN

KUNGSHÖJDSGATAN

LÄROVERKS-GATAN

Feskekörka ⑭

PUSTERVIKSGATAN

ROSENLUNDSG.

SAHLGRENSGATAN

BASARGATAN

Vasabron

RAOUL WALLENBERGS GATA

Viktoriabron

Kungs-parken

NYA ALLÉN

KUNGSPORTSAVENYEN

STORGATAN

TEATERGATAN

CHALMERS-GATAN

Röhsska museet ⑪

FÖRSTA LÅNGGATAN

ANDRA LÅNGGATAN

TREDJE LÅNGGATAN

FJÄRDE LÅNGGATAN

PLANTAGEGATAN

OLOF PALMES PLATS

JÄRN-TORGET

NYA ALLÉN

NORRA ALLÉGATAN

HAGA

SÖDRA ALLÉGATAN

Hagakyrkan

HAGA ÖSTER GATA

PARKGATAN

STORGATAN

ERIK DAHLBERGSGATAN

KARLGUSTAVSGATAN

ASCHEBERGSGATAN

VASAGATAN

GÖTABERGSGATAN

VIKTORINGATAN

Vasaparken

⑥

④

VARMLANDSGATAN

NORDHEMSGATAN

LINNEGATAN

LANDSVÄGSGATAN

FRIGÅNGSGATAN

BERGSGATAN

Gamla Haga ⑲

HAGA NYGÅRD

KAPONJÅRG.

ÖSTRA SKANS

SKOLGATAN

NYGATA

PILGATAN

HUSARGATAN

SPRÅNGKULLSGATAN

HAGA KYRKOGATA

VASA-GATAN

LILLA BERGSGATAN

Skansparken

Skansen Kronan ⑯

LILLA RISÅSGATAN

RISÅSGATAN

KASTELLG.

BULTEKLUBBG.

ÖVRE HUSARGATAN

VÄSTERGATAN

FÖRENINGSGATAN

SÖDR VIKTORIA-GATAN

MOLINSGATAN

ASCHEBERGSGATAN

ENGELBREKTSGATAN

OLIVEDAL

③

GOTHENBURG

Experience
1. Maritiman
2. Gustav Adolfs torg
3. Kronhuset
4. GötheborgsUtkiken
5. Barken Viking
6. GöteborgsOperan
7. Göteborgs Stadsmuseum
8. Domkyrkan
9. Ullevi
10. Trädgårdsföreningen
11. Röhsska museet
12. Liseberg
13. Universeum
14. Feskekôrka
15. Världskulturmuseet
16. Skansen Kronan
17. Götaplatsen
18. Gathenhielmska huset
19. Gamla Haga
20. Sjöfartsmuseet Akvariet
21. The Harbour
22. Slottsskogen
23. Botaniska Trädgården
24. Nya Älvsborgs Fästning

Eat
1. Ahlströms konditori
2. Brogyllen
3. Doktor Glas

Drink
4. Brewers Beer Bar
5. Haket
6. The Rover

Shop
7. Välkommen Åter, Antikt Retro Design
8. Café Asti
9. Holmen's Marknad

1

Maritiman

📍B3 🏠Packhusplatsen 12
🚋 🕐Apr: 11am-4pm Sat &
Sun; May & Sep: 11am-4pm
daily; Jun-Aug: 10am-6pm
daily 🌐maritiman.se

Located in Gothenburg's inner harbour, Maritiman is said to be the world's largest floating ship museum. Built in 1987, the site reinvigorated the harbour that was then lying empty after Gothenburg's ships moved to the city's new port facilities further out to sea.

The interactive and family-friendly museum comprises of 13 historic vessels at anchor. Highlights include the iconic destroyer *Småland*, built in 1952 at Eriksbergs shipyard on the other side of the river, the submarine *Nordkaparen* (1962), and the monitor *Sölve* (1875), as well as lightships, fireboats and tugs.

2

Gustav Adolfs torg

📍C3 🚋

Gothenburg's famous founder, Gustav II Adolf, gave his name to the city's central square. Since 1854 Bengt Erland Fogelberg's statue of the "hero king" has gazed imperiously over the square and Rådhuset (the town hall), Börsen (the Stock Exchange) and Stadshuset (the City Hall).

Rådhuset, closest to Norra Hamngatan, was designed by Nicodemus Tessin the Elder and completed in 1673. It has a Functionalist extension designed in 1937 by Gunnar Asplund (*p94*).

Both the 18th-century Stadshuset and Wenngrenska Villa, located on the north side of the square, are used by the city administration. Börsen, designed by P J Ekman in 1849, is the city's main venue for receptions and council meetings.

You can celebrate Gustav II Adolf's legacy beyond his statue with a special marzipan cake on 6 November, the date on which the king died in 1632, which is made in his honour. It is topped with a piece of chocolate in the shape of the king's head.

3

Kronhuset

📍C2 🏠Kronhusgatan 1D
📞031 368 40 00 🚋

A grand brick building in Dutch style, Kronhuset was built in 1643–55 and is Gothenburg's oldest preserved secular building. This part of town was originally a storage area for the artillery. The ground floor was converted into a chamber for the parliament of 1660.

Today, the building is a living craft centre and is used regularly for events such as concerts and exhibitions.

Around the square are a number of small buildings known as Kronhusbodarna (the Kronhus sheds), which create a pleasant setting for crafts people whose wares include pottery, leatherwork, glass, clocks and homemade sweets. There is also an old-fashioned country store with a café.

←

Statue of Gustav
II Adolf, in the
square that is
named after him

↑ *Viking* reflected in
the water, next to
GöthesborgsUtkiken

4

GötheborgsUtkiken

📍C2 🏠Lilla Bommen 2
📞031-156 147 🚋 🕐11am-
3pm daily (Jul & Aug: 10am-
4pm); access by lift every
hour

This red and white building has dominated the Lilla Bommen harbour area since 1989. Architects Ralph Erskine and Heikki Särg's daring design was soon christened "the Lipstick" by Gothenburg wits. Standing 86 m (282 ft) above sea level, it offers great views over the harbour.

5

Barken Viking

📍C2 🏠Gullbergskajen
🚋 🕐Daily 🕐22-31 Dec
🌐barkenviking.com

One of the world's few preserved four-masted

barques from the great age of sail is permanently moored in Gothenburg. The *Viking* was constructed in 1906 by the Copenhagen shipyard Burmeister & Wain. She sailed the wheat route to Australia and shipped guano from Chile in South America. A fast and beautiful vessel, she logged a record speed of 15.5 knots in 1909. Her days as a merchant ship ended in 1948 and in 1950 she became a training centre for sailors and chefs.

Today, the *Viking* provides an unusual setting for a hotel and conference centre. During summer the 97-m (318-ft) deck becomes a popular harbourside café, restaurant and bar, which radiates a very lively, bustling atmosphere.

GöteborgsOperan

📍 B2 🏛 **Christina Nilssons Gata** 🚋 🕙 **In conjunction with performances; check website for details** 🕙 **1 May, Good Friday, 24h, 25 Dec** 🌐 **opera.se**

The 1994 opening of this very impressive Opera House had been most eagerly anticipated by western Sweden's music lovers. This is demonstrated by the vast donation wall listing the names of the 6,000 people who contributed towards the funding of the new building.

The city's main venue for opera, musicals and ballet, the theatre is designed on a grand scale and is reflected in the water of the Göta Älv river. The Classical-style octagonal auditorium seats 1,300 people, all able to enjoy the excellent acoustics. The main stage is complemented by a further four equally large areas for storing sets. Using advanced technology, it is possible to switch quickly and efficiently between productions, thus enabling the Opera House to stage an extensive repertoire of opera, musicals and con-temporary dance.

Architect Jan Izikowitz was inspired by Gothenburg's har-bourside location – ships, hulls, sails, bridges and cranes are echoed in the building's design. The aim of his creation was for the "building to be posses-sed by a lightness, which encourages thoughts to soar like seagulls' wings over the mighty river landscape".

SHOP

Välkommen Åter, Antikt Retro Design
This shop is filled with antiques and retro design.

📍 A2 🏛 **Älvsborgsgatan 50** 🕙 **Sun & Mon**

Café Asti
This spot is known for its unique blend of coffee, antiques and new age items for sale.

📍 A1 🏛 **Karl Johansgatan 36A** 🕙 **Sat & Sun**

Holmen's Marknad
Here you will find everything from antique crystal glass to retro gadgets and clothes.

📍 D1 🏛 **Ryttmästare-gatan 3** 🕙 **Sun** 🌐 **holmensmarknad.se**

EAT

Ahlströms konditori

Relax in the inner courtyard and savour the fresh baked goods.

📍C3 🏠Korsgatan 2
🌐ahlstromskonditori.se

Ⓚ ⓀⓇ Ⓚⓒ

Brogyllen

Try the freshly baked bread made with raw ingredients or the traditional princess cake.

📍B3 🏠Västra Hamngatan 2
🌐brogyllen.se

Ⓚ ⓀⓇ Ⓚⓒ

Doktor Glas

Serves a variety of dishes, as well as baked goods and smoothies.

📍A5 🏠Linnégatan 56
🌐doktorglaslinne-gatan.se

Ⓚ ⓀⓇ Ⓚⓒ

---

7 🔄 🎧 🖥 🛍

Göteborgs Stadsmuseum

📍B3 🏠Norra Hamngatan 12
🚇 ⏰10am–5pm Tue–Sun (to 8pm Wed) 🚫Public hols 🌐stadsmuseum.goteborg.se

The City Museum is located in the Ostindiska Huset (East India House). The building, designed by the Swedish architects Bengt Wilhelm Carlberg and Carl Hårleman, was constructed in 1747–62 as management premises, auction rooms and a warehouse for the East India Company. When trading ceased in the early 19th century the building became a natural history museum, and in 1861 the City Museum was founded.

The permanent exhibitions show the early history of western Sweden and the importance of the Göta Älv river as a route to Europe from the Viking period onwards. Displays focus on the history of the first inhabitants of Gothenburg and the industrialization and social upheavals of the 20th century. The work of the East India Company and its trade in exotic goods such as Chinese porcelain, silk and lacquer work, is also featured.

---

8 🎧 🖥

Domkyrkan

📍C3 🏠Kyrkogatan 28
📞031-731 61 30 🚇 ⏰Daily

Gothenburg's cathedral, Gustavi Domkyrka, was designed by C W Carlberg in Neo-Classical style in 1815–25. It stands on the ruins of its two predecessors, which were both destroyed by fire.

The elegant gilded interior behind the Domkyrkan's Neo-Classical façade *(inset)*

The pristine interior is dominated by an impressive gilded altarpiece. In front of the cathedral in Domkyrkoplan is one of the city's preserved watering places: from the late 18th century water was transported here in hollowed-out oak logs from the well of Gustafs Källa to the south of the city.

⑨ 🍽️
Ullevi

📍E3 🚪Skånegatan 📞031-368 45 00 🚽 🕐During events

Sweden's largest outdoor arena, Ullevi, opened for the 1958 football World Cup and over the years has hosted numerous other international events. Designed by Swedish architect Fritz Jaenecke, the elegant wave-shaped ellipse has been erected and modernized several times. The arena is mostly used for sporting events and concerts.

In front of the arena, a statue has been erected in honour of the great Swedish boxer Ingemar "Ingo" Johansson (1932–2009).

↑ Fireworks erupting from the Ullevi arena during an event

⑩ ⚫⚫⚫⚫
Trädgårds-
föreningen

📍D3 🚪Slussgatan 1 🚽1-5, 7, 9-11, 13 🕐7am-6pm daily (May-Sep: to 8pm) 📅24, 25 & 31 Dec 🌐tradgardsforeningen.se

Gothenburg has many parks, but Trädgårdsföreningen is in a class of its own. In 1842 work began to transform a marshland south of Vallgraven into beautiful parkland for the benefit of the city's residents.

The flora of five continents are represented in the magnificent **Palmhuset** (Palm House) built in 1878. The building is filled with flowering camellias, giant bamboo, exotic orchids and palm trees. Vattenhuset (the Water House) is carpeted by the twisting roots of mangrove trees and the 2-m- (6-ft-) wide petals of the giant water lily. The Rosarium has become a leading world collection, with more than 1,900 rose varieties.

There are cafés in the park and Trägår'n, a restaurant and nightclub that has founded in the 19th century. It is now housed in a new building with a large open-air terrace.

Palmhuset
🕐Jun-Aug: 10am-8pm daily; Sep-May: 10am-4pm daily

⑪ ⚫⚫⚫⚫
Röhsska museet

📍C4 🚪Vasagatan 37-39 🚽3, 4, 5, 7, 10 🕐11am-6pm Tue & Wed, 11am-8pm Thu, 11am-5pm Fri-Sun 📅Some public hols 🌐rohsska.se

The country's leading museum of applied art and design, Röhsska Museet contains a marvellous collection of 20th-century Nordic domestic and decorative items. Other parts of the museum are devoted to European applied art, and antiquities from the ancient world, Japan and China. A mere fraction of the total of 50,000 objects can be displayed at any one time. Specialist temporary exhibitions are also mounted here.

The museum was founded with donations from financiers Wilhelm and August Röhss. It opened in 1916 as the Röhss Museum of Handicrafts in the brick building designed by architect Carl Westman.

Rather appropriately, standing next to the museum is the University College for Arts and Crafts Design.

Entrance to Liseberg amusement park, with its thrilling rides *(inset)*

12

Liseberg

E5 Örgrytevägen 5 Times vary, check website Mon & public hols liseberg.se

The people of Gothenburg are rightly proud of their amusement park, which attracts huge numbers of visitors. Apart from the latest exhilarating rides, Liseberg is the place to come for dancing and entertainment, shows and theatre performances. It is also a green park where garden design has always played a major role.

The park's history began in the 18th century, when financier Johan Anders Lamberg bought the land and built the first magnificent house, Landeriet, in 1753. He had two passions in life – gardening and his wife Lisa, after whom the new house on the hill was named, Liseberg.

The City of Gothenburg purchased the site for the Gothenburg Exhibition in 1923 and founded the amusement park with the installation of a wooden roller-coaster. Other rides followed, attracting more than 140 million visitors over the past 80 years. "Balder" is said to be the best wooden roller-coaster in the world. It reaches a speed of 90 km/h (56 mph) from a top height of 36 m (118 ft). This retro ride is reminiscent of the park's very first roller-coaster.

Technology has introduced rides that test courage to the limit. The impressive "Helix" accelerates to 4.3 G forces, while "Valkyria" has a huge vertical drop. Less adrenalin-fuelled rides are suitable for children, where they can captain their very own Viking ship or get wet on the log-flume ride.

Apart from the latest exhilarating rides, Liseberg is the place to come for dancing and entertainment, shows and theatre performances.

13

Universeum

E5 Södra Vägen 50 10am-6pm daily universeum.se

Along the Mölndalsån river, not far from Kungsportsavenyn, is an area encompassing several of Gothenburg's major sights, including Liseberg, Ullevi and Universeum, the largest science centre in Scandinavia. While the aim of Universeum is to stimulate the interest of children and young people in science and technology, it provides a fun, educational experience for the entire family.

The daily catch from the North Sea is brought here directly, which guarantees the freshest mackerel and the most delicious shellfish. These days, however, there is more to the market than simply selling fish over the counter – the hall provides a colourful setting for restaurant tables at which seafood specialities can be sampled.

15 ⊗ ⊗ ⊗ ⊗ ⊗

Världskulturmuseet

📍 E5 🏛 Södra Vägen 54 🚃
🕐 Noon–5pm Tue–Fri (to 8pm Wed), 11am–5pm Sat & Sun (mid-Jun–mid-Aug: 11am–6pm Tue–Sun)
❌ Some public hols
🌐 varldskulturmuseet.se

Designed by the London-based architects Cécile Brisac and Edgar Gonzalez and completed in 2005, the ice cube-like Världskulturmuseet is a museum of world cultures. The exhibitions, like the building, are far from traditional; they are intended to surprise and question stereotyped attitudes towards culture and subculture, and are complemented by an extensive programme of concerts, films, dance and poetry.

The centre was built largely with recycled or ecologically friendly materials, and solar panels on the roof ensure that the building has a low impact on the environment. Exhibits are often interactive and include a tropical rainforest populated by snakes and frogs; a large aquarium, as well as a Swedish West Coast tank filled with local sea life; and a space station where you can learn about the life of an astronaut.

14 ⊗ ⊗

Feskekôrka

📍 B4 🏛 Fisktorget 4 🚃
📞 046-31 46 81 🕐 10am–6pm Tue–Fri, 10am–3pm Sat ❌ Public hols

Nicknamed Feskekôrka (the fish church), the architect Victor von Gegerfelt borrowed from Gothic church architecture when he designed this market hall in 1874, incorporating a steeply pitched roof and large oriel windows.

DRINK

Brewers Beer Bar
This bar offers a rotating tap list and tasty sourdough pizza to enjoy your beer with.
📍 A5 🏛 Tredje Långgatan 8
🌐 brewersbeerbar.se

Haket
A large selection on tap and in bottles and a lovely outdoor area for summer evenings.
📍 A1 🏛 Första Långgatan 32 🕐 Sun
🌐 linnestaden.nu/Haket

The Rover
Choose from a wide variety of 32 taps and a revolving selection.
📍 A4 🏛 Andra Långgatan 12
🌐 therover.se

An impressive variety of fish and seafood at Feskekôrka fish market ↓

Skansen Kronan

📍 B5 🚇 Skansberget 🚏
🕐 10am–3pm Tue–Fri
🔒 Public hols 🌐 skansen kronan.se

Topped by a golden crown, the octagonal Skansen Kronan fortress dates from Sweden's Age of Greatness. It sits enthroned on the peak of Skansberget, a leafy park offering excellent views. Like its counterpart Skansen Lejonet, near the station area,

> 💬 INSIDER TIP
> ### Boat Charter
>
> Gothenburg's beautiful location by the sea is best taken advantage of by renting a boat and exploring the serene archipelago or canal on a sunny day. Check out www.boatcharter-sweden.com for more details about trips.

Kronan is one of the most striking survivors of military engineer Erik Dahlbergh's fortifications. It was built in 1687 to protect the city from attack from the south. During the 1850s it was used as a shelter for homeless citizens and has also been a prison.

17

Götaplatsen

📍 D5 🚏

The focal point of the city is Götaplatsen. In the centre of this grand square lies Carl Milles's giant statue *Poseidon*, which has become the symbol of Gothenburg. Götaplatsen was built for the Gothenburg Exhibition in 1923.

Gothenburg's bastions of culture sit in state on this square. Wide steps lead up from the southeastern side to **Konstmuseet** (Art Museum), designed by Sigfrid Ericson. It contains a collection of Nordic art, with key works by Carl

Larsson and the Gothenburg Colourists. The Danish golden age, Dutch painting and French Modernists are also on show. Pride of place is taken by Fürstenbergska Galleriet, a copy of the gallery which the great patron of the arts had in his private palace in the late 19th century. The neighbouring **Konsthallen** (Art Hall) shows temporary exhibitions. The bronze lion on the façade is by Swedish sculptor Palle Pernevi.

Konserthuset (Concert Hall) on the southwestern side of the square was designed by architect Nils Einar Eriksson and opened in 1935. The foyer is decorated with murals by Prince Eugen (*Grove of Memories*) and Otte Sköld (*Folk Song*).

Konstmuseet

😊 🎨 🕐 11am–5pm Tue–Sun (to 6pm Tue & Thu, to 8pm Wed) 🔒 1 Jan, Good Friday, 1 May, Midsummer, 6 Jun, 24, 25 & 31 Dec 🌐 goteborgs konstmuseum.se

Konsthallen
🕐 11am–5pm Tue–Sun (to 6pm Tue & Thu, to 8pm Wed)
🌐 konsthallen.goteborg.se

Konserthuset
🕐 For concerts
🌐 gso.se/konserthuset

18
Gathenhielmska huset

📍 A1 🏠 Stigbergstorget 7
🚇 🔒 To the public

The western side of the Stigberget hill was formerly the site of the Amiralitetsvarvet shipyard, and it was here in the early 1700s that Privateer Captain Lars Gathenhielm was granted land by Karl XII. His widow built a two-storey manor house here in 1740. It is one of Sweden's best examples of a Carolian wooden house designed to imitate stone.

Next door is an open-air museum of wooden houses showing an 1800s suburb.

The unique exterior of Skansen Kronen and its golden crown

19
Gamla Haga

📍 B5 🚇

The former working-class area of the city south of Vallgraven is one of the few places left to experience old Gothenburg. The cobbled streets, courtyards and wood-and-stone houses of Gamla Haga are home to crafts-people and lined with small shops, cafés and restaurants.

Haga was Gothenburg's first suburb as early as the 17th century and was mainly populated by harbour workers. During the industrialization of the 19th century a small town grew up here and tenements filled with people flocking in from the countryside for work.

In the 1960s and 70s Haga was fast becoming a slum and threatened with demolition. Public opposition to the plans ensured that important parts were saved and the houses renovated. Some of the *landshövdingehusen* ("county governor's houses") typical of the area can be seen. These were built in the 1880s, when rules set in 1854 banning wooden houses in the centre more than two storeys high were circumvented – with the governor's approval. Providing the building had a ground floor in brick, as these do, it could have two wooden floors above and not constitute a fire risk.

---

20 ♻️ 🚫 💻 🛍️
Sjöfartsmuseet Akvariet

📍 A1 🏠 Karl Johansgatan 1-3 🚇 🔒 For renovation until 2021 🌐 sjofarts museetakvariet.se

The maritime history of Gothenburg and Bohuslän is one of the subjects of the Sjöfartsmuseet (Maritime Museum). Set up in 1933, it was funded by the Broström shipping family and is situated on Stigberget, high above the

↑ Pavement café on a cobbled street in picturesque Gamla Haga

Göta Älv river. The fascinating displays also explore the sometimes complex relation-ship between man and sea, and demonstrate how the port has adapted to a changing world.

Akvariet (the Aquarium) is the best spot to find out more about marine life, with 25 tanks covering both Nordic and tropical waters. Here, it is possible to see how crabs, starfish and sea anemones live 40 m (130 ft) below the surface. A touch-pool allows you to come into close contact with some creatures.

After undergoing an extensive renovation and extension, the museum and aquarium will reopen with a new entrance and underground exhibitions in autumn 2021. The Gamla Varvsparken, containing various busts, will gain a brilliant new café and extra green space.

Sjömanstornet tower out-side the museum is topped by Ivar Johansson's bronze sculpture *Woman by the Sea*, 1933, in memory of the sailors from western Sweden who died in World War I. There is a viewing platform at the top.

←

Älvsborgsbron suspension bridge crosses the Göta Älv river below at the harbour

㉑
The Harbour

📍B3 🧭 N of the centre between Götaälvbron and Älvsborgsbron bridges 🚢 From Lilla Bommen or Paddan sightseeing boat from Kungsportsplatsen bridge, up to 3 times an hour 🌐 stromma.se/en/Gothenburg

Seafaring has been of immense importance to Gothenburg and the harbour and shipyard have long dominated the area along the Göta Älv river. Now the shipbuilding industry is a shadow of its former self and apart from ferry traffic, the major shipping activities have moved down to the mouth of the river. Yet, although there is little loading and unloading to be seen in the centre of the city these days, three times more goods are shipped today than in the 1960s.

The inner harbour and shipyard area bordered by the imposing Älvsborgsbron bridge have been transformed to provide housing, offices and centres for research and education. Nevertheless, the pulse of seafaring can still be experienced either on a regular ferry from Lilla Bommen to Eriksbergsvarvet shipyard, or on the white, flat-bottomed Paddan boats that run from Kungsportsplatsen bridge (about a 10-minute walk away) via 17th-century Vallgraven down the river to the inner harbour. The round trip takes about 50 minutes.

Many of the city's sights are best viewed from the water. Eriksbergs shipyard on Hisingen is the home port of the spectacular East Indiaman *Götheborg*, which is often out on voyages all around the world. Tours also operate around the island of Hisingen and the outer harbour, and to the Gothenburg archipelago. Ever since 1910, the Fishing Harbour has held an auction Tuesday to Friday at 6:30am.

㉒ 🍴 🖼
Slottsskogen

📍A2 🧭 Museivägen 10 🚌

Since the 1870s, Slottsskogen has been one of the city's finest green spaces. Criss-crossed by paths, it features dazzling planting, ponds and a zoo. In spring the azalea valley is ablaze with colour. In 1999, what was then the world's longest border, with more than 90,000 flowering bulbs, was created. There are a number of old cottages from western Sweden to be seen in the park. Areas for sport and outdoor activities include Slottsskogsvallen. The park has several good cafés and a restaurant.

Gothenburg's oldest museum, **Naturhistoriska museet** (the Museum of Natural History), lies in the northern part of the park. Dating from 1833, it moved to Slottsskogen in 1923. Its vast

> Seafaring has been of immense importance to Gothenburg and the harbour and shipyard have long dominated the area along the Göta Älv river.

collection of more than 10 million exhibits incorporates animals of all sizes from all around the world, including brightly coloured insects and an African elephant.

The most famous of the stuffed animals is Malmska Valen, a blue whale measuring over 16 m (52 ft) long, which was beached in Askimviken in 1865. Today, it can only be seen on special occasions.

Naturhistoriska museet
 ⏱11am–5pm Tue–Sun (to 8pm Thu) Some public hols ⚑gnm.se

23

Botaniska Trädgården

📍A2 🏛Carl Skottsbergs Gata 22 A 🚋 ⏱24 hours daily ⚑botaniska.se

Covering 1,750,000 sq m (432 acres) and containing 16,000 species, the city's Botanical Garden is one of the largest of its kind in Europe.

Just under a fifth of the area has been developed into gardens, while the remainder forms a nature reserve partly consisting of primeval forest. Design of the gardens began in 1916, and they have been expanded continually ever since.

The Rhododendron Valley offers a rich tapestry of dazzling flowers in late spring each year. The Rock Garden, in a former quarry, contains 5,000 alpine plants from around the world. In early summer the Japanese Glade with its scented magnolias is a delight, while autumn sees a riot of colour.

Large greenhouses shelter the impressive plant collection from the sometimes bitter climate, and the controlled environments within recreate a variety of conditions from desert to steaming rain forest. In the tropical greenhouse, bamboo and banana plants stretch more than 10 m (33 ft) up to the ceiling, towering above the other plants.

1,500

The number of orchids in the Botaniska Trädgården's tropical house.

24 🍽

Nya Älvsborgs Fästning

📍A1 🚗8 km (3 miles) W of the centre 🚢From Lilla Bommen 📞031-158 151 ⏱Jul–mid-Aug

In 1660 a new fortress on Kyrkogårdsholmen replaced the dilapidated Älvsborg castle to defend Sweden's precious gateway to the North Sea. It was besieged by the Danes in 1717 and 1719, but never captured. In the late 18th century it became a prison that closed in 1869. Today the fortress is a popular tourist destination.

↑ A glass greenhouse fronted by a riot of colour at Botaniska Trädgården, and palms *(inset)* growing inside

A SHORT WALK
VÄSTRA NORDSTAN

Distance 2 km (1.5 miles) **Nearest train** Gothenburg
Central Station **Time** 25 minutes

This part of Gothenburg is the pulse of the seafaring
city, encapsulating almost 400 years of history. On the
quayside along the Göta Älv river the maritime world
is ever present, with museum ships at anchor and
the constant to-ing and fro-ing of boats and ferries.
Spectacular modern buildings, such as GöteborgsOperan
and GöteborgsUtkiken contrast with the city's more
historic monuments. These include the East India
Company building on Stora Hamnkanalen, a reminder
of the Dutch influence on Gothenburg's design, and
Kronhuset, the city's oldest secular building. Shoppers
should head for nearby Nordstan, which has a range of
department stores and galleries.

*Generous donations
enabled the building
of the long-awaited
GöteborgsOperan (p231),
which opened in 1994.*

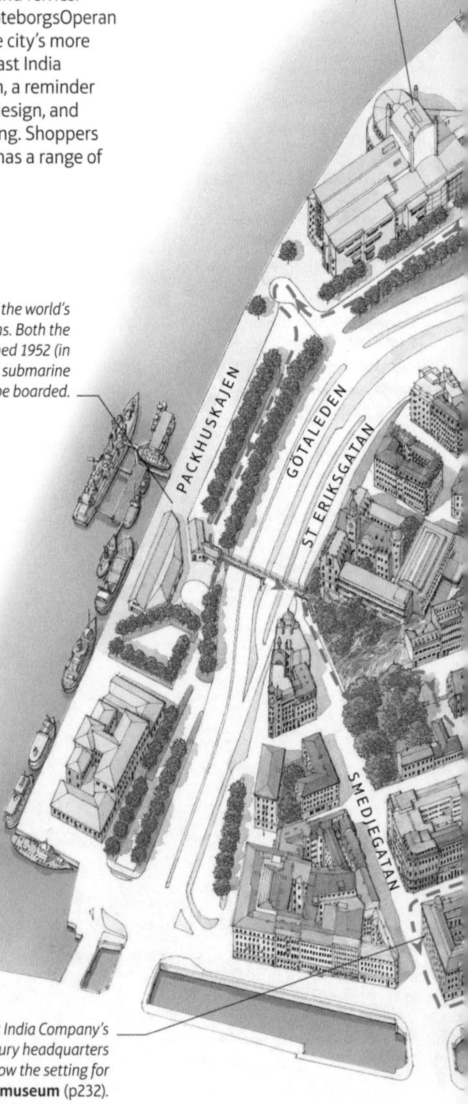

*__Maritiman__ (p230) is one of the world's
largest floating ship museums. Both the
destroyer Småland, launched 1952 (in
the background), and the submarine
Nordkaparen, 1962, can be boarded.*

↑ The striking
architecture of
GöteborgsOperan

*The former East India Company's
classical 18th-century headquarters
building is now the setting for
Göteborgs Stadsmuseum (p232).*

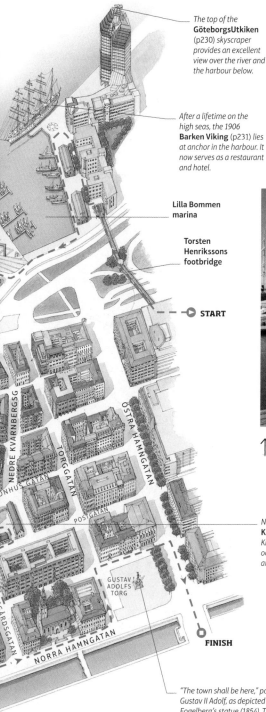

The top of the **GöteborgsUtkiken** (p230) *skyscraper provides an excellent view over the river and the harbour below.*

After a lifetime on the high seas, the 1906 **Barken Viking** (p231) *lies at anchor in the harbour. It now serves as a restaurant and hotel.*

Lilla Bommen marina

Torsten Henrikssons footbridge

- - - **START**

NEDRE KVARNBERGSG

KRONHUS GATAN

TORGGATAN

ÖSTRA HAMNGATAN

POSTGATAN

GUSTAV ADOLFS TORG

YGGÅRDSGATAN

NORRA HAMNGATAN

FINISH

Next to the 17th-century **Kronhuset** (p230), *the Kronhusbodarna sheds are occupied by craft-workers and restaurants.*

"The town shall be here," pointed King Gustav II Adolf, as depicted by Bengt Erland Fogelberg's statue (1854). The anniversary of the king's death is commemorated in **Gustav Adolfs Torg** (p230) *every year.*

Västra Nordstan

GOTHENBURG

Locator Map
For more detail see p228

↑ Lilla Bommen marina, with the GöteborgsUtkiken building in the background

| 0 metres | 100 |
| 0 yards | 100 |

N ↑

WESTERN GÖTALAND

Spanning four provinces – Dalsland, Bohuslän, Västergötland and Halland – this is an attractive and immensely diverse part of Sweden, with the country's largest lake, Vänern, at its heart.

Dalsland in the northwest is one of Sweden's smallest provinces. The landscape is hilly and it is said that the border with Norrland starts here with the mountain area of Kroppefjäll. From the plains of agricultural Dalsland this border can be seen rearing up like a dark forest-clad wall to the west, while the blue expanse of Lake Vänern glistens to the east.

In the southwest, Dalsland borders Bohuslän, a coastal province where the smooth bare rocks are dotted with little wooden houses. Here fishing and the stone industry have been the backbone of the economy since the Middle Ages, but today tourism is the chief money earner.

Västergötland has been inhabited since ancient times and has many prehistoric remains. It was the first region in Sweden to be converted to Christianity and has an abundance of early churches. The country's first Christian king, Olof Skötkonung, is thought to have been baptized at Husaby in 1008 and two of the medieval royal dynasties had their roots in Västergötland.

Halland, the coastal region south of Gothenburg, is a summer paradise, with its long sandy beaches, appealing towns and some of southern Sweden's most interesting castles and manor houses.

WESTERN GÖTALAND

Must See
1 Gunnebo Slott

Experience More
2 Strömstad
3 Åmål
4 Koster Islands
5 Fjällbacka
6 Tanum
7 Nordens Ark
8 Uddevalla
9 Smögen
10 Lysekil
11 Skaftö
12 Bassholmen
13 Gullholmen
14 Kungälv
15 Tjörn
16 Orust
17 Marstrand
18 Vänersborg
19 Trollhättan
20 Lidköping
21 Läckö Slott
22 Tivedens National Park
23 Kinnekulle
24 Karlsborg
25 Mariestad
26 Falköping
27 Hjo
28 Skara
29 Skövde
30 Borås
31 Torpa Stenhus
32 Alingsås
33 Kungsbacka
34 Ulricehamn
35 Laholm
36 Halmstad
37 Varberg
38 Falkenberg

❶ 🕭 🎨 🍴 ☕ 🛍

GUNNEBO SLOTT

🅰 C5 🚗 15 km (9 miles) SE of Gothenburg. E6/E20, then Gunnebogatan
🚌🚊 Mölndal 🕐 For tours only; times vary, check website. Garden: daily
🌐 gunneboslott.se

This beautiful Neo-Classical country mansion and its adjoining landscaped gardens, set among lush hills and two lakes, offers a relaxing break from the bustle of everyday life.

In the 1780s, John Hall, one of the richest men in Sweden at the time, commissioned city architect Carl Wilhelm Carlberg of Gothenburg to design a summer villa and park at Gunnebo. On completion in 1796, it was one of the most beautiful and stylistically pure examples of Neo-Classical Swedish architecture. The French-inspired formal garden surrounding the house was also designed by Carlberg, as was the English park, which makes an ideal setting for a walk. An adjoining farm made the estate virtually self-sufficient.

> ## Did You Know?
>
> Hall is said to have paid the bill for the mansion's construction with 38 barrels of gold.

↑ The beautifully preserved Neo-Classical façade of the mansion

Three magnificent French windows in the hall let in the sunlight, which is reflected on the stunning parquet floor.

Oval vestibule

The frieze on the southern gable is made from lead painted to imitate marble.

The interior design, including exquisite ceramic stoves, is by Carlberg, who adopted the light Gustavian style that pervades the house.

The staircase leads to the park with its parterres and gravel paths.

↑ The grand main building on the estate

The entrance is through the cellar, the starting point for tours.

EAT

Kaffehus och Krog
Housed in the service building at Gunnebo Slott, this spot serves fantastic lunches and coffee. The food is sustainable and seasonal, and there's even an in-house bakery that sells cookies, chocolate muffins and berry pie.

🔲 **gunneboslott.se/ inlagg/kaffehusoch krog**

Ⓚ Ⓚ Ⓚ

Ionian columns frame the sheltered terrace on the northern façade, which opens onto the garden with its neatly clipped trees.

↑ Attractive buildings along the waterfront in the resort town of Strömstad

EXPERIENCE MORE

②
Strömstad

🅰 C4 🏠 Bohuslän E6
➡ From Rygge, Norway
🚌 ⛴ From Sandefjord, Norway 🛈 Norra Hamnen; www.vastsverige.com

Once a small fishing village, by 1676 Strömstad had become a town, acting as a strategic counter to the towns of Halden and Fredrikstad in Norway. In the mid-19th century sea bathing became popular and ever since, Strömstad, with its glorious island archipelago, has been one of Sweden's major holiday resorts.

The **Strömstads Museum** focuses on local history, while **Friluftsmuseet Fiskartorpet** is an open-air museum featuring fishermen's cottages. The harbour, with bars and shops, is in the centre of town and boats from here serve the islands. The Svinesund bridges between Sweden and Norway offer magnificent views.

Strömstads Museum
🏠 Södra Hamngatan 26
📞 0526-102 75 ⏰ 10am–4pm Mon–Fri ⛔ Public hols

Friluftsmuseet Fiskartorpet
😊 🏠 Östra Klevgatan 9
📞 0526-190 00
⏰ Summer: daily

③
Åmål

🅰 D4 🏠 Dalsland Road 45
➡ Karlstad 🚌 🛈 Marinan, Hamngatan 3; www. vastsverige.com/amal

Thanks to its strategic location on Lake Vänern, Åmål became an important marketplace, controlling timber exports to Norway. After fires in the 17th century and one in 1901, a new town was built on the north side of the Åmålsån river. A few 18th-century houses remain around the town park. The local history museum, **Åmåls Hembygdsmuseum**, whose three floors house a dentist's clinic and a flat furnished in 1920s style, can be found in Snarhögsgården.

Åmåls Hembygdsmuseum
🚲 🏠 Hamngatan 7 📞 0532-158 20 ⏰ Mid-Jun-Aug: daily; Sep-mid-Jun: Mon-Fri

④ Koster Islands

🅰C4 🏠Bohuslän
🚢From Strömstad (about
45 mins) ℹ️Norra Hamnen,
Strömstad; 0526-623 30

The islands of Koster, in the middle of the Kosterhavet National Park, are renowned for their beauty and their flora. Together they form a nature reserve. These are the western-most Swedish islands to be inhabited. Sydkoster is the largest island in the group. It is greener than Nordkoster and is best explored by bike. In contrast, Nordkoster is much more barren and can easily be explored on foot.

The highlights of the Koster Islands' calendar include the Kosterhavsfestivalen Chamber Music Festival in July and the lobster festival in the autumn, when you can sample the freshest shellfish and take part in thrilling fishing trips.

> 💬 INSIDER TIP
> ### Kayaking the West Coast
>
> August can often be the best time to kayak around the scenic Koster Islands as the weather is good and the crowds are minimal. Some islands, however, can be occassionally closed off to protect the birds and seals, so it's always best to check your route with a tour operator before you head out.

---

⑤ Fjällbacka

🅰C5 🏠Bohuslän E6/Road
163 🚂To Tanum, then bus
ℹ️Ingrid Bergmans Torg,
(summer only); www.
vastsverige.com/tanum

On the coast between Strömstad and Uddevalla lies the picturesque village of Fjällbacka. There has been a settlement here since the 17th century and like many other villages along this coast the community once made a living from herring fishing and seafaring. Today, holidaymakers come for the swimming and boating.

Attractive low-rise wooden houses and shops line the narrow streets, but it is the harbour that is the heart of the community. Fjällbacka has a stunning location with islands offshore and the 70-m- (230-ft-) high mountain, Vetteberget, creating a precipitous backdrop to the square known as Ingrid Bergmans Torg. Actress Ingrid Bergman spent many summers in Fjällbacka and after her death her name was given to the square and a bust made. Fjällbacka is also the location of author Camilla Läckberg's series "The Fjällbacka Murders", which has sold millions of books worldwide.

Vetteberget, meanwhile, is divided by a huge gorge, known as Kungsklyfta, named after King Oscar II who visited Fjällbacka in 1887 and had his name carved at the entrance. This dramatic setting was also used as a location for the film of Astrid Lindgren's children's book Ronja Rövardotter (Ronja the Robber's Daughter).

← Fjällbacka's popular waterside restaurants, full to the brim

Tanum

⚑ C4 ⚐ Bohuslän E6
🚉 ℹ Tanumshede,
Apoteksvägen 6; www.
vastsverige.com/tanum

The municipality of Tanum has an extraordinary 525 km (326 miles) of coastline indented with fjords and bays. It stretches from Gerlesborg in the south to Resö in the north, and is sheltered by a mass of islets and skerries offshore.

Above all, Tanum is famous for its Bronze Age rock carvings, with the earliest dating from around 1000 BC. Indeed, the concentration of these pictorial images and their contribution to the understanding

Fjällbacka's wooden houses clustering around the harbour ↓

of Bronze Age culture is such that they were designated a UNESCO World Heritage Site in 1994. Subjects include human life, animals, boats and weapons carved onto smooth rock.

The largest carving, covering 200 sq m (2,150 sq ft), can be seen at Vitlycke. **Vitlycke Museum** is well worth a visit for a fascinating insight into this form of rock art, with a reconstructed Bronze Age farm. Guided tours by night, when carvings that are not visible by day emerge in the light of a torch, are especially enthralling for any age group.

Around the region, carvings featuring hunting scenes can be seen at Fossum, east of Tanumshede; Tegneby has images of ships; and Asberget has scenes containing animals, ploughs and axes.

Vitlycke Museum

⊗⊗⊙⊜⊜ ⚑ 3 km (2 miles) S of Tanumshede ⊙ Mid-Apr–Nov 🌐 vitlyckemuseum.se

---

7 ⊘⊗⊜⊡⊕
Nordens Ark

⚑ C5
⚐ Hunnebostrand, 20 km (12 miles) N of Smögen ⊙ Daily; times vary, check website 🌐 nordensark.se

This nature park and zoo caters specifically for endangered species. Located in Åby Säteri, it contains animals from every corner of the world, including ancient Swedish breeds such as Gotland sheep and mountain cows, Nordic wild animals such as wolves and wolverine, and exotic species such as the Amur leopard and a variety of parrots. Many of the creatures are part of programmes to protect them from extinction.

To see the animals up close, follow the 3-km (2-mile) walk around the park – and bring binoculars to spot the wide variety of birds. The route takes you between the enclosures via wooden bridges and

BRONZE AGE ROCK CARVINGS

The rock carvings at Tanum represent a high point in the artistic language of pictures and symbols used by Bronze Age people more than 3,000 years ago. Images reflect daily life and hardships, battles won and lost, weapons and hunting scenes. Mating scenes, fertility symbols and the afterlife are also common. The importance of the sea is reflected in the proliferation of ships and fishing scenes. It is thought that the rock paintings were mainly of ritual significance, but the depiction of animals could have acted as a calendar to show when various creatures could be hunted. Rock carvings are found all over the world, with the oldest dating from 20,000 BC. Those in Sweden are younger, since it wasn't free of ice until 6,500 BC.

along gravel paths, but breeding and quarantine areas are not open to the public. Admission in the summer includes a guided tour.

Nordens Ark is a particularly enjoyable outing for families as there are special children's activities throughout the park. Youngsters – and adults – can find out how animals adapt in relation to their food, enemies and the environment by being active themselves, trying things out and playing. Overnight accommodation is also available.

Uddevalla Bridge, a cable-stayed bridge crossing Sunninge Sound ↑

8

Uddevalla

🅐C5 🅐Bohuslän E6, Road 44 🔼Trollhättan 🅐
🛈Södra Hamnen 2; www. uddevalla.com

The town of Uddevalla was famous for shipbuilding on a grand scale until the 1980s, when an economic crisis forced the closure of its shipyard. Uddevalla's history dates from 1498, when it gained its town charter. Its strategic location helped trade to flourish, but also left it open to attack. It became Swedish in the Peace of Roskilde in 1658, as the statues of Karl X Gustav and Erik Dahlbergh in front of the old town hall testify.

Among the town's museums, the collections at **Bohusläns Museum** focus on the cultural and natural heritage of the region. The museum is situated by the harbour, and includes Konsthallen, a gallery for contemporary art.

Uddevalla also has a pleasant seaside promenade. Nature lovers will enjoy the unusual shellbanks and the museum devoted to them, **Skalbanksmuseet**, in Kuröd, outside Uddevalla.

Bohusläns Museum

🕙🛈🔲🔲🅐 🅐Museigatan 1
🕙Daily 🕙Some public hols
🆆bohuslansmuseum.se

Skalbanksmuseet

🚏 🅐5 km (3 miles) E of Uddevalla 📞0522-138 91
🕙Jun–Aug: 11am–5pm daily

9

Smögen

🅐C5 🅐Bohuslän E6/Road 174 🛈Sotenäs Tourist Office, Kungshamn; www. vastsverige.com/sotenas

One of Sweden's largest fishing communities, Smögen today is a delightful holiday resort. Shrimp trawlers and colourful wooden buildings enhance the waterfront, and the daily fish auction provides popular entertainment. Commerce is particularly lively along the wooden quayside.

Ferries operate to the island of Hållö, a nature reserve south of Smögen where there is a lighthouse, Hållö Fyr, which has guided seafarers since 1842.

The Sotenkanalen links Smögen and Hunnebostrand. Built in the 1930s, the canal is 6 km (4 miles) long and a popular tourist route. Hunnebostrand is a typical west- coast holiday destination and home to Svenska Hummerakademien (the Swedish Lobster Academy). The village's development was based on stonemasonry.

10

Lysekil

🅐C5 🅐Bohuslän E6/Road 162 🚌From Fiskebäckskil 🛈Strandvägen 9; www. lysekil.se

When Lysekil gained its town charter in 1903 it was already an established seaside resort. Buildings in the old part of Lysekil, Gamlestan, are more than 200 years old. A walk along Strandgatan reveals the many charms of this delightful old quarter. The 19th-century sea-bathing area has been beautifully restored, with a cold bath house and the Nordic-style Curmanska Villas. The rest of the town is dominated by the large, Neo-Gothic granite church dating from 1901.

Lysekil lies at the far end of the Stångenäset peninsula, with Gullmarsfjorden – Sweden's only real "fjord" in a Norwegian sense – to the south and Brofjorden to the north, and here the sea has always played a major role. The town's aquarium, **Havets Hus**, is devoted to the marine and plant life found off the Bohuslän coast. Around 100 different species of fish can be viewed in their natural habitats. There is a walk-through aquarium and an interesting multimedia centre. The town's fishing traditions can also be experienced at the Hot Bulb Engine Festival held in August.

Havets Hus

♿🏷️💬🅿️ 🏠Strandvägen 9 🕐Jul–mid-Aug: 10am–6pm daily; mid-Aug–Dec: 10am–4pm daily 🌐havetshus.se

---

⑪
Skaftö

🅰️C5 🏠Bohuslän Road 161 towards Fiskebäckskil 🛈Lysekil Tourist Office; www.skafto.com

The best way to see the island of Skaftö is to walk or cycle around it. The scenery varies between fertile agricultural land, pine forests and bare hills. Skaftö's potatoes and strawberries are justifiably famous. Located in the centre of the island is Gunnesbo, a great spot for children, offering pony rides and a mini-zoo.

In the far south, on the slopes running down towards the sea lies Rågårdsvik, a small community overlooking the wide Ellösefjorden and the village of Ellöse, site of the internationally successful Hallberg Rassy shipyard. Rågårdsvik Pensionat provides an excellent selection of west-coast cuisine.

Between Skaftölandet and Orust are the winding, narrow Malö straits, made famous by the songs of troubadour Evert Taube (*p76*), while the beautiful Snäckedjupet separates Skaftö from the mainland.

Fiskebäckskil is a seafaring community established at the end of the 19th century in Gullmarsfjorden, it features a captain's house, richly decorated wooden cottages and romantic gardens. It is also the site of Kristineberg Marine Research Station.

The village of Grundsund dates from the 17th century. A canal runs through it past the closely packed red fishermen's huts on the lively quayside, so typical of the west coast. The small wooden church, built in 1799, is well worth a look. Delicious fresh seafood is served in the harbourside inn.

⑫
Bassholmen

🅰️C5 🏠Bohuslän Road 161 towards Fiskebäckskil 🚌From Uddevalla daily 🛈Uddevalla; www.onbassdholmen.com/sv

The nature reserve on the island of Bassholmen, between Orust and Skaftö, is one of the highlights of the Bohuslän archipelago. The landscape is one of narrow valleys, leafy meadows and pine forest. It is a particularly attractive area for walking. In the centre of the island an old farm stands amid parkland and trees.

Bassholmen is also home to a number of traditional shipbuilder's yards, which come under the care of the Föreningen Allmoge Båtar, a society that works to preserve and renovate the traditional wooden boats of Bohuslän. Many of these boats can be seen in the museum.

Every summer boating enthusiasts converge on the island to study the craftsmanship in great detail. There is a guest jetty in the former shipyard for visiting craft. In summer boats run to Bassholmen from Uddevalla.

↓ Snow-covered village of Fiskebäckskil on Skaftö island

13

Gullholmen

🅰C5 🏛Bohuslän 🚢From Tuvesvik, Orust 🛈Henåns Tourist Office; www. sodrabohuslan.com

Dating from 1585, Gullholmen is one of the oldest fishing communities in Bohuslän. In the mid-19th century one of Sweden's early canning factories was set up here. Line fishing on the Dogger Bank in the North Sea produced good catches and in 1910 Gullholmen had a fishing fleet of more than 50 cutters. As the fishing industry declined, so did the population and summer residents have taken over many of the houses. Gullholmen is a typical westcoast summer paradise. Sights include the church, inaugurated in 1799, and the pilot's lookout, which was dismantled in 1916 but is now being rebuilt.

South of Gullholmen, as if thrown out to sea, lies the completely barren Käringön. The charming tightly packed houses are mostly used by summer visitors and in the

season the popular guest harbour is bursting with life. A fishing cottage houses a small museum. The island can be reached by boat from Hälleviksstrand or by ferry from Tuvesvik.

14

Kungälv

🅰C5 🏛Bohuslän E6 ✈Landvetter 🚌To Ytterby then bus 🛈www.vasts verige.com

Strategically located between the Nordre Älv and Göta Älv rivers, Kungälv occupies the site of the 10th-century Viking settlement of Kongahälla. It is dominated by the ruins of **Bohus Fästning**, a fortress built by the Norwegian king Håkon Magnusson in 1308. Constructed first in wood and later in stone, the fortress was at the frontline in the constant wars between Sweden, Norway and Denmark. At the Peace of Roskilde in 1658 it became Swedish, but it went on to be besieged no less than 14 times without being captured.

In 1678, some 900 Swedish defenders faced 9,000 Norwegians and 7,000 German mercenaries, but still the castle didn't fall. In the 18th century it became a prison and in 1789 all the towers were destroyed apart from the main one

> **Did You Know?**
>
> Käringön, south of Gullholmen, is so bare that earth for its churchyard had to be brought from Orust.

known as "Fars Hatt" (Father's Hat). Red-roofed Kungälv church, situated in the market square, dates from 1679.

Bohus Fästning
♿♿ 🕐Times vary, check website 🔒Midsummer Eve 🌐bohusfastning.com

15

Tjörn

🅰C5 🏛Bohuslän 🛈Tjörn Tourist Office; www.tjorn. se, www.sodrabohuslan. com

The municipality of Tjörn comprises six inhabited islands. Fishing, boat-building and small businesses are the cornerstones of the economy and in summer the population doubles with the arrival of holidaymakers.

Opened in 1960, the Tjörn Bridges offer great views over land and water. Tjörnbroleden, the road linking the islands of

The impregnable fortress of Bohus Fästning in Kungälv ↑

← Taking a dip in the clear waters around the island of Tjörn

brought poverty, but with the herring's reappearance in the 1750s the population increased, inns opened and refineries for making fish oil from herring developed. The bare rocks of Bohuslän are a reminder of this time; the fish oil refineries needed lots of wood and the coastline was practically deforested.

Most homes had a fisherman's hut on the harbour and even today the houses and huts are closely packed together. There is a smell of stockfish hanging out to dry to produce *Lutfisk* for Christmas.

Today Orust manufactures superior leisure boats. The boatyards display their craft on the "Öppet Varv" open days.

17

Marstrand

🅰 C5 🚌 Bohuslän Road 168
🚢 🌐 www.marstrand.se, www.vastsverige.com

Sun, sailing and the sea are what Marstrand is all about. The little town of pastel-coloured wooden houses has its roots in the herring boom of the mid-16th century, which attracted fortune-hunters. But it really took off in the mid-19th century as a fashionable seaside resort: Marstrand built its baths and society arrived.

The town is crowned by the impressive **Carlstens Fästning**, a fortress built in 1666–73 and redesigned in the 1680s. At one time it was a notorious prison. Tours provide a glimpse into the life and times of the fortress and its inmates in the 18th century. Plays are staged here and feasts held during the summer.

Carlstens Fästning
🏛 ⏱ 🏠 ⏰ Times vary, check website 🌐 carlsten.se

Tjörn and Orust to the mainland at Stenungsund, crosses the bridges of Stenungsöbron, Källosundsbron and Tjörnbron over Askeröfjorden. In 1980 Tjörnbron collapsed when a ship collided with it in thick fog; a new bridge opened the following year. At its northern end is an ideal site for camping with great views. Skärhamn, on the west side of Tjörn, is the island's main town. It has a guest harbour, restaurants and hotel. Sights include the Sjöfartsmuseum (Seafaring Museum) and the popular **Nordiska Akvarellmuseet** (Nordic Watercolour Museum), a stunning building hosting exhibitions and courses for amateur painters.

Pilane Gravfält, a burial site with more than 100 Iron Age mounds, stone circles, rings and standing stones, is in northwest Tjörn. You can reach it by taking the road towards Kyrkesund and turning left to Hällene.

Nordiska Akvarellmuseet
🏛 🎨 🏠 🏛 🅰 Skärhamn Södra hamnen 6 ⏰ 11am–6pm daily 🚫 Some public hols 🌐 akvarellmuseet.org

---

16

Orust

🅰 C5 🚌 Bohuslän
ℹ Hamntorget 18; www.orust.se or www.sodrabohuslan.com

Orust's fortunes over the centuries have been tied to the rise and fall of herring fishing. On the southwest coast, the village of Mollösund dates from the 16th century, when herring fishing was at its height. A decline in stocks

> Today, Trollhättan successfully combines high-tech businesses with a film industry that has earned the town its local nickname, "Trollywood".

18
Vänersborg

🅐C5 🚗Västergötland Road E45 🚅🚌 ℹ️Kungsgatan 9; www.visittv.se

Vänersborg is otherwise known as "Little Paris" after the compositions of local poet Birger Sjöberg (1885–1929). A statue of Sjöberg's muse, Frida, can be seen in the beautiful Skräckleparken on the lake shore, and a reconstruction of his home is in **Vänersborgs Museum**. Other museums in the area focus on medical history, dolls and sport.

Just over 5 km (3 miles) east of the town, the steeply sided hills of Halleberg and Hunneberg rise over the landscape. The hillside forests are a nature reserve home to a large elk population. On top of Hunneberg is the **Kungajaktmuseet Älgens Berg** (Royal Hunt Museum) where the "king of the forest" is presented in fascinating interactive displays.

Vänersborgs Museum
🏛️ 🕐Noon–4pm Thu–Sun (Jun–Aug: also Wed) 🅦vanersborgsmuseum.se

Kungajaktmuseet Älgens Berg
🌐🏛️💬🍽️ 🚗Hunneberg 121, on Road 44 🕐Times vary, check website 🅦algensberg.com

→

Läckö Slott, on the shore of Lake Vänern, and art *(inset)* displayed inside the castle

19
Trollhättan

🅐C5 🚗Västergötland Road E45 🚅🚌 ℹ️Åkerssjövägen 10; 0520-135 09

The opening of the Trollhättan Canal in 1800, linking Lake Vänern and the North Sea, marked the birth of Trollhättan as an industrial town. Today, Trollhättan successfully combines high-tech businesses with a film industry that has earned the town its local nickname, "Trollywood".

The town's main sight is the waterfall area, where four locks regulate the once wild 32-m-(105-ft-) high falls. In summer the sluices are opened several times a week to let the mass of water rush freely down river.

The technology centre **Innovatum Science Center (ISC)** features multimedia exhibits on the development and history of Trollhättan. Leaving from the Innovatum area, a cable car transports you 30 m (98 ft) above the canal to the opposite bank. A short walk leads to the Canal Museum.

Innovatum Science Center (ISC)
🌐💬🍽️🏛️ 🚗Åkerssjövägen 16 🕐11am–4pm Tue–Sun (mid-Jun–mid-Aug: daily) 🅦innovatum.se

20
Lidköping

🅐D5 🚗Västergötland Road 44 🚅🚌 ℹ️Gamla Rådhuset på Nya stadens torg; www.vastsverige.com

The town of Lidköping lies at the heart of the area of Västergötland that is considered to be the cradle of the Svea Kingdom.

Like so many Swedish wooden towns, Lidköping suffered a devastating fire in 1849, though some of the 17th-century buildings around the square of Limtorget survived.

The Lidan river divides the town into old and new, and the two main squares face each other across the water. Nya Stadens Torg (New Town Square) is the site of a former hunting lodge, which the founder of the new town, Magnus Gabriel de la Gardie, brought here to serve as a town hall.

Lidköping is known for the Rörstrands Porcelain Factory and **Rörstrands Museum** attracts visitors to enjoy the museum showpieces.

Vänermuseet with the Paleo Geology Centre is an interactive science museum.

Rörstrands Museum

⊕🖼🏠 🄰Fabriksgatan 4 🄲10am-6pm Mon-Sat (to 4pm Sat), 11am-3pm Sun 🄴Some public hols 🅦rorstrandcenter.se

Vänermuseet

⊕🖼🟡😊🍴 🄰Framnäsvägen 2 🄲10am-5pm Mon-Fri, 11am-4pm Sat & Sun 🄴Some public hols 🅦vanermuseet.se

---

21

Läckö Slott

🄰D5 🄰Västergötland 25 km (15 miles) N of Lidköping 🄲10am-6pm daily 🅦lackoslott.se

In 2001 Läckö was named the most beautiful castle in Sweden. It is surrounded by water on three sides. Originally built in the 13th century, it was remodelled in the 17th century. In 1681 Läckö was claimed by Karl XI in his recovery of crown lands from the nobility and its contents were scattered.

Restoration work in the 20th century has revealed more than 200 rooms, including the ornate apartment of Princess Marie Euphrosyne, wife of Magnus de la Gardie, and the King's Hall with its paintings of the Thirty Years' War.

EAT

Hvita Hjortens
Food prepared with crops from the castle gardens and from local fishermen, farmers and hunters is served here.

🄰D5 🄰Läckö Slott, Lidköping 🄲Oct-Nov: Mon-Fri 🅦lackoslott.se

Ⓚ Ⓚ Ⓚ

Skärets Krog
Small plates are divided between snacks, cold and warm dishes and dessert – only the finest ingredients are used.

🄰C5 🄰Hamnen 1, Smögen 🄲Winter 🅦skaretskrog.se

Ⓚ Ⓚ Ⓚ

㉒
Tivedens National Park

🗺 D5 🏛 Västergötland Road 49 ℹ Tivedens National Park Visitor Centre, Stenkälla; www. nationalparksofsweden.se

On the border between Närke and Västergötland lies Tivedens National Park, an untouched area of rugged wilderness. It was established in 1983 to protect the remaining primeval forest and lakes, of which Fagertärn is the original habitat of the large red water lily.

The area is very hilly and demanding for walkers. You can find information on trails, parking and things to see inside the park at the visitor centre at Stenkälla.

Giant Ice Age boulders, some up to 10 m (33 ft) high, litter the forest around Trollkyrka, the hill east of the road by the visitor centre. The mountain's name, meaning "Troll's Church", is thought to be derived from the fact that the site was used by local people who came here to worship after the ban in 1726 on holding religious services outside churches.

㉓ 🍴
Kinnekulle

🗺 D5 🏛 Västergötland Road 44 ℹ Gamla Rådhuset på Nya stadens torg, Lidköping; www.vastsverige.com

The 306-m- (1,000-ft-) high plateau of Kinnekulle, known as "the flowering mountain", rises from the Västergötland landscape, providing habitats for wild flowers, deciduous woods, pine forests, meadows and pastures. It is topped with bare limestone and a

> GREAT VIEW
> **Dine in Awe**
>
> If you're not up to climbing to the lookout tower at the top of Kinnekulle, you can still enjoy impressive views of the countryside from the restaurant (www. kinnekullegarden.com) on the top of the hill.

20-m- (66-ft-) high lookout tower. Limestone has been quarried here since the 12th century. In summer demonstrations at the remaining quarry show how the work used to be carried out. The area is peppered with ancient Bronze Age and Stone Age sites.

Forshems Kyrka, just to the east, dates from the 12th century and is known for its stone reliefs. The churchyard of the 12th-century church at Kinne-Vedum, 2 km (1 mile) north of Götene, has several lily stones, typical of this area.

↑ Peaceful forests and lakes in Tivedens National Park, and the visitor centre (inset) at Stenkälla

→ The industrial flour mill at Forsvisk Bruk, near Karlsborg

Karlsborg

D5 **Västergötland**
Road 49 **Fortress: 0505-17350** **Times vary, call ahead** **Karlsborg Tourist Office, Storgatan 65; www.karlsborgsturism.se**

In 1819 King Karl XIV Johan decided that a fortress should be built at Vanås on the shore of Lake Vättern. It was named Karlsborg and was to act as an emergency capital in the event of war; a place of safety for the Royal Family, the national bank and the government. The 90 years it took to build meant that by the time it was finally finished the fortress was out of date and it never had any real significance.

Today, however, it is a major tourist attraction. The "town" enclosed within the 5-km- (3-mile-) long walls is always open to visitors but best viewed on one of the hour-long guided adventure tours that run daily in the summer. Action fans can watch *Fästningsäventyret*, an adventure depicting life in the fortress in the 1860s complete with stunt men and special effects. After the tour, the museum offers additional facts about life behind these walls from history to the present time.

Outside the fortress, the Göta Canal wends its way towards Lake Vänern, passing **Forsviks Bruk**, which offers an interesting glimpse into Sweden's industrial heritage, with a blacksmith's forge, sawmill and working flour mill.

Forsviks Bruk

8 km (5 miles) N of centre **Mid-May–mid-Sep: noon–6pm daily (Jun & Jul: from 10am)** **forsviksbruk.se**

Mariestad

D5 **Västergötland**
E20 **Lidköping**
Esplanaden 5; www.vastsverige.com

Duke Karl founded the pretty town of Mariestad in 1583, naming it after his wife, Maria of Pfalz. He built the cathedral and lavishly decorated it in the Baroque style. It is worth exploring the little streets surrounding the cathedral, as these are lined with 18th and 19th century buildings.

In 1660 Mariestad became the county town of Skaraborg. The former royal manor of Marieholm, on an island where the River Tidan flows into Lake Vänern, was the governor's residence. The building now houses the **Mariestads Industrimuseum** (Industrial Museum) and the **Vadsbo Museum**.

Mariestad's location on Lake Vänern and the River Tidan makes it an idyllic summer town. The Göta Canal runs through it and just north in Sjötorp is the **Kanalmuseet** (Canal Museum).

Those interested in rural life should head for Klockarbolet in Odensåker, a reconstructed village dating from the 17th and 18th centuries.

Vadsbo Museum and Mariestads Industrimuseum

Marieholmsbron 3 **0501-755830** **Wed; other days by appt**

Kanalmuseet

Slussvägen 112, Sjötorp (off Road Rv 26) **May–Sep: daily** **gotakanal.se**

TOP 4 ACTIVITIES ON LAKE VÄTTERN IN HJO

Kayak
Rent a kayak or a stand-up paddle-board at the Hjo Tourist Information.

Row Your Boat
Take a trip with a steamboat from 1892 and do a round trip on the lake.

Float Away
The wood-fired floating sauna in the wharf is the perfect way to unwind.

Swim
The sand beach below Hjo Town Park, next to the harbour, is a delight.

Falbygdens Museum is a great stop to learn about the local history.

Ekornavallen, 15 km (9 miles) north of Falköping, is an important historic burial site from the Stone, Bronze and Iron ages. **Dalénmuseet** in Stenstorp, 15 km (9 miles) northeast of Falköping, uses sound-and-light shows to illustrate the life and work of the 1912 Swedish Nobel laureate Gustaf Dalén, who invented the AGA oven.

Falbygdens Museum
🏛 St Olofsgatan 23 📞 0515-885 050 🕐 Tue–Fri & Sun 🚫 Some public hols

Dalénmuseet
📷 🏛 Järnväfsgatan 27, 10 km (6 miles) N of centre 🕐 Mid-Mar–Aug: 10am–6pm Tue–Fri, noon–4pm Sat & Sun (Jul: also Mon) 🚫 Midsummer weekend 🌐 dalenmuseet.se

Bird enthusiasts at Lake Hornborgasjön by Skara, anticipating a glimpse of a dancing crane *(inset)* ↑

26 Falköping

🗺 D5 🚩 Västergötland Road 46 🚍 ℹ Stora Torget 11; www.falkoping.nu

Between the hills of Ålleberg and Mösseberget lies the old town of Falköping. Of particular interest are the medieval wooden houses and the town square, Stora Torget, with Ivar Tengbom's statue *Venus Rising from the Waves* (1931). The

27 Hjo

🗺 D5 🚩 Västergötland Road 193/194 ℹ Bangatan 1B; www.hjo.se

Mention Hjo and Swedes will immediately think of the exquisite little wooden houses dating from the end of the 19th century with their ornately carved verandas. Hjo is a delightful town to visit. On

the shore of Lake Vättern is Stadsparken, a park created when Hjo Spa was founded in the late 19th century. Villa Svea, one of the former spa buildings in the park, houses **Hjo Stadsmuseum** (the Town Museum). It is worth a look for its remarkable calendar clock Hjouret. The park also contains Fjärilsmuseum (the Butterfly Museum) and an aquarium.

Just like the town, the harbour has medieval origins, but the present one was built in the mid-19th century after the construction of the Göta Canal. In summer, the Lok-Hjo-Motivet train takes guided tours (daily except Monday) through the town, starting from the harbour. The steamer S/S *Trafik* (1892) runs Sunday tours to Visingö, and jazz cruises to Vadstena *(p182)* across the lake.

The Hjoån river valley, stretching from Lake Vättern

←

Falköping, sandwiched between snowy hills of Mösseberget and Ålleberg

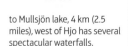

to Mullsjön lake, 4 km (2.5 miles), west of Hjo has several spectacular waterfalls.

Hjo Stadsmuseum
🏠 Villa Svea, Stadsparken
📞 0503-352 55 🕐 May–Aug

28
Skara

🅰️ D5 🏠 Västergötland E20
🛈 Biblioteksgatan 3; www.skara.se/turism

Traditionally an important seat of learning and a bishopric, Skara is one of Sweden's oldest towns. The 11th-century cathedral lies at its heart, enclosed by a network of streets following a pattern set out in the Middle Ages. On Stora Torget stands Krönikebrunnen, a well which on its exterior chronicles important events in the history of Skara and of Sweden.

Stadsparken is the site of Västergötlands Museum with its local history collection, and Fornbyn, an open-air museum.

Axvall, 8 km (5 miles) from Skara on Road 49, is the location of **Skara Sommarland**, the largest amusement park in Scandinavia, with a water park, go-kart track, camp site and cottages.

Just 20 km (12 miles) east of Skara, Lake **Hornborgasjön** is a popular resting place for birds; every year, in March and April, dancing cranes gather here in their thousands. You can spot them from an observation tower.

Skara Sommarland
🅰️ Axvall, Road 49 towards Skövde 🕐 Times vary, check website 🌐 sommarland.se

Hornborgasjön
🏠 Naturum Hornborgasjön, Road 189 🕐 Mar & Apr: daily 🌐 hornborga.com

---

29
Skövde

🅰️ D5 🏠 Västergötland Road 48/49 🚇
🛈 Stationsgatan 3B; vastsverige.com/skovde/matfestivalen

Skövde is set between the two largest lakes in Sweden: Vänern and Vättern. According to local folklore, it became a trading

centre in the 12th century, when pilgrims came here to honour Sweden's first female saint – St Elin, or Helena. Skövde has been destroyed by fire on several occasions; the last time was in 1759. The only building that survived was a 17th-century house, **Helénsstugan**, which today is part of Skövde Stadsmuseum (Town Museum).

Kulturhuset, designed by Hans-Erland Heineman in 1964, houses the library, an art gallery, a cinema and a theatre that often hosts shows featuring popular Swedish musicians and comedians.

The town has a bustling city centre with many independent shops and several large malls.

Rising to the west of Skövde is the 300-m- (984-ft-) high Billingen plateau, with views stretching as far as Lake Vättern. The area offers everything from canoe rentals to mountain-bike trails and a ski slope in winter.

Helénsstugan
🏠 Helénsparken, Skövde Stadsmuseum
📞 0500-498 000 🕐 Summer: by appt

Kulturhuset
🏠 Trädgårdsgatan 9
📞 0500-498 099

30 Borås

🗺️D5 🚗Västergötland Road 40 🚌🚆 🛈Österlanggatan 17; www.boras.com

In 1620 King Gustav II Adolf decided that the textile pedlars of the Knallebygden area should have a town of their own and Borås was founded. Textile factories still line the Viskan river, which winds through the town, although the industry has lost ground.

Borås is a green town with beautiful parks: Stadsparken in the centre is popular, as is Ramnaparken, where the open-air Borås Museum is located. Also in the town centre is **Borås Djurpark**, a zoo with more than 80 species from all corners of the world. Large enclosures and attractive grounds make this zoo a pleasant family park.

Textilmuseet (the Textile Museum of Sweden) is housed in the Textile Fashion Center in Simonsland, just north of Borås. Its collection ranges from displays on industrial history to future textiles via art and design.

Borås Djurpark

🎫😊🅿️ 🚗Boråsparken ⏰Times vary, check website 🌐borasdjurpark.se

Textilmuseet

🎫🎒🕙🅿️ 🚗Skaraborgsv 3A, Simonsland ⏰Noon-5pm Tue-Sun (to 4pm Sat & Sun) 🌐textilmuseet.se

31 🎫🚫🍽️ Torpa Stenhus

🗺️D5 🚗Västergötland 30 km (19 miles) SE of Borås ⏰Times vary, check website 🌐torpas tenhus.se

Standing on a promontory at the southern end of Lake Åsunden is the medieval castle Torpa Stenhus. It belonged to the Stenbock family and from the 14th- to the mid-17th century it was an important stronghold for defence against the Danes. In summer, Torpa Slottsteater stages theatrical performances in a splendid outdoor setting.

32 Alingsås

🗺️D5 🚗Västergötland E20 🚆 🛈Estrad, Bryggaregatan 2; www.alingsas.se

Jonas Alströmer and the textile industry have, between them, left their mark on Alingsås. In the 18th century, Ahlströmer founded his textile factory, and on the proceeds he built Nolhaga Slott, a manor which today has a zoo and bird park.

Alingsås Kulturhus contains Alingsås Museum, an art gallery and library, and organizes regular events.

South of Alingsås on the road towards Gothenburg lies **Nääs Slott**, a 17th-century castle with an impressive 19th-century interior. Here, the handicraft tradition of western Sweden is cultivated through events and exhibitions. The Midsummer celebrations here are fantastic.

Alingsås Kulturhus

🎫 🚗Södra Ringgatan 3 ⏰Times vary, check website 🚫Some public hols 🌐alingsaskulturhus.se

↓ Sculpture by Jaume Plensa outside the Textilmuseet, Borås

Nääs Slott

⊛⊕⊕⊕⊕ 🚗Floda, E20, 30 km (19 miles) N of Gothenburg 🕐Winter: Mon-Fri; summer: daily 🌐naas.se

---

㉝
Kungsbacka

🅰C6 🚉Halland. E6/E20 🚗 ℹ️ Borgmästaregatan 6; www.visitkungsbacka.se

Almost nothing remains of Kungsbacka's 13th-century wooden town: all but two of the houses were destroyed in a devastating fire in 1846. The survivors are the red cottage in Norra Torggatan and the mayor's house at Östergatan 10. The pretty pastel-painted wooden houses that replaced the old at the end of the 19th century can be seen around the square.

Tjolöholms Slott, one of Sweden's more unusual buildings, lies 15 km (9 miles) south of Kungsbacka. This magnificent English Tudor-style mansion was built for a Scottish merchant and completed in 1904. It contained state-of-the-art features such as vacuum cleaners, showers and hot-air heating. The house is surrounded by lovely parkland.

Tjolöholms Slott

🚗10 km (6 miles) S of centre, E6/E20 to Fjärås exit, then Road 939 🕐Feb-mid-Jun & Sep-Nov: Sat & Sun; mid-Jun-Aug: daily; Park: daily 🌐tjoloholm.se

↑ A charming house in the scenic setting of Ulricehamn

㉞
Ulricehamn

🅰D5 🚉Västergötland Road 40 🚗 ℹ️Järnvägs-gatan 2b; www.ulrice hamnsturistbyra.se

The town of Ulricehamn occupies a beautiful setting on Lake Åsunden in an area rich in historic monuments. Originally known as Bogesund, there has been a settlement here since the 14th century. The old coaching road across Västergötland to Halland once ran through the town along Storgatan, the main street.

Textile enterprises dominate the local economy here and in Gällstad the many knitwear shops south of the town are open daily. The town is also a popular area for cycling.

Bystad, a farmstead 30 km (19 miles) south of Ulricehamn, has one of Sweden's oldest wolf traps, a pit measuring about 5 m (16 ft) in diameter and more than 3.5 m (11 ft) deep.

Along the road between Ulricehamn and Mullsjö lies Näs Gård. The manor's six historic red-painted buildings date from the 17th, 18th and 19th centuries and now form a regional cultural centre and art gallery. Concerts and other cultural events are held here, and it's a popular party venue.

Södra Vings Kyrka is a medieval gem of a church, dating in part from the 12th century. The artistic decoration is unusually lavish and includes 15th-century limestone paintings in the nave. The stately lectern was carved in Rococo style in 1748.

←

The former training ship *Najaden* moored in front of Halmstad Castle

Carl Milles' fountain *Europa and the Bull* in Stora Torg and Picasso's *Woman's Head*, which stands between the bridges over the river Nissan, are easily encountered on a stroll.

Halmstad Slott, a 17th-century castle (closed to the public), was built by the Danish King Christian IV. **Hallands Konstmuseum** (the County Museum) has a wide collection of art and cultural history.

Äventyrslandet, 9 km (5.5 miles) west of Halmstad, is a fun destination for kids, with its water park and funfair.

35
Laholm

⌂ D6 ⌂ Halland Road 24 ⌂ 🅸 Teckningsmuseet, Hästtorget; www.visitlaholm.se

The small town of Laholm is primarily associated with the long sandy beaches around the bay of Laholmsbukten. Mellbystrand, 6 km (4 miles) to the west of the town, throngs with holidaymakers in summer.

Laholm itself has winding streets and low houses, reminiscent of Danish rule before 1645. Around the square, the 200-year-old Rådhuset (town hall) is particularly beautiful.

The old fire station, with a beautiful view over the Lagan, houses Teckningsmuseet, a museum of drawings.

36
Halmstad

⌂ D6 ⌂ Halland E6/E20 🚆🚌🚢 From Grenå 🅸 Fattighuset, Köpmansgatan 20; www. destinationhalmstad.se

At the point where the River Nissan flows into Laholmsbukten bay lies Halmstad. Today, the medieval inner city with its half-timbered buildings is classified as being of national interest. Kirsten Munk's house on Storgatan is a 17th-century building in green-glazed Dutch brick. Craftsmen can be seen at work in **Fattighuset**, Lilla Torg, a former poor-house dated 1859.

Several modern artists have left their mark on the town and

Fattighuset
🕐 ⌂ Lilla Torg 📞 035-120 200 🗓 Mon-Sat

Hallands Konstmuseum
🕐📷 ⌂ Tollsgatan 🗓 Tue-Sun 🌐 hallandskonst museum.se

Äventyrslandet
🕐🕐 ⌂ Gamla Tylösands-vägen 1 🗓 Times vary, check website 🌐 aventyrslandet.se

The Moorish-style open-air bath house, Varberg, on stilts over the sea ↓

37

Varberg

C6 **Halland E6/E20**
From Grenå **Västra Vallgatan 39; www.visit varberg.se**

The coastal town of Varberg has, since the 19th century, been famous for its bathing, whether the cold curative baths fashionable of the period or swimming from the rocks and sandy beaches. Though it was founded in the 13th century, little from that time remains after several fires.

Located in the harbour area, Kallbadhuset is a renovated cold bath house in Moorish style with separate sections for men and women. The oriental touch is repeated in Societetshuset, built in the 1880s when the town's popularity as a spa was at its height. Today it houses a restaurant and mini-golf.

Guarding the approach from the sea is the mighty Varbergs Fästning. Most of the fortress was built in the 17th century, with parts dating from the 13th century. Today it houses a museum, **Hallands Kulturhistoriska Museum**,

focusing on the history of Halland. The museum's biggest attraction is the 14th-century Bocksten Man, whose body was discovered in a bog still dressed in an outfit from the Middle Ages. The notorious bullet that killed King Karl XII in 1718 is also on show.

Hallands Kulturhistoriska Museum

⊛⊛ **Varbergs Fästning** **10am–6pm Mon–Fri, noon–4pm Sat & Sun** **museumhalland.se**

38

Falkenberg

D6 **Halland E6/E20**
**** **Holgersgatan 11; www.visitfalkenberg.se**

A town with medieval roots, Falkenberg stands at the mouth of the River Ätran. The oldest areas of the town still have their wooden buildings, including St Laurentii Kyrka (St Laurence's church), partially dating from the 14th century.

The pottery **Törngrens Krukmakeri** (1789) is still in operation, run by the seventh generation of potters. **RIAN**

designmuseum, housed in a half-timbered granary at Söderbron, features a faithful reproduction of an apartment from the 1950s.

Törngrens Krukmakeri

⊚ **Krukmakaregatan 4** **0346-103 54** **Daily**

RIAN designmuseum

⊚⊚ **Skepparesträtet 2** **Jun–Aug: Tue–Sun; Sep–May: Tue–Thu & Sat** **riandesign.se**

EAT

Umai Söndrum
This restaurant serves fantastic sushi and sashimi platters.

D6 **Lars Montins väg 29, Halmstad** **umaisondrum.se**

Ⓚ Ⓚ Ⓚ

STAY

Best Western Varbergs Stadshotell
Pleasant hotel in an old building with an Asian-inspired spa.

C8 **Kungsgatan 24-26, Varberg** **varbergsstads hotell.com**

Ⓚ Ⓚ Ⓚ

Cruising on the ↑
Dalsland Canal by the
Håverud Aqueduct

A BOAT TOUR
THE DALSLAND CANAL

Length 5.5 hours by boat **Boat route** From Bengtsfors to Köpmannabro or reverse

From Bengtsfors the Dalsland Canal, designed by Nils Ericsson in the 1860s, carves its way south towards Köpmannebro on Lake Vänern, passing through 19 locks and dropping 45 m (148 ft) to the lake. The scenery varies from beautiful, almost untouched countryside to modern communities, from old ironworks to historic manor houses. The spectacular aqueduct at Håverud is formed from a series of steel plates joined by 33,000 rivets. Both a rail and a road bridge traverse the deep gorge. When the tour finishes, you can return to Bengtsfors by bus or train in around 1 hour.

The Dalsland Canal
WESTERN GÖTALAND

Locator Map
For more detail see p244

Herrenäs
172
Lelång
Svärdlång
START
Bengtsfors
Ärtingen
164
Billingsfors
Laxsjö
Baldersnäs Herrgård
Grann
Dals Långed
Iväg
Högsbyn
Råvarp
166
Erve
Håverud Aqueduct
Bäckefors
Åsensbruk
Skållerud
Köpmannebro
FINISH
Nären
E45
Mellerud
0 kilometres 8
0 miles 8
N

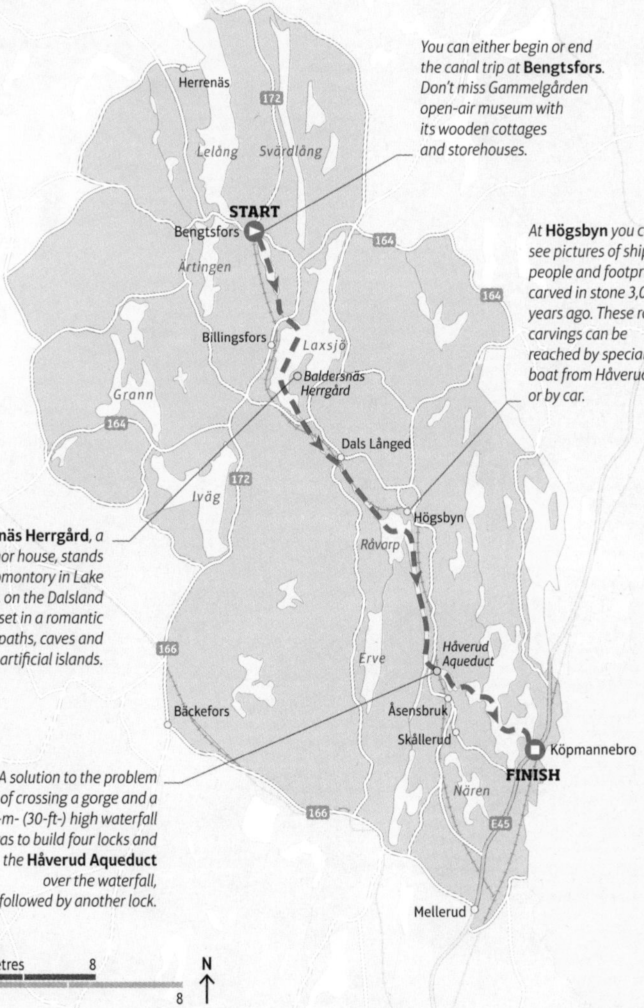

You can either begin or end the canal trip at ***Bengtsfors****. Don't miss Gammelgården open-air museum with its wooden cottages and storehouses.*

At ***Högsbyn*** *you can see pictures of ships, people and footprints carved in stone 3,000 years ago. These rock carvings can be reached by special boat from Håverud, or by car.*

Baldersnäs Herrgård, *a grand manor house, stands on a promontory in Lake Laxsjö, on the Dalsland Canal. It is set in a romantic park with paths, caves and artificial islands.*

A solution to the problem of crossing a gorge and a 9-m- (30-ft-) high waterfall was to build four locks and the ***Håverud Aqueduct*** *over the waterfall, followed by another lock.*

WESTERN SVEALAND

Värmland, Närke and Dalarna, with their rich rural culture, colourful folk costumes, red-painted wooden houses and pastoral scenes, have long attracted visitors. Stretching from the flatlands of Närke to the mountains of Dalarna, this region is known for its industrial heritage based on mining and forestry.

Large expanses of water dominate all three provinces. Southern Värmland encompasses the huge Lake Vänern. The beautiful Fryken lakes provided inspiration for one of the province's well-known authors, Selma Lagerlöf. Her home, Mårbacka, is where many of her adventures are set.

Närke is sandwiched between two large lakes, Hjälmaren and Vättern. The centre of the province is dominated by the fertile Närke flatlands, encircled by forest, including the once infamous haunt of bandits, Tiveden, in the south. Örebro, western Svealand's largest metropolis and Närke's county town, has all the charm of a small town.

Dalarna has the beautiful Siljan lake and the Dalälven river with its arms stretching into the mountains. The province offers more contrasts than most – from the gentle farmland around Siljan to the mountainous north. Every year, on the first Sunday of March, these are linked by the Vasaloppet race, when tens of thousands of skiers head from Sälen down to Mora. Midsummer celebrations on Siljan are emblematic of Dalarna. Villages compete to see who has the most stylish maypole, the most accomplished musicians and the best folk dancers.

WESTERN SVEALAND

Must See
1 Örebro

Experience More
2 Karlstad
3 Värmlandsnäs
4 Borgviks Bruk
5 Arvika
6 Ludvika
7 Hedemora
8 Borlänge
9 Askersund
10 Sundborn
11 Falun
12 Leksand
13 Rättvik
14 Filipstad
15 Hagfors
16 Karlskoga
17 Mora
18 Orsa
19 Sälen
20 Idre and Särna

EASTERN GÖTALAND
p174

WESTERN SVEALAND

Örebro Slott reflected in the Svartån river on a beautiful day ↑

❶
ÖREBRO

🅰E4 ⬛Närke ✈12 km (7 miles) W of town centre 🚉🚌
ℹ️Örebrokompaniet, Olof Palmes torg; www.visitorebro.se

There has been a town on this site since the 13th century, but in 1854 a major fire destroyed the centre of Örebro. This gave scope for a new, more spacious layout on both sides of the Svartån river, and elegant buildings coupled with the castle and St Nicolai Kyrka created a particularly fine townscape. There is also a greener side to Örebro with the promenade that follows the Svartån river to the delights of Wadköping and Karlslund. You can wander or cycle along the river bank, or explore the river in a rowing boat.

Örebro Slott

🏛Kansligatan 1 🕐Mon-Sat; Northwest Tower: Sat & Sun (summer: daily)
🌐orebroslott.se

Örebro Slott has dominated the town since Örebro received its charter in the 13th century. In 1347, King Magnus Eriksson gathered the great and the good at Örebro House, as the castle was then called, to adopt a common law for Sweden. At the end of the 16th century, King Karl IX remodelled the castle to create a Renaissance palace. Today's appearance, however, with its round towers, is due to major rebuilding in the 1890s.

The castle has witnessed a number of historic events, including the adoption of the first Swedish Parliament Act in 1617 and the election of the French marshal Jean-Baptiste Bernadotte as heir to the Swedish throne in 1810. Now it is the official residence of the county governor and has a small tourist information point. An exhibition in the Northwest Tower (entrance fee charged) highlights the castle's interesting history.

❷ Örebro Läns Museum

🏛Engelbrektsgatan 3
🕐For renovation 🌐olm.se

With its roots in the 1850s, the county museum is Sweden's oldest. The main collection of over 100,000 objects is housed in a 1960s' building. The most valuable artifacts, including Viking silver, are housed in the Treasury. During the renovation, the museum has a showroom at Örebro Slott.

❸ Rådhuset

🏛Stortorget 🕐To the public

Built in 1858–63, the Neo-Gothic town hall was

> 🏔 GREAT VIEW
> ### Svampen
>
> Just 2 km (1 mile) north of the town centre is the Water Tower, Svampen. The view from its observation deck is amazing- you can see Örebro, the surrounding landscape, and lake Hjälmaren.

something of a showpiece in its time. Only a fraction of Örebro's administration fits into the building today.

④
Stadsparken

🏠 Floragatan 1 ☎ 019-211 000 ⏰ Daily

Voted the most beautiful city park in Sweden, Stadsparken has a series of themed gardens, including rose, magnolia and herb gardens. There is also a theatre and a children's island with its own railway and a petting zoo.

⑤
St Nicolai Kyrka

🏠 Nikolaigatan 8 ☎ 019-154 500 ⏰ Daily

This church has origins in the 13th century, but has been restyled many times. The north and south entrances are from the original church, while the rest is in Neo-Gothic style.

⑥
Wadköping

🏠 On the Svartån river, 1 km (0.5 miles) E of town centre ⏰ Tue-Sun 🌐 orebro.se/wadkoping

The beautiful promenade along the Svartån river leads to the idyllic wooden houses of Wadköping. This village has a vibrant community with craftworkers and small shops. The oldest building is the early 16th-century Kungsstugan (King's Cabin). Other buildings include Hamiltonska Huset (1844), and Cajsa Warg's Hus (17th century). In summer there are concerts and shows.

⑦
Oset & Rynninge-vikens Nature Reserve

🏠 3 km (2 miles) E of town centre, Oljevägen 15

The nature reserve is located close to central Örebro and be easily reached by bike in just a few minutes. This area was once a rubbish dump, but has been transformed into a scenic place, which is now rich with birdlife and fauna. You can explore the wide bike and foot path that runs through-out the reserve, along the waterfront. There are several barbecue and picnic spots.

> **The beautiful promenade along the Svartån river leads to the idyllic wooden houses of Wadköping.**

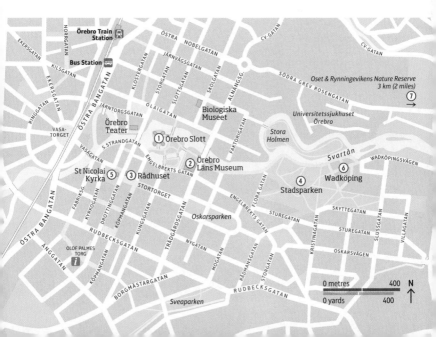

EXPERIENCE MORE

2 Karlstad

🅐D4 🅐 Värmland E18 ➡🚌
🅘 Gustaf Lovéns gata 30;
www.visitkarlstad.se

Karlstad was built on the delta formed by the Klarälven river before it flows into Lake Vänern, and was a market town in medieval times. It received its charter in 1584 along with its name from the then king, Karl IX. The phrase "Sola i Karlsta" (Enjoy the sun in Karlstad) originated from a jovial hostess at the town's inn who brought sunshine into people's lives in the early 1800s – her statue stands outside the Stadshotell.

Karlstad has been devastated by fire on many occasions; the Almen quarter on Västra Älvgrenen is a heritage centre comprising traditional wooden houses that survived. The bishop's palace, built in 1781, also remains, but the cathedral was less fortunate, having to have its exterior rebuilt.

A well-known feature of the town is the 12-arched Östra Bron bridge, built in 1811.

Insight into Värmland's history and folk culture can be gained at **Värmlands Museum** down by the river. **Sandgrund Lars Lerin** is an art gallery devoted to Lars Lerin, one of Sweden's most famous artists. **Alsters Herrgård**, east of Karlstad, is the birthplace of poet Gustaf Fröding in 1860. The manor is a memorial to him and other local poets.

Värmlands Museum
🏊🐟🎭🍽🛏🛍 🅐 Sandgrund-
sudden 🕐 Daily
🆆 varmlandsmuseum.se

Sandgrund Lars Lerin
🍽 🅐 Vastra Torggatan 28
🕐 Tue-Sun 🆆 sandgrund.org

Alsters Herrgård
🏊🐟🎭🍽🛍 🅐 8 km (5 miles)
E of Karlstad 🕐 May-Aug:
daily; Sep: weekends only
🆆 karlstad.se/Alsters-
herrgard

3 Värmlandsnäs

🅐D4 🅐 Värmland 5 km
(3 miles) S of Säffle

Jutting out into Lake Vänern is a large peninsula noted for its excellent agricultural land and the medieval churches of Botilsäter and Millesvik. From the southernmost tip in Ekenäs it is possible to head out to Lurö, Sweden's largest inland archipelago. This is the ideal spot to enjoy countryside well off the beaten track. The boat trip to the main island of Lurö takes an hour.

4 Borgviks Bruk

🅐D4 🅐 Värmland 35 km
(22 miles) W of Karlstad,
Road 45 📞 0555-740 81
🕐 Jun-Aug

The ironworks in the city of Borgvik operated from 1600 to 1925. The foundry ruins and

Did You Know?

Lake Värnen offers Europe's biggest freshwater archipelago with over 22,000 islands.

works buildings along with the striking manor and 18th-century church make Borgvik one of the leading monuments to a bygone industrial age in Värmland. Near Västra Smedbyn is **von Echstedtska Gården**, an impressive 1760s' Carolian manor.

von Echstedtska Gården

🌐🕙🕒🎫 🏠Västra Smedbyn 20 km (12 miles) NW of Säffle 📞0533-630 74 🕐Mid-May-mid-Aug: 11am-6pm Tue–Sun

---

⑤
Arvika

🅰D4 🚆Värmland Road 61 🚌🚲🚗 🛈Storgatan 22; www.visitarvika.se

The people of Värmland are known for their wit and ability to tell funny stories, particularly in Jösse, where Arvika is the main town. It is situated on a hill above the bay of Kyrkviken, which is linked to the lake of Glafsfjorden by a narrow strait. **Arvika Fordonsmuseum**, centrally located next to the

Östra Bron bridge in Karlstad, most appealing when lit up at night

↑ A Messerschmitt KR 200, built in 1957, on display at the Arvika Fordonsmuseum

fire station, has an exciting collection of veteran vehicles, including hundreds of cars, motorcycles and carriages.

The area has long been home to craftworkers and artists, as can be experienced in the **Rackstadmuseet** in Taserud just outside the town. This is where sculptor Christian Eriksson set up his studio, Oppstuhage, in the mid-1890s. For many years it was a magnet for artists attracted by the pristine countryside.

Klässbols Linneväveri, 20 km (12 miles) south of Arvika, is the Nordic region's only damask weaving mill and a rewarding destination for those who want to see how the linen tablecloths for the Nobel Prize banquets, or fabric for the Royal Family, are made.

Arvika Fordonsmuseum

🌐🕙🕒🎫 🏠Thermiavägen 2 📞0570-803 90 🕐Daily

Rackstadmuseet

🌐🕒🎫 🏠Kungsvägen 11 🕐Jun-Aug: 11am-5pm daily; Sep-May: 11am-4pm Tue–Sun 🚫Some public hols 🌐rackstadmuseet.se

Klässbols Linneväveri

🌐🕒🎫 🏠Damastvägen 5, 20 km (12 miles) S of Arvika 🕐May-Sep: daily; Oct- Apr: Mon-Fri & Sat 🌐klassbols.se

---

SELMA LAGERLÖF

In 1909, Selma Lagerlöf (1858-1940) became the first woman to receive the Nobel Prize for literature. Despite the passing of a century since she wrote her first masterpiece, interest in the author's captivating adventures continues unabated. When she made her debut in 1891 with the imaginative novel *Gösta Berling's Saga*, she put the estate of Mårbacka and the Värmland countryside around the Fryken lakes on the literary map. Numerous film and TV versions of her works have been produced, including *The Treasure* and *Jerusalem*. Even more remarkable was the success of *The Wonderful Adventures of Nils*. The tale of the boy's epic journey with wild geese was translated around the world.

Traditional-style houses by the lake in Hedemora ↑

6
Ludvika

🅰E3 🏠Dalarna Road 50
🚆🚌 ℹ️Bergslagsgatan 10;
www.visitsodradalarna.se

The western part of Bergslagen has foundries, mines and mining magnates' estates around every corner. The industry has also left its mark on the main town, Ludvika. **Ludvika Gammelgård och Gruvmuseum** offers a good impression of mining as it was in bygone times, as does the surrounding countryside.

For years Grängesberg, 16 km (10 miles) southwest of Ludvika, was central Sweden's largest iron ore mine. It was

---

🔍 HIDDEN GEM
Church Paths of Mårtens and Kullens

Located near Ludvika, this ancient 30-km (19-mile) trail between two Old Finnish villages is marked with orange paint on tree trunks and the occasional signpost.

---

closed in 1989. Ore deposits beneath the settlement meant that in places buildings had to be abandoned to allow mining to continue. **Grängesbergs Lokmuseum** (the Locomotive Museum) is believed to house the world's only operational steam turbine locomotive.

Ludvika Gammelgård och Gruvmuseum

♿️🅿️🚻 🏠Ludvika 📞0240-100 19 🕐1–15 Jun & 18–31 Aug: Mon–Fri; 16 Jun–17 Aug: daily

Grängesbergs Lokmuseum

♿️🅿️🚻🚽 🏠Grängesberg 📞0240-207 35 🕐Mid-Jun–mid-Aug: 10am–4pm daily 🚫Midsummer Eve

---

7
Hedemora

🅰E3 🏠Dalarna Road 70 🚆
ℹ️Hökargatan 6; 0771-626 262

This small Dalarna town is the oldest in the province with a charter dating from 1446. The 13th-century church and the pharmacy built in 1779 are

---

among the few buildings that survived a major fire in 1849. **Theaterladan** from the 1820s also survived. It was built by a theatre-loving merchant above a granary. Performances take place here in the spirit of the early 19th century and there is also a museum.

Husbyringen, north of Hedemora, is the location for a 60-km (37-mile) circular tour, taking in the countryside and local culture. There are mining centres en route and Kloster has the ruins of an abbey. The star feature is Stjärnsund's 18th-century mining settlement, where the father of Swedish mechanics, Christopher Polhem, worked. **Polhemsmuseet** exhibits the work of this inventive genius, including the Stjärnsund clock and ingenious Polhem lock.

Theaterladan

♿️ 🏠Gussarvsgatan 10 🕐Times vary, check website 🌐teaterladanhedemora.se

Polhemsmuseet

♿️🅿️🚻🚽 🏠Stjärnsund, 15 km (9 miles) S of Hedemora 📞0225-801 31 🕐Mid-Jun–4 Aug: noon–4pm Tue–Sun

Ornässtugan

🖐🖐🖐🖐 ⏸ 8 km (5 miles)
NE of Borlänge 📞 0243-648
35 🕐 May: book ahead; Jun–
Aug: Tue–Sun

---

⑨
Askersund

🅰 E4 🔹 Närke 🔹
ℹ Hamngatan 4; www.
visitaskersund.se

On the north shore of Lake
Vättern lies Askersund, the
main town of southern Närke,
offering easy access to the
forests of Tiveden and islands
on the lake. A devastating
fire struck the town in 1776,
but many wooden buildings
constructed since then have
been preserved.

The brick-built church,
Landskyrkan, designed by
Jean de la Vallé in 1670, survived the fire. It is one of
the most splendid religious
buildings from Sweden's
Age of Greatness, with its
magnificent Baroque pulpit
and altarpiece. The notable
Oxenstierna-Soopska chapel
designed by Erik Dahlbergh
contains a tin sarcophagus.

Lake Vättern's northern
archipelago comprises around
50 islands, most of which are
a nature reserve. The islands
can be reached by boat from
Askersund. Plying the route is
the S/S Motala Express, which
entered service in 1895 and
is known as "the prisoner of
Vättern" as it is too big
to leave the lake
via the Göta
Canal.

⑧
Borlänge

🅰 E3 🔹 Dalarna Road 50/
E16 🔹ℹ Sveagatan 1;
www.visitsodradalarna.se

The town of Borlänge came to
prominence in the 1870s when
an ironworks was established
and several railway lines came
together here. In recent years
it has gained a university to
add to its iron and paper industries. **Jussi Björlingmuseet**
celebrates the town's greatest
son, the renowned tenor Jussi
Björling (1911–60). His record-
ings can be enjoyed here.

Nearby is **Ornässtugan**, a
wooden inn. It is said that in
the 16th century the future
king, Gustav Vasa, fled from
Danish knights via the privy.

Jussi Björlingmuseet

🖐🖐🖐 ⏸ Borganäsvägen 25
📞 0243-742 40 🕐 Times vary,
check website 🚫 Some public
hols

→

A quaint ceramic shop
in the rural village
of Sundborn

Stjernsunds Slott 4 km
(2 miles) south of Askersund
was the home of the "singing
prince" Gustaf (1827–52), the
song-writing son of Oscar I.
It was so lavishly decorated
that today it is considered
to contain Sweden's finest
mid-19th-century interiors.

Stjernsunds Slott

🖐🖐🖐 ⏸ 4 km (2 miles) S of
Askersund 📞 0583-100 04
🕐 House: mid-May–late Aug:
daily, other times by appt;
Park: daily

---

⑩
Sundborn

🅰 E3 🔹 Dalarna 12 km
(7 miles) NE of Falun
ℹ 023-600 53

In the village of Sundborn
is **Carl Larssongården**, the
home of the artist Carl
Larsson (1853–1919). It was
once known as Lilla Hyttnä.
The well-preserved interior
contains wooden furniture,
traditional Swedish textiles
and influences from the Arts
and Crafts movement and Art
Nouveau. Sundborn's shingled
wooden church, built in 1755,
features paintings by Larsson
(1905) and the graveyard contains the artist's family plot.

Carl Larssongården

🖐🖐🖐 🕐 Jan–Sep: 10am–
5pm Mon–Sun; other times
by appt 🚫 Public hols
🌐 carllarsson.se

⓫ Falun

🅰 E3 🚗 Dalarna Road 50/ E16 🚆🚌 ℹ Trotzgatan 10-12; www.visitdalarna.se

It goes without saying that Falun still has a colourful impact on Sweden. Wooden buildings painted in the distinctive Falun Rödfärg (Falun Red) can be seen everywhere.

The paint has been made since the 17th century from powdered ore containing ferrous sulphate from the **Falun Gruva** (Falun copper mine), on the back of which the town was founded. Falu Gruva was the country's treasure chest – at its peak, two-thirds of the world's copper was mined here. The entire area, including Stora Stöten (the Great Pit formed by a collapse in 1687), Falun's historic buildings and industrial remains, and outlying settlements, was designated a UNESCO World Heritage Site in 2001. Guided tours take you underground, and warm clothing is advised as the temperature below is freezing. There is a lot to discover above ground as well. The Mining Museum has fun interactive displays and the Mine Art Gallery hosts exhibitions. Take a peep at the eagle owl in the Great Pit with the binoculars provided at the lookout point.

Dalarnas Museum gives an insight into the cultural history of the region with extensive collections of folk costumes, local paintings and traditional craftwork. Dalarnas is the origin of the Dala Horse. The museum houses the world's largest collection of these brightly painted, hand-carved wooden figures, including the smallest one – to see the detail you'll need a magnifying glass.

Falu Gruva

🚫🔘🏞🍴🛍🅿 🚗 1 km (half a mile) S of Falun 🕐 Times vary, check website 🔒 1 Jan, Good Friday, Midsummer, 24 & 25 Dec 🌐 falugruva.se

Dalarnas Museum

🚫🏞🍴 🚗 Stigaregatan 2-4 🕐 10am–5pm Tue–Sun (from noon Sat & Sun) 🔒 1 Jan, Good Friday, Midsummer Eve, Midsummer Day, 24, 25 & 31 Dec 🌐 dalarnas museum.se

⓬ Leksand

🅰 E3 🚗 Dalarna Road 70 🚌ℹ Norsgatan 28; www.siljan.se

The landscape around Siljan lake is especially beautiful, but the Leksand area is the most striking. One of the best times to see the lake is during the annual rowing race in church boats in early July.

Another event worth visiting Leksand for is Himlaspelet, one of Sweden's oldest rural pageants. First performed in 1941, Rune Lindström's

play about a path that leads to heaven depicts the witch trials of the 1670s.

The impressive onion dome belonging to Leksand's 18th-century Baroque church can be seen from far and wide. Parts of the church date from the 13th century.

Younger visitors to Leksand will be attracted by **Äventyret Sommarland**, which is made up of three amusement parks on the banks of Siljan lake: Waterland, Motorland and Summerland. Action activities include high-rope courses with zip lines, BMX tracks, trampolines, go-karts and a water park. "Drop'n Twist" is a bit more stomach-churning, as it rapidly goes up and down while the carousel spins. There are several food and drink options and a picnic area where you can eat your own.

Insjön, 8 km (5 miles) south of Leksand, was the birthplace in 1899 of the Swedish mail

← Painted in the distinctive Falun Red is Kristine Church, the parish church of Falun

↑ Audience enjoying a concert at the Dalhalla amphitheatre, Rättvik

> **The landscape around Siljan lake is especially beautiful, but the Leksand area is the most striking. One of the best times to see the lake is during the annual rowing race.**

order business run by Åhlén & Holms. The commercial tradition lives on with Clas Ohlson, whose store attracts so many DIY enthusiasts that Insjön has become Dalarna's most visited tourist destination.

Äventyret Sommarland
⊛⊛⊛⊛⊛ 🕐 Mid-Jun–mid-Aug: 10am–5pm daily (later at peak times) 🕐 Midsummer Eve 🌐 leksandresort.se/sommarland

---

13

Rättvik

🅰 xx 🕐 Dalarna Road 70
🚃ℹ Vasagatan 6; www.siljan.se

You can't fail to notice Rättvik's landmark, Långbryggan pier. After docking at the pier on the M/S *Gustaf Wasa*, passengers have a 628-m (690-yd)

walk to reach the mainland. The pier was built in 1895 to allow steam boats to moor near the shallow shore. Rättvik also has a medieval church, beautifully situated on a promontory surrounded by former church stables – the oldest dating from the 1470s.

A search for older Dalarna buildings, rural communities and paintings will be rewarded at Gammelstan in Norrboda, 35 km (22 miles) north of Rättvik. The village street is lined with old buildings, some of which date back to the 17th century.

Tällberg, 12 km (7 miles) south on the shore of Lake Siljan, has many preserved timber houses in the classic Dalarna style. It is also known for its top-class hotels and guest houses, including the renowned Åkerblads with its excellent restaurant. Located at the top of the village, Holens Gammelgård

features workshops selling traditional handicrafts.

At **Dalhalla**, 7 km (4 miles) north of Rättvik, a limestone quarry has been converted into an auditorium. The quarry forms an amphitheatre with unique acoustics that have been praised by the world's top opera singers. Concerts are held in summer, and Dalhalla can also be toured in the day. The area was formed 360 million years ago when a meteor landed here, creating a crater which encompasses the whole of the Siljan region.

Dalhalla
⊛⊛⊛⊛⊛ 🕐 7 km (4 miles) NW of Rättvik, Road 70
🕐 For performances and tours 🌐 dalhalla.se

Did You Know?

Dalhalla, near Rättvik, is one of three places in the world where you can see the impact of a meteorite.

THE INVENTOR JOHN ERICSSON

Swedish-American inventor John Ericsson (1803–89) was born in Långban, Värmland. Aged 13, he was employed in the construction of the Göta Canal *(p178),* together with his brother, Nils (1802–70). Wrestling with the development of a steam engine, he went to England to exploit his invention. He constructed a groundbreaking engine, *Novelty* (1829), which took part in the Manchester-Liverpool race and was narrowly beaten by George Stephenson's *Rocket.* Ericsson's ultimate triumph came in the American Civil War with the design of the armour-plated warship *Monitor,* with a rotating cannon tower.

14

Filipstad

⬛D4 ◉Värmland Road 63
🚌ℹ Viktoriagatan 8; www.
visitfilipstad.se

Karl IX founded Filipstad in 1611, naming it after his son Karl Filip. Mining, ironworking and blacksmithing were the mainstay of the town, but today it is known for a very different type of industry – it is home to the world's largest crispbread bakery, which bakes the famous Wasabröd. A bread museum is combined with the bakery, and both are open from Monday to Saturday.

Two of the town's great sons have contrasting memorials. A life-size sculpture by K G Bejemark of the popular poet and songwriter Nils Ferlin (1898– 1961) has been placed on a park bench, while John Ericsson's imposing mausoleum stands next to Daglösen lake. Two *Monitor*-type cannons stand next to it.

John Ericsson grew up along with his equally illustrious brother Nils in the mining community of **Långban**, 20 km (12 miles) north of Filipstad. Here an entire community built around iron has been preserved, including a foundry, gaming house and pithead buildings. Mineral hunters investigating the slag heaps of Långban have unearthed an exceptionally diverse collection of no fewer than 312 minerals.

Långban

🔵🔵🔵🔵 ◉20 km (12 miles)
N of Filipstad 📞0590-221 81
◉Mid-Jun- mid-Aug: daily

15

Hagfors

⬛D3 ◉Värmland Road 62
ℹDalavägen 10; www.
visithagfors.se

In the heart of Värmland on the Klarälven river lies Hagfors, which is a centre for the steel and forestry industries. It is a good starting point for trips up the Klarälven valley. Places upriver offer raft and boat launch areas, providing the

The sun rising over a lake in the serene countryside around Filipstad ↓

opportunity to spend a few days drifting at 1–2 knots. Ekshärad, 20 km (12 miles) north of Hagfors, has a red shingled church built in 1686. The churchyard is known for its 300 iron crosses with "leaves" that play in the wind.

Southwest of the town is Uddeholm, a village with an original 1940s mill that houses a museum and art gallery, **Stjärnsfors Kvarn**. You can enjoy a ride on an inspection trolley from the mill to Hagfors, a 6-km (3.5-mile) round trip.

Stjärnsfors Kvarn

⌂ Uddeholm   ☏ 0563-234 00; trolley rides: 0563-187 50   ⏰ Jun-Aug: daily; Sep-May: by appt

---

⑯
Karlskoga

⧉ D4   ⌂ Värmland E18 ⧉ Kungsvägen 34; www. visitkarlslogadegerfors.se

Iron ore has been mined and processed in this area since the 13th century, but it was not until Alfred Nobel (p91) bought the Bofors ironworks and cannon factory in 1894 that the foundation was laid for Karlskoga's expansion. During the 20th century, Bofors expanded to become one of the world's leading arms manufacturers.

The **Nobelmuseet** in Björkborns manor, Nobel's last home, offers an insight into the life of the inventor. Nobel's laboratory is just as he left it when he died. The stable where he kept his Russian stallions is now an industrial museum displaying the history of the ironworks.

At the end of the Ice Age water poured out from a lake at Sveafallen near Degerfors, 15 km (9 miles) south of Karlskoga. The landscape it created can be seen in the Domedagsdalen (Doomsday valley) and from walking trails through the nature reserve.

Nobelmuseet

⊘ ⊘ ⏲   ⌂ 2 km (1 mile) N of Karlskoga   ⏰ Tue-Sun (Jun-Aug: daily)   ⊗ Some public hols ⓦ nobelkarlskoga.se

⑰
Mora

⧉ D3   ⌂ Dalarna Road 70 ➜ ⧉ ⧉ Siljan Tourism Mora, Köpmannagatan 3 A; www. siljan.se

Beautifully situated between Orsasjön and Siljan lakes, Mora is particularly associated with King Gustav Vasa (1496–1560) and artist Anders Zorn (1860–1920). Gustav Vasa's travels in Dalarna in 1520 have left many traces. The Vasaloppet ski race (p281) is the main memorial to the king, and the history of the famous race is detailed at **Vasaloppsmuseet**.

Anders Zorn was a collector of local handicrafts. In his **Zorngården** estate, he revelled in National Romanticism. On the estate there are many older buildings which have been moved here, such as the 12th-century bakehouse that was used as a studio.

Tomteland in Gesunda is the home of Father Christmas and his workshop, which is busy all summer making presents for children.

Vasaloppsmuseet

⊘ ⊘ ⏲   ⌂ Vasaloppets Hus ⏰ Mon-Fri (mid-Jun-mid-Aug: daily)   ⊗ Some public hols ⓦ vasaloppet.se

Zorngården

⊘ ⊘   ⌂ Vasaloppsspäret 36 ⏰ Daily   ⊗ Good Friday, 24 & 25 Dec   ⓦ zorn.se

Tomteland

⊘ ⏲   ⌂ Gesundaberget 12 km (7.5 miles) S of Mora   ⏰ Times vary, check website ⓦ tomteland.se

⑱
Orsa

Ⓐ E3 **Ⓐ Dalarna Road Rv 45**
**ⓘ Dalagatan 1; www.
siljan.se**

The Orsa region extends from the gentle agricultural landscape around Orsasjön lake to the desolate lands of Finnmark in the north.

In the past many of the local inhabitants made grindstones as a sideline, a skill that can now be studied at **Slipstensmuseet**, 12 km (7 miles) northeast of Orsa.

In this part of Sweden animals are still taken to the mountains for summer grazing. Around Djurberga, Fryksås and Hallberg it is possible to see how dairy-maids used to live, far from their villages, churning butter and making cheese from the milk of hornless mountain cattle and goats.

In Våhmus, on the western side of Orsasjön, two crafts are practised, which in the past were a major source

The lush landscape around Lake Orsasjön, dotted ↓ with houses, Orsa

of income locally: basket weaving and making jewellery out of hair. The women used to walk as far afield as St Petersburg in Russia, and Germany, to sell their work.

Orsa Grönklitt, which is situated 14 km (9 miles) north of Orsa, is the main destination for outdoor activities. At Orsa Björnpark (Orsa Bear Park) specially designed paths and ramps allow a close-up view of the bears, wolves, lynx and wolverines that live here in large enclosures.

Slipstensmuseet

🅐🅐🅐🅐🅐 **Ⓐ Mässbacken**
Ⓒ 0250-550 255 **Ⓒ Summer:** times vary, call ahead

Orsa Grönklitt

🅐🅐🅐 **Ⓐ Grönklitt 15 km** (9 miles) NW of Orsa **Ⓒ Daily**
ⓦ orsagronklitt.se

---

⑲
Sälen

Ⓐ D3 **Ⓐ Dalarna Road 71**
**ⓘ Centrumhuset;
www.salenfjallen.se**

Like the majority of Dalarna's mountains, Transtrandsfjällen, with Sälen at their heart, are rounded and undulating and

INSIDER TIP
Husky Tour

There is no better way to experience the snowy mountains than by taking a husky tour through the stunning countryside. Sälen, Idre, and Orsa all offer dog sledding adventures and the chance to meet these incredible dogs.

less dramatic than those located further to the north. The highest peak, Östra Granfjället, is 949 m (3,114 ft) above sea level. However, the terrain is excellent for both downhill and cross-country skiing and this, combined with its relative proximity to Sweden's cities, has made the area one of the country's leading destinations for winter sports enthusiasts.

Whether it's black runs for advanced skiers, spines or jumps for snowboarders, or family slopes for children, there is plenty to choose from in Sälen. Around 200 km (124 miles) of trails are marked for cross-country skiers and summer hikers alike.

Berga, just south of Sälen, is the starting point of the 90-km (56-mile) Vasaloppet ski race to Mora.

---

⑳

Idre and Särna

🅰D2 🔵Dalarna Road 70 🔴Framgårdsvägen 1, Idre; Högenvägen 2, Särna; www.visitidre.se

Northernmost Dalarna, with the towns of Idre and Särna, belonged to Norway until 1644 and the local dialects still sound Norwegian. This is a mountainous region, with impressive views. On Nipfjället mountain it is possible to drive up to a height of 1,000 m (3,280 ft) for a good view of Städjan, a peak 1,131 m (3,710 ft) high. The STF mountain station at Grövelsjön on Långfjället, to the north, is an ideal starting point for mountain tours.

Idrefjäll is a year-round mountain resort with excellent slopes and lifts. It offers great skiing in winter and a range of activities in the summer. Särna has a beautiful wooden church dating from the late 17th century and the rural museum of Buskgården.

Fulufjället National Park contains Sweden's highest waterfall, Njupeskär, with a drop of 90 m (295 ft). The effects of a violent storm in August 1997 can still be seen at Göljån, where 400 mm (16 in) of rain fell in 24 hours. Streams became torrents and fallen trees dammed the water, ploughing wide furrows through the forest.

Competitors gearing up to start the legendary Vasaloppet ski race

THE VASALOPPET SKI RACE

The world's longest and oldest ski race was first held in 1922 when 122 competitors skied the 90 km (56 miles) from Sälen to Mora. Today more than 15,800 skiers take on the challenge on the first Sunday in March. The race also includes spin-off events such as TjejVasan (for women, 30 km/18 miles) and HalvVasan (half-course, 45 km/28 miles). A staff of 3,000 support the skiers by providing blueberry soup, ski waxing and blister plasters.

THE FIRST VASALOPPET

In 1520 Gustav Vasa fled on skis from Mora towards Norway to escape Danish troops. Near Sälen, local men caught up with him and persuaded the future king to turn back. Since 1922 almost 750,000 skiers have repeated the achievement, albeit skiing in the opposite direction.

BERGA

Just south of the village of Sälen, Berga is the starting point for the skiers, who are let loose in the early dawn in several stages, top skiers first.

EVERTSBERG

Lying halfway between Sälen and Mora, Evertsberg is where the competitors fortify themselves with blueberry soup. Those only skiing half the race can leave the track at this point.

MORA

The winning time at the end of the race in Mora is usually just over four hours, but some entrants can take ten hours. The text on the finishing line reads: "In the footsteps of our forefathers for the victories of tomorrow."

Sunne lies on the sound
between Övre Fryken
and Mellanfryken lakes ↑

A DRIVING TOUR
THE FRYKEN LAKES

Length 90 km (55 miles) **Stopping-off points** Tosseberg, 20 km (12 miles) north of Sunne on the road to Torsby

Author Selma Lagerlöf *(p273)* called the Fryken lakes the "smiling leaves", and it is the natural surroundings, the glittering waters, the flowering meadows and the dark forests on the horizon that strike visitors most. The author's spirit is a constant presence, and no more so than at the Rottneros estate, which is Ekeby in *Gösta Berling's Saga*, and the author's home, Mårbacka, across the water. The best ways to experience the lakes are aboard the vintage steamer *Freja af Fryken*, or by bicycle or car from Sunne, the main centre of the area.

WESTERN SVEALAND

The Fryken Lakes

Locator Map
For more detail see p268

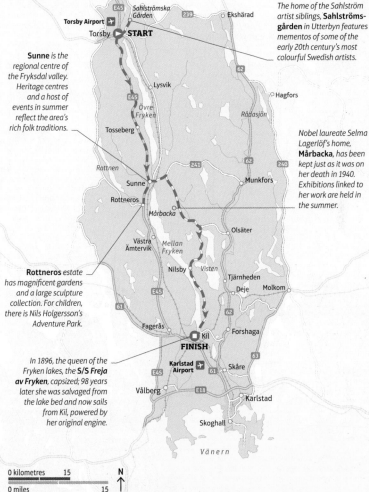

The home of the Sahlström artist siblings, **Sahlströms-gården** in Utterbyn features mementos of some of the early 20th century's most colourful Swedish artists.

Sunne is the regional centre of the Fryksdal valley. Heritage centres and a host of events in summer reflect the area's rich folk traditions.

Nobel laureate Selma Lagerlöf's home, **Mårbacka**, has been kept just as it was on her death in 1940. Exhibitions linked to her work are held in the summer.

Rottneros estate has magnificent gardens and a large sculpture collection. For children, there is Nils Holgersson's Adventure Park.

In 1896, the queen of the Fryken lakes, the **S/S Freja av Fryken**, capsized; 98 years later she was salvaged from the lake bed and now sails from Kil, powered by her original engine.

Sahlströmska Gården — Ekshärad — Torsby Airport — Torsby — **START** — Lysvik — Övre Fryken — Tosseberg — Rottnen — Sunne — Rottneros — Mårbacka — Västra Ämtervik — Mellan Fryken — Nilsby — Visten — Fagerås — Kil — **FINISH** — Karlstad Airport — Vålberg — Skåre — Karlstad — Skoghall — *Vänern* — Hagfors — Rådasjön — Munkfors — Olsäter — Tjärnheden — Deje — Molkom — Forshaga

0 kilometres 15
0 miles 15
N ↑

Skier on the slopes near Sundsvall

SOUTHERN NORRLAND

The six provinces of southern Norrland cover almost a quarter of the country. In the Middle Ages, the southeasterly province of Gästrikland belonged to Svealand and its gently rolling landscape is more akin to that of neighbouring Uppland than Norrland. An offshoot of the Bergslagen mining district extends into this area and ironworking formed the basis of today's manufacturing industry. The trading port of Gävle has long been a gateway to Norrland.

The pass between Kölberget and Digerberget in the province of Hälsingland is another gateway to the north, beyond which the mountainous Norrland landscape becomes more evident. Huge wooden mansions stand proud with their ornate porches. These houses are evidence of the successful trade in the green gold of the local forests in a landscape of which 80 percent is covered with productive woodland. Exploitation of the forests had an even bigger impact on the provinces of Medelpad and Ångermanland. At the end of the 19th century, the timber barons of Sundsvall and Ådalen had made themselves a fortune. Today, processing wood into pulp and paper is still a key industry. The smell of sulphur can be quite striking.

The provinces of Jämtland and Härjedalen belonged to Norway until 1645. The mountains stretch out to the west, attracting visitors to the ski resorts and to the upland areas where the wildlife and countryside can still be enjoyed undisturbed.

↑ View from the High Coast Bridge, across the Ångermanälven river

❶
THE HIGH COAST

🅰F1 **🅾Ångermanland** **🆆hogakusten.com**

Sweden's spectacular High Coast is best experienced on a light summer evening, when the hills are reflected in the bay waters, or on the quay in Ulvöhamn during the *surströmming (p297)* season in August. A boat is ideal for getting around, but the Högakustenbron bridge provides easy access and ferries sail regularly from several ports. The dramatic landscape is the main attraction. Declared a UNESCO World Heritage Site in 2000, it is the result of the land rising 300 m (984 ft) since the ice receded around 9,600 years ago.

WALK THE HIGH COAST TRAIL

The High Coast Trail stretches 130 km (80 miles) from Hornöberget in the south to Örnsköldsvik in the north. It covers a mixture of forest and coast, and stretches the entire World Heritage Site, taking in flora and fauna along the way. Enjoy the mountaintop views, sandy beaches, and unspoilt nature. There are sections for seasoned hikers and beginners.

---

① ⓜ
Skuleskogens National Park

🚹 High Coast Naturum Visitor Centre; www. varldsarvethogakusten.se

Watched over by Skuleberget hill, the Skuleskogens National Park covers 30 sq km (12 sq miles) of wilderness, with walking trails through magical ancient forest and over the clifftops along the coast. It is a roadless, wild and imposing section of the High Coast with views of dense forest and sea, lovely lakes, and lush valleys. The intriguing geological phenomena make it apparent, here more than anywhere else, that parts of Sweden have emerged entirely from the sea.

②
Hogakustenbron

Högakustenbron (the High Coast Bridge) is a mighty piece of architecture that you cross on the main road, the E4. Completed in 1997, the 1,800-m (6,000-ft) bridge, suspended on 180-m- (600-ft-) high pylons, offers travellers stunning views. It is Sweden's longest suspension bridge and was modelled on San Francisco's Golden Gate Bridge.

③
Högbonden

The 100-year-old lighthouse on the island of Högbonden warned shipping of the rocky coastline. Today it is a youth hostel, reached by ferry from either Barsta or Bönhamn, Both of these old fishing villages are good places to savour local specialities such as fresh river salmon, whitefish and, of course, *surströmming* (fermented herring). The whole island is a nature reserve with quite a few trails for hiking and exploring. The barren cliffs that rise sharply out of the sea are ideal observation points.

④
Nordingrå

🏠 Häggvik 109 📞 0613 202 90 🕒 Apr–Sep

"Fair Nordingrå" was a tourist destination long before the term High Coast was coined. Beautiful roads lined with steep hills pass through stunning scenery. Many people visit Nordingrå to find tranquility, whether it is to sunbathe on the warm slopes of Rotsidan or to hike up one of the magnificent mountain peaks. Meander through Mannaminne, a unique museum, full of many oddities.

↓ Trysunda's timber-framed chapel with its painted panels

⑤
Ulvöhamn

Ulvöhamn is the spiritual home of the herring speciality, *surströmming*. Norrland's largest fishing fleet made its home in the sheltered harbour lying between Norra and Södra Ulvön. This picturesque fishing village offers unspoilt nature and steep cliffs that plunge straight into the sea. Take a stroll along the harbour street, where there are many iconic red fishing stalls. Boats run year-round from Köpmanholmen and in the summer boats also leave from Docksta, Ullånger and Mjällomslandet. The chapel dates from 1622.

⑥
Trysunda

Some say that this is Sweden's most beautiful island and one of the best-preserved villages. It's like being in a living postcard. There are no roads or vehicles on this small island and you can walk around it in about an hour. Take the trail up to Kapellberget and admire the stark contrasts between the mountainous mainland and the picturesque fishing village. On a sunny day, a visit to Björnviken is a must, with its beautiful sandy beach. The small 17th-century fishermen's chapel, richly decorated with stunning frescoes, is well worth a visit too. Part of the island is a nature reserve.

⑦
Ullångersfjärden

Ullångersfjärden Bay, with its high, sheer cliffs, is one of the deepest fjords in Sweden. Fäberget is perfect for a quick outing because the hike is short. The views from the top are magical, with Ullångersfjärden inlet spread out below.

2

THE HÄRJEDALEN MOUNTAINS

🗺️D1 🏠Härjedalen Road 84 ✈️Sveg or Östersund 🚉to Ljusdal or Östersund, then bus ℹ️Jämtland Härjedalen Tourism, Rådhusgatan 44, Östersund; www.jht.se

This region is full of adventure and beauty all year long. Visit in summer for hiking, fishing, biking and golfing with the mountains as a majestic backdrop. The wintertime is a paradise for skiers, offering alpine or cross-country skiing. Raise your adrenaline levels dog sledding, on a snowmobile safari or reindeer sleigh ride as you take in the awe-inspiring landscape.

The tree line in Härjedalen is at 900 m (2,950 ft) and even in the forested lowlands in the east there are mountains with bare summits, such as Sånfjället and Vemdalsfjällen. But the mightiest mountains loom in the west towards Jämtland, with Helagsfjället the highest peak at 1,797 m (5,900 ft). Funäsdalen is the local hub, from where in summer Sweden's highest road runs via the Sami village of Mittådalen and the plateau of Flatruet to Ljungdalen. The Sami culture has had a major influence on the region. Jämtland Härjedalen has 12 Sami villages and around 44,000 reindeer. Lake Storsjön is the country's fifth largest lake and is home to the Storsjö Monster – a legend from 1635 that today has gathered some 200 witness reports.

💬 INSIDER TIP
Driving

Route Z531, over the Flatruet (Flatruetvägen) mountain pass, is closed during bad weather and from 10pm to 6am in the winter. Note that it's a dirt road for about 100 km (60 miles).

TOP 4 SPECTACULAR SKI SLOPES

Åre
Many World Cup events have been hosted on the scenic slopes here *(p299)*.

Funäsfjällen
Scandinavia's largest ski area, with six resorts available on one ski pass.

Lofsdalen
Offers several ski trails over 10 km (6 miles) long, with an electric illuminated slope.

Vemdalsfjällen
A skiers' paradise with a joint lift system for the main resorts: Klövsjö, Vemdalskalet, Björnrike and Storhågna.

1 The nature reserve around Härjedalen's largest lake system has unusual flora and fauna.

2 The Sami village of Mittådalen has reindeer pastures in the western mountains.

3 Ski touring in the Härjedalen mountains is a popular activity.

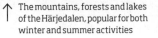

↑ The mountains, forests and lakes of the Härjedalen, popular for both winter and summer activities

EXPERIENCE MORE

❸
Gävle

F3 Gästrikland
Södra Skeppsbron 15;
www.visitgavle.se

The mouth of the Gävleån river made Gävle an ideal port, so traders set up base here to conduct business in the north. The harbourside warehouses along Skeppsbron bear witness to this. Gävle remains one of Sweden's larger ports, although operations have moved out into the bay.

Gävle has attractive 19th-century buildings and tree-lined esplanades. The jewel is the splendid theatre on Rådhusesplanaden, built in 1878. Boulognerskogen, which features Carl Milles' famous sculpture, *Five Playing Geniuses*, is the most popular of Gävle's city parks.

South of the Gävleån river is Gävle Slott, dating from the 16th century. This is also the location of the old town,

"Gamla Gefle", with fine streets of wooden houses from the 18th century. Joe Hill Gården on N Bergsgatan is the birthplace of the Swedish-American union agitator, and is now a museum. Other museums include **Länsmuseet Gävleborg**, with extensive collections relating to the history of Gästrikland. **Sveriges Järnvägsmuseum** offers a delightful selection of old locomotives and carriages, from mining titans to neat little narrow-gauge carriages. **Fängelsemuseet** is a small museum housed in 17th-century prison cells, and details prison life at the time.

Länsmuseet Gävleborg
Södra Strandgatan 20 Tue-Sun Public hols
lansmuseetgavleborg.se

Sveriges Järnvägsmuseum
Rälsgatan 1
Times vary, check website
jarnvagsmuseet.se

Fängelsemuseet
Hamiltongatan 1
Noon-4pm Wed-Sun
Public hols sveriges-fangelsemuseum.se

❹
Dalälven Delta

F3 Gästrikland, Uppland Gavle Tourist Office; www.visitgavle.se

Before the mighty Dalälven river empties into the bay at Gävle, it forms an expansive delta with hundreds of small islands. The flora and fauna

are abundant and the area offers great sport fishing.

Least affected by forestry and farming is the area around Färnebofjärden, part of which was declared a national park in 1998. The birdlife is incredibly diverse, with more than 100 breeding species, including several different endangered woodpeckers and owls.

Gysinge, on road Rv 67, 38 km (24 miles) south of Gävle, is a good place to start exploring the area. The falls between Hedesundafjärden and Färnebofjärden attracted ironworking here at the end of the 17th century. The industrial community has a main street dating from the 1770s and a manor from 1840. **Dalälvarnas Flottnings-museum** shows just how important the river once was for timber transportation.

Another important feature of the Dalälven river is hydro-electric power, which manifests itself in Älvkarleby, further down-river. The imposing power station, built in 1915, is an attraction in itself, but the most impressive sight is when the water is released at full-flow on Weir Day.

Dalälvarnas Flottningsmuseum

⊛ 🏠 Gysinge Bruk 📞 0291-210 00 🕐 Mid-May–mid-Aug: daily

↑ Hikers admiring the view over Storsjön lake from the high ground in the town of Sandviken

---

5
Sandviken

🅰 E3 🗺 Gästrikland
🚉 ℹ Folkets Hus, Köpmangatan 5-7; www.sandviken.se

The town of Sandviken grew up with the establishment of an ironworks on the shore of Storsjön lake in 1860. Using

---

← Elegant 19th-century buildings running alongside the Gävleån river at Gävle

---

the groundbreaking Bessemer production process, Sandviken soon gained a reputation for its steel. In the 1920s it began making stainless steel and by the 1940s it was the world's leading producer of steel for tools and drill bits.

Evidence of Sandviken's ironworking roots can be seen in Högbo, west of Sandviken. Nearby in Kungsgården is **Rosenlöfs Tryckerimuseum**, which has a still-functioning printing press from the 1890s.

Rosenlöfs Tryckerimuseum

⊛ 🕑 🏠 Kungsgården, 10 km (6 miles) W of Sandviken 🕐 Jul-late Aug: Tue-Fri 🔒 Midsummer 🌐 rosenlofsvanner.se

---

6
Söderhamn

🅰 F2 🗺 Hälsingland 🚉
ℹ Norra Hamngatan; www.visitsoderhamn.se

Sweden's need for power and armaments led to the foundation of Söderhamn in

---

1620. Hälsingland's weapon-makers were brought together from around the region to work in the town. The gun and rifle-making factory (1748) now houses the **Söderhamns Stadsmuseum**.

A series of parks create a green patchwork around the city. Söderhamn's landmark is the Oscarsborg tower, which rises proudly on Östra Berget. Anyone braving the 125 steps is rewarded with breathtaking views of the archipelago. Today Söderhamn is a thriving coastal community that offers great opportunities for swimming, boating and fishing.

Miles of the inlet of Söderhamnsfjärden were lined with sawmills during the industrial boom of the late 19th century. **Bergviks Industrimuseum** tells the story.

Söderhamns Stadsmuseum

🏠 Oxtorgsgatan 5 📞 070-327 69 14 🕐 By appt

Bergviks Industrimuseum

⊛ 🕑 🏠 15 km (9 miles) W of Söderhamn 📞 070-692 23 76 🕐 By appt

❼ Bollnäs

🗺 E2 📍 Hälsingland 🚉
ℹ Kulturhuset, Odengatan
17b; www.bollnas.se/
turism

Located in the heart of Hälsingland's rich farming land, Bollnäs is the gateway to the valleys of the Voxnan and Ljusnan rivers. The town itself has a semi-modern centre, with some wooden mansions. The church, built in the 1460s, contains ornate medieval sculpture work. The Classical-style **Bollnäs Museum** (1929) is worth a visit to explore the city's history, as is Kulturhuset next door, which has a room devoted to Onbacken, an Iron Age settlement just a stone's throw away. Also interesting is Kämpen rural heritage centre, a 16th-century farm displaying local culture.

Hälsingland was a major flax-growing area in the 1700s, and local landowners displayed their wealth in lavishly decorated wooden mansions. These farmhouses are now a designated UNESCO World Heritage Site. Some of Hälsingland's finest estates and farms can be seen around Alfta, about 20 km (12 km) into the Voxnadalen valley. Alfta rural heritage centre, Löka, in Gundbo, comprises three farm buildings, some with beautiful murals. Hansers farm has wall hangings from the 15th century.

Bollnäs Museum

🕐 📍 Odengatan 17 📞 0278-253 26 🕐 During exhibitions Tue-Sat

❽ Hudiksvall

🗺 E/F2 📍 Hälsingland 🚉
ℹ Storgatan 33; www.
visitgladahudik.se

Fishing, seafaring and trade have been the mainstay of Hudiksvall throughout its 400-year history. In the late 19th century the timber industry boomed and the town became known for its high living, giving rise to the phrase "Happy Hudik".

Despite attacks by Russian forces fires, a number of older buildings remain, giving the town charm and character. The Sundskanal in the centre, a canal linking Lillfjärden and Hudiksvallsfjärden inlets, is lined with red huts and merchants' warehouses from the mid-19th century.

East of the inlet is Fiskarstan (Fishermen's Town), with its partly preserved wooden houses from the early 19th century. Along Hamngatan there are fine old merchants' yards featuring the elegant wood-panelled architecture of the time. They have terraces on the waterside and shops on the parallel street of Storgatan.

An example is the Bruns Gård pharmacy, which has an ornate pharmacy entrance on Storgatan and a winged house on the terraces of Hamngatan.

Dominating the skyline is St Jakobs Kyrka, a church built in the 17th and 18th centuries, although its onion dome dates from 1888.

Hälsinglands Museum, in a former bank building, provides a good picture of the colourful history of the area.

Hudiksvall municipality covers a large area of northern Hälsingland, including Delsbo and the beautiful Dellensjö lakes to the west.

Hälsinglands Museum

🕐🕐🕐 📍 Storgatan 31
📞 0650-196 01 🕐 Mon-Sat
🚫 Public hols

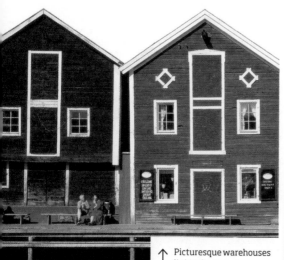

↑ Picturesque warehouses lining the quay on Sundskanal in Hudiksvall

↑ Looking down over Järvsö, south of Ljusdal, from the snow-clad hills

❾ Ljusdal

🅐 E2 🏔 Hälsingland 🚉
ℹ Lill-Babs torg, Järvsö;
www.ljusdal.se

On the Ljusnan river is Ljusdal. Settlers have long been attracted to this fertile valley and their history is explored at **Ljusdalsbygdens Museum**.

South of Ljusdal, at Järvsö, wildlife from the north can be seen at **Järvzoo Djurpark** and the adjacent Rovdjurscentret (Predator Centre). Järvsö village has Sweden's largest provincial church; when built in 1838 it had space for 2,400 people. Also here is **Järvsö Bergscykel Park**, which offers downhill mountain biking facilities.

Ljusdalsbygdens Museum

🄰 🏛 🄰 Bostallsgatan 5,
Ljusdal 🕐 Mon–Wed & Sun
🚫 Public hols 🌐 ljm.se

Järvzoo Djurpark

🐾 🄰 🏛 🄰 1 km (half a mile)
south of Järvsö centre
🕐 Daily 🌐 jarvzoo.se

Järvso Bergscykel Park

🄰 Vallmovägen 20
🕐 Jun–Sep: daily 🌐 jarvso
bergscykelpark.se

❿ Ljungadalen

🅐 E2 🏔 Medelpad E14
ℹ Sundsvalls Tourist Office;
060-658 58 00

The 350-km (220-mile) Ljungan river rises at Helagsfjällen mountain and flows into the Gulf of Bothnia just south of the town of Sundsvall. The E14 follows stretches of the river, offering good views. The great Norrland forests loom on the horizon and the river was an important timber route.

Stöde Kyrkby on Stödesjön lake, 40 km (25 miles) west of Sundsvall, has a long history, illustrated at the Huberget rural heritage centre.

Borgsjö, 40 km (25 miles) further upriver, has a Rococo church built in 1768, with a superb wooden bell tower. Next to the church is Borgsjö rural heritage centre featuring Jämtkrogen Inn, relocated here from the Jämtland border.

Ånge, a railway junction 100 km (60 miles) west of Sundsvall, is an ideal starting point for exploring the area. To the west, the countryside of Haverö spreads out around the Havern and Holmsjön lakes, which are good for canoeing.

Haverö Strömmar is an 8-km (5-mile) stretch of rapids with streams where dams, mills and huts have been preserved.

STAY

Quality Hotel Statt
Beautifully restored, this 19th century building is now a conference hotel with a spa, gym and pool.

🅐 E/F2 🄰 Storgatan 36,
Hudiksvall 🌐 nordic
choicehotels.se

Ⓚ Ⓚ Ⓚ

Best Western Hotel Baltic
This eco-friendly hotel is close to the main street, Storgatan. Relax in the sauna or enjoy a meal in their restaurant, Mamma Augustas Kök.

🅐 F2 🄰 Sjögatan 5,
Sundsvall
🌐 baltichotell.com

Ⓚ Ⓚ Ⓚ

←

The carefully restored
Elite Hotel Knaust's
staircase, Sundsvall

⑪ Sundsvall

🗺 F2 🏛 Medelpad
✈ Midlanda ⓘ
ⓘ Stora Torget; www.
visitsundsvall.se

The view from Norra and
Södra Stadsberget hills shows
Sundsvall sandwiched between
the Ljungan and Indalsälven
rivers. The sheltered inlets
attracted traders to this spot
in the 6th century, as can be
seen from the Högom burial
ground near Selånger. Alongside Selånger's 12th-century
church lay St Olofs Hamn, the
starting point pilgrimages to
Norway's Nidaros (Trondheim).

Sundsvall took off in the
mid-1800s with the advent of
the steam-powered sawmill.
In 1888 fire destroyed large
parts of the town centre. The
railway station survived, and
the attractive wooden building
is now a casino. A grand "stone

town" rose from the ashes.
Stora Torget square is flanked
by the town hall and the
Hirschska Huset with its
extravagant pinnacles and
towers. A notable building on
Storgatan is the renovated
Elite Hotel Knaust, built
in 1890, with a superb
marble staircase. On Norra
Stadsberget lies **Sundsvalls
Stadspark**, which has a
collection of buildings from
Medelpad, as well as lookout
towers. Södra Stadsberget's
outdoor recreation centre has
adventure trails for children.

Sundsvalls Stadspark

🐾🚲🎿🍴🏛 🏛 Norra
Stadsberget ⏰ Daily 🚫 Eves
of public hols 🌐 sundsvalls
stadspark.se

⑫ Örnsköldsvik

🗺 F1 🏛 Ångermanland
✈ 🚂 To Sundsvall or
Mellansel, then bus/taxi
ⓘ Jarnvägsgatan 11; www.
ornskoldsvik.se/turism

Örnsköldsvik, or Ö-vik as it is
often called, was founded in
1842 and named after the

county governor, Per Abraham
Örnsköld. Many of the town's
older buildings have been lost
to modern developments, but
a few exceptions to this
include the delightful town
hall that, thankfully for
Örnsköldsvik's large artists'
colony, was saved as an exhibition space. The restored
junior secondary school
houses **Örnsköldsviks
Museum**, which displays the
history of Nolaskogs.

Attractive new architecture
can be seen in the inner
harbour, where Arken – a
centre for offices, university
buildings and a library – forms
an exciting backdrop. One of
its glass-roofed courtyards
houses the Hans Hedberg
Museum dedicated to the
Swedish sculptor.

Örnsköldsviks Museum

🏛🛗 🏛 Läroverksgatan 1
📞 0660-886 00
⏰ Midsummer-Aug: 11am-
4pm daily; other times:
Tue-Sat 🚫 Public hols

→

The bright and distinctive
Ting1 apartment block
in Örnsköldsvik

INSIDER TIP
Safety First

Hiking in the southern
Swedish landscape is a
real treat, but be sure to
stick to the trails and
book a guide if you lack
experience. Do not
wade in waters if it feels
risky, as conditions
change quickly.

⑬ Härnösand

🅰F1 🅐Ångermanland
🅑 🅘Hoga Kusten
Turistservice; www.
hogakusten.com

The county town of western Norrland is an interesting place to stroll around. The Russians plundered Härnösand in 1721, but a new wooden town replaced the old, and charming districts such as Östanbäcken and Norrstan still remain. Noteworthy are the old secondary school and the county governor's residence.

Västernorrlands Museum has 18th-century buildings that have been preserved. This large open-air museum also reflects farming culture, with crofts and farms, a blacksmith's and sawmill, and a Norrland church village.

Länsmuseet Västernorrland

🔞 😊 🏠 🅐Murberget
🕙11am–5pm daily (to 8pm Thu) 🚫1 Jan, Easter, 1 May, 24, 25 & 31 Dec 🌐vnmuseum.se

⑭ Ådalen

🅰F1 🅐Ångermanland
Road 90 🅘Hoga Kusten
Turistservice; www.
hogakusten.com

As the forestry industry flourished, Ådalen, the river valley leading to Junsele, became a hotbed of trade unionism and earned the nickname "Red Ådalen". In 1931, the year of the Great Depression, a most unlikely event occurred: the military shot indiscriminately into a peaceful strikers' march in Lunde, killing five people. Lenny Clarhäll's sculpture depicting the drama stands beside Sandöbron bridge.

Already in the mid-18th century, Livonian Christoffer Kramm set up a water-powered sawmill on the site that in 1947 became the town of Kramfors. Cargo ships were able to navigate 50 km (31 miles) up the river and the lower valley became a magnet for the forestry industry. The line of factories is now almost gone. Further up-river, however, there are many power stations. Particularly worth visiting is Nämforsen, where in summer you can view the large power station and occasionally see the mighty waterfall burst into life. The islands in the falls are an outstanding site for rock carvings. From 4000–2500 BC, hunters carved out over 2,500 figures.

SURSTRÖMMING, A FISHY DELICACY

The coast of southern Norrland has a speciality that many consider to be the ultimate delicacy, although it divides opinion. This treat is fermented herring (surströmming), which, after around eight weeks of fermenting, is canned. When the can is opened it unleashes a powerful aroma, which aficionados consider divine. The fishing villages along the High Coast (p288) are the centre of production.

VILDHUSSEN AND THE DEAD FALLS

A drama with a lasting impact unfolded on 6 June 1796 in Ragunda on the Indalsälven river. Magnus Huss, known as Vildhussen, a merchant in Sundsvall, had been building a log flume to bypass the Storforsen waterfall when an unusually high spring flood put pressure on the lake above the falls. The log flume burst as the river forged a new route, emptying the lake in just four hours and sending so much soil and debris downstream that it formed Sweden's largest delta at the river mouth. The Storforsen waterfall had become Döda Fallet (the Dead Falls).

of Norway and flows into Klingerfjärden, north of Sundsvall. The lower stretch of the river from Ragunda in Jämtland includes Döda Fallet (the Dead Falls), now a nature reserve from where you can see the giant basins carved out by stones in the falls. A revolving open-air theatre has been created next to the falls.

Utanede features a lovely Thai pavilion, the **King Chulalongkorn Memorial**, erected in memory of the King of Siam's trip along the river in 1897. The decorative elements of the golden pavilion were built by Thai craftsmen. The interior holds a life-sized bronze statue of the king.

King Chulalongkorn Memorial

🏛🚗🚻♿🅿 🚗Utanede Road 86, 7 km (4 miles) S of Bispgården ⏰Mid-May–mid-Sep: daily 🌐thai paviljongen.se

Enjoying the scenery on Mount Åreskutan above the village of Åre ↑

The county museum, **Jamtli**, with its Historieland feature, offers an exciting picture of life around Storsjön. This time machine transports you to scenes from the 18th and 19th centuries, where history can be felt, heard and even tasted. The museum's showpiece are the oldest preserved Viking *Överhogdal* tapestries. Opened in June 2018, the site incorporates Nationalmuseum Jamtli, with permanent and temporary art and design exhibitions.

A short bridge leads to the rolling, green island of Frösön. Its eastern parts are more urban, but the views across Storsjön to the peak of Oviksfjällen inspired the composer Wilhelm Peterson-Berger to create his distinctive home, **Sommarhagen**, in 1914. The house is now a museum and the rich interior houses decorative paintings by Paul Jonze. Every summer *Arnljot*, Peterson-Berger's drama about the Viking from 11th-century Frösö, is performed in a field a short distance away.

Storsjön lake is best seen on a steamer, such as the 1875 S/S *Thomeé*, Sweden's oldest steamer. Many enthusiasts

15

Indalsälven

🅰E1 🚗Jämtland/ Medelpad Road 86 🚌To Sundsvall, then bus 🛈Ragunda Tourist Office; www.ragundadalen.se

The 430-km- (270-mile-) long Indalsälven river rises in the mountains

16

Östersund

🅰E1 🚗Jämtland ✈🚗 🛈Rådhusgatan 44; www.visitostersund.se

Established on the shores of Storsjön lake in 1786, the town of Östersund lies opposite Jämtland's centre of Frösön.

←

Thai pavilion in Utanede, commemorating the King of Siam's visit in 1897

try to spot the elusive Storsjö Monster, the so-called sister of Scotland's Loch Ness monster.

Jamtli

🎨🎭🎪😊🏛 🅰 Museiplan 2 ☎063-150 100 ⏰11am–5pm daily; Historieland: mid-Jun–mid-Aug 🚫24, 25 & 31 Dec

Sommarhagen

🎨🎭😊🏛 🅰 Frösön, 9 km (6 miles) from Östersund ⏰Mid-Jun–mid-Aug: daily; other times by appt 🌐sommarhagen.com

---

🔟 Sveg

🅰D2 🏔 Härjedalen ➡ 🚂Inlandsbanan (summer), or to Mora or Ljusdal then bus 🛈Ljusnegatan 1; 070-622 05 00

Härjedalen's central town is Sveg, the gateway to the mountains. Forest stretches in every direction and winding waterways provide opportunities for fishing and canoeing.

Around Sveg, villages such as Duvberg, Ytterberg, Äggen, and Överberg are well-preserved, with 18th-century features. Gammel-Remsgården, 15 km (9 miles) north of Sveg, is a typical early-18th-century Härjedalen manor with richly decorated interiors.

🔟 Åre

🅰D1 🏔 Jämtland E14 ➡Östersund 🚂 🛈Sankt Olavs Väg 33; www.are 360.com

Åreskutan is Sweden's most visited mountain peak. The cable car lifts passengers from the village of Åre to within 150 m (490 ft) of the summit. There are 100 pistes, some of which are the longest and steepest in the country. Prominent visitors have included Winston Churchill, who came for the fly-fishing and to hunt elk. Today's range of activities includes scooter safaris, dog sledding, paraskiing, ice-climbing, surfing rapids and mountain biking.

🔟 Storlien

🅰D1 🏔 Jämtland ➡Östersund 🚂 🛈SP Livs & Bensin petrol station, Vintergatan 25; www. storlienturistbyra.se

The arrival of the railway in Trondheim in the 1880s opened up new opportunities for Storlien, which is located near the border with Norway. It is only 60 km (37 miles) to the Trondheim Fjord, and the broad pass between Stenfjället and Skurdalshöjden allows mild Atlantic winds to sweep through. The healthy air attracted spa guests to a mountain sanatorium, and in the 20th century tourists began arriving.

Today, Storlien is a classic ski resort for cross-country and downhill. It is also a starting point for walks in the Jämtland mountains. The mountains can also be reached from Enafors on the E14 and by train.

Nearby Ånnsjön lake is popular with birdwatchers. Handöl, on the western shore, has been a site for soapstone mining since the late Middle Ages. It was also where the surviving Carolean forces gathered in 1799 after Carl Gustaf Armfelt's catastrophic retreat from Norway; a monument on the waterfront is a memorial to the who froze to death in the mountains.

> ⛰ GREAT VIEW
> ### Awe at Åre
> At an altitude of 1,420 m (4,658 ft), the summit of Åreskutan is the perfect viewing spot. The cable-car ride to the peak takes 7 minutes, but you don't have to wait till you're there to enjoy the stunning views.

NORTHERN NORRLAND

The three provinces of Västerbotten, Norrbotten and Lappland make up Sweden's most northerly region. Västerbotten, on the Gulf of Bothnia, is the most southerly. Its coast and river valleys had booming settlements for many centuries. But today commercial activity is concentrated in towns such as Umeå, with its university and youthful population, and Skellefteå, known as the "Town of Gold" because of its proximity to two of Europe's largest gold deposits. Inland, the wilderness takes hold with vast tracts of forest and marsh.

North of Västerbotten, Norrbotten's coastline harbours features of rural culture such as the church village in Gammelstad. The Norrbotten archipelago is renowned for being the sunniest place in the country and its beach resorts lure holiday-makers. The border with Finland lies along the Torne river, and here the phrase "two countries, one people" is the most applicable.

Lappland borders Norway in the west and Finland in the northeast, but for the Sami (Lapp) people their land extends beyond official boundaries, across the mountains and forests and down to the coast, where their thriving culture of reindeer herding, hunting and fishing prevail. Known as Laponia, this area is a UNESCO World Heritage Site. The main towns of Kiruna and Gällivare in northern Lappland owe their existence to the mining industry.

NORTHERN NORRLAND

Must See
❶ The Kungsleden Trail

Experience More
❷ Umeå
❸ Holmöarna
❹ Lövånger
❺ Blå Vägen
❻ Skellefteå
❼ Boliden
❽ Luleå
❾ Piteå
❿ Storforsen
⓫ Tornedalen
⓬ Kalix
⓭ Boden
⓮ Kiruna
⓯ Arvidsjaur
⓰ Gällivare
⓱ Jokkmokk
⓲ Arjeplog

NORTHERN
NORRLAND

SOUTHERN
NORRLAND
p284

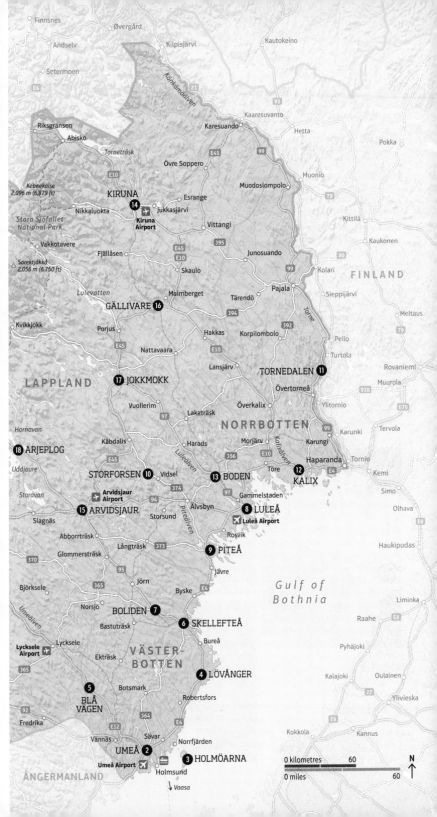

❶

THE KUNGSLEDEN TRAIL

🗺 A2–B1 📍 Lappland; E12 to Hemavan, E10 to Kiruna and Abisko 🚆 Storuman or Kiruna, then bus 🚌 To Kiruna and Abisko ℹ Kiruna Tourist Office; Abisko Tourist Station; Tärnaby Tourist Office; www.svenskaturistforeningen.se

The king of all trails offers vast open areas, lakes and streams, and some of the highest mountains in Sweden. Here you can pick cloudberries, spot an elk or even a bear, and enjoy unspoilt nature sleeping in a tent or hut.

The best way to experience the magnificence of the Swedish mountains is to hike a few stages of the Kungsleden Trail. In 1900, the Swedish tourism organization, Svenska Turistföreningen (STF), drew up plans for a network of marked walking trails and huts for overnight stays through the mountains from Lappland south to Grövelsjön lake in Dalarna. Today the 440-km (275-mile) long stretch between Abisko mountain station and the Malmbanan railway line in the north and Hemavan in southern Lappland forms the Kungsleden Trail. The simple huts have given way to mountain stations and rest cabins, which offer hikers shelter in bad weather and overnight accommodation. Some also have a ferry service to help people on their way.

TOP 5 HIKES ON THE TRAIL

Abisko to Nikkaluokta
Home to high peaks with wide-open areas, lakes and fast-flowing water.

Nikkaluokta to Vakkotavare
Passing through birch forest followed by steep slopes with valley views.

Saltoluokta to Kvikkjokk
Roams through alpine bearberries, willows and mountain birch.

Kvikkjokk to Ammarnäs
A lesser walked part of the trail that is more challenging because of its steep inclines.

Ammarnäs to Hemavan
Views punctuated by dramatic valleys, steep slopes and high peaks.

① Elk are a common sight in Sarek, perhaps the most spectacular of Sweden's national parks.

② The well-marked mountain trails are a big draw for hikers.

③ Views of the Northern Lights from Sarek National Park are spectacular.

GREAT VIEW
Hike to Skierfe

Some of the most scenic parts of the Kungsleden are in Sarek National Park. Hike to the summit of Skierfe for perhaps the finest panoramic view in Sweden, looking across the rivers of the Rapadalen below.

Mountains appreciated ↑
from the Kungsleden Trail, often capped with snow

EXPERIENCE MORE

❷
Umeå

🅰B3 🔘 Västerbotten
🔜🚆🚌 From Vasa, Finland
ℹ Renmarkstorget 15;
www.visitumea.se

With 3,000 birch trees lining the streets, it is not surprising that Umeå is known as "The City of Birches". Umeå dates back to the 16th century. An important trading and administrative centre, it became a county town in 1622. After a major fire in 1888, a new city was built with broad, tree-lined esplanades and parks to prevent fires spreading. Post-fire buildings of interest include Scharinska villa on Storgatan, designed by Ragnar Östberg, and Moritska Gården, Umeå's grandest residence for a local timber baron. The city's Neo-Gothic church was completed in 1894.

The opening of a university in 1965 prompted an expansion that transformed Umeå into a city – Norrland's only one. With 40,000 students and lecturers, it is very much a young persons' place (the average age is 38).

The splendid **Bildmuseet**, on the Arts Campus, is a great showcase for international contemporary art and design.

In Gammlia, a 10-minute walk from the centre, the **Västerbottens Museum** focuses on the history of Umeå and Västerbotten. It includes Svenska Skidmuseet, covering the history of skiing, and the fishing and maritime museum Fiske-och Sjöfartsmuseet. In summer, the open-air museum Gammlia Friluftsmuseum shows off its historic farm buildings, complete with pets, and there are activities for children.

Bildmuseet

🌐🌐🌐 🅰 Umeå Arts Campus, Östra Strandgatan 30B 🕐 Tue-Sun
🚫 Midsummer Eve, 24 & 31 Dec 🌐 bildmuseet.umu.se

Västerbottens Museum

🌐🌐 🅰 Helena Elisabeths väg, Gammlia 🕐 Tue-Sun (mid-May-mid-Aug: daily). Gammlia Friluftsmuseum: mid-May-mid-Aug: daily
🚫 24, 31 Dec 🌐 vbm.se

❸
Holmöarna

🅰B3 🔘 Västerbotten
ℹ Umeå Tourist Office: www.visit.umea.se

A 45-minute free ferry trip from Norrfjärden leads to the Holmö archipelago. There are four main islands – Holmön, Grossgrundet, Angesön and Holmögadd – and several smaller ones. Most of the group forms part of Sweden's largest archipelago nature reserve. It is an area of exciting geological formations and extensive fields of rubble stones, and

Did You Know?

The forest and shorelines of Holmöarna provide habitats for 130 species of birds and a variety of flora.

is ideal for cycling, bathing and fishing. The islands have been inhabited since the 14th century and **Holmöns Båtmuseum** focuses on the lives of the local fishermen, seal hunters and farmers.

Holmöns Båtmuseum

🌐🌐 🅰 At the ferry quay
🕐 Mid-Jun-mid-Aug: daily
🌐 holmonsbatmuseum.se

❹
Lövånger

🅰 xx 🔘 Västerbotten E4
ℹ Lövångers Kyrkstad; www.lovangerkyrkstad.se

The church village at Lövånger is one of the largest in the country with 117 cabins. It dates from the Middle Ages, although the oldest surviving cabin is from 1746. The village

← Mehmet Ali Uysalat's peg sculpture outside Bildmuseet in Umeå

↑ The amazing Northern Lights over Västerbotten's main town, Umeå

was built to accommodate churchgoers from remote outlying areas during church festivals. A number of cabins have been converted into hotel rooms. The 16th-century granite church of St Anne is decorated with various fine medieval sculptures.

Sockenmuseet, just north of the church, illustrates how the people of Lövånger lived in the 19th century.

Sockenmuseet
🕙 🅰 Kungsvägen 31 📞 0913-100 40 🕐 Times vary, call ahead

---

❺
Blå Vägen

🅰 B2/3 🅰 Västerbotten, Lappland E12 🛈 Umeå Tourist Office: www.visit. umea.se

From Lake Onega in Russia to Träna on Norway's Atlantic coast, the Blå Vägen (Blue Highway, E12) stretches 1,700 km (1,050 miles). The Swedish section follows the Umeälven river from Umeå through the towns of Lycksele, Storuman and Hemavan.

Klabböle, near Umeå, is the site of the river's first power station, built in 1899. It now

houses the museum of **Umeå Energicentrum**, which is well worth a visit. There is something for everyone here, and children will enjoy the "Playing with Energy" exhibit and trying to balance on logs like a log driver.

At Vännäs, 26 km (16 miles) from Umeå, the unspoilt Vindelälven river joins the Umeälven, and a detour can be made to the mighty Mårdsele falls to ride the rapids or fish for salmon, salmon trout and grayling.

Lycksele, the only town in southern Lappland, lies

123 km (76 miles) from Umeå. The local zoo, **Lycksele Djurpark**, specializes in Nordic wildlife.

Umeå Energicentrum
🕙 ⊜ 🅰 10 km (6 miles) W of Umeå 📞 090-160 020 (090-160 000 in winter) 🕐 2nd week in Jun–3rd week in Aug: 10am–5pm daily

Lycksele Djurpark
🕙 🕙 🛈 🍴 🛍 🅰 Brännbergsvägen 🕐 Times vary, check website 🅦 lycksele djurpark.com

200 YEARS OF PEACE
Sweden has had over 200 years of peace. The last battles here took place north of Umeå in 1809. Russian troops had been plundering the coast and a Swedish force landed at the port of Ratan to attack the Russians from the rear. The Swedes were defeated and withdrew to Ratan, where another battle was fought the next day. This time the Swedish troops stood their ground, but 1,000 men died in the conflict.

The oldest wooden bridge in Sweden crossing the river at Skellefteå ↑

⑥
Skellefteå

**⒜B2 ⒩Västerbotten E4
⬆️⒨ To Bastuträsk, then
bus ⒤Nygatan 49; www.
visitskelleftea.se**

Northern Västerbotten's first town, Skellefteå, originated in 1845. It was with the boom in the mining industry in the 1920s that Skellefteå's development took off, fuelled by the smelting plant at the mouth of the Skellefteälven river.

The town's green lung is the Nordanå Centrum of Culture, a park on the northern bank of the river. It houses an art gallery and the historical **Skellefteå Museum**.

Skellefteå Museum

⊛⊙⊙⊙⊙ ⒜Ernst Wester-
lunds Alle ⊙Tue-Sun
⊗Some public hols
ⓦskellefteamuseum.se

⑦
Boliden

**⒜B2 ⒩Västerbotten E4/
Road 95 ⬆️Skellefteå, then
bus ⒤Skellefteå Tourist
Office; 0910-452500**

The Kingdom of Gold is the name given to Skellefteå's ore field, which, with Boliden at its heart, runs from Bottenviken towards the mountains of Lappland. Europe's two largest gold deposits are mined here.

Bergrum Boliden, in the old mining office, traces the formation of the sulphide ores more than 4,600 million years ago to their extraction today.

In World War II, the world's longest cable-car system was constructed to transport the ore 96 km (60 miles) from the mines in Kristineberg. It is possible to travel along a 13-km (8-mile) stretch, swinging over the beautiful countryside at a sedate 10 km/h (6 mph).

Bergrum Boliden

⊛⊙⊙⊙ ⒜1 km (half a
mile) NW of Boliden ⒞0910-
60060 ⊙Jun-Aug: daily
⊗Midsummer

⑧
Luleå

**⒜B2 ⒩Norrbotten E4
⬆️⒨ ⒤Skeppsbrogatan 17;
www.visitlulea.se**

The county town of Luleå is surrounded by water as the Luleälven river flows into glittering bays with a lush archipelago beyond. A good harbour was the reason for the town's location here in the mid-17th century, when the site upstream became too shallow.

→

Exploring the traditional red cabins *(inset)* in Luleå church village

Gammelstads Kyrkstad, the church village, and its church, Nederluleå Kyrka, form a unique monument to the old trading centre and are a designated UNESCO World Heritage Site. The 15th-century granite building with its perimeter wall is upper Norrland's largest medieval church. The white steeple towers over a group of 408 small red cabins. This is where churchgoers from remote villages would stay overnight and stable their horses. The magnificent altar-screen from Antwerp dates from 1520.

The ore-loading harbour and SSAB's steelworks are the cornerstones of Luleå. They also influence the science museum, **Teknikens Hus**, where technical experiments can be attempted, such as drilling in a mine and launching a space rocket.

Gammelstads Kyrkstad

⊛⊙⊙⊙ ⒜10 km (6 miles)
NW of Luleå ⊙Times vary,
check website ⓦvisit
gammelstad.se

Teknikens Hus

⌖ ⓘ ☺ 🖨 🅰 Teknikens
Hus väg 2 🕐 Tue–Sun
🔲 teknikenshus.se

---

⑨
Piteå

🅰 B2 🅰 Norrbotten E4
🚆 Luleå 🚌 ℹ Bryggargatan
14; www.visitpitea.se

Originally next to Öjebyn, Piteå
was moved after a fire to the
mouth of the Piteälven river.
The new town was burned
by the Russians in 1721 and
rebuilt. Picturesque wooden
buildings from the 19th century, such as the town hall, can
be found on the square of
Rådhustorget. But it is the
coast that is the main draw.
The "Nordic Riviera" offers

sandy beaches and Sweden's
best chance of sun. There's
also a fun indoor pool.

---

⑩
Storforsen

🅰 B2 🅰 Norrbotten 80 km
(50 miles) NW of Piteå, Road
374 ℹ Älvsbyn Tourist
Office; Jun–Aug: daily;
www.alvsbyn.se/visit

Europe's mightiest untamed
stretch of white water can be
found on the Piteälven river,
where the rapids drop 82 m
(270 ft) over 5 km (3 miles).
Efforts to channel the rapids
into a single course created
Dead Falls (p298). Log floating
may have ceased, but a visit to
the **Skogs-och Flottningsmuseet** will reveal how things
looked when Storforsen's
huge log jams were formed.

Skogs-och
Flottningsmuseet
⌖ ☺ ⓘ ☺ 🅰 Storforsen
☎ 070-296 68 88
🕐 May–Aug: daily

STAY

Clarion Collection
Hotel Uman
Centrally located in
Umeå, with a sauna.

🅰 B3 🅰 Storgatan 52
🔲 nordicchoicehotels.se

Ⓚ Ⓚ Ⓚ

Mansion of Filipsborg
Rooms in two buildings;
continental breakfast.

🅰 C2 🅰 195 Nyborgs-
vägen, Kalix
🔲 filipsborg.se

Ⓚ Ⓚ Ⓚ

Piteå Stadshotell
This four-star hotel in
Piteå offers top dining.

🅰 B2 🅰 Olof Palmes Gata
1 🔲 simlochotell.se

Ⓚ Ⓚ Ⓚ

⑪ Tornedalen

🅰C1/2 🚗Norrbotten Road 99 ⓘKrannikatu 5, Travel Center; www.kukkola forsen.se

The Torne river and its tributary, Muonio, form the border with Finland, but culturally the areas along both shores are united. Place names are in Finnish, and many of the inhabitants speak a local form of Finnish.

Haparanda, at the mouth of the river, was created as a border town when Torneå became part of Finland in the peace treaty of 1809. A bridge links the sister towns and they share a tourist office. The disproportionately large train station, with both normal and Russian wider-gauge tracks, is a legacy from its time as a Russian border town.

Fishing is an important part of life on the Torne. Whitefish has been caught in the Kukkola rapids 15 km (9 miles) upstream since the 13th century, using large nets fixed to piers. The best fishing is to be had in late July, when the whitefish festival is held.

Övertorneå, 70 km (43 miles) north of Haparanda, is a fertile

The serene Kalixälven river flowing through the Kalix area ↓

horticultural area. The long light summer nights help berries, fruit and vegetables to develop an exceptional flavour. There is a church dating from the 17th century and a good view from the top of the mountain, Luppioberget.

Pajala is the centre of northern Tornedalen. The area is popular for fishing and wilderness camps and it is possible to shoot the rapids on the Torne and Tärendö rivers. **Laestadius Pörte** attracts Laestadian Lutherans on a pilgrimage to the log cabin of the revivalist preacher and botanist Lars Levi Laestadius (1800–61).

Laestadius Pörte

🕑🕑🕑 🚗Karesuando ☎0981-202 05 🕐May–Aug: Mon–Sat

⑫ Kalix

🅰C2 🚗Norrbotten E4, 50 km (31 miles) W of Haparanda ✈Kallax 🚆 ⓘStrandgatan 10; www. heartoflapland.se

The Kalix area to the north of the Gulf of Bothnia has been inhabited since Stone Age times. Nederkalix became a parish in the 15th century, but its church has had a turbulent history, with fires and plundering by the Russians. During the 1809 war, it served as a

Did You Know?

Father Christmas is said to live in Luppioberget, north of Tornedalen.

stable for Russian horses. Englundsgården Cultural Heritage Centre is a good example of Norrland's lovely wooden architecture.

The Kalixälven, which flows through Kalix, is one of Sweden's few unregulated rivers, ensuring good catches of salmon trout and salmon.

⑬ Boden

🅰B2 🚗Norrbotten 35 km NW of Luleå, Road 97 ✈Kallax 🚆 ⓘKungsgatan 40; www.upplevboden.nu

Its strategic location on the Luleälven river, at the intersection of two main train lines, has made Boden a centre for Sweden's northerly defences. It became the country's largest garrison town at the beginning of the last century and countless young men from across the country have completed their military service here. Five artillery forts circled the town, and the nuclear bunker deep in the rock was top secret until only a few years ago. Now **Rödbergsfortet** is a national monument open to the public who can experience life in the fort and even stay in rooms carved out of the rock.

The central Björknäs area is worth a visit for its open-air heated swimming pool and to see historic Norrbotten farms.

Rödbergsfortet

🕑🕑🕑 🚗5 km (3 miles) W of Boden 🕐Late Jun–early Aug; other times by appt 🌐fastningsguiden.com/ the-red-mountain-fort

14

Kiruna

A B1 **⌂** Lappland E10 **→** **⊞**
ℹ Kiruna Lappland Tourist
Office, Folkets Hus, Lars
Janssonsgatan 17; www.
kirunalapland.se

The large town of Kiruna is the
site of Sweden's highest
mountain, Kebnekaise, 2,014 m
(6,607 ft) above sea level,
from where, on a clear day,
you can see one-eleventh of
the country. For 50 days in
summer the sun never sets,
and for 20 winter days it never
rises. In January a snow
festival has exciting activities
such as a scooter jump show,
kick-sled racing and reindeer
racing. Kiruna is also one of
the best places in the world
to see the Northern Lights.

Kiruna's development is
due largely to the local iron
ore deposits. Older buildings
include the church, a gift of
the mining company LKAB
in 1912, whose shape was
inspired by a Sami hut, and
which is richly decorated by
artists of the time, including
Prince Eugen, Christian
Eriksson and Ossian Elgström.
LKAB Visitor Centre lies 540 m
(1,772 ft) below ground and
paints a picture of mining in
the region. With work in the
Kirunavaara mine causing
subsidence, both Kiruna and
the town of Malmberget are
gradually being moved to a
safer location.

The space centre Esrange,
which is 40 km (25 miles)
east of Kiruna has, since the
first rocket was launched in
1966, been a vital link in the
European space programme.

The former Sami village of
Jukkasjärvi, 17 km (11 miles)
east of Kiruna, has Lappland's
oldest church, dating from
1607. It houses Bror Hjorth's
altar-screen in wood depicting
the charismatic 19th-century
preacher Lars Levi Laestadius'
missionary work among the
Sami and Swedish pioneers.

Jukkasjärvi is renowned
for **ICEHOTEL**, first created
in 1989. In mid-November

↑ The ICEHOTEL in
   Jukkasjärvi, east
   of Kiruna

each year, a team of builders
constructs a hotel with ice
blocks and snow. Drinks are
served in the hotel's cool Icebar
and guests sleep on ice beds,
wrapped in furs, even though
it is -40°C outside. As spring
arrives, the structure slowly
thaws. In 2016, ICEHOTEL 365
was opened, a solar-powered
hotel with a bar, art gallery and
luxury art suites, all sculptured
by selected artists. This additional facility offers guests a
permanent sub-zero ice experience year-round. ICEHOTEL
also offers summer activities,
which include whitewater
rafting, cross-country cycling,
fishing and ice-sculpting and
major ice art exhibitions.

Kiruna's vast mountain
landscape is traversed by
the Kungsleden trail (p304).

LKAB Visitor Centre

🎨 🕐 **⊙** Daily; book tours
online **W** kirunalapland.se

ICEHOTEL Jukkasjärvi

🎨 🕐 🍴 ⓘ **◨** 17 km (10 miles)
E of Kiruna **⊙** 10am-6pm
daily **W** icehotel.com

> **The large town of Kiruna is the site of
> Sweden's highest mountain, Kebnekaise,
> 2,014 m (6,607 ft) above sea level.**

which can be relived at Kåkstan in Malmberget and experienced from 1,000 m (3,280 ft) down in the LKAB iron ore mine (contact Gällivare Tourist Center for information). LKAB's Gruvmuseum focuses on 250 years of mining history. The area's intense mining has left Malmberget standing on unstable ground, so buildings are gradually being moved to a more solid terrain.

The Gällivare municipality stretches to the Norwegian border, covering parts of the Laponia UNESCO World Heritage Site.

15
Arvidsjaur

B2 **Lappland Road 94 & 45** **To Jörn, then bus** **Östra Skolgatan 13; www.visitarvidsjaur.se**

This community in central Lappland was founded in the early 17th century when King Karl IX set up a church here to bring Christianity to the Sami. Arvidsjaur's Sami church village contains 80 huts and cabins from the 18th century.

Located in Glommersträsk, a small village southeast of Arvidsjaur, is **Hängengården**, a homestead dating from the 1800s. It is now a museum with 12 old buildings and around 3,000 items of interest.

In the summer a steam train operates on the Inlandsbanan line to the **Rallarmuseet** in Moskosel, which has informative displays that tell of the pioneers who built the railway.

Hängengården

⊚ Glommersträsk, 45 km (28 miles) SE of Arvidsjaur, Road Rv 95 ☎070-607 64 20 ◷Early Jun–mid-Aug: bookings only

Rallarmuseet

⊚ Stationsvägen 16, Moskosel, 40 km (25 miles) N of Arvidsjaur, Road Rv 45 ☎070-339 83 53 ◷Mid-Jun–mid-Aug: 11am–5pm daily

↑ Gällivare's attractive main church, built in the late 1800s

16
Gällivare

B1 **Lappland E10** **Railway station, Centralplan 4; www.welcometogallivare.com**

The twin communities of Gällivare and Malmberget grew rapidly from the late-19th century as the mining industry developed. But there was a settlement here long before that time: a chapel was built for the Sami in the 17th century and the Sami church on the Vassaraälven river opened in 1751.

A bigger replacement church was built in the 1800s set back from the main road. If it's unlocked, it's worth taking a peek inside. The wood-panelled ceiling and atrium are impressive, and above the altar a tapestry depicting the Sermon on the Mount adds a splash of colour to the mostly white interior.

The arrival of the railway in 1888 sparked an iron ore rush,

→
Crowds gathering after dark at the annual Jokkmokk winter market

17
Jokkmokk

B2 **Lappland Road 97 & 45** **Stortorget 4; www.destination jokkmokk.se**

The town of Jokkmokk is known for its winter market, which dates back to 1605 and is the oldest in Sweden. It is held the first Thursday until

> **Jokkmokk's annual reindeer race through the town often causes chaos, but things are even faster at the reindeer race on the frozen Lake Talvatissjön.**

Saturday in February every year, Snow, darkness and cold give way to light, warmth and sparkling colours, when more than 30,000 people arrive to browse among the 500 market stalls and join in the festivities. There are also special events, dancing and concerts.

Jokkmokk's annual reindeer race through the town often causes chaos, but things are even faster at the reindeer race on the frozen Lake Talvatissjön.

The life of the Sami and the pioneering Swedish settlers is depicted in **Ájtte, Svenskt Fjäll-och Samemuseum**. Unfortunately in 1972 the Sami church built in 1753 burned down. The exterior of the new church replicates the original, but it has a modern interior.

The municipality includes the magnificent national parks of Padjelanta, Sarek, Stora Sjöfallet and a section of Muddus, which is part of the Laponia UNESCO World Heritage Site.

Porjus, located 40 km (25 miles) north of Jokkmokk, is known for having Sweden's first major hydroelectric power station (1910–15). In the early 1970s, a new power station was built but the old monumental building has been kept as a heritage site. Its story is related in **Porjus Expo,** which has a power station museum 50 m (164 ft) underground.

In Vuollerim, which is 43 km (26 miles) south of Jokkmokk, Stone Age settlements have been uncovered on the Stora Luleälv river.

Ájtte, Svenskt Fjäll-och Samemuseum

⊛🕐♿ 🏠Kyrkogatan 3
🕐Jun-Aug: daily; Sep-May: Tue-Sat 🌐ajtte.com

Porjus Expo

⊛♿ 🏠Porjus 40 km (25 miles) N of Jokkmokk, Road 45 ☎020-820 000
🕐Times vary, call ahead

⓲ Arjeplog

🅱B2 🏠Lappland Road 95
🚆Arvidsjaur 🛈Torget 1;
www.visitarjeplog.se

On the "Silver Road" between Hornavan and Uddjaur lies Arjeplog, which is home to the **Silvermuseet**. The museum was created by the "Lappland doctor" Einar Wallquist, whose home, Doktorsgården, is open to the public in July. The collection features 16th-century Sami silverwork, including collars and belts worn by their proud owners, and chronicles silver passed from generation to generation over the centuries. In addition the museum looks at the life of the Sami and the pioneering incomers.

The area around Arjeplog has much to offer hunting and fishing enthusiasts.

Silvermuseeet

⊛🕐♿ 🏠Torget 🕐Jun-mid-Aug: 9am-5pm daily; Sep-May: times vary, check website 🌐silvermuseet.se

NEED TO KNOW

A row of trams in Gothenburg

BEFORE YOU GO

Forward planning is essential to any successful trip. Be prepared for all eventualities by considering the following points before you travel.

AT A GLANCE

CURRENCY
Krona (SEK)

AVERAGE DAILY SPEND

ON A BUDGET	MODERATE SPENDER	SPLASH OUT
600Kr	**1,200Kr**	**2,500Kr**

BOTTLED WATER	COFFEE	BEER	DINNER FOR TWO
25Kr	**40Kr**	**80Kr**	**400Kr**

ESSENTIAL PHRASES

Hello	Hej
Thank you	Tack
Please	Snälla
Goodbye	Hej Då
Do you speak English	Pratar du Engelska?
How much is this	Vad kostar den?

ELECTRICITY SUPPLY

Electricity Supply: Power sockets are the Europlug (type C and F). Standard voltage is 230v.

Passports and Visas

Passports are required for everyone, except citizens of Nordic countries and EU nationals with valid ID cards from the countries that are part of the **Schengen** Area. North Americans, Britons and Australians do not need visas for visits lasting up to 90 days. Those arriving from other countries should check their visa requirements with their local Swedish embassy or with the **Swedish Migration Agency**.
Schengen visas
ⓦ schengenvisainfo.com/sweden-visa
Swedish Migration Agency
ⓦ migrationsverket.se

Travel Safety Advice

Visitors can get up-to-date travel safety information from the **UK Foreign and Commonwealth Office**, the **US State Department** and the **Australian Department of Foreign Affairs and Trade**.
AUS
ⓦ smartraveller.gov.au
UK
ⓦ gov.uk/foreign-travel-advice
US
ⓦ travel.state.gov

Customs Information

There are no restrictions for EU citizens if goods are for personal use. For non-European residents, an individual is permitted to carry the following for personal use:
Tobacco products 200 cigarettes, or 100 cigarillos, or 50 cigars or 250 g tobacco.
Alcohol 1 litre of spirits or 2 litres of fortified wine, including sparkling wine, 4 litres of wine and 16 litres of beer.
Money All travellers entering or leaving with €10,000 or more in cash must declare the sum to Swedish Customs.
Tullverket provides up-to-date information in several languages on its website.
Tullverket
ⓦ tullverket.se

Language

Swedish is the official language of Sweden, while five national minority languages are also recognised by law. These are Finnish, Yiddish, Meänkieli, Romani and Sami. Additionally, a number of indigenous languages are spoken and English is widely understood.

Insurance

It is wise to take out a comprehensive insurance policy covering theft, loss of belongings, medical problems, cancellation and delays before travelling. As Sweden has a government-funded, free national health service, citizens of EU countries are entitled to emergency medical care if they produce a European Health Insurance (**EHIC**) card and a valid passport or other form of identification. Tourists from non-EU countries should arrange personal cover in advance of a visit and show proof of medical insurance from their country.

EHIC
w gov.uk/european-health-insurance-card

Vaccinations

No inoculations are necessary for Sweden.

Booking Accommodation

Sweden offers a range of accommodation options, from luxury five-star hotels to simple, remote cabins in the wild. Online booking is prevalent, but tourist offices can also help locate inexpensive and private-home accommodation not otherwise advertised. In remote areas, it is essential to book ahead. Thanks to the Allemansrätten, Sweden's legal right to roam, wilderness camping is allowed anywhere as long as campers are sensible, respectful and leave no trace.

Money

Credit and debit cards, as well as prepaid currency cards are accepted in almost all shops and restaurants. Contactless payments are common. Nowadays, cash is used only for small purchases. Sweden is increasingly becoming a cashless society.

Travellers with Specific Needs

Stockholm prides itself on being one of the most accessible capital cities in the world and Sweden is a long away ahead of many other countries. Public areas have to be accessible for physically or visually disabled people, as well as those suffering from allergies. All new buildings have wheelchair ramps and spacious toilets for disabled people. In Stockholm, for example, the *tunnelbana* underground network and local trains are adapted for disabled passengers. A great portal for information is the **Visit Sweden** website, which provides a database where you can find information about the physical accessibility of stores, restaurants and outdoor areas.

Visit Sweden
w visitsweden.com/accessible-travel

Closures

Lunchtime A few shops and museums close for lunch during the working week.
Monday Museums are sometimes closed.
Saturday or Sunday Most shops and offices close on Sunday with exemptions in tourist resorts. Museums and restaurants tend to stay open, but banks are closed on weekends.
Public holidays All offices and banks are closed, but many museums and attractions remain open. It is best to check with individual venues ahead of a visit.

PUBLIC HOLIDAYS	
1 Jan	New Year's Day
Mar/Apr	Good Friday
Mar/Apr	Easter Sunday
1 May	Labour Day
May	Ascension Day
31 May	Whit Sunday
6 Jun	National Day of Sweden
End June	Midsummer
Oct/Nov	All Saints' Day
25 Dec	Christmas Day

GETTING AROUND

Whether you are visiting for a short city break or for a tour of the forests and far north, discover how best to reach your destinations and travel like a pro.

AT A GLANCE

PUBLIC TRANSPORT COSTS

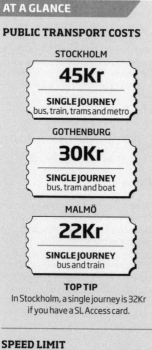

STOCKHOLM

45Kr

SINGLE JOURNEY
bus, train, trams and metro

GOTHENBURG

30Kr

SINGLE JOURNEY
bus, tram and boat

MALMÖ

22Kr

SINGLE JOURNEY
bus and train

TOP TIP
In Stockholm, a single journey is 32Kr if you have a SL Access card.

SPEED LIMIT

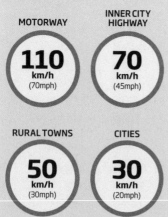

MOTORWAY

110 km/h
(70mph)

INNER CITY HIGHWAY

70 km/h
(45mph)

RURAL TOWNS

50 km/h
(30mph)

CITIES

30 km/h
(20mph)

Arriving by Air

Most major European cities have direct flights to one of Stockholm's four airports: Arlanda, Skavsta, Västerås and Bromma. The main airport used by most carriers is Arlanda. It is located 40 km (25 miles) north of Stockholm and is set to become the biggest airport in Scandinavia. Landvetter, near Gothenburg, and Sturup outside Malmö also have many international connections. Scandinavian airlines SAS and Norwegian are the leading providers. For information on transport from Stockholm's airports, see the table opposite.

Train Travel

International Train Travel
There are excellent train links from across Europe to various destinations in Sweden and the network connects the temperate south to the wilds of the Arctic. Modern couchettes are available on many routes and plenty of services operate at high speed. Students and budget travellers with **Eurail** or **Interrail** multi-country passes have access to the entire Swedish network. Eurail also offers a budget pass limited to Sweden.
Eurail
W eurail.com
Interrail
W interrail.eu

Domestic Train Travel
There is a well-developed train network covering parts of Sweden from the Öresund Bridge in the south to Riksgränsen in the north. The state-run **SJ** operates most long-distance routes, while other operators include **Tågkompaniet** and **MTR Express**. There are two daily high-speed services between the main southern cities (Stockholm, Malmö, and Gothenburg), while overnight ski services run to Åre and Vemdalen in winter.
MTR Express
W mtrexpress.travel
SJ
W sj.se
Tågkompaniet
W tagkompaniet.se

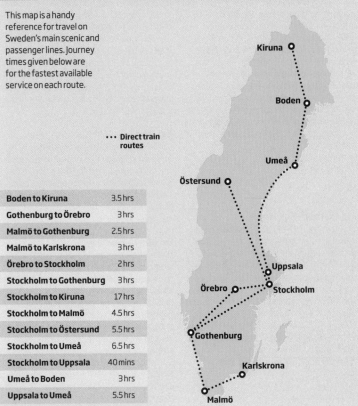

GETTING TO AND FROM THE AIRPORT

Airport	Public Transport	Distance	Taxi Fare
Arlanda	Arlanda Express train	18 mins	299Kr
Arlanda	Commuter train	45 mins	45Kr
Arlanda	Flygbussarna Airport Coach	45 mins	99Kr
Arlanda	Flixbus	40 mins	65Kr
Arlanda	Taxi	40 mins	675Kr (max)
Bromma	Flygbussarna Airport Coach	20 mins	89Kr
Skavsta	Flygbussarna Airport Coach	80 mins	159Kr
Västerås	Flygbussarna Airport Coach	80 mins	159Kr

RAIL JOURNEY PLANNER

This map is a handy reference for travel on Sweden's main scenic and passenger lines. Journey times given below are for the fastest available service on each route.

••• Direct train routes

Boden to Kiruna	3.5 hrs
Gothenburg to Örebro	3 hrs
Malmö to Gothenburg	2.5 hrs
Malmö to Karlskrona	3 hrs
Örebro to Stockholm	2 hrs
Stockholm to Gothenburg	3 hrs
Stockholm to Kiruna	17 hrs
Stockholm to Malmö	4.5 hrs
Stockholm to Östersund	5.5 hrs
Stockholm to Umeå	6.5 hrs
Stockholm to Uppsala	40 mins
Umeå to Boden	3 hrs
Uppsala to Umeå	5.5 hrs

Public Transport

As eco-conscious as anyone on the planet, Swedes are enthusiastic supporters of public transport. In smaller cities outside Stockholm it is often more practical to walk or cycle rather than negotiate buses. Travel cards, allowing you to make as many journeys as you like throughout the county for the duration of the card, are generally the best buy for those who plan to use public transport regularly.

Metro

Stockholm Public Transport, **SL**, is responsible for underground trains in Greater Stockholm. Operated by **MTR Nordic**, the *tunnelbana* is just over 100 km (60 miles) in length with around 100 stations – over one million commuters use it every weekday. Tickets can be purchased at SL Centres, underground ticket booths, newsagent kiosks, or via the SL app.

MTR Nordic
ⓦ mtrnordic.se
SL
ⓦ sl.se

Busses and Trams

In many places buses are the only public transport available. Local timetables can be found on **Samtrafiken**'s website and, in Stockholm, Stockholm Public Transport (**SL**) is an invaluable resource for getting around. Bus tickets should be purchased online or from kiosks and ticket machines, as buying on board incurs a surcharge. Tickets can be bought for a single journey to specific zones or for unlimited travel for periods of a day or longer. Stockholm, Gothenburg and Malmö offer discounted city passes for tourists.

Samtrafiken
ⓦ samtrafiken.se
SL
ⓦ sl.se

Long-Distance Bus Travel

Express buses compete with trains and airlines on lengthy routes. Journey times are longer, but ticket prices are lower and buses are modern and comfortable. Many express bus companies arrange special excursions in the tourist season and trips are also on offer to the southern Fjällen where there is no train line. **Fjällexpressen** is one operator running ski buses from Stockholm and Gothenburg. For domestic and international bus travel, **Flixbus** has an extensive network connecting Sweden's major towns and cities with over 20 other European countries.

Flixbus
ⓦ flixbus.se
Fjällexpressen
ⓦ fjallexpressen.se

Taxis

Taxis are expensive; the price you see displayed is the cost of a 10-km (6-mile), 15-minute journey, and the rate starts at about 300Kr. While it's easy to hail an empty taxi, indicated by the illuminated sign on the car roof, you can also order a taxi by smartphone or app. Some reputable companies include **TaxiKurir** and **Taxi Stockholm**. **Uber** is also popular in cities.

TaxiKurir
ⓦ taxikurir.se
Taxi Stockholm
ⓦ taxistockholm.se
Uber
ⓦ uber.com

Driving

Sweden has safe roads with well-mannered drivers. Cars are not really necessary in the city centres because of the short distances between sights and excellent public transport; however, a car is an advantage for exploring further afield.

Driving to Sweden

It is possible to drive from London to Stockholm in well under 24 hours using the Channel Tunnel, then following major roads through Belgium, Germany and Denmark before connecting on to the E4 at Helsinborg. Drivers approaching from other points in Europe have a variety of routes to choose from, but are likely to end up on the E47 through Denmark, before driving the cable-stayed Øresund bridge that crosses the border into Malmö in Sweden.

Car Hire

A valid driving licence from any country is accepted in Sweden, although drivers must be at least 18 years of age and must have held a license for two years. Drivers under the age of 25 who plan to rent a car may incur a young driver surcharge. Hire rates are more expensive than elsewhere in Europe.

Driving in Sweden

Sweden has an extensive road network, with more than 210,000 km (130,500 miles) open for public use. The national road network comprises *europavägar* (European motorways), *riksvägar* (national roads) and *länsvägar* (county roads). With the exception of the Öresund and Svinesund bridges, roads are generally toll free. In Sweden, all vehicles including foreign-registered vehicles, are obliged to pay congestion taxes in Stockholm and Gothenburg, as well as infrastructure charges in Motala and Sundsvall. The system is administered electronically by **EPASS24** and taxes (invoiced at a later date) cost between 9 and 35Kr depending on the time of day and distance travelled.

Road conditions in the winter vary depending on the severity of the weather and the location. Studded tyres are permitted in Sweden and their use is recommended, at least from central Sweden northwards. Anyone not used to winter driving should not venture out if there is a risk of snow and ice. The major roads are gritted, and ploughing is generally good, but even in Skåne, in the far south, snow storms can cause traffic chaos. For road information, see **Trafikverket**'s website.

EPASS24
Ⓦ epass24.com
Trafikverket
Ⓦ trafikverket.se

Rules of the Road

Despite occasionally dense traffic and severe weather conditions, road safety is generally good. The most common breach of the rules relates to speed limits, despite the presence of cameras and radar patrols. Fines are high and there is a risk of losing your licence for serious offences.

Swedish road signs mostly follow the European standard, but the country has some signs of its own. Those carrying the symbol for elk, reindeer or deer warn that there is a major risk of colliding with wildlife. In rural areas, drive slowly, particularly at dawn and dusk when visibility is poor.

A driver is guilty of drunk driving with a blood alcohol level of only 0.2 per mil. Gross drunk driving (from 1.0 per mil) is punishable by imprisonment

In case of breakdown, **Assistancekåren**, **Breakdown Service Sweden** and **Falck** provide emergency assistance 24 hours a day.

Assistancekåren
Ⓦ assistancekaren.se
Breakdown Service Sweden
Ⓦ bdss.se
Falck
Ⓦ falcksverige.se

Hitchhiking

Hitchhiking is not uncommon in Sweden, but the weather and distances add to the risks. As a result, hitchhiking is not advised.

Bicycle and Motorbike Hire

The freedom to roam, a principle protected by Swedish law, applies to cycling and **Visit Sweden**'s website is a great resource for inspiration and bike itineraries. Stockholm's network of cycle paths is increasing all the time, while its surrounding areas are tailor-made for cycling. **City Bikes** offers a pay-and-go subscription, letting you pick any bike and drop it off at stands located throughout the capital. In Gothenburg or Malmö, you can book bikes with **BimBimBikes**. For longer, more immersive country tours, hire a motorbike from **Svensk MC-uthyrning**.

BimBimBikes
Ⓦ bimbimbikes.com
City Bikes
Ⓦ citybikes.se
Svensk MC-uthyrning
Ⓦ svensk-mc-uthyrning.se
Visit Sweden
Ⓦ visitsweden.com/enjoy-day-your-bike-sweden

Boats and Ferries

There are a number of ferry companies operating direct services across the North Sea and the Baltic to Sweden. **Stena Line** covers the Grenå–Varberg and Fredrikshavn–Gothenburg routes from Denmark, while the busiest passenger route is from Finland with regular crossings from Helsinki, Turku and Mariehamn to Stockholm and Kapellskär. Both **Viking Line** and **Tallink Silja Line** have terminals in Stockholm at Stadsgarden and Värtahamnen respectively. **Wasaline** operates ferries between Vaasa in Finland and Umeå in northern Sweden, making it the world's northernmost all-year-round passenger route. From Estonia, Tallink Silja Line operates routes between Tallinn and Stockholm.

Stena Line
Ⓦ stenaline.nl
Tallink Silja Line
Ⓦ tallinksilja.com
Viking Line
Ⓦ vikingline.com
Wasaline
Ⓦ wasaline.com

On a Cruise

Sweden's splintered coastline, vast lakes and fragmented archipelagos make for busy boat services. In addition to the scheduled services, sightseeing trips and tours are offered in summer, occasionally on classic old steamers. The Dalsland, Strömsholm and Kinda canals attract plenty of charming boats, but the best tourist trail is the **Göta Canal**. Sweden's blue ribbon cruise takes three days, negotiating 65 locks, the country's three largest lakes and some of Sweden's most attractive scenery.

Boat services to the Baltic Sea's largest island, Gotland, are run by **Destination Gotland**; its high-speed ferries take less than three hours on either the Nynäshamn–Visby or Oskarshamn–Visby routes. In peak summer, there are up to eight departures a day. Although the ferries can take 500 cars per trip, it can be difficult to get a place during holidays, so book in advance.

Destination Gotland
Ⓦ destinationgotland.se
Göta Kanal
Ⓦ gotakanal.se

PRACTICAL
INFORMATION

A little local know-how goes a long way in Sweden. Here you will find all the essential advice and information you will need during your stay.

EMERGENCY NUMBERS

GENERAL
EMERGENCY

112

POLICE
NON-EMERGENCY

1 14 14

TIME ZONE
CET/CEST: Central European Summer time runs from the last Sunday in March to the last Sunday in October.

TAP WATER
Unless stated otherwise, tap water in Sweden is safe to drink.

TIPPING

Waiter	Service included
Hotel Porter	10Kr per bag
Housekeeping	Not expected
Concierge	Not expected
Taxi Driver	10Kr per bag

Personal Security

Sweden is a safe destination compared with most countries in the world. Crime does occur, with some cities suffering more than others, but this is rarely a concern for tourists. Be wary of pickpockets and avoid the empty, commercial parts of city centres late at night. Reasonable care should also be taken not to leave smartphones and cameras on tables or benches.

The Swedish police are generally extremely helpful and speak good English: any incidents should be reported to them and an official crime report obtained for insurance claims.

Health

In case of accident or emergency, treatment is swift in Sweden's excellent hospitals. EU citizens with an EHIC card are considered of equal status with Swedish citizens. Patients should not report to emergency clinics with minor ailments. First, contact the healthcare information service **1177 Vårdguiden** for instructions in English.
1177 Vårdguiden
w 1177.se

Smoking, Alcohol and Drugs

Smoking in Swedish bars and restaurants has been banned since 2005, but additional laws now limit smoking in public places, including in playgrounds, railway stations, and in outdoor sections of restaurants and bars. Beware of the strict rules regarding alcohol, drugs and some medications when driving. The possession of drugs is illegal and the country's marijuana laws are some of the harshest in Europe; the country outright bans any and all possession and sale, including medical marijuana, with few exceptions.

ID

Visitors are not required to carry passports or ID cards on their person but, in the case of an incident, you must be able to produce suitable identification at a police station within 12 hours.

Local Customs

Swedes are usually friendly and pleased to help visitors. The use of first names is the norm and a friendly *"Hej!"* is the common greeting. Casual clothing is acceptable almost everywhere, including restaurants. One Swedish drinking custom to watch out for is the tradition of *"skåling"*, which confounds many. To *"skål"*, look the person in the eye, raise your glass, drink, then repeat the eye contact before putting your glass down.

LGBT+ Safety

As across Western Europe, diversity and inclusion are crucial to the Swedish way of life and Swedes are enthusiastic supporters of LGBT+ rights – laws prohibit discrimination and hate speech in all forms. Sweden hosts a number of LGBT+ events annually, including more Pride festivals per capita than in anywhere else in the world, and the Gay Happiness Index ranks Sweden consistently high, alongside its Scandinavian neighbours.

Visiting Churches and Cathedrals

Sweden does not have any dress codes or head covering rules for visiting churches. Simply show respect when visiting.

Mobile Phones and Wi-Fi

On most phone networks, travellers from the EU can use their data allowance without being charged an additional fee. However, it is wise to contact your phone provider, prior to travelling, to clarify whether international roaming is activated on your mobile. Most businesses, hotels, restaurants and bars have open Wi-Fi networks.

Post

There are small post service points, primarily in supermarkets and at petrol stations, which are in the evenings and at weekends. Most international courier services, such as DHL, FedEx and TNT, are represented in the cities, and special services are also operated by the Swedish post office, **PostNord Sverige**.
PostNord
ｗ postnord.se

Taxes and Refunds

The standard VAT rate in Sweden is 25 percent, making it one of the highest in the world, with reduced rates of 12 percent and 6 percent for food, books, newspapers and other goods and services. If you reside outside the EU and are leaving Europe, you can get a refund for the items you purchased in Sweden via **Global Blue** before departing from an international airport.
Global Blue
ｗ globalblue.com

Discount Cards

Many destinations offer a visitor's pass or discount card for events, museum entry, guided tours, activities and transport. They can be purchased from tourist information offices and many hotels. Family cards are usually available and a great money saver. Consider how many of these offers you are likely to take advantage of before purchasing, as this might not be the most cost-effective purchase. The following offer good value:
Gothenburg Pass
ｗ goteborg.com
Stockholm Pass
ｗ stockholmpass.com

WEBSITES AND APPS

goteborg.com
The main information portal for Sweden's second city.
sj.se
A useful website and app that provides information on all major train routes in Sweden.
sl.se
This website and app will help guide you around Stockholm.
visitstockholm.com
Provides plenty of helpful information about Sweden's capital city.
visitsweden.com
Sweden's official tourist board website.
vasttrafik.se
Use this website and app for public transport informtion in Västergötland, including Gothenburg.

INDEX

Page numbers in **bold** refer to main entries.

PHRASE BOOK

When reading the imitated pronunciation, stress the part which is underlined. Pronounce each syllable as if it formed part of an English word, and you will be understood sufficiently well. Remember the points below, and your pronunciation will be even closer to the correct Swedish.

ai:	as in 'fair' or 'stair'
ea:	as in 'ear' or 'hear'
ew:	like the sound in 'dew'
ew:	try to say 'ee' with your lips rounded
oo:	as in 'book' or 'soot'
OO:	as in 'spoon' or 'groom'
r:	should be strongly pronounced

SWEDISH ALPHABETICAL ORDER

In the list below we have followed Swedish alphabetical order. The following letters are listed after **z**: **å**, **ä**, **ö**.

YOU

There are two words for 'you': 'du' and 'ni'. 'Ni' is the polite form; 'du' is the familiar form. It is not impolite to address a complete stranger with the familiar form.

IN AN EMERGENCY

Help!	Hjälp!	yelp
Stop!	Stanna!	stanna!
Call a doctor!	Ring efter en doktor!	ring efter ehn doktor
Call an ambulance!	Ring efter en ambulans!	ring efter ehn ambewlanss
Call the police!	Ring polisen!	ring poleesen
Call the fire brigade!	Ring efter brandkåren!	ring efter brandkawren
Where is the nearest telephone?	Var finns närmaste telefon?	vahr finnss najrmasteh-telefawn
Where is the nearest hospital?	Var finns närmaste sjukhus?	vahr finnss-najrmasteh shewkhews

COMMUNICATION ESSENTIALS

Yes	Ja	yah
No	Nej	nay
Please (offering)	Varsågod	vahrshawgOOd
Thank you	Tack	tack
Excuse me	Ursäkta	ewrshekta
Hello	Hej	hay
Goodbye	Hej då/adjö	haydaw/ahyur
Good night	God natt	goongtt
Morning	Morgon	morron
Afternoon	Eftermiddag	eftermiddahg
Evening	Kväll	kvell
Yesterday	Igår	ee gawr
Today	Idag	ee dahg
Tomorrow	I morgon	ee morron
Here	Här	hair
There	Där	dair
What?	Vad?	vah
When?	När?	nair
Why?	Varför?	vahrfurr
Where?	Var?	vahr

USEFUL PHRASES

How are you?	Hur mår du?	hewr mawr dew
Very well, thank you.	Mycket bra, tack.	mewkeh brah, tack
Pleased to meet you.	Trevligt att träffas.	treavlit att traffas
See you soon.	Vi ses snart.	vee seas snahrt
That's fine.	Det går bra.	dea gawr brgh
Where is/are ...?	Var finns ...?	vahr finnss...
How far is it to ...?	Hur långt är det till	hewr lawngt ea dea till
Which way to ...?	Hur kommer jag till ...?	hewr kommer yah till ...
Do you speak English?	Talar du/ni engelska?	tahlar dew/nee engelska
I don't understand	Jag förstår inte.	yah furshtawr inteh
Could you speak more slowly, please?	Kan du/ni tala långsammare, tack.	kan dew/nee tahla lawng-ssamareh tack
I'm sorry.	Förlåt.	furrlawt

USEFUL WORDS

big	stor	stOOr
small	liten	leeten

hot	varm	varrm
cold	kall	kall
good	bra	brah
bad	dålig	dawleeg
enough	tillräcklig	tillraikleeg
open	öppen	urpen
closed	stängd	stgngd
left	vänster	vainster
right	höger	hurger
straight on	rakt fram	rahkt fram
near	nära	naira
far	långt	lawngt
up/over	upp/över	ewp/urver
down/under	ner/under	near/ewnder
early	tidig	teedee
late	sen	sehn
entrance	ingång	ingawng
exit	utgång	ewtgawng
toilet	toalett	too-alett
more	mer	mehr
less	mindre	meendre

SHOPPING

How much is this?	Hur mycket kostar den här?	hewr mewkeh kostar dehn hair
I would like ...	Jag skulle vilja ...	yah skewleh vilya
Do you have?	Har du/ni ...?	hahr dew/nee...
I'm just looking	Jag ser mig bara omkring	yah sear may bahra omkring
Do you take? credit cards	Tar du/ni kreditkort?	tahr dew/nee kredeetkoort
What time do you open?	När öppnar ni?	nair urpnar nee
What time do you close?	När stänger ni?	nair stainger nee
This one.	den här	dehn hair
That one.	den där	dehn dair
expensive	dyr	dewr
cheap	billig	billig
size (clothes)	storlek	stOOrlek
white	vit	veet
black	svart	svart
red	röd	rurd
yellow	gul	gewl
green	grön	grurn
blue	blå	blaw
antique shop	antikaffär	anteek-affair
bakery	bageri	bahgeree
bank	bank	bank
book shop	bokhandel	bOOkhandel
butcher	slaktare	slgktareh
cake shop	konditori	konditoree
chemist	apotek	apoteak
fishmonger	fiskaffär	fisk-affair
grocer	mataffär	maht-affair
hairdresser	frisör	frissurr
market	marknad	mgrrknad
newsagent	tidningskiosk	teednings-cheeosk
post office	postkontor	posstkontOOr
shoe shop	skoaffär	skOO-affair
supermarket	snabbköp	sngbbchurp
tobacconist's	tobakshandel	tOObaks-handel
travel agency	resebyrå	reasseh-bewraw

SIGHTSEEING

art gallery	konstgalleri	konnst-galleree
church	kyrka	chewrka
garden	trädgård	traidgawrd
house	hus	hews
library	bibliotek	beebleeotek
museum	museum	mewseum
square	torg	tohrj
street	gata	gahta
tourist information office	turist-informations-kontor	tureest-informashOOns-kontOOr
town hall	stadshus	stgtshews
closed for holiday	stängt för semester	staingt furr semester
bus station	busstation	bewss-stashOOn
railway station	järnvägsstation	yairnvaigs-stashOOn

STAYING IN A HOTEL

Do you have any vacancies?	Har ni några lediga rum?	hahr nee nawgra legdiga rewm
double room with double bed	dubbelrum med dubbelsäng	doobelrewm med doobel-seng
twin room	dubbelrum med två sängar	doobelrewm med tvaw sengar

alternatives for a female speaker are shown in brackets

single room	**enkelrum**	_enkelrewm_
room with	**rum med**	_rewm med_
a bath	**bad**	_bahd_
shower	**dusch**	_dewsh_
key	**nyckel**	_newckel_
I have a	**Jag har**	_yah hahr_
reservation	**beställt rum**	_bestellt rewm_

EATING OUT

Have you got a	**Har ni ett**	_hahr nee ett_
table for...	**bord för...?**	_bOOrd furr..._
I would like	**Jag skulle vilja**	_yah skewleh vilya_
to reserve	**boka ett**	_bOOka ett_
a table.	**bord.**	_bOOrd_
The bill, please.	**Notan, tack.**	_nOOtan, tack_
I am a	**Jag är**	_yah air_
vegetarian.	**vegetarian**	_vegetariahn_
waitress	**servitris**	_sairvitreess_
waiter	**servitör**	_sairviturr_
menu	**meny/**	_menew/_
	matsedel	_mahtseadel_
fixed-price	**meny med**	_menew med_
menu	**fast pris**	_fast prees_
wine list	**vinlista**	_veenlista_
glass of water	**ett glas**	_ett glahss_
	vatten	_vatten_
glass of wine	**ett glas vin**	_ett glahss veen_
bottle	**flaska**	_flaska_
knife	**kniv**	_k-neev_
fork	**gaffel**	_gaffel_
spoon	**sked**	_shead_
breakfast	**frukost**	_frewkost_
lunch	**lunch**	_lewnch_
dinner	**middag**	_middahg_
main course	**huvudrätt**	_hewvewdrett_
starter	**förrätt**	_furrett_
dish of the day	**dagens rätt**	_dahgens rett_
coffee	**kaffe**	_kaffeh_
rare	**blodig**	_blOOdee_
medium	**medium**	_medium_
well done	**välstekt**	_vailstehkt_

MENU DECODER

abborre	_abborreh_	perch
ansjovis	_anshOOvees_	anchovies
apelsin	_appelseen_	orange
bakelse	_bahkelse_	cake, pastry, tart
banan	_banahn_	banana
biff	_biff_	beef
bröd	_brurd_	bread
bullar	_bewllar_	buns
choklad	_shooklahd_	chocolate
citron	_sitrOOn_	lemon
dessert	_dessair_	dessert
fisk	_fisk_	fish
fläsk	_flaisk_	pork
forell	_fooraill_	trout
frukt	_fruckt_	fruit
glass	_glass_	ice cream
gurka	_gewrka_	cucumber
grönsaksgryta	_grurnsahks-grewta_	vegetable stew
hummer	_humm-er_	lobster
kallskuret	_kall-skuret_	cold meat
korv	_koorv_	sausages
kyckling	_chewkling_	chicken
kött	_churtt_	meat
lamm	_lamm_	lamb
lök	_lurk_	onion
mineralvatten	_minerahl-vatten_	mineral water
med/utan	_mehd/ewtan_	still/sparkling
kolsyra	_kawlsewra_	
mjölk	_m-yurlk_	milk
nötkött	_nurtchurtt_	beef
nötter	_nurtter_	nuts
ost	_oost_	cheese
olja	_olya_	oil
oliver	_oleever_	olives
paj/kaka	_pa-y/kahka_	pie/cake
potatis	_potahtis_	potatoes
peppar	_peppar_	pepper
ris	_rees_	rice
rostat bröd	_rostat brurd_	toast
räkor	_raikoor_	prawns
rökt skinka	_rurkt sheenka_	cured ham
rött vin	_rurtt veen_	red wine
saft	_safft_	lemonade
salt	_sallt_	salt
sill	_seell_	herring
skaldjur	_skahl-yewr_	seafood
smör	_smurr_	butter

stekt	_stehkt_	fried
strömming	_strurmming_	baltic herring
socker	_socker_	sugar
soppa	_soppa_	soup
sås	_saws_	sauce
te	_tea_	tea
torr	_torr_	dry
ungsstekt	_ewngs-stehkt_	baked, roast
vinäger	_vinaiger_	vinegar
vispgrädde	_veesp-graiddeh_	whipped cream
vitlök	_veet-lurk_	garlic
vitt vin	_veett veen_	white wine
ägg	_aigg_	egg
älg	_ail-y_	elk
äpple	_aippleh_	apple
öl	_url_	beer

NUMBERS

0	**noll**	_noll_
1	**ett**	_ett_
2	**två**	_tvaw_
3	**tre**	_trea_
4	**fyra**	_fewra_
5	**fem**	_fem_
6	**sex**	_sex_
7	**sju**	_shew_
8	**åtta**	_otta_
9	**nio**	_nee-oo_
10	**tio**	_tee-oo_
11	**elva**	_elva_
12	**tolv**	_tolv_
13	**tretton**	_tretton_
14	**fjorton**	_f-yoorton_
15	**femton**	_femton_
16	**sexton**	_sexton_
17	**sjutton**	_shewton_
18	**arton**	_ahrton_
19	**nitton**	_nitton_
20	**tjugo**	_chewgoo_
21	**tjugoett**	_chewgoo-ett_
22	**tjugotvå**	_chewgoo-tvaw_
30	**trettio**	_tretti_
31	**trettioett**	_tretti-ett_
40	**fyrtio**	_furrti_
50	**femtio**	_femti_
60	**sextio**	_sexti_
70	**sjuttio**	_shewti_
80	**åttio**	_otti_
90	**nittio**	_nitti_
100	**(ett) hundra**	_(ett) hewndra_
101	**etthundraett**	_ett-hewndra-ett_
102	**etthundratvå**	_ett-hewndra-tvaw_
200	**tvåhundra**	_tvawhewndra_
300	**trehundra**	_treahewndra_
400	**fyrahundra**	_fewrahewndra_
500	**femhundra**	_femhewndra_
600	**sexhundra**	_sexhewndra_
700	**sjuhundra**	_shewhewndra_
800	**åttahundra**	_ottahewndra_
900	**niohundra**	_nee-oohewndra_
1,000	**(ett) tusen**	_(ett) tewssen_
1,001	**etttusenett**	_ett-tewssen-ett_
100,000	**(ett) hundra-**	_(ett) hewndra-_
	tusen	_tewssen_
1,000,000	**en miljon**	_ehn milyOOn_

TIME

one minute	**en minut**	_ehn meenewt_
one hour	**en timme**	_ehn timmeh_
half an hour	**en halvtimme**	_ehn halvtimmeh_
ten past one	**tio över ett**	_teeoo urver ett_
quarter past one	**kvart över ett**	_kvahrt urver ett_
half past one	**halv två**	_halv tvaw_
twenty to two	**tjugo i två**	_chewgoo ee tvaw_
quarter to two	**kvart i två**	_kvahrt ee tvaw_
two o'clock	**klockan två**	_klockan tvaw_
13.00	**klockan tretton**	_klockan tretton_
16.30	**sexton och trettio**	_sexton ock tretti_
noon	**klockan tolv**	_klockan tolv_
midnight	**midnatt**	_meednatt_
Monday	**måndag**	_mawndahg_
Tuesday	**tisdag**	_teesdahg_
Wednesday	**onsdag**	_oonssdahg_
Thursday	**torsdag**	_toorsdahg_
Friday	**fredag**	_freadahg_
Saturday	**lördag**	_lurrdahg_
Sunday	**söndag**	_surndahg_

ACKNOWLEDGMENTS

The publisher would like to thank the following for their kind permission to reproduce their photographs:

Key: a-above; b-below/bottom; c-centre; f-far; l-left; r-right; t-top

Alamy Stock Photo: Mauricio Abreu 89br; Adventure Pictures / Marcin Jamkowski 204–5t; age fotostock / Jörgen Larsson 294–5t, / Peter Lilja 304clb, / Nils-Johan Norenlind 179tl; AGF Srl / Algol 97br; Archive PL 76bl, 121tl, 135bc; ARCTIC IMAGES / Ragnar Th Sigurdsson 45cr, 276–7t; ART Collection 48t; Arterra Picture Library / Arndt Sven-Erik 200–201b, 216–17b; Auk Archive 106bl; Stuart Black 34tl, 220cra; blickwinkel / McPHOTO / G. Streu 40bl; Paul Carstairs 137bl; Frank Chmura 146tr, 248–9b; Kee Pil Cho 2–3, 189br; Ian G Dagnall 24t, 116–17t, 170–71t, 232cr; Damkier Media Group 148–9b; Mikael Damkier 182bl; Deco Images 36b; Digital-Fotofusion Gallery 76–7t, 79br; dleiva 104bl; DuncanImages 43cl, 305; Jakub Dvořák / detail *House of Knowledge* (2008) by Jaume Plensa © DACS 2019 260b; E.D. Torial 311t; eFesenko 122tl; Chad Ehlers 87tr, 166tr, 291tl; Greg Balfour Evans 24bl; Folio Images / Calle Artmark 308tl, / Gustaf Emanuelsson 213bl, / Jonas Gunnarsson 306–7t, / Isabelle Hesselberg 20tr, 242–3, / Helena Karlsson 11br, / Werner Nystrand 92–3b, 125tr, / David Schreiner 21tr, 284–5, / Jonas Tulldahl 110bl; GL Archive 157bl; Manfred Gottschalk 217tr; Grace Lou Images 121br; Bjorn Grotting 249tr; Jeppe Gustafsson 181b, 182–3t, 232–3b, 257tr; Hamperium Photography 293tr; Fredrik Hedberg 282; hemis.fr / Bertrand Gardel 22crb, 45cl, 61, 121c, 135cr, 140, 143cra, 144–5t, / Ludovic Maisant / paintings © Niki de Saint Phalle Charitable Art Foundation / ADAGP, Paris and DACS, London 2019 103tl, / Jacques Pierre 261tr, / Bertrand Rieger 306bl; Shawn Hempel 74t; Heritage Image Partnership Ltd / Göran Algård Collection / Historisk Bildbyrå / Mustang media 49cra; Heritage Image Partnership Ltd / Historisk Bildbyrå / Mustang media 51cb, / Torkel Lindeberg 184bl; Stefan Holm 139tl; Ian Dagnall Commercial Collection 117bl; Image Professionals GmbH, / Sabine Lubenow 43t, / TravelCollection 26tl, 85t, 132–3b, 220–21b, 234cr: imageBROKER / Angela to Roxel 296–7b, / Robert Haasmann 10ca, 304br, / Sonja Jordan 235br, / Daniel Kreher 21br, 300–301, / Olaf Krüger 184–5t, / MLNG 201tr,/ Thomas Robbin 70–71b, 72br, 88–9t, 108–9b, / Tobias Veser 273tr; Janzig / Europe 32tl; jbdodane 53tr; jejim120 275br; Lars Johansson 33t, 246cl, 254cr, 256cl, 258bl, 258–9t; Johner Images 41crb, 290–91b, 294bl, / MattiasJ Josefsson 233tr, 310bl; Inge Johnsson 214t; Jon Arnold Images Ltd 8clb; KI Editorials 134bl; David Kleyn 296tcl; christian kober 46cra; Matus Korman 163tl; Joana Kruse 308–9b; Leslie Garland Pictures 187bc; Look / Franz Marc Frei 238–9b; Johnny Madsen 203t; Martin Thomas Photography 170tc; mauritius images GmbH / Julian Birbrajer 107cra, / Thomas Ebelt 205br, / Hans-Peter Merten 230bc; Henk Meijer 45t, 186–7b, 250t, 272–3b; Hercules Milas 67cra, 68bl, 78bl; Uwe Moser Moser 179tr; Nature Picture Library / Wild Wonders of Europe / Unterthiner 259cla; NJphoto 26tr, 198cl, 199br; Nathaniel Noir 10clb, 22cr; NordicImages 298–9t; Nordicphotos / Berndt-Joel Gunnarsson 291cra; hugh nutt 30bl; Gunnar Österlund 168–9t; Panther Media GmbH / Dagmara 222–3t; Panther Media GmbH / Umo 27tl; Dusica Paripovic 60tl, 112–13; Kenneth Pellfolk 22t; Peter Adams Photography Ltd / Peter Adams 253tl, 312–13b; Bildapoteket Per Petersson 264; The Picture Art Collection 307crb; Pictures Colour Library 33cl, 237tr; Mihai Popa – Travel 121cra; Premium Stock Photography GmbH / Dagmar Richardt 289bl; Prisma Archivo 50cr, 92cl, 117crb; Prisma by Dukas Presseagentur GmbH / Frank Chmura 6–7, 94–5t, 247tr; Jaroslaw Pyrih 312tl; Realy Easy Star / Tullio Valente 106–7t; Matthias Riedinger 220tl; Robert Matton AB / Björn Andrén 230–31t; Robert Matton AB / Håkan Pettersson 298bl; robertharding / Stuart Black 241cra, / Armand Tamboly 213crb; Olle Robin 72bl; Rolf_52 28tl, 162–3b, 164–5t, 167b; Stefan Sollfors 200cl; Kumar Sriskandan 219t; Linus Strandholm 11t; Goran Strandsten 170bl; Thomasvy 291tr; roger tillberg 169bl; Anders Tukler 17t, 152–3, 180–81t, 270–71t; Rohan Van Twest 24cr; Knut Ulriksson 249cl; Urbanmyth 251br; Utterström Photography 27tr; kavalenkava volha 67tl; wanderworldimages 236–7b; Westend61 GmbH 276bl, / Biederbick&Rumpf 280b; Scott Wilson 86–7t, / Åke Pallarp © DACS 2019 and Enno Hallek 39cla; World History Archive 183br; Yegorovnick 274–5t; Zuma Press; Inc. / Polaris / Rob Schoenbaum 22bl.

AWL Images: Marco Bottigelli 39cr.

Bridgeman Images: 48bc; Calmann & King Ltd 49cb; © Look and Learn 50cb; Peter Newark American Pictures 51tr.

Dreamstime.com: Allard1 28tr; Almgren 190bl; Tommy Alvén 26–7ca; Anderm 4; Anikasalsera 18, 192–3; Rui Baião 13cr, 158–9t, 162tl; Bernard Bialorucki 124b; Magnus Binnerstam 178–9b; David Hjort Blindell 188t; Blojfo 187tr; Panom Bounak 144bl; Ryhor Bruyeu 136t; Hans Christiansson 160clb; Dairon655 37cl; Mikael Damkier 41cl; Dutchscenery 44tl; Kalin Eftimov 44–5b, 145cl; Stefan Holm 160–61b; Balachandra Gurumurthy Jois 238tl; Lars Ove Jonsson 288t; Kerstin700 139br; Vichaya Kiatyingangsulee 127tc; Bernhard Klug 35tr; Kennerth Kullman 46cr; Nicole Langener 173tr; Magnus Larsson 29tr; Ingemar Magnusson 47tr; Thomas Males 49tr; Mariagroth 309cl; Mikhail Markovskiy 70cr; Antony Mcaulay 29tl, 224bl, 252b, 262tl, 262–3b; Sophie Mcaulay 218bl, 225; Minnystock 96bl; Multiart61 36cla; Niklas Norberg 86bl; (null) (null) 34–5b; Olgacov 84cl; Radiokafka / La Parisienne II exhibition Secret times. Photograph Cathleen Naundorf 134–5t; Magnus Renmyr 188cr; Rolandm 12t, 214br, 273br; Rolf52 172bl, 196–7t, 202b, 240clb, 254–5b; Jonas Rönnbro 278–9b;

Main Contributers Susan Danielsson,
Mike MacEacheran, Kathleen Sauret,
Steve Vickers, Ulf Johansson,
Mona Neppenström, Kaj Sandell

Senior Editor Alison McGill

Senior Designer Tania Da Silva Gomes

Project Editor Zoë Rutland

Designers Jordan Lambley, Kitty Glavin

Factchecker Mike MacEacheran

Editors Alice Fewery, Emma Grundy Haigh,
Lydia Halliday, Jackie Staddon, Lucy Sara-Kelly

Proofreader Stephanie Smith

Indexer Helen Peters

Senior Picture Researcher Ellen Root

Picture Research Sophie Basilevitch,
Susie Watters, Sumita Khatwani,
Rituraj Singh, Manpreet Kaur

Illustrators Stephen Conlin, Gary Cross,
Urban Frank, Claire Littlejohn,
Jan Rojmar, John Woodcock

Senior Cartographic Editor Casper Morris

Cartography Ashutosh Ranjan Bharati,
Simonetta Giori, Zafar ul-Islam Khan,
Stig Söderlind

Jacket Designers Tania Da Silva Gomes,
Maxine Pedliham

Jacket Picture Research Susie Watters

Senior DTP Designer Jason Little

DTP Designer Rohit Rojal

Producer Rebecca Parton

Managing Editor Rachel Fox

Art Director Maxine Pedliham

Publishing Director Georgina Dee

MIX
Paper from
responsible sources
FSC
www.fsc.org   FSC™ C018179

**The information in this
DK Eyewitness Travel Guide is checked regularly.**
Every effort has been made to ensure that this book
is as up-to-date as possible at the time of going to
press. Some details, however, such as telephone
numbers, opening hours, prices, gallery hanging
arrangements and travel information, are liable to
change. The publishers cannot accept responsibility
for any consequences arising from the use of this
book, nor for any material on third party websites,
and cannot guarantee that any website address
in this book will be a suitable source of travel
information. We value the views and suggestions
of our readers very highly. Please write to: Publisher,
DK Eyewitness Travel Guides, Dorling Kindersley,
80 Strand, London, WC2R 0RL, UK, or email:
travelguides@dk.com

First edition 2005

Published in Great Britain by Dorling Kindersley Limited,
80 Strand, London, WC2R 0RL

Published in the United States by DK Publishing,
1450 Broadway, Suite 801, New York, NY 10018

Copyright © 2005, 2020 Dorling Kindersley Limited
A Penguin Random House Company
19 20 21 22 10 9 8 7 6 5 4 3 2 1

A CIP catalog record for this book
is available from the British Library.

A catalog record for this book is available
from the Library of Congress.

ISSN: 1542 1554
ISBN: 978 0 2414 0837 7

Printed and bound in China.

www.dk.com